Europe and Refugees

Towards an EU Asylum Policy

EUROPEAN MONOGRAPHS

Editor-in-Chief Prof. Dr. K.J.M. Mortelmans

In the series *European Monographs* this book
Europe and Refugees: Towards an EU Asylum Policy
is the thirty-first title.

The titles published in this series are listed at the end of this volume

EUROPEAN MONOGRAPHS

Europe and Refugees

Towards an EU Asylum Policy

Ingrid Boccardi

KLUWER LAW INTERNATIONAL

THE HAGUE – LONDON – NEW YORK

Published by Kluwer Law International
P.O. Box 85889
2508 CN The Hague, The Netherlands
sales@kli.wkap.nl
http://www.wkap.nl

Sold and distributed in the USA and Canada by
Kluwer Law International
101 Philip Drive
Norwell, MA 02061, USA
kluwerlaw@wkap.com

Sold and distributed in all other countries by
Kluwer Law International
Distribution Centre
P.O. Box 322
3300 AH Dordrecht, The Netherlands

A C.I.P. Catalogue record for this book is available from the Library of Congress.

Cover design: Bert Arts

Printed on acid-free paper

ISBN: 90-411-1709-1

Printed and bound in Great Britain by MPG Books Limited, Bodmin, Cornwall.

To my parents

TABLE OF CONTENTS

Preface and Acknowledgements

This book is based on my Ph.D, *Towards an EU Asylum Policy: "Protection" for Whom?*, which I defended at University College London in October 2001. I had the privilege to be supervised in this research project by a distinguished expert in this field, Professor David O'Keeffe. I am much indebted to him for his strong encouragement, invaluable advice, unfaltering dedication and constant support throughout many difficult moments.

I am also very thankful to my two Ph.D. examiners, Professors Marise Cremona and Alan Dashwood, for their discerning comments and helpful suggestions with regard to the final version of this work. In addition, my gratitude also goes to Professor Klaus Nanz, Mr Jon Payne and Dr Valeria Galandini for their valuable insights into the way Germany, Britain and Italy respectively have contributed to EU asylum co-operation. Many thanks also to James Michael for his help with issues relating to the European Convention of Human Rights and to Dr Danesh Sarooshi for sharing his expertise on questions concerning the United Nations.

I owe a special debt of gratitude to Belén Martínez Carbonell and Angela Martini for their invaluable help in tracking down and supplying me with EU sources and documentation. Many thanks also to ECRE (London), UNHCR (Brussels) and the British Refugee Council for letting me access their documentation centres and supplying me with important research material. I am also indebted to the Italian Centre for National Research (CNR) and the UCL Postgraduate School for their generous financing of this project.

Finally, many heartfelt thanks also to Katie Lambert for her careful language editing and to my husband Mark for his invaluable technical editing and critical comments. I remain eternally grateful to my parents for their unfaltering support without which this project could have not been possible. It goes without saying that all errors, omissions and opinions are, of course, mine alone.

Ingrid Boccardi
November 2001

Table of Abbreviations

Bull. EC	Bulletin of the European Communities
BYIL	British Yearbook of International Law
CAT	1984 UN Convention against Torture and other Cruel, Inhuman or Degrading Treatment or Punishment
CEAS	Common European Asylum System
CFSP	Common Foreign and Security Policy
CIREA	Centre for Information, Discussion and Exchange on Asylum
CIREFI	Centre for Information, Discussion and Exchange on the Crossing of Borders and Immigration
CIS	Commonwealth of Independent States
CML Rev.	Common Market Law Review
COREPER	Committee of Permanent Representatives to the European Community
CRISP	Centre de Recherche et d'Information Socio-Politique
CUP	Cambridge University Press
DC	1990 Dublin Convention determining the State responsible for examining applications for asylum lodged in one of the Member States of the European Communities
EC	European Community
EC	(If following a Treaty Article) Treaty establishing the European Community as amended by the Maastricht Treaty)
ECHR	European Convention of Human Rights
ECJ	European Court of Justice
ECR	European Court Reports
ECRE	European Council of Refugees and Exiles
ECOSOC	UN Economic and Social Council
ECtHR	European Court of Human Rights
EEC	Treaty establishing the European Economic Community (post-SEA, pre-Maastricht)
EHR	European Human Rights
EHRR	European Human Rights Reports
EL Rev.	European Law Review
EP	European Parliament
EPC	European Political Co-operation
EURODAC	European Automated Fingerprinting System of Asylum Applicants
FRY	Former Republic of Yugoslavia
GC	1951 Geneva Convention on the Status of Refugees
HRQ	Human Rights Quarterly

IA Rev.	Immigration Appeals Review
ICCPR	International Covenant of Civil and Political Rights
ICJ	International Court of Justice
ICLQ	International and Comparative Law Quarterly
ICRC	International Committee of the Red Cross
IGC	Intergovernmental Conference
IJRL	International Journal of Refugee Law
ILPA	Immigration Law Practitioners Association
INLP	Immigration and Nationality Law and Practice
IOM	International Organisation for Migration
JCMS	Journal of Common Market Studies
JHA	Justice and Home Affairs
NGOs	Non-governmental Organisations
NQHR	Netherlands Quarterly on Human Rights
OAS	Organisation of American States
OAU	Organisation of African Unity
OJ	Official Journal of the European Communities
OUP	Oxford University Press
QUANGO	Quasi Non-Governmental Organisation
SC	1990 Schengen Convention
SEA	Single European Act
SIS	Schengen Information System
TEC	Treaty establishing the European Community as amended by the Amsterdam Treaty
TEU	Treaty on the European Union
TP	Temporary Protection
UNGA	United Nations General Assembly
UNHCR	United Nations High Commissioner for Refugees
YEL	Yearbook of European Law

Introduction

'The twentieth century saw the developed world descend into a paroxysm of ideological violence, as liberalism contended first with the remnants of absolutism, then bolshevism and fascism, and finally an updated Marxism that threatened to lead to the ultimate apocalypse of a nuclear war. But the century that began full of self-confidence in the ultimate triumph of Western liberal democracy seems at its close to be [...] the end of history as such: that is, the end point of mankind's ideological evolution and the universalisation of Western liberal democracy as the final form of human government'.[1]

Back in 1989 the 'new world order' rising from the ashes of the Cold War might well have seemed the 'end of history', but it certainly did not mean the end of the refugee cycle. Throughout the world liberal democracies based on the respect for fundamental Human Rights have remained a privilege for the few. Refugee crises have, without a doubt, been one of the most tragic occurrences of the 20th Century, a terrible phenomenon that looks set to continue well into the next one. In the five decades following the end of the Second World War, the global refugee population experienced a tenfold increase. The UNHCR estimated that on the eve of the third millennium there were 22.3 million refugees in the world.[2] One tenth of them were in Europe. During the last decade heated political discussions about asylum trends dominated national agendas across the EU, despite the fact that refugees only represented on average 0.07 per cent of the total population.[3] Following the end of the Cold War's polarisation and the ensuing proliferation of localised conflicts, the number of asylum applications in Europe has risen steeply since the middle of the 80s. The pressure on national asylum systems was further enhanced by the restrictive immigration policies EU Members introduced in the aftermath of the 70s economic slump. Most Member States, in an attempt to stem the asylum flows, repeatedly tightened their national refugee admission policies and progressively looked to the EU for a comprehensive regional solution.

This research has focused on the gradual development of a co-ordinated EU response to the pressing asylum issues that have affected most Member States

---

1. F. Fukuyama, 'The end of history?' (1989) 16 *The National Interest*, p. 3.
2. In 1951 the UNHCR estimated the existence of 2,116,200 refugee worldwide. This figure had grown to 22.3 million by 31 December 1999. See UNHCR, *The state of the world's refugees*, 2000.
3. UNHCR estimates for end of 2000, see Table 2 of Annex.

in the past two decades. This EU involvement in the asylum field has been analysed following a historical/evolutionary approach that has concentrated on two main aspects. On the one hand, the analysis has attempted to monitor the rise since 1985 of a common interest among EU Member States in co-ordinating their national asylum policies. It has focused on explaining the reasons for this rise and the shape this asylum co-ordination has progressively taken. It has also attempted to assess whether such asylum co-ordination has been characterised by an identifiable pattern of evolution, for instance in the choice of priorities or of an overall strategy. Most importantly, this analysis has tried to ascertain whether these initial efforts have developed effectively into a fully-fledged EU asylum policy. On the other hand, this research has concentrated on the impact of these initiatives on the levels of refugee protection in the EU. In particular, it has tried to assess whether European initiatives in the asylum field have been compatible with previous international refugee and Human Rights obligations. Finally, this work has attempted to suggest ways in which enhanced levels of refugee protection could be integrated in the development of an efficient EU asylum policy.

The concept of refugee protection was essentially a 20th Century creation. At the beginning of the 50s Europe took the lead in dealing with the consequences of large-scale refugee movements resulting from the devastation of the Second World War. The drafting of the 1951 Geneva Refugee Convention – to date the international cornerstone of refugee protection – was essentially driven by European nations in the midst of their efforts to build a regional system of Human Rights. Since implementation of the Refugee Convention was essentially remitted to each signatory State, this led to extensive and, at times, widely differing national asylum policies. It would be impossible in this context to examine in detail each EU Member State's asylum legislation and their related practices. Therefore, this research will limit itself to analysing asylum initiatives undertaken at intergovernmental and EU level. Whenever possible, reference to national asylum policies has been made for the purpose of clarifying both the background and the implications of EU intervention.

Research for this book has often been complicated by the sensitive nature of some of the material. The Maastricht Third Pillar and Schengen frameworks were repeatedly criticised for their excessive secrecy. Only after the entry into force of the Amsterdam Treaty has documentation on EU initiatives been made more widely available. The European Parliament is the only EU institution that has obviously made public its numerous interventions on asylum matters since the middle of the 80s. Due to the incredible volume of such interventions, in the context of the present research they could only be analysed in a limited manner. EP contributions were included if they represented a valuable survey of national policy aspects, or if they were part of the ongoing legislative process. Other valuable sources of EU information were provided by Member States' national representations in Brussels and, in the UK case, by the Home Office representatives in London. In this respect, personal interviews proved extremely useful for gathering insight into the most obscure aspects of both EU and national asylum policies, despite the fact that few officials were willing to talk on the record. The assistance of the UNHCR and NGOs such as ECRE, Amnesty, ILPA and the national Refugee Councils was also essential in obtaining feedback on the impact of EU asylum initiatives on refugee protection levels. Due to the only very recent involvement of the ECJ in asylum matters, its jurisprudence in the field is still very limited. Most of the jurisprudence analysed in this research stems from the European Court of Human Rights, national Courts and other small international tribunals, such as the Committee against Torture. Finally, assembling reliable statistical data has proved very difficult because asylum estimates vary widely according to their source. This work has relied essentially on data provided by EUROSTAT and the UNHCR.

The beginning of this book sets the general framework for this research by outlining the international foundations of refugee protection such as the 1951 Geneva Convention, the 1967 New York Protocol and the UNHCR, and the way they have evolved in the last four decades. At the same time it outlines other examples of regional refugee protection initiatives, such as the African and South American ones, as well as Human Rights instruments that have had important implications for refugee protection in Europe. Particular attention is given in this respect to the far-reaching jurisprudence of the European Court of Human Rights. This research then concentrates on its main focus by shifting to the European regional dimension and analysing the initial attempts of EC countries to co-ordinate their asylum measures through the burgeoning European Political Co-operation as well as the reasons behind the need for such co-ordination. The role played by parallel asylum initiatives, adopted by a smaller number of EC Members within the Schengen framework, is also examined as an important precursor to subsequent EU developments.

The Maastricht Treaty was of fundamental importance for the enhancement of EU asylum co-operation. This work analyses the nature of the Third Pillar provisions on asylum, the operating structures set up for asylum co-ordination and the resulting patterns of interaction between Member States and the Union's institutions. The Third Pillar codification of an intergovernmental asylum co-operation framework led to the adoption of a number of asylum initiatives, mostly relating to the implementation of the 1990 Dublin Convention on the criteria assigning State responsibility over asylum applications. However, these measures presented several problems of effectiveness and implementation, as well as indicating a gradual shift of asylum objectives by the mid-90s.

The Amsterdam Treaty attempted to overcome the inefficiencies of the Third Pillar by radically reshaping Member States' asylum co-operation. This research analyses in detail the new complex asylum framework that emerged at Amsterdam. A new asylum competence was inserted into the First Pillar and subjected to a strict five-year timetable. However, this competence was limited by a series of opt-ins, opt-outs, restricted jurisdictional controls and finally the possibility of enhanced co-operation among a smaller number of Member States.

The roles played by the subsequent Tampere European Council and the recent Nice Treaty are also explored as they provided both a development path and a fine-tuning of decision-making processes of the new EU asylum co-operation. Finally, attention is given to the possible impact that the EU Charter of Fundamental Rights, approved at Nice, might have on strengthening the Human Rights dimension of asylum in future EU action.

Throughout this research, particular attention has been given to analysing the evolutionary dynamic that shaped the motivations of Member States' asylum co-operation and the impact of such co-operation on refugee protection levels in Europe. This co-operation appears to have produced an inevitable dichotomy between the security implications generated by the reality of regional economic integration within a competitive world market and the need to guarantee effective protection from persecution as an expression of those Human Rights principles that constitute the very foundations of the Western democratic model that emerged triumphant from the ideological battles of the 20th Century. Striking an equitable balance between these two elements remains to date a very arduous task.

1 The International Protection of Refugees

I.1. GENERAL PRINCIPLES

All the asylum initiatives undertaken by Community Member States in the past fifteen years did not happen in a situation of legal vacuum. In this respect, Member States were bound by a series of pre-existing international obligations arising both from specific asylum provisions and from other Human Rights instruments. Moreover, other countries in the world had adopted their own regional approaches to refugee protection. The purpose of this Chapter is to outline the various ways in which the concept of refugee protection has been developed in the international context and thus to set a useful background for better understanding the evolution of EU asylum co-operation that will be analysed in the following Chapters.

'Refugees', in the broader sense of the term are by no means a twentieth century phenomenon. However, only at the end of the First World War did the Western world focus its attention on the plight of people obliged by adverse circumstances to flee their own homes and seek refuge elsewhere. Thus began a slow process of legal definition that eventually led to the drafting of universal international instruments such as the 1951 Geneva Convention on the Status of Refugees (GC) and the creation of organisations such as the UN High Commissioner for Refugees (UNHCR).

This lengthy process started with the numerous special arrangements concluded under the auspices of the League of Nations to protect Russian, Armenian and later German refugees.[1] These Treaties were characterised by the adoption of a 'group' or 'category' approach, in so far as they protected people defined on the basis of ethnic or nationality criteria. Contemporary legal commentators already highlighted the shortcomings of such an approach, insofar as it lacked an abstract and general definition of the term 'refugee'.[2] It was only after the Second World War that more precise criteria emerged and 'in a little more than five years the preferred approach to refugee definition moved from a basis in

---

1. For an overview of this numerous arrangements see J. Hathaway, 'The evolution of refugee status in international law' (1984) 33 ICLQ 348. These agreements included for instance a 1926 Convention concerning Russian and Armenian refugees and the 1938 Convention on German refugees that after the *Anschluss* was also extended to Austrian nationals.
2. See for instance J.H. Simpson, *The refugee problem* (Royal Institute of International Affairs, OUP, 1939), who stressed that the 'essential quality' of refugees was the fact that political events made it impossible for them to stay in their own country (at p. 28 *et seq.*).

flexible or open groups and categories to an apparently more closed and legalistic one'.[3]

One of the most pressing issues at the end of the Second World War was the necessity of dealing with the millions of people that had been displaced by the conflict. The International Refugee Organisation (IRO), was born out of such necessity and later became the UNHCR. The IRO Covenant constituted the first attempt to codify the term 'refugee' as well as the type of protection such people should be afforded. Refugees thus came to be termed as individuals being 'persecuted' on a certain number of grounds,[4] mainly concerning race, nationality and political or religious beliefs and as being unable to avail themselves of the protection of their country of nationality.[5]

But as the world's post-war geopolitical asset edged more and more towards a bipolar framework, Western States became increasingly concerned by the necessity of narrowing down the definition of the term 'refugee'.[6] Thus, they focused on a strictly legalistic concept of protection and persecution that was rooted in the parallel international codification of universal Human Rights. The Statute of the UNHCR, the 1951 GC and the 1967 Declaration on Territorial Asylum became the fundamental texts in which refugee protection was to be encoded.[7] However, the implementation of the latter two was left to the practice of individual States and therefore national applications differed widely. Therefore, outlining a truly international refugee regime without referring to its specific national applications becomes very difficult. It is nonetheless essential for the purposes of this research to briefly analyse the basic foundations of refugee

---

3. G.S. Goodwin-Gill, *The refugee in international law* (2nd edn, Clarendon Press, Oxford, 1996), p. 6.

4. On such grounds see further in I.2. The definition of these grounds was clearly linked with the parallel ongoing discussions on the definition of universal Human Rights. On these links and for an in-depth analysis of how these grounds came to be included in the IRO definition see L.W. Holborn, *The International Refugee Organisation: a specialised agency at the United Nations. Its history and work 1946–52* (OUP, Oxford, 1956).

5. Since UN Member States also had to abide by the principle of non-interference in domestic affairs the definition of a 'refugee' logically entailed the necessity of crossing an international frontier in order to flee from the persecution of the State of origin. In this sense, the very essence of refugee protection already constituted a fundamental exception to the international law regime on nationality whereby each State was traditionally responsible for its own citizens.

6. The main concern derived from the fear that a broad obligation of assistance to persecuted people would have proven impossible and potentially politically explosive in the context of the precarious Cold War equilibrium.

7. Other international conventions had an indirect impact on the international protection of refugees. Those were the 1966 International Covenant on Civil and Political Rights (ICCPR) and the 1984 Convention against Torture (CAT). See Chapter I.2. On a regional level the 1950 European Convention on Human Rights (ECHR) contained similar provisions. See Chapter I.4.

protection as it is laid down in international law, both in the form of conventions and in the evolving mandates of specific organisations.

I.2. PRINCIPAL INTERNATIONAL INSTRUMENTS FOR THE PROTECTION OF REFUGEES: THE 1951 GENEVA CONVENTION AND THE 1967 NEW YORK PROTOCOL

The five years that followed the end of the Second World War were of pivotal importance for the development of the current international refugee regime. The establishment of the United Nations marked the beginning of a new era in the globalisation of international law issues such as the respect of Human Rights. The 1948 Universal Declaration of Human Rights represented the first impressive step in this direction. Art. 14.1 stated that 'everyone has the right to seek and to enjoy in other countries asylum from persecution'. Although powerful, this statement concealed the enormous differences of opinion that had begun to emerge between UN Members, some of whom were increasingly worried about the potential liabilities of having to protect large numbers of refugees. It transpired from the *travaux préparatoires* that the majority of States had no intention of assuming any moral or legal obligation on these matters. The granting of asylum was perceived as an entirely discretionary exercise of States' sovereignty. Only the duty to respect the decision to grant asylum was seen as an international obligation.[8] In the end, the only right effectively being recognised was the right to flight, rather than the one to asylum.[9]

The 1951 Geneva Convention on the Status of Refugees was the direct result of a recommendation by the newly established UN Commission on Human Rights.[10] By then it had become obvious that the old IRO definition of refugee

---

8. Any suggestion to substitute the expression 'to enjoy [...] asylum from persecution' with the one 'to be granted asylum from persecution' was quickly dismissed, as well as the idea that the power to decide on matters of refugee protection should be delegated to the IRO. See the original draft of Art. 14: UN Doc. A/C.3/285/Rev.1 and the UK objections in UN Doc. A/C.3/SR.121, pp. 4–6. See also P. Weiss, *The travaux préparatoires of the 1951 Geneva Refugee Convention*, UN Documentation series, XII/1995.

9. In this sense refugees were entitled to leave their country to escape persecution, but were not necessarily given any guarantees of protection in law.

10. The UN Commission on Human Rights was established in 1946 by the UN Economic and Social Council on the basis of the Art. 68 of the UN Charter and it played an important role in assisting the drafting of the 1948 Universal Declaration of Human Rights. It would be impossible in this context to deal with the complex evolution of the international discipline of Human Rights that took place in those crucial post-war years. Nonetheless, it is important to recall the burgeoning idea of 'intangible' rights, in order to understand the transition from a 'category' definition of refugees towards a more general one. In principle, all Human Rights were considered of equal importance. However, some particular rights could never be the subject of any derogation (see, for instance, the 1966 UN ICCPR, where derogation from the freedoms granted was allowed in cases of life-threatening public emergencies, with the exception of seven fundamental rights – incidentally, the

– still based on a 'category' approach – needed updating.[11] However, no overall consensus had yet been built on the scope to be given to the legal definition of a refugee.[12] In the end, after intense negotiations, a compromise was reached whereby a rather general definition of the term 'refugee' was accompanied by a restrictive temporal clause, limiting the application of the GC only to those who acquired refugee status as 'a result of events occurring before 1 January 1951' (Art. 1.B.1). Furthermore, there was the optional possibility of geographically limiting 'events' to those 'occurring in Europe' prior to 1951 (Art. 1.B.1.*a*).[13] In order to overcome these draconian limitations a Recommendation was added to the GC (n° E) inviting Member States to extend protection to refugees within their territory beyond the contractual scope of the Convention. Many States actually relied on this Recommendation to broaden their national refugee protection regimes until 1967, when these restrictions were officially lifted.

The 1951 Geneva Convention dealt with the recognition of refugee status by States.[14] It was widely accepted that such a formal recognition was merely of a 'declaratory' nature, since anybody became a refugee as soon as they fulfilled the definition.[15] According to Art. 1, 'Convention' refugees were characterised by four elements: a) they had fled their country of origin; b) they were unable or unwilling either to return to it, or to avail themselves of its protection; c) this impossibility was due to past persecution or to a well-founded fear of possible persecution; d) they feared persecution on the grounds of race, religion, nationality, political opinion or membership of a particular social group. The assessment of such elements was entirely remitted to Member States and their national

---

same limited derogation appeared in the ECHR). Such freedoms were the right to life (Art. 6), the protection against torture and cruel or inhuman treatment (Art. 7), the prohibition of slavery and servitude (Art. 8), the right not to be submitted to retroactive criminal penalties (Art. 15), the right to recognition as a person before the law (Art. 16) and the freedom of thought, conscience and religion (Art. 18). These fundamental freedoms became in turn the very grounds on which the international regime of protection from persecution came to be based (see further).

11. The definition had already been updated when the Statute of the UNHCR was drafted (see later Chapter I.3).

12. The United States expressed concerns that too vague a definition would inevitably result in lengthy interpretation disputes and too many unforeseeable responsibilities. The United Kingdom tried to introduce a more wide-ranging definition that focused on the situation where a person, having been persecuted – or fearing persecution – was unable or unwilling to return to his country of origin. See G. Goodwin-Gill, *supra* n° 3, p. 18.

13. It appears that a truly 'international' definition of refugee protection was doomed from the very beginning. Only a small number of States that had supported the draft Convention in the UN Assembly showed up in Geneva to actually sign it and most of them were European States.

14. Also the UNHCR can 'recognise' refugees, see Chapter I.4.

15. Problems obviously arose when, for instance, the recognition by a State and by the UNHCR didn't coincide or if States declined to even 'initiate' the procedure for determining refugee status (see further on the Schengen and Dublin Conventions, Chapters II and III).

adjudication systems and, in the absence of any international control, their application or interpretation differed widely.[16]

The term 'persecution', for instance, was not defined by the GC nor by any other international convention,[17] leaving States with a wide margin of appreciation. This in turn resulted in a very disparate national jurisprudence. Art. 1 GC established, however, a clear link between persecution, or the mere fear of it, and the absence of protection.[18] In this context the notion of fundamental Human Rights could be assumed as an effective base for assessing the existence of persecution.[19] 'Means' of persecution also proved difficult to assess since they assumed so many different historical forms. Therefore, its interpretation had to rely on an ill-defined concept of proportionality.[20] The assessment of persecution was further complicated by the fact that the oppression was often not carried out directly by the State itself, but the State in question was unwilling or unable to provide protection to the individual.[21]

---

16. It is impossible in the framework of this research to examine all the different national refugee determination procedures implemented following Art. 1 GC. This analysis will restrict itself to general problems of interpretation and application. Likewise, the provisions relating to the juridical status of 'recognised' refugees, their benefits and travel arrangements, shall be only briefly examined in so far as they have not proven particularly controversial.

17. See G. Goodwin-Gill, *supra* n° 3, p. 66.

18. See the reasoning followed by G. Goodwin-Gill, *supra* n° 3, p. 67 where he states that '[t]he persecuted clearly do not enjoy the protection of their country of origin, while evidence of the lack of protection on either the internal or the external level may create a presumption as to the likelihood of persecution and to the well-foundedness of any fear'.

19. See *supra* n° 10. Since the preservation of these rights was intrinsically connected with the dignity and integrity of the human being, any measure that would threaten the life (and physical/mental integrity), freedom and recognition as a person of an individual would necessarily have amounted to persecution.

20. The notion of when the nature and severity of a measure becomes oppressive and persecutory was by definition open to infinite interpretations. However, some guidance could be found in the principle of non-discrimination, whereby any measure that could, even indirectly, lead to the singling out of an individual with the purpose of oppression could be considered paramount to persecution (on non-discrimination as a principle of general international law, see the *Barcelona Traction* case, ICJ Rep. 1970 3, at p. 32). For a comprehensive review of all the different interpretations of the term 'persecution', see D.J. Steinbock, 'The refugee definition as law: issues of interpretation' in F. Nicholson and P. Twomey (eds), *Refugee rights and realities*, (CUP, Cambridge, 1999), p. 13.

21. The last 50 years of international history have been full of such tragic circumstances spanning the entirety of the globe. Unfortunately, for a refugee the formal existence of a State can sometimes mean the difference between recognition and rejection. Some countries – notably, within Europe, France and Germany – do not recognise the principle of 'non-State agent' persecution. In the past, for instance, Algerians targeted by the Islamic Front (FIS) have failed to obtain refugee status in some countries even though it was clear that their own government was unable to protect them. Somalis too have often been rejected because no clear government was identifiable. This responsibility-based approach did not,

The level of proof required by the GC to sustain a claim of persecution (or the fear of it) was equally left open to States' interpretation. Given the gravity of the issues at stake (the possibility, for individuals, of being left without protection against their own State and the denial of their most fundamental freedoms) the burden of proof could reasonably be expected to be in favour of the refugee.[22] Furthermore, it would be unfair to apply the standard of proof required for criminal cases, because it would be very difficult for someone who has been the object of persecution to present the level of proof necessary to make his case 'beyond any reasonable doubt'. However, the question remained of whether the 'balance of probability' test could be usefully applied to a future speculation of fear of persecution.[23]

Problems of proof were further complicated in cases where persecution had not actually taken place but the applicant was claiming a 'well-founded fear' of persecution. National jurisprudence seemed to have diverged remarkably on the value to be given to subjective fear.[24] The UNHCR clearly stated on a number of occasions its belief that a fear of persecution had to be founded on an objective situation that could reasonably give rise to concerns about future oppression.[25] In general, most national Courts endorsed the principle that the level of proof required should be assessed on a case-by-case basis. This individual approach was justified by the fact that 'fear' in itself could not be objectively quantified, whereas the real subject of the judicial assessment was in fact the degree of the 'risk of persecution' involved.

Interpretation of the grounds for persecution listed by the GC was equally controversial. 'Race' and 'religion' gave rise to the least divergence, having been widely defined in other international texts.[26] 'Nationality' in the context of the

---

however, appear to be in conformity with the actual GC. Assessment in such cases should not have focused on whether it was possible to establish the 'responsibility' of the State in the international meaning of the sense, but whether there was a likely risk of persecution for the refugee

22. This is, however, almost never the case in Europe (see Chapters III and IV).

23. On this point see the interesting 'theory of the three scales' by J.Y. Carlier, 'The Geneva refugee definition and the 'theory of the three scales", in F. Nicholson and P. Twomey (eds), *supra* n° 20, p. 37.

24. See, on this point, M. Gibney, 'A well-founded fear of persecution' (1988) 10 HRQ, p. 109 *et seq.*

25. See UNHCR, *Handbook on procedures and criteria for determining refugee status*, para. 42, where it states that '[I]n general the applicant's fear should be considered well-founded if he can establish, to a reasonable degree, that his continued stay in his country of origin has become intolerable for him for the reasons stated in the definition, or would for the same reasons be intolerable if returned there'.

26. 'Race', for instance, was clearly defined in the 1965 Convention on the Elimination of All Forms of Racial Discrimination, which included all distinctions based on 'race, colour, descent, or national or ethnic origin' (Art. 1). Throughout history racial persecution appeared to be the most common origin of the refugee phenomenon. In the case of 'religion', such freedom necessarily had to include the possibility of holding no religious belief at all

GC was always interpreted rather broadly as including membership of a community characterised by particular ethnic, religious, cultural and linguistic ties.[27] There were frequent and inevitable overlaps between these grounds of persecution in the way they were applied by Member States, and sometimes this cumulation actually resulted in a strengthening of the applicant's claim.

Persecution on grounds of 'political opinion', although quite precisely described in international texts, gave rise to an ample display of different interpretations. Art. 19 of the Universal Declaration of Human Rights stated that 'everyone has the right to freedom of opinion and expression; the right includes freedom to hold opinions without interference and to seek, receive and impart information and ideas through any media and regardless of frontiers'.[28] Typically, a 'refugee' within the GC meaning would be someone persecuted by his government or other national agents on account of opinions that could be perceived as threatening to the institutions, political programme or objectives of the latter. In this context, it would be irrelevant whether the political opinion in question constituted an actual threat or merely a perceived one, or if the opinion was wrongly attributed to the refugee. It was primarily the subjective perception of the persecutor that gave rise to the oppressive measures.[29]

Finally, the most controversial point of interpretation proved to be the 'membership of a particular social group' clause. The *travaux préparatoires* offered no insight into the reasons why such definition came to be included. It was highly likely that the drafters were concerned by the 'restructuring of societies' that

---

(see the Declaration on the Elimination of All Forms of Intolerance and Discrimination Based on Religion or Belief, adopted by the UN General Assembly (UNGA) on 25/11/1981 res. 36/55).

27. A useful reference in this respect can be found in Art. 27 of the 1966 ICCPR with respect to the rights of minorities (which are defined on ethnic, religious or linguistic grounds). On this point see also A. Grahl-Madsen, *The status of refugees in International Law* (Sijthoff, Leiden, 1966, vol. I & II), vol. I, pp. 218–219.

28. Art. 19 of the 1966 ICCPR echoed this wording, although a derogation was allowed for 'special duties and responsibilities'. This represented a further evolution in the field of Human Rights whereby certain opinions were no longer regarded as acceptable, as, for instance, all those in favour of racial discrimination.

29. The boundaries of the concept of 'political opinion' have proven very difficult to define, especially if the expression of such opinions entailed breaching the law in the country of origin. For instance, most extradition treaties carried an exception for 'political' offences, but often the State seeking the extradition would not see the offence as 'political' at all. Similarly, there might be a very fine line between a legitimately held political opinion and an act of violence tending to affirm such opinion (see, for instance, the problem of distinguishing a 'freedom-fighter' from a 'terrorist'). Other areas where discrepancies in the application of this ground have been frequent concern the issue of conscientious objectors (G. Goodwin-Gill, *supra* n° 3, pp. 54–59) and cases where the opinion held went against the 'public interest' (as in China's 'one-child' policy). See also P. Shah, 'Taking the 'political' out of asylum: the legal containment of refugees' political activism' in F. Nicholson and P. Twomey (eds), *supra* n° 20, p. 119.

were taking place at the time in the socialist States, where entire classes of citizens were being targeted by the State and persecuted. The UNHCR Handbook (para. 78) justified the inclusion on the grounds that 'membership of a particular social group may be at the root of persecution because there is no confidence in the group's loyalty to the government or because the political outlook, antecedents or economic activity of its members, or the very existence of the social group as such, is held to be an obstacle to the government's policies'. Formulating a widely accepted definition of 'social group' across national interpretations would prove impossible. In most instances, particular attention was given to the presence of linking factors of a cultural, ethnic or economic nature, to shared backgrounds, values and visions of life. However, the notion lent itself to a virtually endless evolution and was stretched to include very different circumstances.[30] Again, actual membership of the group was not essential if it could be demonstrated that the individual was perceived as being a member of the group by the persecutor.

Only Art. 1 of the GC closely concerned the attribution of refugee status. Most of the rest of the Convention dealt with the status itself and the benefits and obligations that it entailed.[31] The overall spirit of such provisions was inspired by the wish to afford recognised refugees a treatment as similar as possible to the State's own nationals. Thus, numerous articles regulated the refugees' juridical status, the conditions of their employment,[32] welfare, administrative assistance, freedom of movement, identity and travel papers, fiscal charges and transfer of assets.

A special provision was made for 'refugees unlawfully in the country of refuge' (Art. 31 GC) in the instance that they were fleeing directly from somewhere where their life or freedom was at risk. Provided that they alerted the authorities to their presence and the reasons for their illegal entry, no penalties could be

---

30. In a world where the roots of the refugee phenomenon had undergone a dramatic change in the last three decades, the concept of 'social' group was often seen as a 'catch-all' for adjusting to the evolving historical context. On the whole, Courts leaned towards a characterization of the individual based on traits that were innate or unchangeable (such as, for instance, 'gender'). Other times they found admissible associations dictated by reasons of fundamental human dignity (for example Human Rights associations). For a review of national jurisprudence on these characteristics, see G. Goodwin-Gill, *supra* n° 3, pp. 356–66.

31. For the purpose of this research the analysis of these provisions shall be brief as their application was essentially non-controversial. Most of the problems surrounding the international protection of refugees actually concerned recognition of the status itself and the issues of people who didn't fall within the scope of the GC definition, but were nonetheless perceived to be in need of protection.

32. Interestingly, in the case of employment, refugees were only granted 'the most favourable treatment accorded to nationals of a foreign country in the same circumstances' (Art. 17.1), although in respect to labour legislation and social security they were to be treated as a national of that host country (Art. 24). The same discrepancy appeared in other provisions such as non-elementary education (Art. 22.2).

applied to them. The drafting of this provision proved quite controversial as Member States tried to balance the necessity of guaranteeing protection with their efforts to thwart abuses of the asylum institution.[33] As a consequence the scope of application of Art. 31 varied considerably. Countries who were mostly concerned with restricting their alternative immigration channels imposed a very narrow definition of the 'transit time' refugees were allowed in other countries in the course of their flight and also developed a wide-ranging notion of the 'country of first asylum'.[34]

According to the second part of Art. 31 GC, the movements of refugees coming directly from the territory of persecution should be restricted as little as possible and only until either their status has been regularised or they have obtained admission into another country. Also in this instance the scope of application has varied considerably. In most EU countries imprisonment – in special detention camps or in regular jails – was normally imposed on asylum seekers during at least some of the stages of their assessment by the asylum authorities and justified by the possibility that they might abscond into the host country and thereby bypass immigration requirements.

The provisions regulating expulsion and the return of refugees were undoubtedly the ones that generated the most varied and extensive body of national practices and jurisprudence.[35] Art. 32 GC dealt with the expulsion of refugees lawfully resident in a Member State ('recognised' refugees), whereas Art. 33 GC contained broader clauses concerning the minimum protection against forcible

---

33. In the *travaux préparatoires*, the High Commissioner for Refugees strongly pointed out that flight very rarely happened in a straight path and that most of the time transit through other countries was inevitable. The actual wording of the article represented a compromise between countries such as France, who wanted to restrict the application of this provision only to refugees coming directly from the country of origin and others who favoured a more liberal approach. This wording should have also covered instances of transit through countries where refugees would still be at risk of persecution or where they could not be afforded adequate protection. On these points, see G. Goodwin-Gill, *supra* n° 3, pp. 88–91.

34. This concept refers to the country responsible for examining an asylum claim and affording protection to the refugee. EU Member States have been at the forefront of such developments, notably with their Schengen and Dublin Conventions and the 1992 Edinburgh initiatives (see later Chapters II and III). It should be clear, though, that such restrictions on the ability to seek protection from persecution were not directly implied by Art. 31. Instead, these restrictions derived from the fact that the negative prescription of Art. 31 GC could not adequately deal with the instance of refugees not arriving directly from the country of persecution. Eventually, the main problem became the identification of who was responsible for examining an asylum claim, affording protection and under what circumstances. Otherwise countries could indefinitely push onto each other such responsibility and the refugees would remain in an eternal limbo. However, the EU solutions to this problem did not appear to be entirely compatible with the GC (see Chapters II and III).

35. Although the GC definition of 'refugee' was quite limited, all prospective asylum seekers who were in the territory of a Member State were protected by these provisions. This lead to a large volume of national jurisprudence.

returns to be granted to all asylum seekers present on the national territory. According to Art. 32 no refugee 'lawfully in their territory' could be expelled by the Contracting States except for reasons of national security or public order. The decision should be reached in 'accordance with the due process of law' and the refugee should be granted all the minimum judicial guarantees.[36] Additionally, refugees should be given the option to seek admission into another country.

Art. 33 GC affirmed the principle of the prohibition of refoulement.[37] In broad terms this could be defined as the prohibition on returning refugees to countries where they would be likely to face persecution. This principle was generally interpreted as covering all people seeking protection and present in the territory of a Contracting State, regardless of whether they had been recognised as refugees or whether they had gained illegal entry. Since the application of this provision necessarily relied upon an assessment of a risk (the possibility of persecution), national implementations varied considerably.[38] Furthermore, the magnitude of such protection did not coincide with the narrow definition of Art. 1 GC. Thus, the application of non-refoulement led to vast numbers of people – seeking protection on grounds outside of Art. 1 GC – being allowed to remain on the territory of Contracting States under a multitude of legal statuses, unfortunately often under very inadequate conditions.[39]

---

36. These are the typical guarantees found in most international Human Rights covenants such as the right to defence and legal representation and the right to appeal. Exceptions were generally made to these rights, though, in the case of 'compelling national security reasons'. However, such conditions were generally subjected, in the case of most Western countries, to the close scrutiny of the Courts and there have been virtually no instances in Europe where a refugee has been successfully removed on national security grounds (if one excludes a few cases concerning alleged terrorists). The highest profile case of the recent past was no doubt the attempt by the British Government in 1996 to remove Dr Al Masari from Britain and deport him to the Dominican Republic on grounds of national interest. This attempt, however, was quashed by the Courts. See P. Shah, *supra* n° 29.

37. The term derives from the French were it was used in the military sense of an enemy being repelled or thrown back from one's own line of defense. In the immigration controls context it has come to indicate both the act of forcibly escorting someone to the border with the purpose of expelling them or the refusal to admit people without proper documentation.

38. These discrepancies were largely the same as those encountered in setting national standards for the 'well-founded fear of persecution' prescribed by Art. 1 GC. Most States drew a parallel between Art. 1 and Art. 33 and applied the same standard of proof (such as a likely risk of persecution rather than a clear probability of it) to both instances.

39. These people have come to be termed in the last two decades as 'de facto refugees'. Although they would be allowed to remain their conditions were often very harsh (no benefits, no working rights and no social services). The need to devise some international instruments to cover these cases – often the result of civil wars – was constantly stressed by the UNHCR and other relevant organisations. Some efforts have since been undertaken at the EU level (see Chapters IV.6, VI.3 and VI.5).

The principle of non-refoulement was relatively recent. It was introduced in an international text only after the First World War, but adhesion to this instrument was still very limited.[40] Only after 1945 did the principle appear to have been more widely accepted[41] and it was finally incorporated into Art. 33 GC. Its wording gave rise to numerous controversies on the extent of its scope, namely regarding both the recipients of protection against refoulement and the value of this principle in general international law. The fact that officially 'recognised' refugees were certainly covered by the provision was never disputed. The main issue concerned the extent to which other asylum seekers were to be protected against refoulement and sometimes a distinction was drawn between people already present in the territory of the Contracting State and those seeking admission at the border.[42] In practice, most Contracting States adopted a broad interpretation of the non-refoulement principle and allowed large numbers of asylum seekers to cross their borders and to remain in their territories until a solution to their plight could be found. Similarly, the UNHCR consistently supported this broad interpretation[43] and although its Conclusions did not have legally-binding force they certainly influenced the way Member States viewed their obligations in this respect. The correctness of this interpretation was further backed by other international texts, such as the Declaration on Territorial Asylum adopted unanimously by the UN General Assembly in 1967.[44]

---

40. Art. 3 of the 1933 Convention relating to the International Status of Refugees prohibited refoulement for reasons other than national security or public order. But only eight countries ratified it and some with considerable limitations on this principle.

41. In 1946 the General Assembly of the United Nations (UNGA) issued a statement against returning refugees against their will. The International Refugee Organisation was established soon after and charged with resettling thousands of European refugees that could not be returned to their homes. See G. Goodwin-Gill, *supra* n° 3, p. 119.

42. It emerged from the *travaux préparatoires* that a number of States were concerned that the prohibition of refoulement would implicitly mean an obligation for the Contracting Parties to automatically admit people claiming persecution into their territory. This could have made any national immigration control completely redundant, especially in the case of mass migrations (G. Goodwin-Gill, *supra* n° 3, p. 122). Therefore, the wording of Art. 33 was arguably left deliberately vague, so as to hide this lack of consensus.

43. See, for instance, Executive Committee Conclusions n° 6 (1977); n° 19 (1980); n° 22 (1981) and n° 65 (1991).

44. Art. 3.1 of the Declaration stated that 'no person [...] shall be subjected to measures such as rejection at the frontier or, if he has already entered the territory in which he seeks asylum, expulsion or compulsory return to any state where he may be subjected to persecution'. All of the above examples seemed to support the notion that the prohibition of refoulement could have become a principle of general international law. However, it remains unclear whether this notion has become established enough to be considered a norm of jus cogens, although most commentators seem inclined to believe so. For a summary of these arguments, see G. Goodwin-Gill, *supra* n° 3, p. 167 *et seq.* The author argues that all international texts concerning the non-refoulement principle (as the ones mentioned above by the UNHCR or the UN General Assembly) were always adopted unanimously and without any opposition. In his view 'Art. 33 [..] is of a "fundamentally

However, the protection against refoulement was not absolute. Art. 33.2 GC recognised that a refugee 'whom there are reasonable grounds for regarding as a danger to the security of the country [...] or who, having been convicted by a final judgment of a particularly serious crime, constitutes a danger to the community of that country' could be exempted from protection against refoulement. The wording of the provision and the *travaux préparatoires* seemed to indicate that the assessment of both the risk posed by the refugee to the community and of the eventual seriousness of the crime committed was left to the judgment of the Contracting States. Different national perceptions inevitably entailed different uses of this discretionary power, although most Western countries always relied on principles such as proportionality, natural justice and the possibility of judicial review in assessing individual cases.[45]

The two exceptions contained in Art. 33.2 GC were by no means unique. They were part of the wider context of exception clauses to the granting of refugee status established by Art. 1.F.[46] The provision excluded the possibility of claiming refugee status for those who had committed 'a crime against peace, a war crime, or a crime against humanity' (Art. 1.F.a), those who had 'committed a serious non-political crime outside the country of refuge prior to his admission to that country as a refugee' (Art. 1.F.b), and those who had 'been guilty of acts contrary to the purposes and principles of the United Nations' (Art. 1F.c).

The idea to exclude war criminals or other criminals from availing themselves of the asylum institution typically asserted itself immediately after the end of the Second World War. The 1946 International Refugee Organisation (IRO) constitution already included such a clause. Similarly, the 1948 Universal Declaration of Human Rights excluded people who committed non-political crimes or acts against UN principles.[47] The exceptions provided by Art. 1.F.*a* GC – war crimes, crimes against peace and crimes against humanity – could only be defined on the basis of the relevant international instruments. To this purpose, national practice constantly relied on an ever-widening body of international Treaties,

---

norm creating character" in the sense in which that phrase was used by the International Court of Justice in the North Sea Continental Shelf cases' (p. 168).

45. The 1967 UN Declaration on Territorial Asylum reinforced this exception by authorizing a further exception in the case of situations of mass influx (Art. 3).

46. Art. 1.F was not the only exception to the application of Art. 1.A GC. Art. 1.C-E referred to other instances where the Convention might not have been applicable. These instances concerned: voluntary acts of the individual whereby refugee status would effectively be given up (Art. 1.C.1-5); the fact that the circumstances which lead to persecution had ceased to exist (Art. 1.C.6); refugees who were protected or assisted by United Nations agencies (Art. 1.D); and naturalised individuals (Art. 1.E). These cases will not be considered in this context because of their less controversial nature and their minor relevance to the scope to this research.

47. Art. 14.2 states that '[t]his right [to invoke asylum] may not be invoked in the case of prosecutions genuinely arising from non-political crimes or from acts contrary to the purpose and principles of the United Nations'.

such as the 1949 Geneva Conventions and the 1977 Additional Protocols,[48] or the 1948 UN Convention on the Prevention and Punishment of the Crime of Genocide.[49] In the case of crimes against peace their definition relied more on the international widespread interpretation of other texts, such as the UN Charter and the above-mentioned Conventions.[50] In all cases the criteria of 'individual responsibility' was always applied, even in the case of individuals allegedly carrying out superior orders.[51]

Art. 1.F.b raised a few difficulties of interpretation, although its introduction was by no means a novelty.[52] Firstly it was not made clear whether such a non-political crime was to be a permanent impediment to claiming asylum, or if other circumstances[53] might attenuate such an impediment. In this respect State practice appeared to have followed an approach based on the consideration of each individual case.[54] Secondly, the wording 'serious' and 'non-political' crime was inevitably open to very different interpretations. With regards to the 'seriousness' of the crime, the French version of the GC offered some enlightenment,[55]

---

48. These Conventions dealt with the treatment of prisoners of war, of the wounded or shipwrecked, of the civilian population and their property etc. Any breach of such Conventions or of the customs of war would be considered a 'war crime'. Additionally, the 1946 London Charter for the Establishment of the International Military Tribunal included relevant indications in the field of war crimes (see specific crimes listed under Art. VI).

49. The crime of genocide is similar in essence to war crimes, but committed on a larger scale. Art. II of the Genocide Convention defines it as the commission of certain enumerated acts, such as killing, maiming or imposing oppressive measures 'with the intent to destroy, in whole or in part, a national, ethnical, racial or religious group, as such'. Typical recent examples of the exercise of such jurisdiction have been the 1993 International Tribunal on Yugoslavia and the 1994 International Tribunal of Rwanda.

50. For a very comprehensive overview see I. Brownlie, *International law and the use of force* (Clarendon Press, Oxford, 1963).

51. The principle of 'individual responsibility' was clearly included in most Western States' military manuals. The Statutes of both the Yugoslavia and Rwanda Tribunals set out clear rules of responsibility, whereby none of the following could be considered a mitigatory circumstance: a) having an official position; b) the fact of acting under orders; and c) the failure of superiors to monitor their subordinates (Arts 7 and 6 respectively).

52. See the above mentioned Art. 14.2 of the 1948 Universal Declaration and the 1946 IRO Constitution which excluded ordinary criminals extraditable by treaty.

53. Such as, for instance, having been prosecuted and already served the relevant sentence, the passing of considerable time, an amnesty or a pardon. The UNHCR Handbook at para. 149 specifies that all of the above should be taken into account and that if these conditions were to be fulfilled the exclusion clause should no longer be applicable, unless it could be proven that the 'applicant's criminal character still predominates'. This ample national discretion was justified by the fact that it was paramount to protect the community and this was precisely the reason why the exception clause of Art. 1.F was inserted in the first place.

54. However, the transposition of this principle in some of the EU asylum initiatives has been riddled with controversies (see later Chapter III.3 on the 1992 Edinburgh Initiatives).

55. The French version reads '*un crime grave de droit commun*'.

since it stated that each State was entitled to weigh the crime in question against its own standards. The majority of national jurisprudence seemed to indicate that 'serious crimes, above all, are those against physical integrity, life and liberty'.[56] The term 'non-political' crime was equally hard to define. A steady evolution in international law meant that certain violent crimes, committed in the name of political or ideological ideals and greatly disproportionate to their objectives were eventually categorised as 'terrorist acts' because of their cruel or horrifying nature.[57] The overall States' practice seemed to indicate a case-by-case approach where considerable leeway was exercised in the definition of what was to be considered 'political', with the result that application has been very inconsistent.

The exclusion from refugee status based on acts contrary to the purposes and principles of the UN provided by Art. 1F.c GC was based on Art. 14.2 of the 1948 Universal Declaration of Human Rights. Although these principles and purposes were already clearly stated in the first two articles of the UN Charter,[58] they were subsequently considerably developed especially in the Human Rights field. The Universal Declaration of 1948, the 1966 ICCPR and another dozen Conventions in different Human Rights areas greatly enlarged the scope for 'acts contrary to the principles and purposes on the UN'. As in the other exclusion clauses of Art. 1.F, the definition of the boundaries of individual responsibility remained an open question. The main issue in this case concerned whether responsibility was limited to those in a position of authority or whether it also regarded relationships between individuals.[59] The UNHCR interpreted this provision strictly in the context of the other two exclusion clauses, therefore limiting

---

56. G. Goodwin-Gill, *supra* n° 3, p. 105. See also the selection of national jurisprudence quoted by the author, as well as the commentators on this point mentioned in the same context. The author also supplies interesting first-hand information acquired during his co-operation with the US Government and the UNHCR. In 1980, when 125,000 Cubans asylum seekers arrived in the US, the UNHCR's co-operation was requested in assessing their criminal records. 'With a view to promoting consistent decisions, UNHCR proposed that, in the absence of any political factors, a presumption of a serious crime might be considered as raised by evidence of commission of any of the following offences: homicide, rape, child molesting, wounding, arson, drugs trafficking, and armed robbery' (p. 107).

57. The same problem of interpretation arose in respect to the definition of persecution on 'political' grounds (as mentioned earlier in this paragraph).

58. The UN main objectives were, in broad terms, the maintenance of peace, the upholding of Human Rights and justice, the promotion of social progress, better standards of life and greater freedom. To achieve these aims the principles and purposes of the UN included collective action to preserve peace; respect for equal rights and the self-determination of peoples; international co-operation in all fields; and promotion and encouragement of Human Rights.

59. The question was of particular importance as most of the acts that could give rise to exclusion from refugee status under Art. 1F.c GC were generally Human Rights violations This was further demonstrated by the creation of International Tribunals such as the Yugoslav or Rwandan ones.

individual responsibility only to those in a position of authority.[60] National practices were, however, at times inclined to extend the scope of individual responsibility.[61] During the first two decades of the GC this exclusion was very rarely invoked. Recently, its use has become more frequent, probably as a direct consequence of the expansion of the purposes of the UN.[62]

Art. 1 of the 1951 GC subjected the definition of 'refugee' to two limitations, the most important one being the historical dateline of fearing persecution because of 'events occurring before 1 January 1951' (Art. 1.A.2). The GC also offered the option of further restricting such provision with a geographical clause, whereby the above events had to have occurred in 'Europe' before 1951 (Art.1.B.*a*). By the end of the Sixties in a world plagued by the Cold War regional confrontations and the legacy of the post-colonial conflicts the strain of such limitations was becoming increasingly apparent. Many States had relied on Recommendation n° E to the 1951 GC to enlarge the scope of their asylum obligations, but time for an amendment to the GC finally seemed ripe.

Although the 1967 New York Protocol relating to the Status of Refugees was always referred to as an 'amendment' to the 1951 GC, it was in fact a totally independent international instrument. It was not necessary to be a party to the GC to accede to the 1967 Protocol. In ratifying it, Contracting States agreed to apply the 1951 GC, but without the temporal or optional geographical limitations contained in Art. 1.[63] Small differences between the two texts meant that there were some advantages in acceding only to the 1967 Protocol in respect of arbitration. According to Art. 36 of the 1951 GC the International Court of Justice had jurisdiction over any disputes arising from the Convention, and no reservations were allowed on this point. The parallel provisions in Art. IV of the Protocol instead allowed for reservations and a number of countries took advantage of this possibility.[64]

---

60. UNHCR Handbook, para. 162–163.
61. See G. Goodwin-Gill, *supra* n° 3, pp. 110–111 for a review of this jurisprudence. In brief, instances where individual responsibility was extended included cases of people who denounced others to the occupation forces during WW II (France), terrorist acts, membership of special police forces renowned for their brutality (although no individual charge of brutality was alleged) etc. Other cases reviewed have, however, kept in line with the UNHCR theory of responsibility, such as, for instance, the French denial of asylum to Mr Duvalier, Haiti's former dictator.
62. Human Rights aside, the UN has also become involved in totally new fields, such as the fight against the trafficking of drugs and international crime, which has inevitably given rise to new individual responsibilities.
63. In fact, the geographical limitation could still be upheld, but only by those Contracting parties that originally invoked it in 1951. In 1996, six States including Hungary, Monaco, Malta and Turkey, still maintained this geographical limitation. The United States, for instance, is only party to the 1967 Protocol.
64. Among these are China, Venezuela, Rwanda and the Congo.

I.3. REFUGEE PROTECTION THROUGH INTERNATIONAL ORGANISATIONS: THE UNHCR

International bodies for the protection of refugees were an initiative of the 20th Century. In the period between the two World Wars numerous so-called High Commissioners for Refugees were nominated to deal with refugees fleeing different sources of persecution.[65] In 1938 32 States convened at the Evian Conference and decided to create the Intergovernmental Committee on Refugees, but unfortunately its operational abilities were severely hampered by the onset of the Second World War.[66] As soon as the UN structure was put into place ECOSOC prompted the institution of the International Refugee Organisation (IRO) whose tasks included identification and repatriation; protection, care and assistance; and transport and resettlement of war refugees.[67] As the IRO mandate was limited to war refugees it was clear that a more permanent institution had to be created. The main issues under discussion were the definition of the subjects for protection and the ways in which to ensure it. The High Commissioner for Refugees and the Statute of the UNHCR embodied the outcome of this debate.[68]

The mandate of UNHCR comprised two main aims. Firstly, to provide international protection to those in need as defined by the Statute and secondly to seek permanent solutions to the plight of refugees, either by voluntary repatriation or by assimilation in countries of refuge. The office of the High Commissioner was to be of 'an entirely non-political character; it shall be humanitarian and social and shall relate, as a rule, to groups and categories of refugees' (Art. 2). Several ways were identified to provide protection, but they mainly focused on: a) promoting the conclusion of international conventions in the refugee field, supervising their application and proposing amendments to

---

65. In the same way that the evolution of the concept of 'refugee' was characterised by an initial 'category' approach, likewise the various High Commissioners were appointed specifically to deal with one particular group of persecuted people. In 1921 Dr Nansen was appointed by the League of Nations High Commissioner for the Russian Refugees and his mandate was later extended to cover Armenian refugees. In 1933 another High Commissioner's Office was established for German refugees and finally in 1938 all these posts were unified in one single mandate for 'all' refugees.

66. Some of its work was effectively taken over in 1943 by the UN Relief and Rehabilitation Administration (UNRRA) which was to cope with the millions of people displaced by the conflict.

67. The IRO carried out its tasks remarkably well considering the storm of accusations it was subjected to in the few years of its existence. These accusations stemmed mainly from members of the Soviet block who were increasingly accusing it of exploiting refugee issues for the purpose of ideological confrontation.

68. The High Commissioner's Office and the Statute of the UNHCR were approved in 1949 and 1950 respectively (for the entire text see UNGA Resolution 428 (V) of 14/2/1950).

them, or bringing them up to date;[69] b) promoting co-operation with States in order to improve the situation of refugees; and c) promoting the admission of refugees (Art. 8). According to Art. 2 of the Statute the UNHCR should have dealt mainly with a 'group' approach. However, the greatest caseload to date has consisted mainly of individual cases and no national objection to this practice has ever been recorded.

The UNHCR was attributed the legal status of subsidiary organ of UNGA, following of Art. 22 of the UN Charter, and its mandate was renewable every five years. It was to follow policy directives formulated both by UNGA and by ECOSOC and it enjoyed international personality.[70] This personality assumed particular importance in the context of States' obligations towards refugees. Unfortunately, individuals were never considered subjects of international law and therefore they could not enforce their rights against a State. The UNHCR international legal personality allowed it to act on behalf of the disempowered individual. In the event of difficult situations, the High Commissioner could request the opinion of the Executive Committee of the High Commissioner's Programme.[71]

The UNHCR participated in national procedures involving the determination of refugee status by virtue of its supervisory role, although with considerable national variations.[72] In broad terms the UNHCR's fundamental role was to help States identify those in need of protection and to ensure that the interpretation of international criteria was as consistent as possible. To this end it was to provide States with an assessment of the applicant's credibility and conditions in the country of origin, information on similar cases in other jurisdictions and

---

69. The UNHCR actively encouraged and participated in the revision of the 1951 GC that lead to the adoption of the 1967 New York Protocol. See V. Türk, 'The role of UNHCR in the development of international refugee law' in F. Nicholson and P. Twomey (eds), *supra* n° 20, p. 153, at pp. 161–164.

70. Its personality could be traced to the UN overall legal personality. On this issue see the 1949 *Corfu Channel Reparations case*, ICJ Rep. 1949 174, at pp. 178–79. Following on from the conclusions of the Court, the UNHCR was entitled to carry out its protective function on the basis of a 'universal jurisdiction' (p. 184). Specific authority was also granted to the UNHCR by the 1951 GC and the 1967 Protocol. According to Art. 35 GC, for instance, Member States pledged to cooperate with it and to facilitate its supervision of the application of the Convention.

71. This was established by UNGA in 1958, Resolution 1166 (XII), of 26/11/57. Over the years the Committee adopted regular Conclusions, which acquired considerable weight as 'soft law' in the field of refugee protection. Although States were not legally bound to accept them, they had an undeniable impact on the shaping of refugee issues.

72. In 1989, UNHCR broadly identified five levels of participation in national procedures, ranging from no formal role, to observer, to acting as an *amicus curiae*, to voting member of an appeal body or even a joint decision-maker (Note on procedures for the determination of refugee status under international instruments, UN doc. A/AC.96/INF.152/Rev.8, of 12/9/89).

interpretation of fundamental concepts such as 'persecution' or 'well-founded fear' etc.

The definition of who was entitled to protection from persecution contained in the UNHCR Statute was broadly similar to the one of the 1951 GC, notwithstanding two small differences. Firstly, there were no temporal or geographical limitations to the definition of persecution and secondly, the UNHCR Statute did not list 'membership of a particular social group' among the grounds of persecution. These differences had no impact on the way the UNHCR eventually exercised its mandate: the frequency and the large scale of world-wide refugee crises in the last half century required a notable increase in the flexibility of its mandate. In this respect, the concept of who was to be considered a 'refugee' was considerably broadened by new humanitarian concerns. Less than a decade after its creation, the UNHCR was already entrusted to assist specific refugees outside its mandate.[73] By 1959, the proliferation of crises meant that UNGA was forced to give the UNHCR a general mission to use its good offices in assisting all kinds of refugees, even if they fell outside its mandate.[74]

Slowly, throughout the Sixties, amidst world-wide violent internal or international conflicts, a new broader 'working' notion of refugee began to emerge for the UNHCR. It concerned people affected by the same two basic events. They had crossed an international border fleeing an internal civil, political or social conflict and the sheer scale of their numbers made a case-by-case assessment impossible or impractical. Increasingly, these refugees were being termed as 'displaced persons',[75] and this terminology applied both to people fleeing countries divided in fact but not by law (such as Sudan or Vietnam) or to those outside their country of origin. The fact that this term remained in use for decades throughout horrifying humanitarian crises, such as the Indo-Chinese conflict, indicated the reluctance of States to recognise such cases as 'Convention refugees'. By the end of the 70s, the UNHCR's mandate firmly included 'displaced persons' and 'victims of man-made disasters'. In the last two decades its mandate has been further enlarged to include other categories of people in need of assistance, such as returnees, women, children and asylum seekers.[76]

---

73. This was necessary in order to assist Hungarian refugees in 1956 (UNGA Resolution 1129(XI) of 21/11/1956). The following year the High Commissioner was charged to assist Chinese refugees in Hong Kong who were fleeing the civil war on the mainland (UNGA Resolution 1167(XII) of 26/11/1957). In the following few years other crises followed that required urgent intervention in Algeria and in the Congo.

74. UNGA Resolution 1388(XIV) of 20/11/1959.

75. This terminology was developed in the 70s and employed for the first time to define refugees fleeing the Sudan conflict in 1972 (ECOSOC Resolution 1655(LII) of 1/6/1972). It was later applied in 1974 –75 to refugees from the India-Bangladesh conflict and from Cyprus.

76. As of late, the UNHCR competence ratio personae comprised 'five main categories: (i) refugees and asylum seekers; (ii) stateless persons; (iii) returnees; (iv) the internally displaced; and (v) persons threatened with displacement or otherwise at risk' (V. Türk, *supra* n° 69, at p. 155).

The new humanitarian roles the UNHCR was forced to assume were not devoid of criticism. The Agency was often accused of poor co-ordination and of being unable to take the lead on the field. Several commentators laid the blame on the lack of a clear mandate to undertake these new functions and on the increased politicisation of the Agency as a result of having to cooperate with leading donor States.[77] Unfortunately, the UNHCR's considerable expertise in the refugee field did not appear to function properly in crises such as the Yugoslav ones, which entailed the deployment of considerable military force. Other evidence pointed to the fact that the UNHCR was at times manipulated by donor States into pursuing 'internal displacement' solutions at the expense of more effective protection.[78] Hence, given the continuous proliferation of refugee crises, one of the most pressing challenges of future international refugee protection would no doubt be the reform of the UNHCR's mandate.

I.4. OTHER INTERNATIONAL INSTRUMENTS OF PROTECTION AND REGIONAL INITIATIVES

I.4.A. Other international organisations involved in the protection of refugees

Although the UNHCR was specifically designed to deal with the protection of refugees, numerous other UN agencies also cooperated with it for particular tasks, especially in providing relief aid.[79] Among other non-UN international organisations dealing with refugee problems there have been the IOM (International Organisation for Migration) and the International Committee of the Red Cross (ICRC). The IOM was founded in 1951 and currently comprises some 83 States. Its main activities have focused on ensuring planned migration, but it also dealt with the organised transfer of refugees, displaced persons and other persons obliged to leave their country of origin. It has also been assisting asylum seekers in various countries and refugees who elected to be voluntarily repatriated.[80] Although the IOM did not have a real protective function, its presence in countries where refugees were being returned – voluntarily or not – brought considerable advantages and often amounted to informal protection.

The ICRC mandate included protection responsibilities similar to those of the UNHCR. They were regulated by the four 1949 Geneva Conventions and the

---

77. See S.A. Cunliffe and M. Pugh, 'UNHCR as leader in humanitarian assistance: a triumph of politics over law?' in F. Nicholson and P. Twomey (eds), *supra* n° 20, p. 175.

78. See E. Mooney, 'In-country protection: out of bounds for the UNHCR?' in F. Nicholson and P. Twomey (eds), *supra* n° 20, p. 200.

79. These are mainly specialised agencies such as the FAO (Food and Agriculture Organisation), UNICEF (The UN Children's fund), UNBRO (UN Border Relief Organisation) and WHO (World Health Organisation).

80. Successful IOM initiatives have included helping to resettle Ugandan refugees in 1972, helping people displaced by the Iraqi invasion of Kuwait in 1990 and helping Vietnamese refugees resettle in Vietnam after 1991.

1977 Additional Protocols, and such responsibilities were, as a rule, exercised during conflicts.[81] Other institutions involved with the protection of refugees have been operating on more regional bases, such as the Organisation of African Unity (OAU), the Organisation of American States (OAS) and the Council of Europe. ECOSOC also developed an effective system of co-operation and consultation[82] with a number of non-governmental institutions such as Amnesty International, the Anti-Slavery Society, the Minority Rights Group and the European Council of Refugees and Exiles, an umbrella organisation encompassing more than 60 European NGO's and Refugee Councils dealing with refugee protection.

I.4.B. Other international instruments of protection

After the signing of the 1967 New York Protocol little progress was done to further the scope of refugee protection through universal international agreements. That same year UN Members approved a Declaration on Territorial Asylum,[83] that laid down the principles on which national asylum policies should be based. The Declaration was, in fact, of very little substance, as it mainly reiterated principles already contained in the 1951 GC, such as the prohibition of refoulement.[84] The only new concept appeared to be the necessity of showing 'a spirit of international solidarity' in cases where excessive burdens might be placed on any particular receiving State (Art. 2.2). The drafters of this Declaration expressed the hope that it would eventually be turned into an international convention.[85] But despite a decade of efforts, the 1977 UN Conference on Territorial Asylum ended in complete failure and no further effort was ever made towards reconvening another conference. Given the emerging divisions on matters of principle between UN Members,[86] it was thought best to leave the UNHCR to deal with the emerging refugee crises.

In the meantime other instruments in the field of Human Rights emerged that were going to have a collateral effect on refugee protection. Overall, their main impact consisted in an enhancement of the right of non-refoulement. The first

---

81. The modes of protection for both organisations were similarly defined, but the subjects of this protection were different. In the case of the ICRC it mainly concerned itself with prisoners of war and wounded armed forces personnel. One area where the mandates of both institutions did overlap was the protection of civilians during conflicts. In these case there have been frequent and very successful instances of co-operation.

82. This was achieved under Art. 71 of the UN Charter which granted official 'consultative' status to any organisation named by ECOSOC.

83. The Declaration was adopted unanimously by the UNGA (UN doc. A/CN.4/245).

84. Unfortunately, the Declaration also expanded the previous exception clauses of the GC (see above Chapter I.2)

85. See UN docs. A/C.6/SR. 983–9.

86. On these differences see P. Weiss, 'The Draft Convention on territorial asylum', (1979) 50 BYIL, p. 151, at p. 176 et seq.

of such instruments was the International Covenant on Civil and Political Rights of 1966 (ICCPR) and the activities of the Human Rights Committee that was set up to monitor its implementation. Although the ICCPR was modeled on the 1948 Universal Declaration, some important rights, such as the right to seek asylum, were omitted.[87] Art. 7 of the Covenant contained a prohibition on subjecting anybody to 'torture or to cruel, inhuman or degrading treatment or punishment'. The Human Rights Committee interpreted this provision so as to include a prohibition on expelling individuals to a country where they could face such treatment.[88] An optional Protocol allowed the Committee to hear individual complaints, but some major international actors – such as the United States – did not adhere to it, making the complaints procedure rather ineffective.

The 1984 UN Convention against Torture and other Cruel, Inhuman or Degrading Treatment or Punishment (CAT) possessed an even greater potential to improve refugee protection, especially with regards to the prohibition of refoulement. The Committee against Torture set up by the Convention was given the power to investigate cases on its own initiative upon receiving reliable information that torture was being systematically practised by a Member State. The Convention also contained an express prohibition against returning anyone to a State 'where there are substantial grounds for believing that he would be in danger of being subjected to torture' (Art. 3.1). To determine if such risks existed Member States had to consider whether the State where the person was to be returned to displayed 'a consistent pattern of gross, flagrant or mass violation of Human Rights' (Art. 3.2). The principle of non-refoulement was reinforced by a Protocol allowing individual petition that States could ratify. In this case, the Committee could act as a further opportunity to appeal for asylum seekers facing removal. Since the Convention only entered into force in 1987, the Committee has not had sufficient time yet to develop a large body of jurisprudence. A few cases so far have concerned asylum seekers and reinforced their right to non-refoulement.[89]

---

87. Most of the rights that are similarly phrased to those of the European Convention of Human Rights will be examined further on. Only some are of interest to refugees, such as the right not to be tortured (Art. 3) or the right to leave one's country or to re-enter it (Art. 12), but the Human Rights Committee has produced to date very little case law on the subject of refugees (probably because the countries that have signed the optional protocol have other regional fora where they can take their disputes).

88. See R. Plender and N. Mole, 'Beyond the Geneva Convention: constructing a *de facto* right of asylum from international Human Rights instruments' in F. Nicholson and P. Twomey (eds), *supra* n° 20, p. 81, at pp. 91–92.

89. See R. Plender and N. Mole, *supra* n° 88, at pp. 86–87. The first of those cases centered on the necessity of establishing a 'personal' risk of torture to the asylum seeker and the fact that the absence of a 'consistent pattern of gross, flagrant or mass violations of Human Rights' in the country of origin (Art. 3.2) did not necessarily entail the impossibility of the applicant being tortured if returned (*Balabou Mutombo* v. *Switzerland*). In another case (*Kisoki* v. *Sweden*) the Committee decided that an applicant's credibility should not be damaged by the fact that he withheld information about his experience as it would be

I.4.C. Regional approaches to protection

Although the 1951 GC and the 1967 Protocol were the only world-wide instruments for the protection of refugees, a number of other initiatives were undertaken at the regional level, especially in the African and Latin American contexts.[90] Latin America, in particular, had a long asylum tradition. Art. 16 of the 1889 Montevideo Treaty on International Penal Law had already recognised that political refugees were to be granted 'inviolable asylum'. The subsequent 1954 Caracas Convention on Territorial Asylum extended protection to all those persons 'persecuted for their beliefs, opinions, or political affiliations, or for acts which may be considered as political offences' (Art. 2). The tragic refugee crises of the 80s prompted further initiatives that led to the 1984 Cartagena Declaration where a significant broadening of the refugee definition was proposed.[91] The Declaration was not a formally binding treaty, but it was repeatedly endorsed by the OAS and closely mirrored the expanding scope of protection supported by the UNHCR.

The African continent also developed regional instruments of protection that included a very broad definition of 'refugee'. Art. I.1 of the 1969 OAU Convention on Specific Aspects of Refugee Problems largely echoed the wording of the parallel article in the 1951 GC. Art. I.2, however, considerably broadened the scope of protection by extending it to 'every person who, owing to external aggression, occupation, foreign domination or events seriously disturbing public order in either part or the whole of his country of origin or nationality, is compelled to leave his place of habitual residence in order to seek refuge in another place outside his country of origin or nationality'. Remarkably, this was the most comprehensive international definition of refugee protection ever conceived. The same Convention also contained an express clause on solidarity with other States in the event that they might be unable to cope with an excessive burden of refugees (Art. II.4).

---

normal for someone subjected to torture to be severely traumatised. In the latest case (*Ismail Alan* v. *Switzerland*) the Committee reviewed the possibility of an 'internal flight' option for the applicant and found this not to be possible in Turkey. On the basis of this jurisprudence, CAT appeared to considerably enhance the principle of non-refoulement of Art. 33 GC.

90. It is impossible at this stage to analyse these initiatives in depth. For some general insights on these instruments, see E. Arboleda, 'Refugee definition in Africa and Latin America: the lessons of pragmatism' (1991) 3 IJRL, p. 185; and by the same author 'The Cartagena Declaration of 1984 and its similarities with the 1969 OAU Convention – A comparative perspective' (1995) 7 IJRL, p. 87.

91. Art. 3 reads '[h]ence the definition or concept of a refugee to be recommended for use in the region is one which, in addition to containing elements of the 1951 GC and the 1967 Protocol, includes among refugees persons who have fled their country because their lives, safety or freedom have been threatened by generalized violence, foreign aggression, internal conflicts, massive violations of Human Rights or other circumstances which have seriously

In Europe no regional refugee arrangement comparable to those of South America or Africa was undertaken. This was probably due in part to the fact that the 1951 GC was perceived as a European initiative anyway.[92] Nonetheless, much along the same lines as the 1966 ICCPR and the 1984 CAT, the 1950 European Convention on Human Rights and Fundamental Freedoms (ECHR) contained some rights that indirectly reinforced refugee protection. Unfortunately, no specific provision on asylum on the model of Art. 14 of the 1948 Universal Declaration was included in the ECHR.[93] The most relevant provision for asylum seekers proved to be the prohibition of torture and cruel or inhuman treatment contained in Art. 3.[94] As in the case of Art. 7 ICCPR, although there was no specific mention of the prohibition of refoulement, the principle was nonetheless inferred from the contents of the article.[95] Interestingly, there was at times a considerable discrepancy between the Decisions of the EHR Commission and the EHR Court (ECtHR). The Commission frequently found for a 'favourable' application of Art. 3 towards asylum seekers, often using its powers to suspend an imminent national measure of expulsion, whereas the Court was always more circumspect. The latter also set a high standard of proof by stressing that the ill-treatment had to attain a minimum level of severity.[96]

---

disturbed public order'. The same article also contains a reference to the formulation of a 'refugee' contained in the 1969 OAU Convention.

92. Some smaller initiatives by the Council of Europe in the early 80s will be reviewed in Chapter II.

93. The European Court of Human Rights pointed out on several occasions that the right of asylum was not 'as such' protected by the ECHR (see for instance *Vilvarajah and others v. UK* (1992) 14 EHRR 248, at para. 102). For a general overview of the application of the ECHR to refugees see Council of Europe, *Problems raised by certain aspects of the present situation of refugees from the standpoint of the European Convention on Human Rights* (Strasbourg, 1997, Human Rights files n° 9).

94. The 1984 CAT contained a stronger provision (Art. 3.1) because it explicitly mentioned the prohibition of refoulement.

95. See the Decision of the European Human Rights Commission in the *Kerboub* case (1972) Collection of Decisions, p. 62; also the judgment of the ECtHR in *Cruz Varas* v. *Sweden* (1992) 14 EHRR 1.

96. In the *Vilvarajah* case, *supra* n° 93, para. 111, the Court held that 'mere possibility of ill-treatment [...] in such circumstances, is not in itself sufficient to give rise to a breach of Art. 3'. It also stressed that the applicants had to present 'substantial grounds' and there had to be 'real risk' of ill treatment (para. 103–107). This constant line of interpretation was strongly criticised, given that asylum seekers were unlikely to ever meet such stringent levels of proof. Overall, the Court seemed to be motivated by a general fear of opening the floodgates of extradition; see, for instance, C. Van Den Wyngaert, 'Applying the European Convention on Human Rights to extradition: opening Pandora's box?' (1990) 39 ICLQ, p. 757. In contrast, see the Decision of the Commission in *Chahal* v. *United Kingdom*, application n° 22414/93, 27/6/95 where it noted that the guarantees of Art. 3 are of such an absolute character, not permitting any exception, that they are in fact wider than Art. 33 of the 1951 GC.

However, in a landmark judgment in 1996,[97] the Court established that the prohibition of Art. 3 ECHR was absolute and therefore applied both to asylum seekers and extradition cases. It was also non-derogable and thus broader than the prohibition contained in Art. 33 GC. In fact, the Court had previously already stated that Art. 3 ECHR applied to everyone 'however heinous the crime allegedly committed'.[98] It then further expanded this concept in *Chahal* by affirming that '[i]n these circumstances the activities of the individual in question, however undesirable or dangerous, cannot be of material consideration. The protection afforded by Art. 3 is thus wider than that provided by Arts 32 and 33 on the United Nations 1951 Convention on the Status of Refugees'.[99]

In so far as the right to family life (Art. 8) was concerned, the Commission adopted a fairly wide interpretation, thereby protecting relatives of asylum seekers threatened with deportation.[100] However, on the whole, the Court often seemed to subscribe to the national governments' concerns about 'population manageability' and did not yet exploit the full potential offered by the EHRC for refugee protection.[101]

I.5. CONCLUDING REMARKS

This Chapter's purpose was to give a brief outline of the fundamental tenets of international refugee protection. To date, the only truly universal texts on international refugee protection remain the 1951 GC and the subsequent amendments included in the 1967 New York Protocol. Despite the universality of such texts, it remains difficult to outline a real international refugee regime

---

97. *Chahal* v. *UK* (1997) 23 EHRR 413.

98. *Soering* v. *UK* (1989) 11 EHRR 439, at para. 88.

99. See *Chahal, supra* n° 97, para. 80. The protection afforded by Art. 3 ECHR was broader because none of the exception clauses contained in Art. 33.2 GC applied. Art. 15.2 ECHR specifically excluded any derogation from Art. 3 ECHR. Subsequent jurisprudence further expanded the principle by claiming that protection did not depend on the source of harm, or on whether the persecution derived from non-State agents (see *Ahmed* v. *Austria*, (1996) 26 EHRR 278 and *HLR* v. *France* (1996) 24 EHRR 423).

100. See *Fadele* v. *UK*, Application n° 13078/87 reported in R. Plender and N. Mole, *supra* n° 88, at p. 91. The case involved the case of a Nigerian asylum seeker with three British children. The Commission found that obliging the children to follow their father to Nigeria to live in conditions of extreme poverty would have amounted to a breach of Art. 3 ECHR. The case was settled before the Court could examine it.

101. The Court found it necessary to mention the concerns expressed by the United Kingdom in *Vilvarajah* by the fact that 'the consequences of finding a breach of Art. 3 in the present case would be that all other persons in similar situations facing random risks on account of civil turmoil in the state in which they lived, would be entitled not to be removed, thereby permitting the entry of a potentially very large class of people with the attendant serious social and economic consequences'. This constituted a strong indication of the intentional adoption of policy considerations limiting the scope of the Court's decision-making ability.

because the implementation of the above Conventions was remitted purely to the Signatory States. The ICJ was never asked to clarify interpretation problems and hence national implementations varied widely. The growing number of refugee crises of the last few decades differed greatly from the refugee scenarios the drafters of the GC had in mind. In the past few years it has therefore been questioned whether the refugee definition of the GC has not become obsolete.[102] In the face of so many different national interpretations, the answer to this issue remains uncertain.

The UNHCR, as the leading global refugee protection agency, has thus become the only instrument capable of ensuring some uniformity in the international refugee regime. Its mandate lacks, however, any way to enforce its uniformity drive through binding interpretations. The demand for increasing flexibility in the UNHCR's exercise of its mandate has also put the latter under increasing strain. On the one hand, it has allowed its working definition of 'refugee' to adapt to the intervening historical events, such as the proliferation of international and civil conflicts or natural and man-made disasters. On the other hand, though, the UNHCR has not always been successful in the new roles that it has been obliged to perform. This is mainly due to the emerging overlap between humanitarian and military interventions that has characterised all the latest refugee crises. In order to deal effectively with such events in the future the UNHCR will need a clear modification of its old mandate.

Both the 1951 GC and the 1967 Protocol were, in most respects, European creations. Other subsequent regional initiatives generously expanded the narrow 1951 refugee definition, notably in South America and in Africa. The OAU's introduction of a most comprehensive concept of refugee protection quickly became a leading example of human solidarity. Other international conventions, most notably the ECHR, had a considerable effect on the reinforcement of the principle of non-refoulement. Europe, however, was notable in its inability to follow the examples of other regional initiatives and expand its own concept of refugee protection. On the contrary, a restricting trend has slowly taken place since the 70s, otherwise termed 'Convention fundamentalism'.[103] Instead of allowing a certain degree of flexibility in the interpretation of the GC, European States championed a very narrow implementation of the Convention with the explicit aim of reducing refugee flows. It is in this context of shrinking refugee protection that the European initiatives analysed in the next Chapters should be understood.

---

102. See J. Sztucky, 'Who is a refugee? The Convention definition: universal or obsolete?' in F. Nicholson and P. Twomey (eds), *supra* n° 20, p. 55.
103. See J. Sztucky, *supra* n° 102, p. 68.

2 The Beginnings of European Political Co-operation on Asylum and the Schengen Laboratory

II.1. THE BEGINNINGS OF EUROPEAN POLITICAL CO-OPERATION ON ASYLUM

The analysis contained in the previous Chapter clearly indicates that the origins of refugee protection can be traced to the evolution of international Human Rights law during the 20th Century. The 1951 GC and all subsequent refugee initiatives were adopted as international conventions and transposed by Signatory States into their respective legal orders. Since there was no provision for an international jurisdictional control over the application of such instruments, national implementations varied considerably. As a consequence, up to the end of the 70s refugee protection was, by and large, perceived as a purely national responsibility.

By the middle of the 80s two factors led to a change in this perception. The first one involved the dawning of a new geopolitical reality as the Cold War world order slowly started to disintegrate. This inevitably led to dramatic changes in refugee flows. With the crumbling of the Soviet empire what had been a steady but small trickle of politically persecuted refugees became first a stream and later a flood.[1] Localised conflicts started to erupt, no longer contained by the logic of super-power nuclear confrontation.[2] The considerable expansion of global communications and transport networks further increased cross-border refugee mobility. The impact of these increased refugee flows on the West was further compounded by the 70s economic crisis, which left most States unable to absorb the high level of immigration they had encouraged in the two previous decades. With the closing down of traditional immigration channels, claiming asylum became the only avenue left to gain access or refuge in the West. Thus, national asylum adjudication procedures began to be increasingly unable to

---

1. Asylum applications in Western Europe increased as much as a hundred times in the span of a decade. On this point see D. Joly, 'The porous dam: European harmonisation on asylum in the Nineties' (1994) 6 IJRL, p. 159, at p. 160 *et seq*. See also Annex, Table 1.

2. These conflicts meant the appearance of new persecutory factors, such as ethnic cleansing and victims fleeing civil wars. Most Signatory States maintained that the provisions of the 1951 GC could not cover such instances, but they were nonetheless bound by the non-refoulement clause of Art. 31 GC. Thus, thousands of refugees ended up in a legal status limbo that inevitably encouraged them to move from country to country in the hope of more comprehensive protection.

cope, leading to an almost total paralysis of European asylum systems by the beginning of the 90s.[3]

In the face of ever increasing cross-border refugee mobility it gradually became apparent that purely national asylum strategies would inevitably be doomed to failure. The need for an international approach was further highlighted in Europe by a second factor, namely the onset of the Single European Act (SEA). In order to overcome the political stagnation of the early 80s EC countries decided to promote the creation of a European shared identity. The Adonnino Committee was instituted by the Fontainebleau Council of June 1984 and charged with initiatives relating to a Citizens' Europe. Among its various tasks was the drawing up of a plan to achieve the abolition of all police and customs formalities across intra-Community borders.[4] Hoping to increase the momentum, Germany and France signed an agreement at Saarbrücken on 13 July 1984 to ease border controls between them.[5]

However, it quickly transpired from the internal discussions of the Adonnino Committee that border controls were such an important aspect of public security that they couldn't simply be removed. Member States came to the conclusion that a set of compensatory measures had to accompany any initiative to abolish border controls among the Twelve. The Brussels European Council of March 1985 therefore stressed the parallelism between the abolition of border controls and compensatory measures.[6] Such measures related mainly to visa policy, common external border controls, a common information system, judicial and police co-operation and principles on assigning States' responsibility for asylum applications. Following the Committee's recommendations, and building on the Saarbrücken agreement, in June 1985 France, Germany and the Benelux countries signed the Schengen Agreement on the gradual abolition of controls at internal borders.[7]

Following the renewed impetus in European integration, negotiations on the

---

3. This was the case most notably for Germany, Austria and to a smaller extent for France, especially after the fall of the Iron Curtain and during the Bosnian crisis. See D. Joly, *supra* n° 1.

4. See R. Plender, 'Competence, European Community law and nationals of non-Member States' (1990) 39 ICLQ, p. 599.

5. This agreement was the first step in what later became the whole Schengen initiative. The Benelux countries joined the Saarbrück agreement soon after Germany and France.

6. See K.-P. Nanz, 'The harmonisation of asylum and immigration legislation within the Third Pillar of the Union Treaty – a stocktaking' in J. Monar and R. Morgan (eds.), *The Third Pillar of the European Union* (European Interuniversity Press, Brussels, 1994), p. 123, at p. 124.

7. This Convention and its follow-up in 1990 was the first (and to this date the only) example of an integrated text containing both the goal of abolishing internal border controls and the necessary flanking measures. In this sense, Schengen has been defined a 'laboratory' for further European integration in the field of free movement of persons. See Chapter II.2 for an analysis of the Convention.

SEA were progressing rapidly. The new Art. 8A EEC was to prove of fundamental importance in the development of a new transnational approach to asylum matters. The second paragraph of this provision stated that 'the Internal Market shall comprise an area without internal frontiers in which the free movement of goods, persons, services and capital is ensured in accordance with the provisions of this Treaty'. In his White Paper, presented in June 1985 to the Milan summit, Lord Cockfield listed the areas which needed to be dealt with in order to achieve the free circulation of persons. In this context, he mentioned the right to asylum and the status of refugees, as well as the subsequent intention of the Commission to present some directive proposals in this field.[8] The White Paper also envisaged the adoption of a common visa policy by 1990.

It was soon apparent, however, that interpretation of Art. 8A EEC varied widely among the Twelve. The Commission and a large number of Member States were of the opinion that the free movement of persons necessarily entailed the abolition of all internal border controls, for both EC and third country nationals.[9] Other Member States – the UK being the most vocal among them – understood the provision as only concerning EC nationals, and argued that it had to be applied 'according to the provisions of the Treaty',[10] thus maintaining border controls on third country nationals.[11] They also relied on a Declaration

---

8. See Document COM(85)310 final.

9. See 'Communication of the Commission on the abolition of border controls', Doc. SEC(92)877 final, of 8/5/92. The Commission put forward the idea that Art. 8A EEC entailed an 'obligation of result', i.e. it specified the final result to be achieved (the abolition of border controls) without detailing the means by which this result was to be achieved

10. The UK maintained that this provision necessarily entailed that the exceptions listed elsewhere in the EEC Treaty on grounds of public policy, health and security should apply. See D. O'Keeffe, 'Non-accession to the Schengen Convention: the cases of the United Kingdom and Ireland' in A. Pauly (ed.), *Schengen en panne* (European Institute of Public Administration, Maastricht, 1994), p. 145, at p. 149. The article also highlights the reasons why the two countries found it particularly difficult to adhere to the set of flanking measures necessary for the abolition of internal border controls. It lists among other factors the insular nature of both countries (which favours efficient border controls) and the lack of a system of compulsory ID cards which would make internal spot checks impossible (see pp. 147–148).

11. For a sample of these arguments, see House of Lords Select Committee on the European Communities, *Border control of people*, 22nd Report, session 1988–1989, HL Paper 90. For a more theoretical discussion of the implications of Art. 8A EEC see C. Timmermans, 'Free movement of persons and the division of powers between the Community and its Member States – Why do it the intergovernmental way?' in H. Schermers *et alia* (eds), *Free movement of persons in Europe* (Martinus Nijhoff, Dordrecht, 1993), p. 352, or K.-P. Nanz, 'Free movement of persons according to the Schengen Convention and in the framework of the European Union' in A. Pauly, *De Schengen à Maastricht: voie royale et course d'obstacles* (European Institute of Public Administration, Maastricht, 1996), p. 61. The British interpretation was eventually endorsed many years later by the ECJ, *Wijsenbeek* v. *The Netherlands*, case C-378/97 [1999] ECR I-6207.

annexed to the SEA, which stated that the Treaty did not 'affect the right of Member States to take such measures as they consider necessary for the purpose of controlling immigration from third countries' and that 'the date of 31 December 1992 does not create an automatic legal effect'. The same Declaration, however, contained a compromise of sorts by announcing that '[i]n order to promote the free movement of persons, the Member States shall cooperate, without prejudice to the powers of the Community, in particular as regards the entry, movement and residence of nationals of third countries'. Over the years, those Member States that agreed with the Commission interpretation gradually joined the Schengen Convention.[12]

Even before the entry into force of the SEA it was abundantly clear that the above differences of interpretation were not likely to be resolved soon. The Commission's attempts to promote its own interpretation were invariably frustrated. While attempting to respect the schedule of measures provided by the White Paper, in December 1988 the Commission put forward a proposal to abolish internal border controls on people and elaborated a proposal for a 'Directive co-ordinating rules concerning the right of asylum and the status of refugees'.[13] The Commission based its proposal on Art. 100 and Art. 8A of the EEC Treaty, but the text was far too ambitious to be acceptable to Member States. Its adoption would have entailed a complete co-ordination of national asylum laws on combating abuse of asylum procedures and exchange of information (Title I); the rules governing responsibility for examining applications for asylum (Title II); provisions applicable during the period of examination of a request for asylum (Title III); and the free movement of recognised refugees (Title IV). The whole process would have been governed by a Community Committee for Asylum Questions made up of national representatives with limited consultation powers. The level of opposition to the draft asylum Directive was such that the Commission never formalised its proposal, officially announcing instead that the legal debate over the competence to adopt measures in the asylum field should be postponed to a later date.[14]

In the asylum and migration field in particular, Member States had already showed equal determination not to be led by the Commission by mounting a legal challenge against the latter's Decision of 8 July 1985.[15] This Decision, based

---

12. Thus, the Schengen framework became a 'laboratory' to implement Art. 8A EEC (see *supra* at n° 7). To this day it has been impossible to reconcile these opposing interpretations. However, the Amsterdam Treaty found a pragmatic solution to this dispute by, on one hand, incorporating the Schengen framework into the EU and, on the other hand, by allowing the elective participation of the UK and Ireland in selective measures in this field (see further Chapter V).

13. This Directive proposal is reported by R. Plender, *supra* n° 4, at p. 600. See also J.J. Bolten, 'The right to seek asylum in Europe' (1989) 4 NQHR, p. 381, at pp. 398–99 and p. 402 *et seq.*

14. See COM(88)640 final of 7/12/1988.

15. Decision 85/381/EEC of 18/7/85, OJ 1985 L217/25.

on Art. 118 EEC Treaty, instituted a notification procedure of national measures concerning the entry, residence and employment of non-EC nationals, thus prompting Member States to accuse the Commission of trying to bring migration policy under Community control. The ECJ accepted the applicants' argument that migration matters fell outside the Community scope and to that purpose it declared the Decision void because it concerned, inter alia, the cultural integration of migrants. The Court maintained, nonetheless, that Art. 118 EEC conferred certain implied powers to the Commission to arrange the consultations provided by the article, underlining that certain aspects of national migration policies were liable to influence employment conditions in the Community and therefore fell under the social policy provisions.[16]

Notwithstanding the controversies over the interpretation of Art. 8A EEC, the article nonetheless had a definitive 'knock-on effect'[17] in so far as it developed the idea that asylum matters were to be regarded as an area of 'common interest' for a Community without internal borders. Taking stock of their inability to reach a unified interpretation, the Twelve decided to concentrate their efforts on exploring their common ground. This consisted of the belief that a true free movement of persons inevitably depended on effective compensatory measures, such as those listed in the Adonnino Committee report. Member States that supported the abolition of internal border controls hoped that the setting up of strict flanking measures first, together with the possibility of a good example of internal security to be offered by the Schengen framework, might in future persuade the more reticent Member States.

In order to facilitate co-operation on the compensatory measures, the British Presidency organised a meeting in London, in October 1986, of the Ministers of the Interior and/or Justice, who decided to set up an 'Ad Hoc Immigration Group'. This working group comprised five working parties: border controls, visa policy, asylum policy, illegal immigrants and information technology. It was composed of senior civil servant representatives of the Twelve and was in charge of dealing with all matters relating to asylum and immigration, particularly in connection with the achievement of the Single Market. Remarkably, the Commission was ab initio associated with the works of the Committee in an observer capacity,[18] and the Secretariat of the Council was responsible for ensuring the continuity of the agenda. The Presidency of the Group rotated according to the EC Presidency.

The first achievement of the Ad Hoc Group in April 1987 was the agreement to impose sanctions on carriers responsible for bringing improperly documented

---

16. *Germany, France, Denmark and United Kingdom* v. *Commission* joined Cases 282, 283–285, 287/85 [1987] ECR 3203.

17. See W. De Lobkowicz, 'Intergovernmental co-operation in the field of migration – from the Single European Act to Maastricht, in J. Monar and R. Morgan (eds.), *supra* n° 6, p. 99, at p. 101.

18. The role the Commission effectively managed to play in this body has been highly controversial; see W. De Lobkowicz, *supra* n° 17, at pp. 107–08.

aliens into the Community.[19] Concerned by the growing number of intergovernmental groups dealing with free movement of persons issues in the European context,[20] the European Council of Rhodes, in December 1988, decided to institute a 'Group of Co-ordinators'. It was made up of senior national civil servants, with the participation of the vice-president of the Commission[21] and it had the task of co-ordinating the activities of the various fora in the field of the free movement of persons as well as having to put a fresh impetus into the 1992 project. The 'Group of Co-ordinators' lived up to its task by presenting a very detailed programme of measures to be implemented by January 1993. This document, adopted by the Madrid European summit of June 1989 and better known as the 'Palma Document',[22] was to be the platform for any subsequent initiative in the field of free movement of persons and contained several propositions relating to asylum matters. The document listed the following measures as essential:

1. a common visa list for the Community, to be updated every six months;
2. a common list of inadmissible persons;
3. appropriate measures to deal with the 'asylum shopping' phenomenon;
4. abbreviated procedures for 'manifestly unfounded' asylum claims;
5. harmonised interpretation of international commitments;
6. common measures for external border control;
7. the establishment of a common information system;
8. combating illegal immigration and common expulsion policies.

The Palma document indicated that in defining compensatory measures the Twelve had also agreed to prioritise certain areas. Co-ordination in the asylum field had obviously taken an overall priority, due mainly to two reasons. Firstly,

---

19. On this point see further in Chapter II.3.
20. The oldest of such groups being TREVI, instituted by a Dutch initiative in 1975, with the strong support of the German and British Governments. It was originally intended as an intergovernmental co-operation framework for combating terrorism, but it was gradually developed into a complex three-tier structure including civil servants and police officers as well as ministers. Eventually TREVI's objectives included combating organised crime and drugs and general police affairs. For a survey of TREVI's activities and other European co-operation structures in the field see M. Den Boer and N. Walker, 'European policing after 1992' (1993) 31 JCMS, p. 3; and also J. Peek, 'International police co-operation within justified political and juridical frameworks: five theses on TREVI' in J. Monar and R. Morgan (eds.), *supra* n° 6, p. 201.
21. See COM(88)640 final of 7/12/1988. The Commission participated in the meetings as an 'observer'. The reason for this important concession was probably to compensate for Member States' constant opposition to Commission initiatives in this field within the Community framework.
22. See F. Webber, 'European conventions on immigration and asylum' in T. Bunyan, *Statewatching the new Europe: a handbook on the European State* (Statewatch, London, 1993), p. 142, at p. 143.

asylum applications were rising steeply and carrier sanctions were only marginally effective. Secondly, cross-border refugee mobility was perceived as a pressing problem by a large number of Member States. Thus, the probability of reaching some agreement in a reasonable time framework appeared high. There was, however, a dangerous side-effect to this process. By framing asylum matters in the context of a border-free Europe and the inevitable necessity of controlling internal movements of aliens, asylum policy became increasingly identified as a mere part of immigration controls. Member States appeared to lose sight of the fundamental aspect of protection and increasingly subjected the refugees to the same restrictive trends they imposed on prospective migrants.

This attitude was exemplified by the two initiatives taken by the French Presidency in the summer of 1989. It submitted two draft Conventions to the Ad Hoc Group, one on responsibility for the processing of asylum applications and the other on the crossing of external borders.[23] The main points of the first one had already been included in the Palma Document and endorsed by the 1989 Madrid Council. The Commission on its part decided to lend its full support to this initiative, following a strictly pragmatic approach. The Commission Vice-President Bangemann, in a debate at the European Parliament on 14 March 1990, justified such a choice by pointing out the necessity of working out the conditions for the free movement of persons before the deadline and avoiding sterile and abstract debates on the proper juridical base.[24]

II.2. THE SCHENGEN 'LABORATORY'

The Strasbourg European Council of December 1989 asked the Immigration group to carry out an inventory of asylum policies with a view to their harmonisation and also fixed the deadline for the signature of a Convention on States's responsibility for asylum applications by the end of 1990. The Ad Hoc Group had already completed the draft by early 1990 and the 'Convention determining

---

23. For the contents of both Conventions, see Chapter II.2. A Convention on the control of external borders was seen as a prerequisite to any lifting of internal controls. It aimed at achieving high levels of common controls at the external perimeter of the Community, so that in theory internal controls would become redundant. In essence, it was the transposition of the traditional national public security function of border checking to the wider Community level. In the same way, immigration controls were also seen as a vital function of public security. A Convention on the responsibility for asylum applications should in theory have been about protection from persecution and access to protection. However, by linking the two Conventions, the principle of States' responsibility for asylum applications became primarily a function of public security and the protection aspect was inevitably played down. Thus, the implementation of a Community goal – the free movement of persons – brought about a trend in asylum harmonisation, but unfortunately at the same time it changed the very essence of refugee protection in Europe.

24. See full report of the European Parliament proceedings (A4–085/90) 14 March 1990, pp. 203–208.

the State responsible for examining the applications for asylum lodged in one of the Member States of the European Community' (DC) was eventually signed in Dublin on 15 June 1990 by 11 Member States (Denmark signed and ratified it on 13 June 1991).[25] It was signed only four days before the Schengen Convention (SC) and the two texts were almost identical in so far as asylum provisions were concerned.[26] But whereas the DC only dealt with one particular compensatory measure, the SC aimed at dealing with the whole issue of free movement and the abolition of internal borders. Therefore, since it represented a far more comprehensive approach to the establishment of an area of free movement of persons, in the context of the present research the SC will be analysed first.

The setting up of the Schengen free circulation framework took approximately ten years (until March 1995). As previously recalled, it began in June 1985 with the Schengen Agreement or Accord (SA) between Germany, France and the Benelux Countries. The General Secretariat of the Benelux assumed the secretariat of the Schengen Group. The SA consisted of 33 articles outlining the principal measures necessary to achieve a border-free area. The majority of such measures were specifically designated as 'applicable in the long term' (Title II) and mainly concerned the establishment of common external frontiers; police co-operation; international judicial assistance and extradition agreements; harmonisation of laws on drugs, arms, visa policies and taxes. Art. 32 provided for the entry into force of the agreement without necessarily requiring ratification by national legislators and only the Netherlands felt that it was necessary to do so. As for the others, they considered the SA as being only a declaration of intent and did not submit it for parliamentary ratification.

---

25. Negotiations on the Draft Convention on the Crossing of the External Borders lasted until June 1991. Thereafter the signing was indefinitely delayed, officially because of a dispute between Spain and the United Kingdom over the external border controls to be applied at Gibraltar. Eventually, after the entry into force of the Maastricht Treaty, the Commission presented a 'Communication to the Council and the European Parliament on 10 December 1993 for a Decision on the crossing of the external border controls of the Union' based on Art. K.3 of the TEU (COM(93)684 final). The Communication was accompanied by the 'Proposal for a Regulation establishing the third countries whose nationals needed a visa to enter the EU', based on Art. 100c of the EC Treaty. The Commission also proposed to allow the European Court of Justice jurisdiction over matters of interpretation and disputes regarding implementation. This proved to be a major stumbling block. For an assessment of these two proposals and their respective texts see D. O'Keeffe, 'The new draft external frontiers Convention and the draft visa Regulation' in J. Monar and R. Morgan (eds.), *supra* n° 6, p. 135. The dispute remained unsolved until the Amsterdam Treaty, when the need for a separate convention was in fact superseded by the integration of the Schengen *acquis* into the Community/Union framework (see Chapter V.4.B). It was, however, a pragmatic settlement as, in fact, both parties 'agreed to disagree'.

26. The DC was to a large extent a copy of Arts 28–38 of the 1990 SC. There were, however, a number of differences; see Chapter II.4.

As the five Members began their efforts to implement the 'long term measures' of the SA, it rapidly became clear that a supplementary treaty was necessary. The ensuing negotiations lasted for more than four years and were surrounded by a much criticised climate of secrecy.[27] By June 1989, the five Members announced their intention to sign an additional convention before the end of the year,[28] but another 12 months of negotiations were necessary to approve a final text.[29] The 'Convention applying the Schengen Agreement of 14 June 1985' (generally referred to as the Schengen Convention – SC) was signed on 19 June 1990. It consisted of 142 articles divided into eight Titles. The original membership of the Convention subsequently expanded to include Italy (November 1990), Spain and Portugal (June 1991), Greece (November 1992) and Austria (March 1995) and Denmark, Finland and Sweden (December 1996).[30]

Although taking the shape of intergovernmental conventions, both the 1985 SA and the 1990 SC were intrinsically connected to the Community framework. The preamble of the 1990 SC specifically recalled Art. 8A EEC by stating the

27. See J.J. Bolten, 'From Schengen to Dublin: the new frontiers of refugee law' in H. Meijers *et alia* (eds), *Schengen, Internationalisation of central chapters of the law on aliens, refugees, security and the police* (Kluwer Law International, The Hague, 1991), p. 8. The author claims that the existence of the text of the 1985 Agreement 'has only been known in select gatherings' (p. 9) in all Member States except the Netherlands. See also A. Cruz, *Schengen, Ad Hoc Immigration Group and other European intergovernmental bodies* (CCME Briefing Papers n° 12, Brussels, 1993), and H. Meijers, 'Refugees in Western Europe 'Schengen' affects the entire refugee law' (1990) 2 IJRL, p. 428. Meijers in particular highlights how it had become highly unusual not to publish drafts of multilateral conventions as discussions in national Parliaments would generally produce useful criticism and amendments (p. 429). Not even the UNHCR was allowed access to the proceedings (see further in Chapter II.3).

28. The signing of the supplementary treaty, scheduled for 15 December 1989, was unexpectedly called off one day before by the Bonn Government, which was occupying the Presidency. The official reason was the problem of the transition of the two Germanies, but as A. Cruz (*supra* n° 27, p. 5) points out, other Member States had various reasons to be reluctant.

29. The European Parliament contributed to the delay by passing a Resolution (doc. B3–583/89) on 23 November 1989 in which it expressed deep concern about the secrecy of the negotiations and the decision to opt for an intergovernmental framework. It criticised in particular the 'negative effect on refugees and migrant workers by reinforcing the already considerable restrictions applied to such persons' (p. 8); the principle of a common visa list; the expansion of police powers and the risks of privacy infringement by data collection. As a result of the protests some articles of the SC were modified (Arts 10.1, 23, 26, 117.2, 132.3) in order to allow a better protection of Human Rights.

30. It took five years for the Schengen Executive Committee to establish that the conditions for implementation had been fulfilled by a sufficient number of Members. The abolition of internal borders became effective only in March 1995, after France had persistently refused to go ahead (see P. Keraudren, 'Réticences et obstacles français face à Schengen: la logique de la politique de sécurité' in A. Pauly (ed.), *Schengen en panne, supra* n° 10, p. 123).

belief that 'the Internal Market shall comprise an area without internal frontiers'. Thus, it highlighted the role of Schengen as a way to overcome the national differences of interpretation over Art. 8A EEC by allowing progress on this matter on a parallel track along the Community one. In this respect the SC was imaginatively qualified as a sort of 'laboratory',[31] where different alternatives to the abolition of physical internal border controls could be experimented with. To this purpose, membership of the SC was open to any EC Member (Art. 140.1). The connection with the Community framework was further highlighted by stating that 'the aim pursued by the Contracting Parties coincides with that objective [i.e. the establishment of the Internal Market], without prejudice to the measures to be taken to implement the provisions of the Treaty' (preamble). Art. 134 reinforced the principle of the Schengen dependency on Community rule by establishing that Schengen provisions would only apply if compatible with Community law. Finally, Art. 142.1, specifically allowed for future Community conventions, concluded 'with a view to the completion of an area without internal frontiers' to replace or modify the relative SC.

In describing the SC the image of a 'wheel with a hub and spokes' has been used.[32] The hub of the SC is to be found in the total abolition of internal border controls. Around this hub are the compensatory measures, positioned like the spokes of a wheel. These consist mainly of measures aiming at controlling the movement of aliens inside the common area. They therefore include[33] common visas, external border controls, police and judicial co-operation, a central data-bank and provisions establishing States' responsibility for asylum applications (Title II Chapter 7, Arts 28–38). In this context, the inclusion in the SC of specific provisions concerning refugees appeared to follow the overall purpose and logic of the treaty. Moreover, it had been argued that the need for further provisions in this field had been felt for some time and that Title II Chapter 7 of the SC represented the continuation, on a smaller scale, of the initiative of the CAHAR.[34] However, contrary to the other aspects covered in the

---

31. The number of authors that have employed this definition are countless. It is impossible to trace the original inventor; as an example see N. Guimezanes, 'La Convention de Schengen: une présentation française' in A. Pauly (ed.), *Schengen en panne, supra* n° 10, p. 5, at p. 8.

32. See K.-P. Nanz, 'Free movement of persons according to the Schengen Convention and in the framework of the European Union', *supra* n° 11, p. 64.

33. In line with the recommendations of the *Adonnino* Committee.

34. The CAHAR *(Comité ad Hoc sur les Aspects juridiques del'Asile territorial et des Refugiés)*, established by the Committee of Ministers of the Council of Europe, developed in 1987 a Draft Convention on the determination of the State responsible for examining an asylum application. On this point see both J.P.H. Donner, 'Abolition of border controls' in H. Schermers *et alia* (eds), *supra* n° 11, p. 5, at p. 14, and H.U. Jessurun D' Oliveira, 'Fortress Europe and (extra-communitarian) refugees: co-operation in sealing off the exter-nal borders' in H. Schermers *et alia* (eds), *supra* n° 11, p. 166, at pp. 170–171. For an analysis of the circumstances which determined a surge of interest and concern for refugee issues, see Chapter I.

Convention, asylum matters were not specifically mentioned in the SA of 1985. The subsequent insertion of asylum provisions was justified by a passage in Art. 17 of the SA which enabled the Parties 'to take complementary measures to safeguard security and combat illegal immigration'. As pointed out earlier, the decision to include refugee issues in a text concerning mainly police matters, border patrolling and illegal immigration was highly controversial.[35]

The prevailing concern in the drafting of Chapter 7 of the SC was to address the problem of Member States' responsibility for asylum applications. The fundamental idea was based on a 'solidarity' criterion, according to which the State bearing the biggest responsibility for the entry into the Schengen territory of an asylum seeker should also be the one in charge of processing his or her asylum application.[36] The competence for the examination of asylum applications was intended to be of an exclusive nature, so as to prevent the phenomenon of 'refugees in orbit'.[37] Under the Schengen criteria only one Member State could, in theory, be responsible for the examination of any particular application. Conversely, the SC also introduced the possibility of an 'optional negative binding effect',[38] i.e. the acceptance of another Member State's negative decision on an asylum application.

Art. 30 laid down in great detail and in hierarchical order the criteria for determination of responsibility.[39] The principle being followed was that primary responsibility should have rested first with those States that knowingly allowed access to the applicant, followed by the cases where the applicant gained entry without the knowledge or consent of the Party concerned. Thus, according to this hierarchy, responsibility fell primarily on the Contracting State who first issued a visa to the applicant. Distinctions were drawn between different types of visas, so that transit visas were given relatively less weight than other types, which would have allowed longer residence (such as, for instance, tourist visas). Special provisions covered the case of an exemption from visa requirements by some of the Contracting Members, who equated them to the formal concession

---

35. See *supra* n° 23. For a review of the main criticisms on this point, see R. Dedecker, *L'asile et la libre circulation des personnes dans l'Accord de Schengen* (CRISP, Brussels, 1993), at p. 40.

36. This principle has also been defined as an 'authorisation' one. See A. Hurwitz, 'The 1990 Dublin Convention: a comprehensive assessment' (1999) 11 IJRL, p. 646, at p. 648.

37. Refugees are defined as in 'orbit' when they are constantly reshuffled from one host country to another without ever finding a stable refuge. On the subject, see G. Melander, *Refugees in Orbit* (International University Exchange Fund, 1978) and J.J. Bolten, 'From Schengen to Dublin: the new frontiers of refugee law', *supra* n° 27, at pp. 18–19.

38. K. Hailbronner and C. Thiery, 'Schengen II and Dublin: responsibility for asylum applications in Europe', (1997) 34 CML Rev., p. 957, at p. 964.

39. In laying down the responsibility criteria the SC was not exactly a model of clarity. Criteria were listed in hierarchical order in Art. 30, but numerous exceptions appeared in the susequent articles. In this respect, the DC was far better structured and its exceptions more comprehensive. A comparison between the two follows in Chapter II.4.

of a visa (only until the harmonisation of visa policy, specifically envisaged in Title II Chapter 3, was achieved). In case no visa was ever issued, the criterion of illegal entry applied, qualified as an entry without being in possession of the documents prescribed by Art. 5 SC. In the event of illegal entry, the responsible State would be the one over whose external borders the illegal crossing took place. The specific choices of the asylum applicant were not given any relevance other than as an accessory to the 'last resort' rule.

Two exceptions derogated from the principles of Art. 30. The first was contained in Art. 35, which dealt with family reunification. A Contracting State was automatically responsible for processing the asylum applications of the family members of a recognised refugee residing in its territory ('provided those concerned are in agreement'). This exception was of an innovative nature since there was no reference to the rights of family reunification in the 1951 Geneva Convention nor in the 1967 New York Protocol. An attempt to introduce such a provision in 1977 within the framework of a UN Draft Convention on Territorial Asylum had failed.[40] The foundations of this provision were probably to be found in the 'right to family life' laid down by Art. 8 ECHR and subsequently developed in the jurisprudence of the European Court of Human Rights. The concept of 'family members' was, however, of a restrictive nature, since only the spouse and any unmarried children under the age of 18 were expressly included by Art. 35.2.[41]

The second exception consisted of the residual right of every Contracting Member to process an asylum application even if not responsible under the terms of the SC, for 'special reasons concerning national law' (Art. 29.4). This provision was needed to accommodate the German constitutional formulation of the right to political asylum at the time (before the substantial reforms of July 1993). However, its formulation constituted a major potential disruption of the whole framework of Art. 30. France, also supported the exception because of its constitutional provisions, which allowed asylum rights for a larger category of refugees than those defined in the Geneva Convention.

Given the importance of the exception of Art. 29.4, it might be useful to briefly outline the German and French constitutional provisions on asylum. Prior to the reforms of 1 July 1993, Art. 16.2.2 of the German Basic Law provided that 'persons persecuted on political grounds shall enjoy the right of asylum'. In its judgment of 7 October 1975, the Federal Administrative Court interpreted this provision as entailing a subjective right for foreigners arriving at the German border and claiming to be politically persecuted to enter the country and have their asylum application examined.[42] Therefore, because of its constitutional

---

40. UN Conference on Territorial Asylum held in Geneva from 10 January to 4 February 1977, UN doc. A/CONF.78/12 (21/4/1977).

41. This exception proved to be highly problematic, both in principle and in its application. See further in Chapters II.3 and II.4.

42. For a critical assessment of the German asylum legislation before the modifications of July 1993 see C. Wisskirchen, 'Germany: assault on the constitutional right to asylum – Part I' (1994) 8 INLP, p. 87 *et seq.*

obligations, Germany could not have delegated a decision on an application for asylum on grounds of political persecution to another Schengen Contracting Member on the basis of the criteria laid down in Art. 30. It should be noted that the German internal debate on the need to change the constitutional provisions in question was a considerable delaying factor in the Schengen ratification process.

In the French case specific references to a constitutional right of asylum could be found in the fourth line of the preamble to the 1946 Constitution envisaging the granting of asylum to people fighting for the cause of liberty. This provision guaranteed a right to asylum for a larger category of refugees than those defined in the Geneva Convention and, similarly to the parallel German constitutional provisions, it entailed a subjective right for prospective refugees to have their applications examined.

In its judgment of 25 July 1991, the French Constitutional Council ruled that the Schengen Convention was entirely compatible with the French Constitution.[43] In a subsequent judgment of 13 August 1993, the French Constitutional Council specified that the fourth line of the preamble of the 1946 Constitution entailed an obligation for the French authorities to examine asylum applications lodged under this provision.[44] The French Government feared this interpretation would endanger the application of the SC in so far as it transformed the discretionary power of national administrations to examine an asylum application according to the exception of Art. 29.4 SC into an absolute obligation on France's part. Even if the obligations on the French authorities were limited to the 'actions in favour of liberty' clause, the potential for a disruptive loophole in the Schengen system was very high. Furthermore, in July 1993 Germany had finally carried through its own constitutional revision, thereby increasing pressure on the French Government to secure the Schengen application. After a very heated internal debate in November 1993, a new Art. 53-1 was introduced into the French Constitution, containing two main provisions. The first paragraph specifically allowed for European agreements to regulate the allocation of States' responsibility over asylum applications. The second paragraph granted discretionary power to the French authorities to consider asylum applications, notwith-

---

43. It is not clear whether at that stage the Constitutional Council had analysed in depth the implications of Art. 30 of the Schengen Agreement on the French constitutional right to asylum for actions in favour of liberty, or whether it had considered the exception of Art. 29.4 a sufficient guarantee. For an analysis of the French Constitutional Council's judgments of 1991 and 1993, see P. Keraudren, *supra* n° 30, p. 132 *et seq.*

44. Following the national elections of March 1993 the new centre-right French Government had introduced, in May 1993, a very controversial new law tightening both the conditions for the acquisition of French nationality and the control of immigration. In its judgment of 13 August 1993 (the longest ever since its creation in 1958) the French Constitutional Council invalidated eight provisions of the new law, provoking a particularly vehement response by the French Government (see P. Keraudren, *supra* n° 43).

standing the relevant European agreements, in the case of 'actions in favour of liberty' or 'other reasons'.[45]

The potential 'loophole factor' of Art. 29.4 was also the subject of careful consideration on the part of the Dutch Government. In a Decision of 29 May 1987, the Dutch Court of Cassation ruled that it was the individual responsibility of the Dutch authorities to autonomously assess the refugee status of an applicant, even if the same applicant had had his application previously rejected by the German authorities. In July 1991, in order to overcome a possible incompatibility with the Schengen Convention a new Art. 15.2 was added to the existing Dutch Aliens Act. The new paragraph specifically excluded the possibility of examining an asylum application if another State was responsible for processing it under an international convention. Examination of the application was to be exceptionally allowed only if the request was grounded on facts that could not have played a role in the previous decision by the competent country. This provision was criticised as 'an unnecessary and unwanted restriction'[46] because it narrowed Dutch discretionary power to advocate the examination of an asylum request well beyond the already limited exceptions granted by the Schengen Convention.

Arts 31 to 36 of the Schengen Convention dealt specifically with the obligations Member States had to meet in order to ensure the correct implementation of the rules concerning the determination of responsibility for asylum applications. The underlying objective was to ensure that the responsible State would take full charge of the applicant. This entailed the duty to 'take him back' (Art. 33) in case of illegal presence in one of the other Contracting Members' territories, even if his application had in the meantime been rejected (Art. 34), or to transfer him to the responsible State (Art.31.2).

The two final provisions of Chapter 7 dealt mainly with exchanges of information, both concerning personal data on asylum applicants and national refugee legislation, statistical analysis of refugee flows and situations in countries of origin. Specific attention was given in Art. 38 to the protection of personal data concerning refugees, with explicit reference to the Council of Europe Convention of 1981 for the Protection of Individuals with regard to Automatic Processing of Personal Data, but the setting up of a computerised data bank was only envisaged as optional.

The provisions of Art. 38 gave rise to concerns that refugees appeared to be less protected than other categories of aliens in relation to the transborder flow

---

45. In fact, the French reform achieved no more than a general clarification of the matter, since France was still bound in a compulsory manner by the exception of Art. 29.4. On this point, see J. Rossetto, 'La Convention de Schengen: controverses et incertitudes françaises sur le droit d'asile' (1994) 378 *Revue du Marché commun et de l'Union Européenne*, p. 315.

46. H.U. Jessurun D' Oliveira, *supra* n° 34, p. 175. The judgment of the Netherlands Court of Cassation of 29 May 1987, (1988) *Nederlandse Jurisprudentie* n° 56, is reported by J.J. Bolten, 'From Schengen to Dublin ...', *supra* n° 27, p. 20.

of data.[47] Art. 126.4 specifically stated that the stringent guarantees for the protection of personal data listed in Art. 126 did not apply to transmission of data concerning refugees, but there was no evident explanation for this exclusion.[48] Furthermore, the setting up of a national supervisory authority instructed to monitor independently the processing of personal data (Art. 128) was again specifically excluded in the case of asylum seekers, while the parallel Art. 38.11 only provided for generic 'effective checks'. No express legal remedy was envisaged for refugees in the case of exchange of incorrect information, as Art. 38.6–7 only established the obligation for Contracting Members to delete or correct wrong information, without even providing for measures to ensure compliance. It was only in the event of the information being automated that refugees might avail themselves of the legal remedies provided for by the Strasbourg Convention of 1981 on the protection of personal data. But since the setting up of a computerised system was only envisaged as optional, these guarantees were by no means sufficient.[49]

II.3. CRITICAL ISSUES OF THE SCHENGEN ASYLUM FRAMEWORK

II.3.A. The 'refugees in orbit' problem

Several of the asylum provisions of Chapter 7 of the Schengen Convention were severely criticised, both by international commentators, the UNHCR[50] and national Parliaments.[51] The national ratification processes in particular highlighted what seemed to be the most striking shortcomings of the Schengen asylum system, notably an alleged breach of international obligations and a failure to deliver an effective solution to the problem of 'refugees in orbit'. Moreover, important doubts were cast upon what ultimate purpose the elaborate system laid down in Art. 30 SC was really serving.

The Schengen asylum provisions and the shortly preceding Dublin Convention were hailed by national representatives and the EC Commission as 'the first text

---

47. On this point see P. Boeles, 'Data Exchange, Privacy and Legal Protection; Especially regarding Aliens' in H. Schermers *et alia* (eds), *supra* n° 11, p. 52, at pp. 53–54.

48. On this point, see D. O'Keeffe, 'The Schengen Convention: a suitable model for European integration?' (1991) 11 YEL, p. 185, at p. 207 *et seq.*

49. The Dublin Convention afforded a much higher level of protection for refugees' personal data. See further Chapter II.4.

50. The UNHCR was consulted only at a very late stage of the negotiations on the final text, and only after the existence of a draft agreement had already been leaked to the press (see *supra* n° 27). This raised serious doubts as to whether EC Members had taken their obligation to cooperate with the UNHCR (laid down both by the GC and the Statute of the UNHCR, see Chapters I.2 and I.3) seriously, despite expressly stating this duty both in Art. 28 SC and in Art. 2 DC. For UNHCR reservations about the Schengen Convention, see their briefing of 16 August 1991.

51. See, for instance, the Advisory Opinion of the Dutch Council of State, The Hague, 8 April 1991 (n° WO2.91.0018), a translation of which is available by ECRE.

in international law which guarantees to asylum seekers that at least one State will process their asylum application, and that they will no longer be shuffled from country to country, with all the human drama that this implies'.[52] Similar displays of intent appeared in the preamble of the Dublin Convention, although surprisingly (or not) they failed to surface anywhere in the Schengen text. Unfortunately, these assertions rested on the incorrect assumption that international law did not protect 'refugees in orbit', whereas the new texts were efficiently geared for this purpose.

The 1951 GC aimed at achieving a uniform level of international protection by laying down a general definition of 'refugee' and by establishing certain standards of treatment for refugees. Asylum seekers did not enjoy an individual right to asylum, but they nonetheless had the right not to be refouled to a country where their life might be at danger (Art. 33). It was widely accepted that the GC implied a general obligation on the Contracting States to examine asylum applications, although the actual assessment of refugee status was left entirely to national authorities. It was precisely this great divergence in national legal practices that lead to the painful phenomenon of 'refugees in orbit'. It was in particular the various national interpretations and developments of the 'country of first asylum' principle[53] that directly contributed to refugees being 'struck to and fro like tennis balls'.[54]

The Schengen Convention did not offer any definite solution to this painful problem, as it specifically stated in Art. 29.2 that '[e]very Contracting Party shall retain the right to refuse entry or to expel any applicant for asylum to a Third State on the basis of its national provisions and in accordance with its international commitments'. Moreover, despite the strong wording of Art. 29.1, which established the States' obligation to process asylum applications, there was no guarantee anywhere in the Convention that the actual content of an application would be examined.[55]

Therefore, it could justifiably be argued that the Schengen Convention was in

---

52. *Europe*, 16/6/1990, n° 5276.

53. This term refers to various national practices of declining responsibility for asylum applicants who were deemed to have been able to apply for protection elsewhere. The legal justification of such practices was ambiguously based on the fact that Art. 31 GC required States not to penalise the illegal entry of refugees, but only if they were 'coming directly from a territory where their life or freedom was threatened'. For an in-depth analysis of this principle and of the diverging national practices, see G. Melander, *supra* n° 37, and G.S. Goodwin-Gill, *The refugee in international law* (2nd, Clarendon Press, Oxford, 1996), p. 129 *et seq.*

54. Sörensen, quoted by J.J. Bolten, 'From Schengen to Dublin: the new frontiers of refugee law', *supra* n° 27, p. 19.

55. J.J. Bolten, 'From Schengen to Dublin: the new frontiers of refugee law' *supra* n° 27, p. 25, supports this argument by demonstrating how, as a consequence of Art. 29.2, the 'examination' of an application 'need not be necessarily be on the merits of the case' (opinion of the UNHCR).

fact only designed to achieve a mere shifting of the 'orbit' outside the Schengen territory. This conclusion seemed to be corroborated by the series of 'Readmission Agreements' the Schengen Members subsequently signed with eastern neighbouring countries. The first agreement of this type was concluded with Poland in 1991 and was operational even before it came into force.[56] The agreement was centred on the undertaking by the parties to readmit aliens who had illegally entered the territory of another Member State via their own external border. The immediate result of such an agreement was, of course, the tightening of the eastern Polish border. Similar agreements were also signed with other Eastern European countries, namely Hungary and both the Czech and the Slovak Republics. Although these agreements did not directly affect refugees as such, they had serious implications for their ability to avail themselves of the protection of Schengen countries.[57]

II.3.B. The 'asylum shopping' phenomenon

In the light of the preceding considerations, the need to solve the plight of 'refugees in orbit' could not plausibly be regarded as the sole justification for the Schengen asylum provisions. Had that been the case, there would have been no need for the complex responsibility rules of Art. 30. Responsibility could have been much more easily allocated to the State where the first asylum application had been lodged. Instead, a far more pressing consideration for Member States would have been the desire to stem what was commonly defined as 'asylum shopping' or 'multiple applications'.[58]

The exclusivity principle[59] that dominated the elaborate structure of Chapter 7 SC did not simply determine which State was to be responsible for a particular asylum application. It also ensured that no further applications could be put forward by the same applicant. This was made obvious by the combined provisions of Art. 30 (f-g), which did not allow a State to process an application if another one was already examining it and prevented an asylum seeker from lodging any further application after a negative decision by a Schengen Party. It remained unclear why national governments consistently branded multiple

---

56. On the implications of this hidden rush, see H.U. Jessurun D' Oliveira, *supra* n° 34, p. 172.
57. Detailed information about the content of such agreements can be found in the UNHCR booklet, *Overview of readmission agreements in Central Europe* of 30/09/1993, and for a recent update, see S. Lavenex, *Safe third countries: extending the EU asylum and immigration policies to Central and Eastern Europe* (Central European University Press, New York, 1999). For a critical appraisal of the impact of such agreements on refugee flows, see M. King, 'The impact of Western European border policies on the control of 'refugees' in Eastern and Central Europe' (1993) 19 *New Community*, p. 183. H.U. Jessurun D' Oliveira (*supra* n° 34, p. 172) did not hesitate to define such agreements as a 'rebuilt Iron Curtain'.
58. Most authors employ such terms; for a reference see J.J. Bolten, 'From Schengen to Dublin: the new frontiers of refugee law' *supra* n° 27.
59. See K. Hailbronner and C. Thiery, *supra* n° 38, p. 964.

applications as 'abusive',[60] as if the lodging of more than one asylum request could be deemed a clear indication of fraudulent intentions or of trying to settle in the richest country. However, it was widely acknowledged that the considerable disparities in national asylum legislation would often lead to completely different judgments regarding the same asylum application.

Nor did the SC offer any solution to such disparities. On the contrary, they actually became the keystone of this incredibly sophisticated system, as Art. 32 stated that '[t]he Contracting Party responsible for the processing of an asylum application shall process it in accordance with its national law' (emphasis added). National asylum adjudication depended almost entirely on the appreciation of the 'persecution' element which would be indisputably conditioned by political, economic and other 'cultural' factors. Comparative studies of identical refugee flows in different European countries showed huge disparities in recognition rates.[61] Such disparities should have been entirely acceptable, as indirectly confirmed by a Conclusion of the Executive Committee of the UNHCR, which encouraged States to examine asylum applications previously turned down by other parties.[62] In the absence of international assessment standards for asylum claims, differences in national asylum legislation could actually have proven to be the less imperfect way of guaranteeing 'protection', the GC's main objective.[63]

II.3.C. 'Jurisdictional' harmonisation and compatibility with the Geneva Convention

Overall, the SC effectively ended up lowering the standard of refugee protection in Europe by upholding the principle of the national assessment of asylum claims while at the same time penalising multiple applications. This was the result of a deliberate choice made by the Schengen partners to proceed with 'jurisdictional' harmonisation, while postponing efforts towards 'substantive' harmonisation of asylum law. Point 5 of the Final Act of the SC contained a common commitment to harmonise national asylum policies, but no timetable was provided for it and the Declaration lacked any binding force. 'Jurisdictional' harmonisation was perceived to be vital for the smooth functioning of a border-free Europe. It was also a far easier objective to agree upon. 'Substantive' (including procedural)

---

60. See J.J. Bolten, 'From Schengen to Dublin: the new frontiers of refugee law' *supra* n° 27, pp. 25–26. The author also attempts an explanation of the phenomenon, which she attributes to a fear that bogus refugees might exploit the advantages of a frontier-free Europe.
61. G. Neuman, 'Buffer zones against refugees: Dublin, Schengen and the German asylum amendment' (1993) 33 *Virginia Journal of International Law*, p. 503, at p. 522, and D. Kanstroom, 'The shining city and the fortress: reflections on the 'Euro-solution' to the German immigration dilemma' (1993) 16 *Boston College International and Comparative Law Review*, p. 201, at p. 222. For average recognition rates, see also Annex, Table 3.
62. Conclusion n° 12 (XXIX) on the Extra-territorial effect of the determination of refugee status, 1978.
63. See G. Neuman, *supra* n° 61.

harmonisation was seen as controversial and too time-consuming to be envisaged other than in the distant future. In the meantime asylum seekers were left to bear the brunt of this 'harmonisation gap'.[64]

Other doubts were also cast upon the conformity of such 'jurisdictional' harmonisation with the obligations imposed by the GC. The Dutch Council of State advised the Dutch Parliament against ratification of the SC precisely because it deemed it incompatible with The Netherlands' obligations under the GC: 'The application of obligations essentially deriving from the Convention on Refugees [...] depends on whether the person is judged to be a refugee in the meaning of Art. 1 of the Treaty. This assessment is reserved for national authorities, taking into consideration the Convention on Refugees, but for the remainder, applying their national law and national procedures. The system in the Convention on Refugees assumes that the obligations apply to each of the States which are signatories to the Treaty separately, when a foreigner seeks asylum. [...] This specific, independent responsibility means that each of the Treaty States makes its own judgment about the basis for a decision about refusal or deportation, without there being any mention of consistency with other Treaty States. The national law on asylum, and the national policy on the issue in the state where the request is made, together with the Convention on Refugees, are always determinant for the question of whether the State complies with its obligations under the Convention on Refugees with respect to individual applicants for asylum. On the other hand, the State to which the application is made can, in case of refusal, expulsion [...], only justify its negative response to the question whether it was guilty of refoulement, by claiming that the decision has been made, and then upheld, in accordance with its national law on asylum [...]. The State cannot pass on to another State its responsibility towards an applicant for asylum, and accordingly it cannot hide behind another State's decision either [...]. Of course, a State can delegate the decision on refugee status wholly or partially to a body which is not a government body, for example to the UNHCR; however, this does not absolve the State of its responsibility. In the opinion of the Council, the system under the Implementing Agreement, in so far as it leads to the transfer of responsibility to another State, which then decides according to its own law on asylum [...] has no basis in the Convention on Refugees. It opens a possibility for Treaty States to back out of the obligations arising from the Convention on Refugees, and thus according to Art. 135 of the Implementing Agreement, it cannot be applied. Still a Treaty State may not transfer an applicant for asylum to another State, unless a reasonable guarantee exists beforehand that the transfer to that State, assessed under the criteria used in the first State to which the application was made, will not lead to refoulement.[65]

The negative judgment of the Dutch Council of State was further supported

---

64. See G. Neuman, *supra* n° 61, at p. 221 *et seq.*
65. See *supra* n° 51, pp. 8–9 of the ECRE translation (emphasis added).

by various other arguments,[66] mainly referring to the lack of recognition of 'positive' decisions in the Schengen text. Since the GC relied on national refugee laws for the assessment of asylum claims, it was generally accepted that Member States were not bound by the decisions of other parties to grant refugee status.[67] The SC did not try in any way to establish a system for the mutual recognition of positive national asylum decisions, yet it explicitly allowed national negative decisions to be recognised by other Parties (optional negative binding effect).[68] To give binding effect to another State's negative decision under these circumstances restricted the rights of refugees and would have been in breach of the 'duty of good faith' GC Members owed to each other.[69]

The Schengen Members could have tried to overcome the objections to the internationalisation of 'negative' decisions by at least trying to ensure a uniform interpretation of the Geneva Convention. However, one of the major shortcomings of the Schengen system was precisely the lack of any sort of 'judicial machinery'. Any problem of interpretation or of implementation was to be referred to the 'Schengen Executive Committee' (Title VII), made up of one representative of each national government. Such a choice of arbiter had obvious problems of legitimacy.[70] Moreover, the standard of refugee protection was clearly unlikely to be questioned, nor strongly guaranteed by those very authorities that had contributed in such a controversial manner to its lowering.[71] The issue of jurisdictional control proved to be a very thorny one, despite numerous

---

66. For a detailed summary of the arguments put forward by the various commentators, see J.J. Bolten, 'From Schengen to Dublin: the new frontiers of refugee law' *supra* n° 27, p. 26 *et seq.*

67. In this sense, see the previously mentioned Conclusion of the UNHCR Executive Committee, *supra* n° 62.

68. See K. Hailbronner and C. Thiery, *supra* n° 38, p. 964.

69. Against this interpretation see, however, K. Hailbronner, 'Perspectives of a harmonisation of the law of asylum after the Maastricht summit' (1992) 29 CML Rev., p. 917, at pp. 925–926. Unfortunately, his argument in favour of the mutual recognition of 'negative' asylum decisions does not seem consistent with his belief that asylum decisions are mainly value oriented and depend heavily on national political and economic considerations.

70. On this point, see D. Curtin and H. Meijers, 'The principle of open government in Schengen and the European Union: democratic retrogression?' (1995) 32 CML Rev., p. 391.

71. During the ratification of the SC, the Dutch Parliament highlighted very strongly the lack of a common judicial machinery. In order to secure ratification, the Dutch Government had to promise to push for some form of international judicial control in future negotiations (see *Europe*, 14/2/92, n° 5668, p. 8). This was an important factor in the drafting of Art. K.3.2.c TEU – see further Chapter III.1. For a review of such initiatives, see. C.A. Groenendijk, 'The competence of the European Court of Justice with respect to intergovernmental treaties on immigration and asylum' (1992) 4 IJRL, p. 531, at p. 532. However, the fact that it proved impossible to reach any compromise on jurisdictional control over the following years meant that the Dutch Parliament refused for seven years to ratify the Dublin Convention.

national initiatives. Only with the Amsterdam Treaty was it finally possible to reach a compromise on this issue.

II.3.D. Visa policy and carrier sanctions

In attempting to establish an internal border-free area, the Schengen Convention necessarily contained a number of provisions regulating the circulation of aliens to and within the common area. Although these provisions did not appear to specifically concern refugees, some of them nonetheless had a huge effect on refugee flows to Europe. The provisions in question related mainly to visas and to carrier sanctions. The entire Chapter 3 of the SC dealt with the establishment of a common visa list (for short-term visas) and a uniform visa format, as well as expressly envisaging the harmonisation of Member States' visa policies.

Measures relating to carrier sanctions[72] were contained in Chapter VI under the heading of 'Measures relating to organised travel' and they immediately preceded the asylum provisions. Art. 26 provided for the compulsory introduction to the Member States' legislation of two types of measures. Firstly, it established the responsibility of the carrier to return the illegal alien to the country of origin, the country of departure, or a third country which would guarantee entry. The carrier also had to assume responsibility for all necessary travel documents. Secondly, it provided for the introduction of penalties against carriers which transported aliens without proper travel documents from a third state into the Schengen territory. Ironically, both types of measures were preceded by an express reference to the obligations arising from the 1951 Geneva Refugee Convention and the 1967 New York Protocol.

National legislation imposing fines and other types of sanctions, in particular against air carriers had been a long-standing practice for countries such as the USA, Canada and Australia, as well as Argentina, Bolivia, Brazil, Thailand, Uruguay and Venezuela. Due to the high numbers of people arriving by air with inadequate or forged entry documents, these states were increasingly obliged to rely on airlines as supplementary immigration control mechanisms. These measures were not intended to affect incoming refugee flows in any way and to this purpose they contained a number of exculpatory provisions.[73] But when the

---

72. The progressive introduction of carrier sanctions in a number of European states in the late Eighties, as well as the specific provisions of the SC and of the DC, have been the subject of a number of analysis; see for instance A. Cruz, 'Compatibility of carrier sanctions in four Community States with international civil aviation and Human Rights obligations' in H. Meijers *et alia* (eds), *supra* n° 27, p. 37; by the same author *Carriers liability in the Member States of the European Union* (CCME Briefing Paper n° 17, Brussels, 1994); also by the Danish Refugee Council, *The effect of carrier sanctions on the asylum system* (Copenhagen, 1991).

73. For a survey of such legislation, see E. Feller, 'Carrier sanctions and International Law' (1989) 1 IJRL, p. 6.

burden on asylum procedures started to increase significantly, the sanctions were stepped up and turned progressively into a complex refugee deterrence system.

In Europe the history of carrier sanctions had been quite different. The genesis of these measures was clearly linked to the sharp rise in the numbers of asylum seekers arriving in Europe since the mid-Seventies. Since most European legislation only allowed an asylum claim to be lodged in the national territory, preventing access to such a territory became a key deterrence factor. European governments justified their deterrence strategy by underlining the connection between the tightening of immigration laws and the rise of asylum claims, thus concluding that most asylum seekers were in fact 'economic migrants'. To support such allegations, governments used a number of different arguments, mainly based on the statistical evidence that asylum seekers increasingly arrived from so-called 'safe countries', which were defined by the low percentage of positive findings in the procedure for the determination of refugee status.[74]

Statistics pointed to the fact that increasingly asylum seekers were entering on commercial carriers. In the UK, for instance, until the beginning of 1987 over 90 per cent of all asylum claims were submitted by persons who had been previously admitted into the country on a temporary basis, but by the end of 1987 50 per cent of all applications were made at the port of entry.[75] In order to face rising illegal immigration and what European governments regarded as an abuse of asylum procedures, stringent visa requirements were imposed on an increasing number of countries, coupled with a complex system of carrier sanctions to ensure the enforcement of the new visa policies.

Visa requirements were a substantial component of the tightening immigration laws enacted by European governments since the mid-Seventies. By the mid-Eighties they had become a useful tool to curb incoming refugee flows. Increasingly, visa requirements were introduced for passengers from countries where statistically most asylum seekers originated from. For example, Germany introduced visa requirements for Afghan citizens in October 1981 after the Soviet invasion and the ongoing civil war had started to generate massive refugee flows. The same criteria applied to Ethiopia in December 1982. Following the increased number of Tamil asylum seekers, the UK imposed visas on Sri Lankan nationals in 1985.[76] In December 1985 Benelux decided to require entry visas for the citizens of the five countries which headed the list of the countries of origin of asylum seekers, namely Afghanistan, Iraq, Iran, Sri Lanka and Turkey.[77]

---

74. When the German Government in January 1987 introduced new heavy penalties on carriers, the authorities' main justification was the decrease of valid asylum claims from 16.1 per cent in the first seven months of 1985 to 10.3 per cent during the same period in 1986. Press Release of the Interior Minister, Bonn, 19/8/87, quoted by E. Feller, *supra* n° 73, p. 49.

75. In A. Ruff, 'The Immigration Carriers' Liability Act 1987' [1989] *Public Law*, p. 222, at p. 223.

76. See E. Feller, *supra* n° 73, p. 52.

77. See A. Cruz, 'Carrier sanctions in four European Community States: incompatibilities between international civil aviation and Human Rights obligations' (1991) 3 IJRL, p. 63, at p. 65.

At the same time, in order to effectively enforce visa requirements, from 1987 onwards European governments started to develop a complex system of heavy fines on airlines which were bringing in improperly documented aliens. A system of 'sanctions' whereby carriers were obliged to return inadmissible passengers at their own costs had long been in place.[78] The first countries to introduce fines were Belgium, Denmark, the UK and Germany, soon followed by most EU Member States. Most countries that introduced fines after 1990 specifically pointed at the obligations imposed by Art. 26 of the Schengen Convention, but a close examination of the wording of the article fails to support such justifications. Only the English translation of the Convention used the term 'penalties' in paragraph 2 of Art. 26, whereas the other linguistic versions only employed the term 'sanctions', which did not necessarily imply fines.[79] As English was not an official working language of the Schengen Group, the English translation provided by the Schengen Secretariat had no official value. Furthermore, the obligation in Art. 26 to 'sanction' carriers only referred to undocumented passengers arriving from outside the Schengen area, but all national legislation on carriers' liability conveniently ignored this point.

A detailed examination of the relevant national legislation would have revealed conspicuous differences, both regarding the application of the fines and their financial amounts. Some countries, such as Germany and Denmark, fined carriers on a basis of strict liability and did not provide at all for the possibility of a waiver of the fine based on exculpatory circumstances.[80] Such circumstances were, however, introduced by the Courts. In Denmark in 1991, the Supreme Court confirmed an earlier ruling of the High Court which had limited the strict liability of carriers by a 'negligence test'.[81] In the case of exceptionally well forged documents or of disposal of travel documents after embarkation, the airline could not be held liable. In Germany too, case law clarified that there were limits as to what control measures could be expected from the carrier. Airlines were expected to check passengers only up to the last stop-over before reaching

---

78. In the UK, for instance, The Immigration Act of 1971, Schedule 2, paragraphs 8 and 9 obliged carriers to remove or make arrangements for the removal of any passengers who are refused entry or are illegal entrants. Furthermore, the carrier was liable for all expenses incurred by the State for the custody, accommodation or maintenance of such persons (Schedule 2, para. 19).

79. A. Cruz, *Carriers liability in the Member States of the European Union, supra* n° 72, at p. 8, poignantly remarks that the German term '*Sanktionen*' is indeed 'an extremely unprecise term for a country whose legislation provides for no less than three distinct kinds of fines'.

80. See, for Germany, Art. 74.2 of the Aliens Act (*Auslaendergesetz*) of 1/1/1991 and for Denmark, the Aliens Act, Law n° 226 of 6/6/1983 as amended by Law n° 574 of 19/12/1985 and Law n° 686 of 17/10/1986.

81. See A. Bodtcher and J. Hughes, 'The effects of legislation imposing fines on airlines for transporting undocumented passengers' in Danish Refugee Council, *supra*, n° 72, p. 6, at pp. 7–8.

German territory.[82] In both countries, neither the law nor the jurisprudence envisaged, however, the subsequent recognition of refugee status as an exculpatory circumstance.

All other Schengen/EU Members' legislation on carriers' liability was based on a negligence criterion, but conditions as to the burden of proof and exculpatory circumstances varied a great deal. British provisions were certainly among the harshest because the law was applied to the letter and the circumstances in which fines were waived were very few and very restrictively interpreted. The burden of proving the absence of negligence was on the carrier and exculpatory circumstances[83] in the case of asylum seekers were only envisaged in so far as final refugee status was granted, but did not include cases of exceptional leave to remain (which constituted 75 per cent of all successful applications).[84] Fines per inadmissible passenger were the highest in Europe (EUR 2,576), whereas most other national fines ranged between EUR 1000–2000.

The Netherlands introduced a new Aliens Law on 1 January 1994, which provided for heavy fines (EUR 2,315) or a six month imprisonment for each inadmissible passenger. The law contained a peculiar provision specifically obliging carriers to photocopy the passport of passengers who boarded flights in countries where great numbers of refugees originated from. In Belgium, the enforcement of carriers' liability legislation was to prove very hard. Although fines were stratospherically high (EUR 3,788), they could not be imposed unless at least five inadmissible passengers were on the same flight (a family being counted as one passenger).[85] Carriers were sanctioned on the grounds of negligence when checking documents upon embarkation, with the burden of proof on the authorities. A Court judgment of 1993[86] further complicated matters by deciding that it was currently impossible to establish which legal person (whether the airline or its employees) was responsible for paying the fine.

Carrier sanctions in Italy, France, Greece, Portugal, Spain and Luxembourg were quite similar. Apparently, in practice most carriers in these countries were not fined if they removed inadmissible passengers immediately, without any cost for the authorities. This practice led to the suspicion that most undocumented passengers were effectively prevented from coming into any contact with the

---

82. See *Verwaltungsgericht Köln*, judgment of 31/05/1988–12 K 1169/87.
83. The Immigration Carriers' Liability Act of 1987 did not explicitly contain exculpatory provisions. These were laid down in the guidelines issued for the exercise of discretion under the 1987 Act. For a list of the Guidelines see I. Macdonald and N. Blake, *Macdonald's immigration law and practice* (3rd edn, Butterworths, London, 1991), at p. 25.
84. See Home Office statistic for 1994 in *The Guardian*, 26/10/1995, p. 2.
85. This quota was introduced to protect spontaneous asylum seekers (see *Migration News Sheet*, August 1991, p. 6). However, it is difficult to imagine how a carrier's personnel would be able to detect and distinguish 'spontaneous asylum seekers' from those who try to board without proper travel documents. Evidence suggests that personnel will not take any risks if faced with the prospect of a substantial fine.
86. Tribunal Correctionnel de Bruxelles, judgment of 15 April 1993

authorities. However, in France, Italy, Luxembourg and the Netherlands the carrier would not be held liable if the passenger without proper travel documents was subsequently authorised to apply for asylum and the case was not deemed 'manifestly unfounded'.

The disparity in carriers' liability legislation across Europe, especially within the Schengen Group, as well as the lack of any attempt towards greater harmonisation meant that reaching certain countries in Europe proved comparatively more difficult than others. This reality, coupled with the provisions of Art. 30 on the allocation of responsibility of asylum claims and the mutual recognition of negative asylum decisions, effectively deprived asylum seekers of the slightest chance of lodging their claim in the country which might have been most sympathetic to their plight.

Carrier sanctions also had other important consequences for refugees. Evidence suggested that some countries would take tougher measures against asylum seekers passing through their territories in an attempt to protect their domestic carriers from being fined. In January 1994, Denmark requested that Sweden improve its borders controls with respect to persons travelling to Denmark. An official at the Danish Ministry of Justice explained that the Danish Government was particularly concerned with the prospective fines that could arise if 25,000 Kosovo Albanians, whose asylum application had been rejected in Sweden, were to succeed in their alleged aim of travelling to Germany.[87]

UNHCR repeatedly stressed that the way European States designed and enforced their carrier sanctions violated their obligations under the 1951 GC and placed an unbearable burden on untrained airline personnel: 'If States consider recourse to carrier sanctions unavoidable they should at least implement them in a manner that is consistent with refugee protection principles, and which does not hinder access to status determination procedures. States should enforce sanctions only in the event that they can establish that carriers are negligent in checking documents, and knowingly brought into the State a person that did not possess a valid entry document and did not have a well founded fear of persecution [...]. It does not require, therefore, any judgment by airlines on the asylum claim or the validity of the documents. [...] In this posture, the burden of proof falls, more appropriately, upon the shoulders of the State, in recognition of the fact that States, not carrier personnel, have the appropriate training and authority to identify those with well-founded claims for refugee and asylum [...]. States should exempt carriers from liability if the person is admitted to the asylum procedure, and should consider waiving penalties if a person is admitted for humanitarian reasons generally.'[88]

From the preceding survey of European carriers' liability legislation and the

---

87. See *Migration News Sheet*, February 1994, p. 5.
88. Conclusions on the International Protection of Refugees, adopted by the Executive Committee of the UNHCR, published by the UNHCR, 1991, pp. 52–53.

above UNHCR critical remarks, it could safely be argued that Schengen governments incorrectly implemented Art. 26 of the SC. After pledging to respect their obligations under the 1951 GC twice in the same article, most Schengen Members subsequently failed to introduce into their legislation exculpatory provisions for prospective asylum seekers travelling with insufficient documents. Nor were the provisions for the waiving of fines in case of subsequent granting of refugee status enough, since the obligation to assess refugee status rested solely on Contracting States and could not be passed onto individual private operators.

UNHCR criticism also addressed the possible negative effects of visa policies: 'The introduction or not of visa requirements for a particular nationality is a legitimate measure of immigration management as is the use of sanctions for carriers who bring passengers without the necessary documentation. When visa requirements are applied in combination with carrier sanctions indiscriminately to persons in need of protection and to persons who are not, they may, however, prevent access to safety for persons in need of it'.[89]

Undeniably, in most cases asylum seekers would not be issued a visa if they were honest about their intentions. Thus, they are forced to either deceive embassy personnel or rely on forged documents. In 1990, even the High Court in London recognised the necessity for asylum seekers to deceive the authorities by stating that 'somebody who wishes to obtain asylum in this country [...] has the option of: 1) lying to the UK authorities in order to obtain a tourist or some sort of visa; 2) obtaining a credible forgery of a visa; 3) obtaining an airline ticket to a third country with a stop over in the UK'[90] The British Government did admit that the Immigration Carriers' Liability Act, in conjunction with extended visa requirements, 'does indeed prevent some asylum seekers from coming to the UK'. It tried to justify this fact by arguing that it has no obligation to encourage or assist would-be asylum seekers [...] to come here and enter our procedures [...]. [G]enuine refugees can always find protection in Third, preferably neighbouring countries'.[91]

The high level of the fines[92] led carriers to react with a series of measures which had potentially disastrous consequences for asylum seekers. Airlines, for instance, were forced to undergo extensive training of their personnel, often with the keen technical support of governments. The UK Home Secretary announced in July 1991 that document specialists had been sent to train airline staff in detecting forgeries.[93] In Germany, officers of the Federal Border Police were

---

89. See *supra* n° 88, p. 60.

90. *R. v Secretary of State ex parte K. Yassine et alia* (1990) IA Rev., p. 354 at pp. 359–360.

91. All extracts from a letter from the Home Secretary's private office, dated 21/11/1991, to Amnesty International; see Amnesty International British Section 1991, p. 5.

92. In Germany, a total of DM 10.5 million had been imposed in fines between 1987 and May 1993 (*Migration News Sheet*, July 1993, p. 5). In the UK carriers had been fined a total of £62.55 million by the end of 1993 (House of Commons Written Answers, col. 639, Mr Charles Wardle, 21 April 1994).

93. See *Migration News Sheet*, July 1991, p. 8.

being dispatched to particularly 'sensitive' places of departure, to assist carriers' personnel in checking travel documents.[94] The same type of co-operation was given to KLM by the Dutch authorities.[95] The agreement benefited both sides because it entailed less expenses at home for the authorities in handling asylum applications and almost no penalties prospects for airlines. However, the dispatched border officer would most of the time have no expertise to assess asylum claims. Thus, once more the real 'losers' of the agreement were prospective asylum seekers.

Despite all possible training, the fact remained that carriers' personnel could not validly substitute immigration authorities. Carriers were expected not only to spot forgeries and ensure the validity of documents, but also to make sure that all passengers were in possession of the right documents requested for the purpose of their entry.[96] Visa requirements, in particular, could vary according to the reasons for seeking entry into a country. Taking into account that (other than tourist visas) the Schengen countries had very different visa policies, it would have been presumptuous to suppose that carriers' personnel could effectively distinguish between the requirements of different legislation. Understandably, carriers would not be willing to take any risks in doubtful situations.[97]

Carrier sanctions were also severely criticised under the international law profile for breaching both the 1951 Geneva Convention on Refugees and Annex 9 of the Chicago Convention on International Civil Aviation (ICAO) of 1944. Fear of disproportionate fines often led airline personnel to the practice of 'kidnapping' passengers found without the necessary travel documents at the moment of disembarkation, in order to prevent them from coming into contact with immigration officials.[98] These unfortunate events constituted a breach of Art. 33 of the 1951 GC which prohibited refoulement to countries where the life of an asylum seeker could be in danger. Although the individual misconduct of carriers could obviously not be directly attributed to the concerned States,

---

94. See R. Marx, *Asylrecht* (5th edn, Nomos, Baden-Baden, 1991), p. 1585.

95. See H.U. Jessurun D' Oliveira, *supra* n° 34, p. 179.

96. See I. Macdonald and N. Blake, *supra* n° 83, p. 24.

97. NGOs and other QUANGOs all over Europe actively sampled cases of persons fleeing persecution who were denied boarding on carriers because the personnel was not convinced about their travel documents (see, for instance, the publication by the Danish Refugee Council, *supra* n° 72, or the numerous reports by Amnesty International, in particular the British Section ones from 1991 onwards, and the Amnesty International EU Association report of June 1994). The disconcerting element that characterised most of these cases was that the persons in question were in fact in possession of all the required entry documents. Therefore, the carriers' concern for penalties had the perverse effect of tightening immigration controls even beyond the requirements of the law.

98. Documented cases concerning forced repatriation or, in luckier cases, failure to do so were collected by several Human Rights organisations. See, for instance, the Danish Refugee Council or Amnesty International (British Section annual reports).

evidence suggested that immigration officials tended to turn a blind eye to carriers' 'kidnappings'.[99]

Furthermore, many national carriers' liability provisions breached the ICAO Convention by imposing far too heavy control responsibilities on carriers. Thus, by excessively burdening carriers, European liability legislation could be interpreted as being indirectly conducive to carriers' misconduct in refoulment cases. Annex 9 of the ICAO Convention, as amended in September 1988, clearly stated airlines' obligations in terms of document controls and limited penal responsibility. In particular, according to paragraph 3.37, the airlines' sole responsibility was 'to take precautions to the end' of passengers being in possession of the necessary documents at the point of embarkation. Contracting States had to cooperate with them in establishing authenticity of documents. The imposition of fines was only allowed where evidence suggested that the carrier had been negligent in carrying out its document control tasks. Therefore, strict liability provisions, such as the ones found in the German or Danish legislation, were in direct contrast with Annex 9, as any other national provision placing the burden of proof on carriers.

II.4. THE 1990 DUBLIN CONVENTION ON STATE RESPONSIBILITY FOR ASYLUM APPLICATIONS AND SCHENGEN

Even if the DC was signed in Dublin four days before the SC, its provisions broadly match those contained in Title II, Chapter 7 of the SC. However, a close comparison of the two Conventions revealed some interesting differences. Overall, the Dublin text was far better structured than Chapter 7 SC. Criteria for determining responsibility over asylum application were clearly stated in Arts 4–8, in order of importance, with the main exception on 'family reunification' (Art. 4) clearly positioned before the remaining criteria. Single criteria were defined with much greater detail so as to leave minimal space for dispute among Contracting Parties. Once the DC had been ratified it would have bound all EC Members. Hence, it would have been on a clear collision course with the Schengen provisions that bound a smaller number of Community Members.[100] To avoid this possible conflict, the Schengen Executive Committee in April 1994 adopted a Resolution stating that Chapter 7 SC would cease to be applicable as soon as the DC came into force.[101]

---

99. See the conclusions drawn by Amnesty International (British Section) in its 1991 report, p. 10.

100. However, Art. 134 SC stated that '[t]he provisions of this Convention shall apply only insofar as they are compatible with Community Law'. Art. 142 referred to the possibility that EC Members could in future conclude conventions 'with a view to the completion of an area without internal frontiers'. In such cases 'provisions which are in breach of those agreed between the Member States of the European Communities shall in any case be adapted in any circumstance'.

101. Schengen Members later signed a Protocol in Bonn along the same lines of the Resolution (see K. Hailbronner and C. Thiery, *supra* n° 38, p. 961).

Several provisions of the DC appeared to allow relatively more freedom to applicants in choosing where to lodge their applications. That was the case, for instance, for expired residence permits or visas. If the applicants had not left the Community territory after a period of two years (for expired residence permits) or six months (for expired visas) they were virtually free to apply anywhere (Art. 5.4). Art. 30.c of the Schengen text specifically excluded such a possibility. Similarly, Art. 6 DC, in the case of irregular entry from outside the Community into a Member State, placed responsibility on that State only for the first six months; thereafter, the applicants acquired the right to lodge their application in the State where they had resided for the last six months. Art. 30.e SC instead maintained the indefinite responsibility of the State where the irregular entry had occurred.

In other respects the Dublin provisions seemed to afford better guarantees for asylum seekers. Art. 29.2 SC, after asserting the obligation of Member States to process asylum applications, affirmed that such obligation did not 'bind a Contracting Party to authorise every applicant for asylum to enter or to remain within its territory'. The compatibility of this provision with the obligation of non-refoulement imposed by Art. 33 GC[102] was highly disputable. Fortunately, no parallel provision appeared in the Dublin text. It remained arguable, however, if the absence of such provision entailed per converso a right of asylum seekers to temporary admission. Refugees' personal data exchange was also far better regulated by the DC. As previously pointed out, the Schengen Convention inexplicably discriminated between the protection of refugees' personal data and other forms of cross-border exchanges of information. The stringent guarantees laid down by Art. 126 SC did not apply to Chapter 7; the special monitoring by an independent body over the processing of data was specifically excluded by Art. 128 in the case of refugees; asylum applicants were not entitled (unlike Union citizens!) to damages in the case of incorrect information being transmitted about them, nor to an effective control over its correction. The application of the guarantees of the 1981 Strasbourg Convention on the Automatic Processing of Personal Data was specifically excluded in their case. On the contrary, Art. 15.12 DC specifically submitted any computerisation of the personal data of refugees to the guarantees afforded by the Strasbourg 1981 Convention.

Similarly to Art. 36 SC,[103] the Dublin text also contained a further exception clause to the general criteria on State responsibility. According to Art. 9 any Party, even if not responsible under the Convention, could request another Member State to examine the application 'for humanitarian reasons, based in particular on family or cultural grounds'. This provision was of particular relevance because it could have allowed the circumvention of the restrictive

---

102. Art. 33 GC imposes an absolute obligation on any Contracting State
103. Art. 36 SC was, however, of a more limited nature insofar as it only allowed the responsible State to put forward the request.

definition of 'family' contained in Art. 4 DC.[104] This definition, which strictly adhered to the Western concept of the 'nuclear' family, posed two orders of problems. Firstly, it only referred to the family members of a recognised refugee, leaving open instead the possibility of splitting up families of asylum seekers. It was a common occurrence that members of the same family were often obliged to flee via different routes and at different points in time. The application of SC/DC rules meant that such individuals would fall under the responsibility of different Member States. Even in the rare event of such applications being successful, the refugees would only have been entitled to reside in the State that had granted them refugee status. The end result would have been a family diaspora and, inevitably, a breach of Art. 8 ECHR.[105]

The DC finally came into force in September 1997. The seven-year delay was due to major resistance from several national Parliaments and other institutions. Since Ireland had never been confronted with a significant number of asylum applications in the past, it had to elaborate a complete asylum bill before being able to proceed with the ratification. In the case of the Netherlands, the complications were due to the inability of the Dutch Government to secure some kind of judicial control mechanism under the DC.[106] The implementation record of the Schengen provisions in the preceding years showed that the exceptions were, by and large, not greatly relied upon. It also proved that the mechanism was far from generating equitable results, both for asylum seekers and Member States that happened to be situated along the external borders of the Community.[107]

II.5. THE 1991 COMMISSION COMMUNICATION

Having settled the most urgent issue, namely the 'access' of asylum seekers to the Single Market, Member States increasingly focused on harmonisation matters

---

104. This definition had already been criticised as being too restrictive. See UNHCR's *Handbook on procedures and criteria for determining refugee status*, para. 185, and UNHCR's Executive Committee Conclusions n° 9 and n° 24 on Family Reunification, where it was recommended that family members, such as parents or adult children, living in the same household should be included for the purposes of family reunion.

105. The ultimate irony of this 'one-shot-only system' was that even in the event of a successful application, the refugee would have been barred from lodging another application in the country where his family was. It would also be worth remembering that the possibility of harmonising the residence rights of recognised refugees was never mentioned until the end of 2000. In practice, given national discrepancies in the adjudication of asylum applications, a family whose members were made to apply in different countries would have found it almost impossible to obtain refugee status for all its members. Hence, the importance of having one State examine all their applications. A breach of Art. 8 ECHR would also be likely to occur in the event of separate national examinations of the asylum applications of members of the same family dragging on for long periods of time (on this point, see K. Hailbronner and C. Thiery, *supra* n° 38, p. 969).

106. See *supra* n° 71.

107. See further in Chapters IV.3 and VI.4.

which were deemed essential for the correct functioning of the Dublin machinery. Since one of the founding principles of the DC was the mutual recognition of national asylum decisions, the Twelve needed to prove that they could confidently rely on each other's asylum adjudication. Therefore, they began to tackle the disparities in national asylum procedures.

The Luxembourg Council of June 1991 gave a fresh impetus to the study of such questions by acknowledging that the completion of the Internal Market and the possible establishment of a political union would certainly necessitate harmonisation of the 'formal' (organisation, length of procedures and means of redress) as well as the 'substantive' aspects of the right of asylum. It also agreed with the objectives underlying the German delegation's proposal regarding immigration and asylum,[108] which had been drawn up with an eye to a Treaty on Political Union. This proposal was twofold: in the first part, it stated that Member States should commit themselves under a Treaty on Political Union to harmonising, both formally and substantively, their policies on asylum, immigration and aliens. In the second part, the Ministers responsible for immigration were asked to submit a report to the Maastricht summit in December 1991 outlining the preparatory work needed for harmonisation. They were also charged of proposing concrete measures to be implemented in the period between signature and entry into force of the Treaty. The Commission was also invited to submit a report on these matters.

The Commission submitted two separate Communications on the right of asylum and on immigration[109] which constituted its first official contributions to the intergovernmental discussions on asylum in the context of the impending Treaty reforms. The detailed analysis of the issue, both on a short- and long-term basis, and the practical measures suggested constituted a good starting point for the drawing up of the report of the Ad Hoc Group on Immigration (WGI930), adopted at The Hague on 3 of December 1991. This report contained the 1992 work-programme and was broadly inspired by the guidelines of the Commission Communication.

The two Communications were linked by the assumption that the recent 'abuses' in asylum procedures stemmed from the need to circumvent the ever-tightening European national immigration laws. It followed that any measures aiming at protecting the right of asylum from possible abuses should be linked to a general plan for controlling economic migration into Europe. The asylum Communication was preceded by a discussion paper which outlined the main issues at stake and the recent efforts of the Twelve. It correctly remarked that the international commitments Member States had entered into entailed a loss of discretion over national power to grant asylum. It was therefore paramount that any common measure should respect the obligations of the 1951 GC.

---

108. See Bull. EC 6–91, pp. 134–135.
109. The 'Communication on the right of asylum' was presented on 11/10/1991, SEC(91) 1857 final; the 'Communication on immigration' on 23/10/1991, SEC(91) 1885 final.

However, the Commission correctly pointed out that it was precisely the inadequacies of the GC's definition of 'refugee' that had determined the current 'crisis of the right of asylum'.[110] On the one hand, the GC failed to include the relatively new phenomenon of people fleeing civil wars (so-called 'de facto refugees') who accounted for the largest number of applications. On the other hand national interpretations of the definition of 'refugee' diverged greatly due to the lack of any international judicial control. Differences in admission criteria, in benefits for asylum seekers and in expulsion legislation meant that a few countries in the Community attracted most of the asylum applications: between 1988 and 1990, 80 per cent of all asylum applications were lodged in two countries, namely Germany and France (60 and 20 per cent respectively). At the same time the recognition rate of refugee status dropped dramatically by more than two-thirds.[111]

The discussion paper included a survey of the past initiatives of the Twelve, adopted either individually or jointly under the framework of European Political Co-operation (EPC). Most of the national measures aimed at controlling and stemming the recent refugee inflows were judged to be quite ineffective. Given the top priority of 'combating abuse of the right of asylum',[112] the Commission advocated strongly in favour of a new set of joint measures ranging from the prompt ratification of the DC to the introduction of accelerated procedures for the examination of asylum applications; information exchange measures; the harmonisation of admission and expulsion legislation; the approximation of asylum seekers' national reception conditions; the creation of a common judicial machinery; and the standardisation of rules concerning 'de facto refugees'.

The truly striking aspect of the Commission's Communication was the lack of any independent position. This document differed from the ones where the Commission played its usual role of legislative initiator, in so far as there was no attempt to mediate between different governmental and non-governmental points of view. The choice of the Twelve to proceed outside the Community framework had clearly obliged the Commission to adopt a non-antagonistic position. If it was to play any role at all in the process, the Commission had to align itself completely with the restrictive national positions on asylum. The outcome was a document which correctly listed all the major problems of this delicate field, but failed to draw the logical – yet politically unacceptable – conclusions on the best line of action. Thus, the Commission correctly highlighted in great detail the vast differences between the national implementations of the GC. However, it then proceeded to praise the DC, a system based on the equivalence of outcome of each national asylum adjudication system, as well as the denial of the mutual recognition of positive asylum decisions. Searching to

---

110. See the asylum Communication, *supra* n° 109, p. 6.
111. See the asylum Communication, *supra* n° 109, p. 4 and Annex II of the Communication. See also Annex, Table 3.
112. See the asylum Communication, *supra* n° 109, p. 52

legitimise the policy decisions of the Twelve, the Commission even claimed that the DC had the full support of the UNHCR. In truth this body had repeatedly stressed its concerns over the conformity of this agreement with the spirit of the GC.[113]

In an attempt to overcome the inherent contradictions of its proposal, the Commission tried to link the necessity of drastic 'anti-refugee' measures in Europe with a better development policy, specifically targeting the roots of the refugee phenomenon in the world. It proposed the adoption of principles such as conditioning the granting of aid to the respect of Human Rights. These principles would be integrated with special co-operation programmes aiming, for instance, at reducing brain-drain and poverty in large urban areas.[114] This contribution (the first of its kind in the field) was certainly of great importance for the development of a long-term asylum strategy for the Community. Ironically, the Twelve did not show the same concern for Human Rights protection within the EPC framework. In fact, by marginalizing the Commission, Member States missed the chance not only to introduce some transparency into a very secretive system, but also to allow an international body to voice the legitimate concerns of non-governmental organisations in the public arena.

II.6. CONCLUDING REMARKS

The aim of this Chapter was to analyse how the asylum field developed from a purely national dimension (subject to an international discipline) into a Community concern. Most importantly, this Chapter also aimed at highlighting how this development impacted on refugee protection in Europe. There is little doubt that by the beginning of the 90s standards of protection across the EC had considerably worsened. Major geopolitical changes meant a large increase in refugee flows into Western Europe, yet recognition rates dropped dramatically.

The Community interest in asylum matters was no doubt spurred by the SEA and the ultimate aim of a frontier-free Single Market. Notwithstanding the differences of interpretation of Art. 8A EEC, the drive towards the Internal Market had a fundamental impact on asylum seekers. Refugee protection became primarily an aspect of the need to control the circulation of aliens within the Single Market. Rather than emphasising the element of protection Member States were increasingly concerned about issues of 'access to territory', residence and 'removal from the territory'. Thus, the distinction between asylum and the traditional area of immigration became progressively blurred.

The fact that at the time most progress on these matters took place outside the Community framework only compounded the negative effect on refugees. The dispute over the interpretation of Art. 8A EEC meant that some Members

---

113. See the asylum Communication *supra* n° 109, p. 10. For the UNHCR criticisms, see *supra* n° 88, pp. 89–104.

114. SEC(91) 1855 final (Communication on Immigration) p. 20 *et seq.*

were reluctant to allow any co-operation to take place within the established Community mechanisms. Moreover, the prevailing general perception was that immigration matters were still an essential national prerogative. The Community framework, with its inevitable publicity and loss of national decision power, was not the ideal playing field for reticent Member States. Traditional intergovernmental co-operation had the added advantage of allowing a very high degree of secrecy in the decision-making process, thus effectively bypassing the scrutiny of national legislators and public opinion.

Against this background, the choice of asylum provisions in the SC or DC became almost inevitable, yet hardly justifiable from the perspective of refugee protection and international obligations. In the name of their ultimate goal, a border-free Europe, Member States sacrificed refugees' rights on the altar of compensatory measures. Since time was of the essence, only minimal co-ordination was possible, just enough to guarantee the smooth functioning of the structures regulating access to the 'Common Territory'. Hence, the main preoccupation had been the laying down of criteria for the determination of States' responsibility on asylum applications.

Minimal harmonisation unjustifiably sacrificed the rights of asylum seekers. National implementation of the 1951 GC without any jurisdictional control was hardly an ideal solution, but at least refugees could take advantage of disparities between national legislation. This option was now precluded by the adoption of the SC/DC principles. These principles meant that similar cases were being treated dissimilarly because national asylum legislation still widely differed, both substantially and procedurally. Minimal co-ordination conveniently required the mutual recognition of negative asylum decisions. However, differences in national implementations of the 1951 GC were still considered important enough to prevent mutual recognition of positive decisions. Asylum seekers were left to bear the brunt of this harmonisation gap.

The progressive shaping of a 'policy of access-prevention' to the Common Territory lead to other tragic consequences. It prompted a downwards spiral of national carriers' liability legislation, all competing to implement the tougher sanctions. Governments obviously bore a large responsibility in the subsequent misconduct and abuses displayed by carriers in response to provisions which were in blatant breach of international obligations such as the ICAO Convention. The use of visa policy as a tool to actively and purposefully prevent access to asylum procedures was probably the best example of the 'practical' approach Members States took for the preservation of their Common Territory.

Unfortunately, Member States did not appear in any hurry to proceed to more comprehensive harmonisation. The subsequent asylum initiatives (see next Chapter) appeared to follow the same Single Market logic as the DC provisions. Nor did the Maastricht Treaty achieve more than an 'institutionalisation' of the previous EPC structure. What some national Parliaments had so keenly advocated, namely a jurisdictional control mechanism that would at least partially redress the balance in favour of refugee rights, would not be on the cards for a long time yet.

3 The Maastricht Treaty and European Co-operation

III.1. THE NEW PROVISIONS OF THE MAASTRICHT TREATY ON ASYLUM CO-OPERATION

EC Member States began cooperating on asylum matters in the middle of the 80s. This co-operation had been prompted by two main sets of events. The first was the dramatic increase in refugee flows in Europe brought about by the end of the Cold War and the consequent eruption of localised conflicts. The second was the introduction by the SEA of the new Single Market objective, which – according to most EC Members – entailed the creation of a border-free Community. This in turn required the setting up of 'flanking measures' to guarantee the safety of the common area and in this context the control of refugee movements was deemed essential. Asylum co-operation was initially undertaken through informal exchanges within the EPC framework, but was eventually institutionalised in the Treaty on the European Union signed at Maastricht, 7 February 1992. The resulting text was widely criticised for its ambiguity, fragmentation and general lack of coherence.[1]

Back in 1988, at the height of economic prosperity, initial proposals to amend the EEC Treaty had only concerned the possibility of introducing a single currency throughout the Community.[2] The exceptional historical events that followed shortly afterwards were to change the face of Europe. In the wake of German reunification, Chancellor Kohl saw the need to firmly anchor the new Germany into a tighter European framework and thus allay French historic fears of an overly powerful Germany.[3] The Dublin European Council of June

---

1. The literature on the Maastricht Treaty is extremely vast. For the purpose of this thesis, only the Third Pillar of the TEU will be examined and, more specifically, the asylum provisions. On the history and general issues of the TEU, see A. Duff J. Pinder and R. Pryce (eds), *Maastricht and beyond* (Routledge, London, 1994); also F. Laursen and S. Vanhoonacker (eds), *The Intergovernmental Conference on the European Union* (European Institute of Public Administration, Maastricht, 1992); by the same authors see also *The ratification of the Maastricht Treaty* (European Institute of Public Administration, Maastricht, 1994).

2. The Member States had been committed (at least formally) to achieve some sort of political union since the beginning of the Seventies. See R. Pryce, *The dynamics of European Union* (Routledge, London, 1989), in particular at p. 138 *et seq.*

3. The German reunification inevitably upset the post-war order based on the relatively equal size of the larger EU Members, particularly France, Germany and the United Kingdom. After October 1990, Germany's population increased by a third, making it overnight the largest – and in economic terms the strongest – State in Western Europe. In this respect the Schengen negotiations also assumed great symbolic relevance as they reaffirmed the German commitment to the European ideal (see Chapter II.2).

1990 endorsed the convening of a second Intergovernmental Conference to deal with political integration matters. The official German unification of 3 October 1990 further spurred the conference machinery into action and the first IGC meeting took place at the December summit in Rome. However, consensus on the scope and extent of new political integration proved to be extremely hard to reach.

Most delegations agreed in principle on the importance of achieving greater coordination on asylum and immigration matters, as the latter were deemed such an essential part of the need to guarantee the free movement of persons in the Community. However, their opinions differed greatly on the framework for such coordination. The attribution of competence in these areas still remained a delicate and politically sensitive subject. Governments regarded immigration and asylum as a vital national competence since they formed an essential part of their home affairs and internal security matters. The main argument put forward by the supporters of closer coordination was that the free movement of persons was one of the principal objectives of the Community (Art. 8A EEC, later Art. 7a EC). Therefore, the Community had to be granted sufficient powers to pursue it, especially since 'compensatory' measures had been shown to be an essential precondition for lifting border controls.[4] However, these arguments were met with exceptional resistance from most EC governments.

The German proposal to transfer comprehensive competence on asylum and immigration policies to the Community did not prevail over the deeply rooted objections of the other delegations. The Federal Government originally suggested that Community activities should include 'standardisation of Regulations in the fields of refugee policy (including asylum policy) as well as policies on foreigners and immigration'.[5] Thus, the Community would have been authorised to pass (subject to a unanimity vote) the necessary acts for the standardisation of national laws and administrative regulations concerning asylum and immigration policies. These acts should have been in accordance with the legal guarantees for the politically persecuted contained in the 1951 GC. Unfortunately, only the Belgian delegation was ready to accept such a proposal without reservations.[6]

The 'Pillar' framework began to take shape under the Luxembourg Presidency in the first half of 1991. It rapidly became clear that most delegations overwhelmingly favoured the old tested formula of intergovernmental co-operation,[7] in so

---

4. See Chapter II.1.

5. See the extracts of the German delegation proposal reported by K. Hailbronner, 'Perspectives of a harmonisation of the law of asylum after the Maastricht summit' (1992) 29 CML Rev., p. 917, at pp. 926–927.

6. See W. De Lobkowicz, 'Intergovernmental co-operation in the field of migration – from the Single European Act to Maastricht in J. Monar and R. Morgan (eds), *The Third Pillar of the European Union* (European Interuniversity Press, Brussels, 1994), p. 99, at p. 117.

7. This formula followed the previous EPC model and in particular the structures and instruments that had been set up to coordinate Member States' foreign policies.

far as asylum and immigration matters were concerned. The following Dutch Presidency made a final attempt to 'communitarise' asylum co-operation, but by December 1991 the idea of a Third Pillar on Home and Justice Affairs was irrevocably agreed.[8] Most provisions were incorporated into Title VI of the TEU, outside the EC Pillar, although the German Government eventually managed to have a few proposals accepted. Two aspects of visa policy were included in the Community framework, a special provision was inserted to allow transfer of asylum competence to the EC Pillar and, in an annexed Declaration, a common asylum policy was made an express priority.

Of the original German proposal to include asylum and visa policies in the EC Pillar, only two provisions concerning a common visa list and a uniform visa format were assigned to the Community competence.[9] Under Art. 100c EC, the Council would decide by unanimity, on the basis of a Commission proposal, the third countries whose nationals should require a visa when crossing the external frontiers of the Member States. Emergency action might have been taken for six months to deal with a sudden crisis. Qualified majority voting would have applied from 1 January 1996. A uniform visa format was to be adopted by that date. A special provision in Art. 100c.4 EC obliged the Commission to examine any request put forward by a Member State. Although the Commission was not obligated to turn these requests into proposals, the duty to examine them constituted a preparatory move in view of an eventual transfer of competence from the intergovernmental field.[10]

The Maastricht Title VI TEU formula was described as a 'hybrid: essentially intergovernmental but with a dash of the supranational, mainly pooling sovereignty but also partly transferring it'.[11] The co-operation framework was still of an intergovernmental nature, but there were important institutional and proce-

---

8. For further details on the troubled history of the Third Pillar negotiations, see R. Price, 'The Treaty negotiations', in A. Duff *et alia*, *supra* n° 1, p. 36.

9. The reasons for this choice were never entirely clear. The common visa list and the visa format were without a doubt the two most immediate 'flanking' measures required for the abolition of border controls. However, this arbitrary separation created an uneasy split both of competence and of frameworks in the visa field, since general visa policy matters fell under Art. K.1.2 and K.1.3.a-b TEU. See further in Chapter IV.2.

10. The fact that competence in this field was to be split between different frameworks had, however, important operational consequences: two separate Committees (K.4 for the Third Pillar and COREPER for the EC one) were to work on different aspects of the same issues. This operational division was accentuated by the fact that the national representatives of the two Committees would not necessarily be from the same national administration (COREPER representatives traditionally belonged to Foreign Ministries, whereas K.4 representatives would have been Interior Ministries' civil servants).

11. M. Anderson, M. Den Boer and G. Miller, 'European citizenship and co-operation in justice and home affairs', in A. Duff *et alia*, *supra* n° 1, p. 104, at pp. 115–116. See also P.-C. Müller-Graff, 'The legal bases of the Third Pillar and its position in the framework of the Union Treaty' in J. Monar and R. Morgan (eds), *supra* n° 6, p. 21, at p. 27, who defined the Maastricht Treaty as 'a developed form of intergovernmental co-operation'.

dural connections to the Community Pillar. Despite the understandable disappointment of the German delegation, the perspective of asylum co-operation among the Twelve had undoubtedly shifted towards the Community framework, if only for reasons of codification.

The first notable achievement was to be found in the broad definition of Art. K.1 TEU, which listed 'asylum policy' as the first matter to be considered of common interest. The mere use of the generic term 'asylum policy' implied a great latitude of possible interventions. This latitude was far from coincidental, as clearly highlighted by the contrast with the greatly detailed immigration policy provisions (Art. K.1.3.a-b-c). Under Art. K.2, all initiatives relating to matters listed in Art. K.1 had to comply with the ECHR, the 1951 GC and take into account the protection afforded by Member States to persons persecuted on political grounds.[12] For the first time in the history of the Community these Conventions were mentioned in an official Treaty, reinforcing in this respect the jurisprudence of the European Court of Justice.[13] Similarly, the Common Provisions of the TEU (Title I, Art. F) stated that the Union should respect fundamental rights, as guaranteed by the ECHR.[14] However, Art. K.2.2 introduced a proviso stating that nothing in Title VI should have affected Member States' responsibility towards the maintenance of law and order and internal security. The scope of this provision was so broad it could have effectively nullified the effects of Art. K.2.1.[15]

Art. K.3 listed the measures to be adopted and the procedures to be followed in the fields listed by Art. K.1. Member States had to inform and consult one another within the Council with a view to coordinating their action. As a programmatic intent, they were to establish a collaboration between the relevant

---

12. It is not clear, however, why the 1967 New York Protocol did not appear in this provision. As recalled in Chapter I, the 1967 Protocol's importance lay in the fact that it lifted the geographical limitation to victims of persecution 'within Europe' contained in the 1951 GC.

13. For a review of the jurisprudence of the ECJ in the Human Rights field, see A. Clapham, *Human Rights and the European Community: a critical overview*, vol.1 of *European Union – The Human Rights challenge* (Nomos, Baden-Baden, 1991); also J. Weiler and N. Lockhart, ' "Taking rights seriously" seriously: the European Court and its fundamental rights jurisprudence', Part I and II, (1995) 32 CML Rev., p. 51 and p. 579 respectively, and finally the extensive work by P. Alston (ed.), *The EU and Human Rights* (OUP, Oxford, 1999).

14. One might interpret such provisions as explicitly pointing to the ECHR and the GC having precedence over other related Conventions agreed between Community Member States. The validity of the latter would therefore become questionable if found in contrast with the two above-mentioned Conventions. See, in this respect, the observations made by L. Drüke, 'Refugee Protection in Post Cold War Europe', in A. Pauly (ed.), *Les accords de Schengen* (European Institute of Public Administration, Maastricht, 1993), p. 105, at p. 132.

15. See the observations of D. O'Keeffe, 'A critical view of the Third Pillar' in A. Pauly (ed.), *De Schengen à Maastricht: voie royale et course d' obstacles* (European Institute of Public Administration, Maastricht, 1996), p. 1, at p. 9.

departments of their administrations. This provision showed that lessons on how to extend the scope of European integration had been learned through previous foreign policy co-operation. Unfortunately, national Home Offices responsible for Third Pillar matters still lacked the European liaising experience their Foreign Office colleagues had acquired through 30 years of Community co-operation. This lack of experience was to have considerable impact on the speed of asylum co-operation in the early 90s. In formulating the common measures to be taken, Art. K.3 contained an explicit reference to the principle of subsidiarity. The Council could adopt 'joint positions', promote co-operation and adopt 'joint actions', in so far as the objectives of the Union would have been better achieved by joint action than by the Member States acting individually, on account of the scale of effects of the action envisaged. The legal force of such instruments, however, remained very unclear, especially when compared to similar instruments in the Second Pillar. Art. J.3.4 TEU clearly stated that 'joint actions shall commit the Member States in the position they adopt and in the conduct of their activity. No such reference appeared anywhere in Art. K.3.[16] In any case, according to Art. L TEU the ECJ had no jurisdiction over Third Pillar asylum initiatives. Therefore, it could be argued that no asylum initiative could have been deemed 'binding' since it was not enforceable.

According to Art. K.3, the Commission shared a right of initiative with the Member States, but its proposals did not enjoy the special procedural protection provided by Art. 148 of the EC Treaty.[17] Nor was the Commission assigned its usual broad tasks as provided by Art. 155 EC, especially the duty to ensure implementation of the initiatives adopted under the Third Pillar.[18] The inclusion of the Commission as a policy initiator in this intergovernmental field rewarded the pragmatic approach it had taken towards the EPC during the late 80s.

---

16. The types of 'joint instruments' listed in Art. K.3 were the same as those envisaged in the Second Pillar, Art. J.1–4. Within the Third Pillar, disputes between Member States on the legal force of such measures quickly followed.S. Peers, *EU Justice and Home Affairs law* (Longman, London, 2000), reports that in 1995 a dispute took place between 13 Member States backing the Council Legal Service and the UK and Portugal. The Legal Service argued that joint actions were always obligatory, whereas the two opposing Member States argued that the obligation depended entirely on the 'actual text' (see pp. 28–29). The ECJ refused to be drawn into the argument when invited to do so in the context of an annulment action by the Council Legal Service (see *Commission* v. *Council* (airport transit visas) case C-170/96 [1998] ECR I-2763). 'Joint positions' seemed to suffer from the same uncertainty (see further Chapter IV.5).

17. On a positive note, however, asylum policy was one of the areas of Art. K.1 where the Commission enjoyed a right of initiative (albeit shared). In matters relating to judicial co-operation in criminal matters, customs co-operation and police co-operation (Art. K.1.7–8–9) only Member States had a right of initiative.

18. This was particularly regrettable in the light of the very poor implementation by Member States of the asylum measures adopted under Third Pillar co-operation. On this point see further in Chapters III and IV and, for instance, S. Peers, *Mind the gap! Ineffective Member State implementation of European Union asylum measures* (ILPA, London, 1998).

However, the lack of exclusive initiative and the sensitivity of the JHA did not allow the Commission the same freedom of proposal as in the EC Pillar. In order to guarantee a high acceptance ratio of its proposals within the Third Pillar, the Commission needed to follow the existing policies and preferred orientations of the Member States almost exclusively. Therefore, it would not have enjoyed its usual ability to forge independent and original proposals, such as those put forward in the context of the First Pillar, which relied heavily on the information and influence exerted by pressure groups and NGOs. Since asylum matters were intrinsically connected with problematic Human Rights issues, the contribution of NGOs and other international organisations such as the UNHCR, should have been welcomed in this traditionally restrictive intergovernmental arena.[19]

Art. K.3 also introduced the possibility for the Council to draw up conventions to be recommended to the Member States for adoption. Such conventions would have been subjected to the jurisdiction of the European Court of Justice, in accordance with such arrangements as they may have laid down. Conventions are a classic instrument of international law and therefore their inclusion in Art. K.3 was by no means exceptional. However, their use in the asylum field had been heavily criticised for a number of reasons, most of which related to the secrecy of their negotiations, the length of their ratification[20] and the different force international law had in the various national legal systems. The fact that Art. K.3 explicitly referred to the optional possibility of an ECJ arbitration on an ad hoc basis highlighted the other important shortcoming of international conventions, namely the lack of judicial machinery.

During the course of the Maastricht negotiations it had proven impossible to agree on a definite role for the ECJ in the context of the Third Pillar. Given the importance that the Court's jurisprudence had constantly had in expanding the rule of Community law, the caution – or sometimes open hostility – Member States had displayed towards its involvement was entirely to be expected. However, by inserting the option of an ECJ arbitration, Member States had taken a small positive step towards filling this jurisdictional gap. They had in principle accepted that arbitration should, if necessary, be undertaken within

---

19. The lack of openness in the Third Pillar raised serious issues of transparency. These were already apparent in the secrecy that surrounded the negotiations of the 1990 SC and the DC. However, some amount of public debate was at least afforded by the subsequent discussions on ratification that took place in national parliaments. The codification of co-operation introduced by the Third Pillar had the perverse effect of actually reducing public scrutiny even further, since most initiatives did not need any ratification. It was hard to dismiss the suspicion that this side effect was in fact the result of an intentional design. The situation was made worse by the totally inadequate provisions relating to the information to be given to the European Parliament and the structure of the K.4 Committee (see further). See the observations on the matter by D. O'Keeffe, 'A critical view of the Third Pillar', *supra* n° 15, p. 8.

20. The 1990 DC took seven years to be eventually ratified.

the Community framework rather than through a typical intergovernmental structure, such as arbitration panels.[21]

The powers of the ECJ to rule on a violation of EC law were, however, unaffected by the Third Pillar provisions. Although Art. L TEU specifically excluded the jurisdiction of the ECJ over measures taken under Art. K, this exclusion did not extend to violations of Community law. If a Council decision or the conduct of a Member State under Art. K were to violate a requirement of Community law, this conduct would have been sanctionable under the jurisdiction of the ECJ. This conclusion was further confirmed by Art. M TEU, which established that nothing in the TEU could affect the EC Treaty, and by subsequent case law of the ECJ.[22]

Art. K.4 provided for a Coordinating Committee of senior officials to organise and contribute to the preparation of the Council's discussions in this area.[23] The subsequent setting up of the Committee entailed a complete restructuring of all the numerous fora for co-operation, introduced during the previous EPC years, into one comprehensive structure.[24] The K.4 Committee would report to COREPER II, which in turn would brief the JHA Council. The EC Commission

---

21. This was the solution that had been put in place within the Schengen and Dublin frameworks by deferring arbitration matters to the respective Executive Committees. As recalled in Chapter II.3.C, the lack of ECJ jurisdiction was one of the reasons the Dutch Parliament hesitated to ratify the Schengen Agreement. The Dutch Government promised to address the problem at EU level, but only managed to push through the meagre provision contained in Art. K.3.2.c during the negotiations. For some general comments, see C.A. Groenendijk, 'The competence of the European Court of Justice with respect to intergovernmental treaties on immigration and asylum' (1992) 4 IJRL, p. 531.

22. See *Commission* v. *Council* (airport transit visas), case C-170/96 [1998] ECR I-3655. The Commission contested the ability of Member States to adopt a Joint Action on transit airport arrangements (OJ 1996 L63/8) under the Third Pillar, by arguing that such competence fell under Art. 100c EC. The ECJ clearly stated that it was entitled to 'police' the boundaries between the First and Third Pillars by virtue of Art. M TEU and that it could also judge the validity of Third Pillar measures that infringed Community competence.

23. This committee was almost the exact equivalent of the Executive Committee provided for by Title VII of the 1990 SC and similar in nature to the Political Committee introduced in the Second Pillar on Foreign and Security Policy. Since the entry into force of the TEU, it substituted the Rhodes 'Group of Coordinators' and within its complex multi-tier structure it also accommodated the former Ad Hoc Immigration Group, as well as all the other structures that had in the past dealt with co-operation against terrorism (TREVI), drug trafficking (CELAD) and the Horizontal Informatics Group.

24. The K.4 Committee had three *comités directeurs* that reported to it. The first was concerned with asylum and immigration matters and represented the old Ad Hoc Immigration Group. It was divided into subcommittees that dealt with asylum; immigration; the CIREA (Centre for Information, Discussion and Exchange on Asylum); visas; external border controls and the CIREFI (Centre for Information, Discussion and Exchange on the Crossing of Borders and Immigration). The second committee dealt with police and customs co-operation and the fight against terrorism and drug trafficking. The third was concerned with judicial co-operation.

was to be associated with this work, but no precise terms for such association were given. Under Art. K.5, within international organisations and international conferences, Member States were obliged to defend the common positions adopted in this area. This provision was also an extension of the parallel practice in the Common Foreign and Security Policy Pillar that had been consolidated in the previous EPC framework.

Art. K.6 provided for the right of the European Parliament to be constantly informed and for its views to be taken into consideration. It could pose questions to the Council or make recommendations to it. Each year it was to hold a debate on the progress made in the implementation of the areas referred to in Title VI. The importance and novelty of such provisions should not be underestimated, since in the past Member States had regarded any interference of the European Parliament as illegitimate, given the intergovernmental nature of this field. The European Parliament on its part welcomed the new provisions as the start of a greater democratic control over this area. Hence, it established a new Committee on Civil Liberties and Internal Affairs to deal with issues related to asylum, immigration, international crime, drug trafficking, fraud and other Human Rights issues, including racism and xenophobia.

However, the wording of Art. K.6 was criticised for being vague and lacking in clarity. In practice, the absence of a clear legal obligation to take the views of the EP into account resulted in the latter being consulted only ex post facto. Even if it could have been argued that such an obligation existed, it would have been unenforceable due to the lack of any ECJ jurisdiction.[25] The only real power the EP might have exerted could have come from the provisions of Art. K.8, which allowed expenses in this area to be charged to the Community budget. In this case, given that normal budgetary procedures would have applied, the EP could have used its considerable powers to exert some form of indirect control. Unfortunately, Art. K.8 also provided for the possibility of charging operational expenditures directly to the Member States, thus bypassing the EP control.[26]

Art. K.7 was designed to take into account the existence of special agreements among a number of EC Members, such as the Schengen Convention. It permitted the establishment or development of closer co-operation between two or more Member States in so far as such co-operation did not conflict with, or impede, the co-operation provided for in Title VI.[27] It could be argued that by encoding the possibility for a smaller number of EU Members to further their co-operation

---

25. On these problems, see D. O'Keeffe, 'A critical view of the Third Pillar', *supra* n° 15, p. 10.

26. A review of the practice in this field did reveal that Member States were aware of the possible implications of the EP budgetary scrutiny and always charged expenditures directly to national budgets. See the comments of D. O'Keeffe, 'A critical view of the Third Pillar', *supra* n° 15, pp. 10–11.

27. A parallel provision was to be found in the 1990 SC Art. 134, which stated that '[t]he provisions of this Convention shall apply only in so far as they are compatible with Community law'.

in these matters outside the Community framework, Art. K.7 constituted the first built-in 'flexibility' clause of the Treaties.[28]

The last provision of Title VI represented an absolute novelty in the history of the Treaties. It constituted the dynamic link that allowed matters of the Third Pillar to be transferred under the competence of the Community without the need to call for a new intergovernmental conference. Under Art. K.9, the so-called *passarelle* clause, the Council, acting unanimously on the initiative of the Commission or of a Member State, could decide to apply Art. 100c of the EEC Treaty to activities in areas referred to in Art. K.1.1–6 – therefore including asylum – and at the same time determine the relevant voting conditions relating to it. The Member States would adopt this decision in accordance with their respective constitutional requirements. This last requirement highlighted the fact that the procedure would have been subjected to a 'double-lock' that presented remarkable obstacles. In many countries, national ratification would have required further referenda.

Art. K.9 was of particular relevance to the asylum co-operation provisions. To underline the importance and the absolute priority of the matter, asylum was the subject of a separate Declaration annexed to the Treaty. Whereas Art. N of the TEU listed the areas to be discussed in an Intergovernmental Conference in 1996 with the ultimate aim of furthering integration, asylum was given a more stringent deadline. The Declaration expressly foresaw that the Council should have examined, by the end of 1993, the possibility of transferring competence over asylum matters, under the *passarelle* procedure of Art. K.9, to the Community Pillar.[29] The Declaration constituted a compromise between the original German proposal advocating full Community competence and the traditional sensibility of other Member States over such instances.

The same Declaration stipulated that 'the Council [would] consider as a matter of priority questions concerning Member States' asylum policies, with the aim of adopting, by the beginning of 1993, common action to harmonise aspects of them, in the light of the work-programme and timetable contained in the report on asylum drawn up at the request of the European Council meeting in Luxembourg [...]'. This passage left no doubts over the absolute priority asylum had been slowly acquiring over the other 'compensatory' measures.

Overall, EU asylum co-operation received a notable boost from the new provisions of the Maastricht Treaty. Whether this new framework implied better protection and stronger guarantees for refugees remained, however, highly arguable. Elements that would have substantially improved refugee protection were

---

28. 'Flexibility' became one of the cornerstones of the architecture of the following Amsterdam Treaty. See further, Chapter V.4.A.

29. By the end of 1993, the Commission, as instructed by the Maastricht Council, duly assessed whether it would have been possible to achieve a consensus in the Council about transferring competence over asylum to the Community, but reached a negative conclusion (SEC (93) 1687 final). In the end, Art. K.9 was never implemented, nor was there ever any attempt to table a vote on the matter.

unfortunately discarded. Had the German proposal been accepted, the Community system would have brought about a higher level of transparency, greater democratic accountability and wider public scrutiny of Council initiatives. The Commission would have enjoyed a far greater scope of initiative, nongovernmental actors could have been more easily involved and, most importantly, the ECJ jurisdiction would have ensured a coherent implementation of all asylum initiatives.

Historically, the Third Pillar constituted the only acceptable compromise of the early 90s. It represented a considerable progress over the loose, purely intergovernmental structures of the EPC, codifying them into a coherent framework that relied on Community institutions. The EP's role was modest but novel, and the Commission's participation, a definite list of different measures to pursue the 'matters of common interest' – albeit all of a 'soft law' nature – constituted important links with the EC framework. The built-in option to transfer competence to the First Pillar, the timid introduction of some majority voting (Art. 100c EC and K.3.2.c) and the mere envisaging of a possible ECJ jurisdiction (Art. K.3.2.c) were also notable advancements towards the development of a true Community asylum competence. Unfortunately, it wasn't the co-operation structures set up at Maastricht that were to let refugee protection in the EU take a subsequent turn for the worst, but rather the contents that Member States chose to give to such co-operation.

III.2. THE IMPLEMENTATION OF THE MAASTRICHT WORKING PROGRAMME ON ASYLUM

The Maastricht Treaty took almost two years to enter into force because of the lengthy national ratification procedures. Some national resistance proved particularly difficult to overcome and in the Danish case, following the first popular rejection of the new Treaty, special exceptions had to be negotiated to secure a second-round popular endorsement.[30] Despite these difficult political negotiations, the months following the signing of the TEU were characterised by intense activity in the asylum field.

The Luxembourg Council of June 1991 had formally acknowledged the importance of achieving a certain degree of harmonisation in the field of asylum in view of the completion of the Internal Market.[31] It had therefore asked the EC

---

30. As far as the Third Pillar was concerned, Danish public dissent focused on the 'passarelle clause' contained in Art. K.9 TEU, which enabled the Council of Ministers, by unanimous decision, to place areas of the JHA co-operation under Community competence. To overcome public resistance, the Danish Government introduced a 'Unilateral Declaration to be associated to the Danish Act of Ratification of the Treaty on the European Union', which specified that in the event of the adoption of a Council Decision based on Art. K.9 TEU this would amount to a transfer of Danish sovereignty and as such would be subjected to a national referendum (Declaration presented at the Edinburgh Council of 12/12/92).
31. Bull. EC 6–91, p. 107.

Immigration Ministers to submit a report to the Maastricht summit in December 1991[32] outlining the preparatory work needed for harmonisation, as well as proposing concrete measures to be implemented before the entry into force of the new Treaty.

The report illustrated the main priorities and fundamental principles which were to shape the asylum initiatives of the Twelve during the following four and a half years. Significantly, it addressed both the issues of asylum and immigration in the same context, the first formal recognition that the two areas were irrevocably linked.[33] The most interesting part of the report was the annexed 'detailed note' setting out the general framework of the asylum harmonisation programme that lay ahead for the Twelve. The document was characterised by a strictly pragmatic approach, viewing co-operation and harmonisation as necessary only in so far as they could be instrumental in achieving more efficient national asylum policies. Considering that the authors were senior national officials, the report could have put forward an extremely restrictive action framework, but instead it contained remarkably innovative ideas and guidelines.[34]

The introduction to the annex sensibly pointed out that 'despite informal contacts made by different Presidencies with the European Parliament, the various non-governmental organisations and each government's contacts with its national parliament, the impression remains that there is insufficient transparency in this area'.[35] The surprised tone of this statement seemed hardly justifiable, given the total secrecy that surrounded the Schengen and Dublin negotiations. It was no doubt symptomatic of the parallel ongoing discussions both on transparency and on the democratic deficit in the Union. Consequently, the document strongly recommended the establishment of links with NGOs and other external organisations and increased involvement of the EP and the respective national parliaments. It was wisely pointed out that 'the more the activities undertaken in the harmonisation process are favourably perceived by society and the political world, the greater will be the chances of success'.[36] However cynical the ultimate motives of such a suggestion might have been, the mere official admission of the need for 'opening up' the asylum field to external

---

32. Report of the Ad Hoc Group on Immigration, Brussels, 3/12/91, SN 4038/91 (WGI 930).
33. The necessity of a more 'comprehensive strategy' that would acknowledge the undeniable links between the asylum and immigration fields was developed over a considerable length of time before finally being officially recognised. In its following 1994 contribution (COM (94)23 final of 23/02/1994), the Commission presented a single proposal outlining an integrated guideline policy for both fields. Later on problems arose, however, in reasserting the conceptual differences between the two fields, since Member States constantly insisted on their key assumption that most asylum seekers were in fact 'bogus' (see Chapter VI.1 and the Austrian Presidency proposal).
34. It should be stressed that this was intended as a confidential report with clear practical policy purposes.
35. See *supra* n° 32, p. 17.
36. See *supra* n° 32, p. 17.

scrutiny was in itself an immense step forward. Unfortunately, none of these suggestions were included in the actual work-programme, nor subsequently implemented.[37]

The report offered no real justification for a harmonised asylum policy. Its preliminary assumption rested on the fact that 'the signing of the Dublin Convention means that a common asylum policy must be defined'.[38] Following this premise, it laid down two possible policy options, defined as the harmonisation of 'formal' asylum law as opposed to the harmonisation of 'substantive' asylum law. The first option referred to procedural issues of asylum law, the latter to the harmonisation of asylum policy rules. While recognising that administrative and judicial asylum procedures in the various Member States differed widely, the Ad Hoc Group clearly indicated its preference for the harmonisation of substantive rules. This choice was justified by the need to avoid delaying the harmonisation process because of the complexity of national administrative procedures. However, the inherent pragmatism of such a choice highlighted its serious shortcomings. Any previous discussion on the compatibility of the 1990 DC with other international obligations was bluntly ignored. Moreover, the entire future harmonisation process was explicitly geared to the effective and rapid implementation of the Dublin 'system'. The differences in national asylum procedures were precisely the factor that seriously undermined the fundamental Dublin assumption of the equivalence of national asylum adjudication systems. However, this objection was obviously being overrun by considerations of pure national interest. Thus, the fundamental ambiguity that pervaded this report resulted in the dichotomy between the frank and open analysis of the annex and the official 'state-oriented' work programme itself. In other words, there was a persistent refusal by the authors to draw the obvious conclusion from the issues that they had so openly analysed.[39]

Despite its *raison d'état* limitations, the report still managed to put forward

---

37. Six more years would prove to be necessary for these suggestions to finally find their way into the Amsterdam TEU revision.

38. See *supra* n° 32, p. 31. It revealed a slow change of perception of the relationship between the asylum field and the ultimate goals of the EU. The initial close connection between asylum initiatives and compensatory measures for a border-free area appeared to be gradually relaxing. The need to continuously build on initial asylum initiatives in order to guarantee their efficient implementation in some ways had a 'snow-ball' effect. In a relatively short time the growing number of initiatives meant that the asylum field came to be regarded as a 'quasi-policy' in its own right.

39. The Ministers tried to some extent to justify their contradictory arguments by frequently recalling Member States' humanitarian and refugee-related obligations, but these quotations were of such a pro forma nature that they sounded utterly unconvincing. There was also a highly disputable 'good faith' presumption that any procedural difference would eventually be compensated by the harmonizing of issues such as the national interpretation of the term 'refugee' as defined in Art. 1 of the 1951 GC. The Twelve did eventually manage to agree on such a definition in 1995 (see Chapter IV.4), but the necessity of opting for the lowest possible common denominator made such a presumption totally inadequate.

innovative harmonisation ideas. The emphasis lay on the need to achieve uniformity, both in the assessment of the situation in the countries of origin of asylum seekers and in the application of a common asylum policy itself. Thus, collection and mutual sharing of country data came to be seen as an essential tool and the setting up of a clearing house was proposed. In order to avoid distortions in asylum application flows the Ministers also supported the idea of harmonising the conditions of treatment of asylum seekers during the asylum procedure.[40] In the field of 'substantive' asylum law the report identified the efficient and rapid processing of asylum applications as the most pressing priority. To this purpose it divided applications in three categories: a) 'clearly justified'; b) 'clearly unjustified'; c) those requiring further examination.[41] Priority was given to the first two categories and continuous reference was made to UNHCR Resolutions, but the document only analysed in-depth procedures to deal with 'clearly unjustified' applications and the related principles of 'first host country' and 'safe third country'. Following the approval of this report at the Maastricht summit, progress on these issues was swift and three Resolutions dealing with these matters were approved within a year.[42]

The actual work-programme did not appear to be entirely consistent with how the priorities were developed in the annex of the report. Concrete working priorities were clearly influenced by national asylum policies aimed at fast and efficient results in regulating and controlling access to territory and to procedures. The most urgent measures were deemed to be the ones necessary for the application and implementation of the DC. These included: common interpretation of the Convention's concepts; exchanges of information; and combating asylum applications submitted under false identity. In the field of harmonisation of 'substantive' asylum law, the main priorities concerned: 1) accelerated procedures for 'clearly unjustified' asylum applications (no mention, however, of 'clearly justified' ones, or of the ones requiring further consideration); 2) definition of the 'first host country' principle; 3) development of the 'safe third country' concept; and 4) harmonised interpretation of Art. 1 of the 1951 GC. The development of a common expulsion policy also featured high on the agenda.[43] Finally,

---

40. Despite introducing the idea, the report carefully avoided dwelling on the issue of which level of treatment be afforded. But if one was to follow the prevailing logic of the report, it would have been obvious that in the context of trying to deflect application flows, the trend would necessarily have had to follow the lowest common denominator.

41. The way in which this distinction was drawn indicated for the first time a comprehensive approach to the asylum issue that took not only a purely governmental point of view, but also tried to include the needs of asylum seekers. The subsequent choice of the Twelve to exclusively focus on the 'clearly unjustified' applications was symptomatic of their overriding concern with the abuse of asylum procedures. It was yet another indicator of the dangerous trend in considering asylum issues almost exclusively in their connection with the need to control immigration.

42. The London Resolutions of December 1992 will be examined in Chapter III.3.

43. By contrast, the annex to the report defined expulsion as a matter that could 'only be addressed in the longer term' (see *supra* n° 32, p. 35).

other priorities listed included the setting up of a Clearing House to ensure the effective exchange of information, and eventually harmonised reception conditions for asylum seekers.

III.3. THE THREE EDINBURGH INITIATIVES OF DECEMBER 1992

The Maastricht Immigration Ministers' report provided the guidelines along which all subsequent EU initiatives were to be undertaken in the following four and a half years.[44] It did not prove possible to tackle all the priorities outlined in the report, nor to follow the order it had laid down. Initiatives proved more likely to be based on a circumstantial ability to achieve a minimum consensus than on the opportunity to follow a certain pattern of harmonisation. International events often seemed to be the real motor behind the flow of initiatives, prompting the well-known criticism that the EU seemed more preoccupied with 'reacting' to events rather than anticipating them.

The beginning of the 90s was characterised by an enormous strain on the ability of Member States to cope with massive inflows of people fleeing situations of extreme danger. The civil war in former Yugoslavia meant that asylum applications in the West virtually tripled in the span of two years, reaching an all-time high in 1992. Other less publicised conflicts also caused further population exoduses, such as the persecution of Kurds both by the Iraqi and the Turkish Governments and the civil unrest in Albania and Algeria. All the initiatives taken by the Twelve in 1992 in the asylum field closely reflected the need to react to these powerful strains, often unfortunately in a manner that entailed a disregard for some of the basic rights of the people concerned.

It took Member States less than a year to adopt the first measures of the Maastricht work-programme. In November 1992, the Immigration Ministers agreed on the text of three measures that were to be approved by the European Council in Edinburgh the following December. The measures consisted in two Resolutions, one on 'manifestly unfounded applications for asylum', the other on 'a harmonised approach to questions concerning host third countries' and finally a Conclusion on 'countries in which there is generally no serious risk of persecution'.[45] The texts were adopted in the shape of legally non-binding agreements for two main reasons. Firstly, the TEU had not yet been ratified, so the choice of legal instruments was limited to the traditional international law 'convention' option. Secondly, it was precisely the 'convention' instrument that

---

44. The next formal work-programme would be presented in October 1996 ('Council Resolution laying down the priorities for co-operation in the field of Justice and Home affairs for the period from 1 July 1996 to 30 June 1998', OJ 1996 C319/1).

45. 'Resolution on manifestly unfounded applications for asylum', Ad Hoc Immigration Group, SN 4822/1/92 WGI 1282 of 2/12/92; 'Resolution on a harmonised approach to questions concerning host third countries', SN 4823/92 WGI 1283 of 19/11/92; 'Conclusion on countries in which there is generally no serious risk of persecution', SN 4821/92 WGI 1281 of 1/12/92.

was displaying its evident limitations in the asylum field, as exemplified by the troubled ratification process of the 1990 DC. Lengthy negotiations and incredibly cumbersome national ratification processes meant that a 'soft law' approach was seen as a more suitable way to achieve consensus and rapid implementation.[46]

III.3.A. The Resolution on manifestly unfounded applications

The first 'Resolution on manifestly unfounded applications for asylum' directly followed one of the priority areas for action identified by the Maastricht report. Its main aim was to introduce a common streamlining tool in the national examination procedures of asylum applications. In this way Member States hoped to lighten the burden on national administrations of what they regarded as illegitimate applications. The preamble to the Resolution set the context for the initiative by recalling the humanitarian tradition of the Member States, their commitment to refugee protection as guaranteed by international instruments and the possibility for Member States to envisage other humanitarian grounds for granting refuge in their national territory. However, this rather grand display of humanitarian commitment was quickly followed by a specific mention of the constant abuse of asylum procedures and the express determination that a European asylum policy should give no encouragement to such abuses. There was also a baffling reminder of Member States' commitment to the DC, which would 'guarantee that all asylum applicants at the border or on the territory of a Member State will have their claim of asylum examined'. This remark appeared highly contradictory if considered in the context of the subsequent Resolution on host third countries, precisely because it exonerated Member States from examining an asylum application in certain given circumstances.

Manifestly unfounded applications were generically defined as applications which 'raised no substantive issues under the Geneva Convention and the New York Protocol' (Art. 1.a). For this purpose, two main grounds were taken into consideration: if the applicant's fear of persecution clearly 'lacked substance' or if asylum procedures had deliberately been 'abused or subject to deception'. Lack of substance could be determined: 1) because the application was based on grounds outside the GC (Art. 6.a); 2) because there was no indication of 'fear of persecution' or no circumstantial/personal details were given (Art. 6.b); or 3) because the application was manifestly not credible being based on an

---

46. The history of the seven-year ratification of the 1990 DC seems to confirm that conventions were not an efficient means of asylum harmonisation. More importantly, the difficulties that emerged during the national ratification process of some Member States (notably The Netherlands) highlighted the problems encountered by Member Governments when the fruit of their 'secret' negotiations was finally subjected to the 'open' scrutiny of their national legislators. As a direct consequence of the lessons drawn from the ratification process of the DC, amendments were introduced to the new Amsterdam Treaty subjecting the entry into force of conventions in this field only to a minimum number of ratifications (see Chapter V).

'inconsistent, contradictory or fundamentally improbable' story (Art. 6.c). Means to ascertain whether there had been a 'deliberate deception or abuse of asylum procedure' included the use of false identity or forged documents and the continued assertion of their genuineness (Art. 9.a); the making of false representations in a claim (Art. 9.b); the destruction, damaging or disposal of any travel documents (Art. 9.c); the deliberate failure to reveal the filing of other asylum applications (Art. 9.d); the submission of an application so as to delay an expulsion procedure (Art. 9.e); flagrant non-compliance with substantive national asylum procedures (Art. 9.f); and the rejection of an asylum application by a third country in compliance with the procedures laid down by the GC (Art. 9.g).

The above provisions raised several strong points of criticism. In so far as 'lack of substance' was concerned, only one provision appeared to be non-controversial, namely the fact that an application was outside the scope of the GC.[47] All the other instances quoted in the Resolution seemed to ignore that persecution was in most instances a highly traumatic experience that could often be conducive to incorrect, inconsistent and contradictory recollections by the applicants.[48] In the instance of 'abuse or deception' of procedures it should be pointed out that most applicants were obliged to resort to false or forged documents as a way of circumventing draconian visa requirements and for the very same reasons they subsequently often proceeded to destroy such false documents. It could hardly have been a coincidence that these draconian visa requirements seemed to target precisely the countries producing the largest flows of asylum seekers.[49]

The provision on 'the non-compliance with substantive national asylum procedures' (Art. 9.f) also raised some serious doubts. The generic wording meant that it could virtually be applied to any situation, while it wasn't exactly clear how an asylum applicant could possibly possess such an in-depth knowledge of the procedural laws of the recipient country. Finally, Art. 9.g contained the most perplexing implications. The article defined as 'deceitful' an application lodged in one of the Member States if a previous application to a third country 'comprising adequate procedural guarantees' had been turned down. Logically, 'adequate procedural guarantees' should have been evaluated by comparing them to those of the Member States. However, this Resolution established the possibility for any Member State to decline examining an application if there

---

47. On this matter, the preamble of the Resolution deceptively affirmed to be 'inspired by Conclusion n° 30 of the Executive Committee of the United Nations High Commissioner for Refugees'. But in this respect, Conclusion n° 30 only referred to applications not related to the criteria for granting refugee status and did not mention any of the other subjective grounds introduced in the Resolution, such as lack of circumstantial and personal details or contradictory/improbable data.

48. The UNHCR Executive Committee has often emphasised in its Conclusions that incorrect information should not be taken as evidence of bad faith by applicants (see for instance the above-mentioned Conclusion n° 30, UNHCR Executive Committee Handbook).

49. On this matter, see Chapters II.3.D and IV.2

was another responsible third country (Art. 1.b – see further on). Hypothetically, the backward chain could have been simply endless if the third country that previously rejected the application had also taken advantage of a similar provision.[50]

On the positive side, the Resolution contained a 'softening' clause on the application of the above-mentioned criteria relating to 'deliberate deception or abuse of asylum procedures'. Art. 10 provided that all the factors listed by Art. 9 should not 'in themselves outweigh a well-founded fear of persecution under Art. 1 of the Geneva Convention and none of them carries any greater weight than any other'. However, the same article also specified that all these factors were to be considered an indication of 'bad faith' – thus justifying the recourse to accelerated procedures – in the event of the applicant being unable to offer a 'satisfactory explanation'. In this way the burden of proof in the case of accelerated procedures was effectively reversed from the State to the applicant.[51] This was the most important practical implication of this Resolution and a similar consequence was also found in Art. 8, which dealt with countries where there was no 'serious risk of persecution'.[52]

The application of accelerated procedures was also envisaged in the event of the so-called 'internal flight option' (Art. 7) being available to the applicant. The drafting of this provision appeared to have been quite troubled. An earlier version[53] of the Resolution contained a rather ill-formulated expression of the concept of internal flight in the preamble, asserting that 'those who fear violations of their Human Rights should if possible remain in their own countries and seek protection or redress from their own authorities or under regional human rights instruments'. This version was somehow leaked to the BBC and caused such a storm of protest[54] that it was subsequently withdrawn. The final version of Art. 7

---

50. This argument recalls the criticism already raised about the 'real' purpose of the 1990 DC. The Convention was hailed by Member States as a means to solve the issue of the so-called 'refugees in orbit', but, as it was pointed out in Chapter II.3, it only achieved the shifting of such 'orbit' outside the Member States' Common Territory. The same 'passing the buck' strategy becomes apparent in this provision.

51. In most Member States the onus to prove that an application was unfounded fell on the State because of the obvious problems for an asylum seeker in providing evidence of his persecution in such a manner as to satisfy normal legal requirements (for an overview of national practices see *Asylum in Europe – review of refugee and asylum law and procedures in selected European countries*, compiled by ECRE, London, 1994). In the event of an application displaying the factors listed by Art. 9 the burden of proof was effectively reversed. Practical experience pointed to the fact that most applications were affected by one of the factors listed. Therefore, this provision ended up reversing the burden of proof for a much larger number of applications than originally intended.

52. The 'Conclusion on countries in which there is generally no serious risk of persecution' was also approved at the Edinburgh Council and will be examined further on.

53. Ad Hoc Immigration Group, Brussels, 1/11/92, SN 3926/92 (WGI 1195).

54. See D. Joly, 'The porous dam: European harmonisation on asylum in the Nineties' (1994) 6 IJRL, p. 159, at p. 167 *et seq*.

made explicit reference to the prohibition of refoulement as contained in Art. 33.1 of the GC, and to the need to consult the UNHCR in these circumstances. However, the disputable principle of the compulsory preference for the 'internal flight' option remained embedded in the text.[55]

On the procedural side, the Resolution provided for the establishment of accelerated national mechanisms for the examination of applications, which fell into the categories laid down by Arts 6 and 9. An explicit exception was made in the case of other humanitarian grounds, allowing for the acceptance of the application according to national legislation. Member States were also given the opportunity to establish 'admissibility procedures' for speedily rejecting applications on 'objective grounds'. The vagueness of this definition raised obvious concerns. In particular, it wasn't clear whether the minimum guarantees set out for the accelerated procedure were also applicable to the admissibility ones, or if the latter constituted a separate category, possibly offering even less procedural guarantees.

The procedural guarantees set out for the accelerated procedures recalled almost entirely the ones laid down by the aforementioned Conclusion n° 30 of the UNHCR Executive Committee. A time delay of one month was suggested to complete the accelerated procedure and appeal or review procedures might have been more simplified than those granted in normal asylum cases. A personal interview of the applicant by a qualified official was recommended and decisions in any case were only to be made by the qualified national authorities. In the event of a negative decision on an application, the Member State concerned was to be put under the obligation of ensuring that the rejected applicant would leave the Community territory.[56]

III.3.B. The Resolution on a harmonised approach to questions concerning host third countries and the problem of readmission agreements

This Resolution attempted to generalise the application of a principle that was probably as old as the GC itself. The concept was also known as 'country of first asylum' or 'safe third country', but the term 'host third country' was chosen

---

55. Recent history has proved on numerous occasions how internal 'safe havens' were in fact exposed to considerable danger. Obvious examples of the failure of such policies were the supposedly UNPROFOR (United Nations Protection Force) protected areas in former Yugoslavia, the Kurdish 'protection zone' in Iraq and the Rwandan UNHCR refugee camps. Ironically enough, the failure to protect these safe havens from what effectively amounted to genocide could be directly imputed to those very powers that so keenly supported the 'internal flight option' in their legislation.

56. This Resolution was followed up by another 'Resolution on minimum guarantees for asylum applications' adopted in 1995 (see Chapter IV.4) that aimed at regulating both 'regular' asylum procedures and 'accelerated' ones. The implementation of these Resolutions was far from comprehensive or uniform across EU Member States (see further, Chapter IV.4).

in order to differentiate it from the 'safe country of origin' term employed by the third Edinburgh initiative. This Resolution stemmed directly from the framework of the DC and was developed in connection with the necessity to establish clear common procedures for determining a State's responsibility to examine an asylum application. The heart of the issue lay in the possibility that the applicant might have had the opportunity to apply or obtain asylum 'before' arriving in the state where the application was eventually lodged. The GC did not contain any provisions on the matter other than a passing reference in Art. 33.1.[57]

The preamble of this Resolution was basically identical to the one contained in the other Resolution on manifestly unfounded applications. The concept of 'safe third country' was defined as a country were, according to Art. 33 GC, 'the life or freedom of the applicant must not be threatened',[58] or where he or she wouldn't be 'exposed to torture or inhuman or degrading treatment'[59] (Art. 2.a-b). In addition, the applicant was either to have already been granted asylum in the third country or to have had an opportunity to present his claim to the authorities of the third country,[60] or else to have been declared inadmissible by that country (Art. 2.c).[61] The host third country had to offer 'effective'

---

57. The article prohibited the imposition of penalties against refugees who entered the territory of asylum illegally when they were 'coming directly from a territory' where they had been subjected to persecution. Some States maintained that the wording of this article implied that refugees were not necessarily to be protected in the GC manner if they had passed through other States before reaching their final destination. This interpretation, however, appeared arguable since it didn't take into account that the ultimate purpose of the GC was precisely to guarantee protection from persecution at all costs.

58. Art. 33 GC's very purpose was to prevent States from returning refugees to situations of danger. In this instance, it was effectively turned around to imply that return to other third states judged 'safe' (as a discharge of the recipient State's obligations under the GC) was instead perfectly reasonable. It should be pointed out that Art. 33 was the main instrument that forced States to develop means of 'temporary protection' in persecution cases outside the scope of the GC, precisely because applicants could not be refouled to their country of origin.

59. This provision replicated the exact wording of Art. 3 of the ECHR. The ECtHR decided on several occasions that expulsion or extradition which could result in exposure to such treatment might have involved the responsibility of the Contracting State for the violation of Art. 3. See, for instance, *Soering* v. *United Kingdom* (1989) 11 EHRR 439 or *Cruz Varas* v. *Sweden* (1992) 14 EHRR 1.

60. This point would prove highly controversial, since many Member States had very different parameters concerning the possibility of submitting an application, especially with regards to what qualified as 'transit' (see Chapter II.3).

61. The logic of this provision was highly questionable. It was impossible to assume that a declaration of inadmissibility by another State necessarily implied that the asylum application has been examined. Austria was a case in point, since it considered all neighbouring countries to be 'safe third countries'. Any asylum seekers who had passed through them would automatically have been considered 'inadmissible', even if in fact no application had been examined. See *infra* n° 62, for references.

protection against refoulement (Art. 2.d) and if two or more countries fulfilled these conditions the Member State could chose which third country to expel the applicant to. In determining the conditions of Art. 2.d, States had to consult the UNHCR and take into account the 'known practice' in third countries.[62]

Art. 1 of the Resolution laid down the way in which the host third country principle should be applied. The identification of a possible third country was to precede all substantive examination of an application, regardless of whether the applicant could have been termed a refugee.[63] Thus, if the conditions contained in the Resolution were fulfilled, the applicant should have been sent to the host third country and only in the event of that proving impossible would the Dublin provisions then have applied. A Member State retained the right to grant the applicant the opportunity to stay on its territory for humanitarian reasons. Art. 3 then tried to specifically integrate the host third country principle in the practical functioning of the DC. In particular, it laid down that a Member State could not decline to examine an application by arguing that another Member State should have returned the applicant to a host third country (Art. 3.b), but it nonetheless still maintained the ability to do so itself (Art. 3.c). Finally, the Resolution contained an interesting section about 'future action', thereby inviting Member States to a prompt implementation of this Resolution before the entry into force of the DC. It also set up a periodic revision procedure of sorts – involving consultation of the Commission and the UNHCR – in order to consider eventual additional measures.

This Resolution was portrayed as a typical example of how European asylum harmonisation efforts inevitably built up consensus at the lowest possible denominator.[64] The Maastricht report had indicated three options for the practical application of the host third country principle. In the first case, the principle would have been applied 'after' a claim had been assessed. The second case involved a preliminary assessment of whether the principle could have been applied before examining an application. Finally, the third possibility consisted of a mixed practice of both which differentiated between applicants already within a State (first case applied) or those at the border (second option). The Ministers admitted that the first option would have been preferable from the refugees' perspective, but that the second one would grant, in their view, a greater 'expediency'. The report recognised that a number of Member States were building up a case law that supported the first option, but in Edinburgh

---

62. This appeared to have been the single least respected provision by Member States when translating it into their respective national legislation. See G. Care, *A guide to asylum law and practice in the European Union* (ILPA, London, 1996). Most States adopted a rather formal approach, whereby only the ratification of the GC was taken into account. Amnesty International over the years collected hundreds of cases of evidence of how tragically the host third country principle could end (see *infra* n° 66).

63. I.e. even before deciding if the application should be considered 'manifestly unfounded'.

64. See P. Boeles *et alia*, *A new immigration law for Europe?: the 1992 London and 1993 Copenhagen rules on immigration* (Dutch Centre for Immigrants, 1993), at p. 16 *et seq.*

in 1992 they still opted for an application of the principle that preceded any substantive examination of applications.

Although this Resolution did represent an agreement based on a minimum political consensus, in practice all Member States' legislation already included the first host country principle in some shape or form. The real issue stemmed from the fact that it was now necessary to apply this principle in a manner compatible with the wider framework of the DC. Thus, a harmonised application of this principle would eventually have a wide-ranging repercussion on the ability of asylum seekers to submit an application virtually 'anywhere'. The Dublin system was based on the arguable (and hypocritical) assumption that an asylum application lodged anywhere in the Community would have had exactly the same outcome.[65] Therefore, a common system allocating States' responsibility for examining applications was justified by the necessity of avoiding 'multiple applications'. Since the majority of refugees generally never arrived directly from the persecuting state, the principle of host third countries contained in this Resolution effectively created a further 'orbit' of asylum seekers around the Community perimeter. This orbit could be indefinitely extended and, in several cases, bounced the applicants right back to the point of departure.[66]

Furthermore, the host third country principle laid down by the 1992 Resolution had other important implications in the context of an international treaties 'web' that came to be known as 'readmission agreements'. Because of their own practical experience, by 1992 European Member States were aware that in the absence of formal agreements with third countries the application of the host third country principle was nearly impossible.[67] The most common result was in fact an endless bouncing back and forth of asylum applicants and an inevitable waste of resources.[68] For a long time, countries with extensive open borders, such as Germany, had concluded numerous agreements with their neighbouring States, whereby they mutually undertook to readmit into their territories certain categories of persons at the other party's request.[69] These

---

65. On these points, see comments in Chapter II.3.

66. Amnesty has widely documented these cases, see for instance *Playing human pinball – Home Office practice in "safe third country" asylum cases* (Amnesty British Section, London, 1995); or *Europe: the need for minimum standards in asylum procedures* (Amnesty EU Section, Brussels, 1994).

67. See A. Achermann and M. Gattiker, 'Safe third countries: European Developments' (1995) 7 IJRL, p. 19.

68. For a case by case analysis of how frequently applicants were bounced back and forth in the United Kingdom, see Amnesty (1995) supra n° 66.

69. See, for instance, the German readmission treaty with Sweden (1955), Denmark (1954), Norway (1955), Switzerland (1955), France (1960), Austria (1961) and the Benelux countries (1966). See M. Schieffer, 'The readmission of third-country nationals within bilateral and multilateral frameworks' in M. Den Boer (ed.), *The implementation of Schengen: first the widening then the deepening* (European Institute for Public Administration, Maastricht, 1997), p. 97, at p. 101.

agreements were based on the premise that each Contracting State should individually bear the brunt for the inefficient patrolling of their borders, but the complexity of their provisions evolved considerably over the years. Four main types of agreement were identified in this field, ranging from the obligation to readmit only one's own nationals to readmitting third country nationals found either illegally crossing the common border or even illegally residing in one of the State Parties as a consequence of entry from the other State Party.

However, the Schengen and Dublin Conventions introduced a totally new dimension in the drafting of readmission agreements. Because of these two Conventions, Member States were to harmonise their approach to the question of host third countries and make it an essential preliminary consideration before considering responsibility for the examination of an asylum application. It followed that multilateral readmission agreements had to be developed in order to ensure that this common policy could be effectively implemented. This led to the signing of the Schengen-Poland readmission agreement in March 1991, a so-called 'second generation agreement' which inspired all subsequent bilateral treaties of this kind.[70] It was originally intended as a 'compensation measure' for the granting of visa-free travel in the Schengen area to Polish nationals and it therefore contained quite extensive provisions on the obligation to readmit unwanted aliens. Unlike previous agreements, readmission was no longer contingent on an 'illegal entry' or on specified periods of residence. Any illegal alien found in the territory of one of the Contracting Parties that could 'reasonably be supposed'[71] to have entered from Poland was to be readmitted there. Art. 7 specifically foresaw the possibility for other Parties to join the agreement in future.[72]

The work of the European Immigration Ministers, since the Resolution on host third countries, continued with great intensity.[73] In late November 1993,

---

70. Germany concluded agreements modeled on this type with Romania (1992), Switzerland (1993), Croatia, Bulgaria, the Czech Republic (all in 1994), Vietnam (1995), Pakistan and Algeria (1997). For a comprehensive review of such agreements, see S. Lavenex (see *infra* n° 72).

71. The means of proof were really quite ample and it was up to the receiving Party to disprove the assumption once it had been made. On the means of proof, see further in the 'Council Recommendation on the guiding principles to be followed in drawing up protocols on the implementation of readmission agreements' (see *infra* n° 76).

72. An overview of readmission agreements published by the UNHCR in 1993 contained at least 23 bilateral treaties between countries of Central or Eastern Europe and Western countries and various other treaties were being negotiated. For an updated review of such agreements, see S. Lavenex, *Safe third countries: extending the EU asylum and immigration policies to Central and Eastern Europe*, (Central European University Press, New York, 1999).

73. The guidelines for such action had been set at the Edinburgh summit in another 'Recommendation regarding practices followed by Member States on expulsion', Ad Hoc Immigration Group, SN 4678/92 WGI 1266, of 16/11/92, where in Part IV the Ministers agreed that '[i]n so far as re-admission agreements do not already exist, consideration

one month after the official entry into force of the TEU, the JHA Council adopted a text on the 'principles for the conclusion of readmission agreements with third countries'.[74] It formed the basis for the 'Recommendation concerning a specimen bilateral admission agreement between a Member State and a Third Country', adopted in November 1994[75] under the initiative of the German Presidency. Another 'Recommendation on the guiding principles to be followed in drawing up protocols on the implementation of readmission agreements' was put forward by the French Presidency in July 1995.[76] The principal aim of all these texts was to achieve harmonisation of repatriation issues concerning illegal aliens found in the territory of the Community. Although Immigration Ministers had always expressed a clear preference for multilateral agreements, they decided to concentrate their efforts on developing a standard bilateral text. This was due to the considerable amount of negotiations multilateral agreements had needed in the past – the Polish agreement required two years of talks. It was also thought that the 'recommendation' form would help Member States to tailor the actual texts of the agreements to their individual needs.

UNHCR expressed serious concerns about both the 1994 and the 1995 initiatives and a specific recall to the GC was inserted into the draft of the specimen bilateral readmission Recommendation only after a complaint by Amnesty and UNHCR had been filed (Art. 11).[77] The heart of the problem lay in the fact that readmission agreements were mainly aimed at illegal immigrants and not at refugees as such. It was only in the context of the principle of host third countries and with the enormous numbers of asylum seekers that they assumed a pivotal role in the 'orbital' mechanism put in place by the Dublin and Schengen Conventions. Readmission agreements provided no particular guarantees for the plight of asylum seekers, as their purpose was simply to deal swiftly with irregular

---

should be given to establishing them with the appropriate State. Where possible, such agreements should be multilateral, but where this is not possible bilateral agreements should be considered. Consideration should be given to preparing agreement in a standard format and, in the case of multilateral agreements, these might be along the lines of that between Poland and the Schengen States, with such adaptation as appear necessary to take account of national situations and practical experience of that agreement' (Art. 1).

74. See M. Schieffer, *supra* n° 69, p. 106. It was also mentioned in the preamble of the 'Council Recommendation on the specimen bilateral readmission agreement' (see *infra* n° 75).

75. Recommendation adopted on 30/11/94, OJ 1996 C274/20.

76. Recommendation adopted on 24/7/95, OJ 1996 C274/25.

77. UNHCR note on 'Readmission agreements, "protection elsewhere" and asylum policy' (Brussels, August 1994); and following the adoption of the Recommendation, 'UNHCR concerned at a document adopted by the EU JHA Council on 30 November 1994 which could enable the transfer of asylum seekers to third countries' (Press Release, Brussels, 1/12/94); 'UNHCR position on standard bilateral readmission agreements between a Member State and a third country' (Note, Brussels, 1/12/94). On the issue of compatibility between the GC and readmission agreements see N. Abell, 'Compatibility of readmission agreements with the 1951 Convention', (1999) 11 IJRL, p. 60.

situations.[78] No particular clauses were inserted aiming at obliging recipient States to examine an asylum application.[79] At the International Refugee Conference in Budapest, held in February 1993, various Eastern European countries stated that, unable to cope with the increasing numbers of refugees themselves, they would expel them to other 'safe third countries'.[80] Objections were also raised about the circumstances surrounding the negotiations of these deals. It was alleged that 'continued development aid, or its defrosting [...] the withdrawal of visa requirements for the nationals of the States involved, contributions to the cost of readmission, lifting of trade barriers',[81] were in fact the main negotiation tool employed by the Twelve. In this respect, it is known that Germany alone paid DEM 60 million to the Czech Republic between 1995 and 1997 as part of their 1994 readmission agreement and double that amount (DEM 120) to Poland after 1993.[82] The distinct feeling that the host third country principle had transformed itself in a sort of 'refugee auction' did not appear too unjustified.

III.3.C. The Conclusion on countries where there is generally no serious risk of persecution

The main principle of this Conclusion was designed to work in close conjunction with the 'Resolution on manifestly unfounded applications' and it was seen as a key instrument in achieving more efficient and speedy asylum adjudication. Once

---

78. See, for instance, Art. 2 of the 1994 'Recommendation on the specimen readmission agreement', which regulated 'accelerated readmission procedures'. It laid down a 'brutal form of readmission. It legalises pushing someone at the border back across it to the other side with few formalities. The person must be returned within 96 hours of being stopped [...] the procedure is carried out by immigration officials without any requirement to report to any other national authority [...] the relevant form is completed, limited to personal details and reasons for rejection, filed and the matter ends. There is no requirement to prove the nationality of the person being returned' (ILPA, 'Update: December 1994', London, p. 3).
79. The UNHCR was particularly critical of this point.
80. See A. Achermann and M. Gattiker, *supra* n° 67, p. 37.
81. H.U. Jessurun D'Oliveira, 'Expanding external and shrinking Internal borders: Europe's defence mechanisms in the areas of free movement, Immigration and asylum', in D. O'Keeffe and P. Twomey (eds), *Legal issues of the Maastricht Treaty* (Chancery Law, London, 1994), p. 261, at p. 275.
82. See M. Schieffer, *supra* n° 69, p. 104. The author states that 'these funds are intended to diminish the financial burden resulting from the amendment of German asylum law and the readmission agreement, and to enable the Czech Republic to enhance its border protection and set up an infrastructure for asylum seekers and refugees'. In November 1995, Community Member States decided to make it standard practice to insert readmission obligations into association or co-operation agreements with third countries (see Chapter IV.3.B).

again, a harmonised approach to the matter was necessary because of the DC and the imperative necessity of ensuring a uniform application of this system. However, this Conclusion could have potentially played an important role in restoring an acceptable level of refugee protection within the Dublin system. Had a common definition of a 'safe country' for the purpose of accelerated procedures been achieved, it would have involved Member States tackling one of the most fundamental objections to the Dublin provisions, namely that an asylum application's chances anywhere in Europe were far from identical. Unfortunately, Member States opted again for the 'lowest common denominator', thus failing once more to redress the balance in favour of refugee rights.

Art. 1 of the Conclusion defined a country where there was generally no risk of persecution as one 'which can be clearly shown, in an objective and verifiable way, normally not to generate refugees or where it can be clearly shown, in an objective and verifiable way, that circumstances which might in the past have justified recourse to the 1951 Geneva Convention have ceased to exist'. Art. 2 portrayed the main purpose of the Conclusion as being the reaching of 'a common assessment' of such safe countries, in order to relieve national asylum adjudication systems overburdened by 'clearly unjustified' applications. However, it transpired from previous deliberations of the Ad Hoc Immigration Group that the original plan would have involved the drafting of a common list of 'safe countries of origin'. The plan had to be abandoned because 'the majority of delegations voiced misgivings for political or diplomatic reasons, or because absence from a list might imply that the country was unsafe'.[83]

Particular controversies also surrounded the development of the common assessment criteria. The Conclusion listed four elements that should have been 'taken together' in assessing countries of origin. They included previous numbers of refugees and recognition rates; observance of Human Rights, formally and in practice; and democratic institutions and stability. In the previous draft the numbers of refugees and recognition rates were called 'the most appropriate criterion'. This could have easily led to a downward spiral where, if an error was made in assessing the situation of a particular country, its low recognition rate would have in turn pushed down subsequent recognition rates even further. Also, the role initially assigned to the UNHCR in the draft report was subsequently modified and an initial clause providing for a right of veto by the UNHCR in the assessment process was removed and replaced by a 'specific space' to be given to UNHCR information in Art. 5.

Art. 3 specified that even in the event of a country being assessed as 'safe', this should not have entailed an automatic refusal of all applications, but at most a channelling through 'accelerated procedures'.[84] In this respect, it should be

---

83. See 'Draft Report on countries where there is generally no serious risk of persecution', SN 4282/92 WGI 1230 of 26/10/92.

84. This, however, had serious implications as the burden of proof was reversed on to the applicant (see Chapter III.3.A).

pointed out that Art. 3 of the 1951 GC forbade any discrimination between applicants because of their 'country of origin'. The extreme importance of this absolute prohibition was further emphasised by Art. 42, which provided that no reservation could be put forward in respect of Art. 3. The very essence of this Conclusion seemed therefore to be in direct contradiction with the letter of the GC.

It probably proved impossible to achieve a sufficient level of consensus on a common list of 'safe countries' because the subject was too politically sensitive and Member States were not ready at that stage to relinquish such an important foreign policy tool. The degree to which these kinds of assessments were determined by political considerations was highlighted by a comparative study of how Member States utilised the criteria in this Conclusion to shape their national lists of 'safe countries'.[85] Out of 15 Member States, only eight introduced the concept in their national legislation and only five had actually compiled an official list of 'safe countries'.

Belgium had tried to introduce the principle by adopting the so-called 'double 5 per cent rule'.[86] The Court of Arbitration declared this rule void in March 1993, because reversing the burden of proof in these cases would have been incompatible with the principle of equal treatment. The immediate consequence, however, was that the immigration act was reformed in May 1993 to reverse the burden of proof for all asylum applicants. In practice, this meant that a country was always deemed safe unless the applicant could prove that his safety was at risk.[87] Other countries where the principle of 'safe country' did not appear were France, Greece, Italy, Ireland, Sweden and Spain. Portugal adopted the principle in 1993 and its criteria were entirely consistent with the 1992 Conclusion, but there was no official list. However, it should be emphasised that even if these countries did not adopt the principle, this did not necessarily entail that no list existed. In these countries, 'lists' were simply considered too politically sensitive

---

85. The comparisons drawn on this matter are based on the study done by the European Parliament in 1997 (PE 166.466), *Asylum in the European Union: the 'safe country of origin principle'*. The aim of this study was to find out five years after the Edinburgh 'Conclusion on safe countries of origin' how many Member States had complied with the assessment criteria listed in the Conclusion. On the same point, see S. Peers, *Mind the gap!*, supra n° 18, pp. 17–20 and also Danish Refugee Council, *Safe Third Country: policies in European Countries* (Copenhagen, 1997).

86. An asylum application would have been deemed inadmissible if the applicant originated from a country which had accounted for less than 5 per cent of the previous year's applications and where less than 5 per cent of those applications had been deemed admissible.

87. On the positive side, however, Belgium did not recognise 'mere transit' as a reason to apply the first country principle. The applicant had to have spent three months in the previous country and left without fear of persecution for the principle to be applied. See S. Peers, *Mind the gap!*, supra n° 18, p. 17.

to be officialised. In other instances, particular legal controls led governments to suppose that the lists would not pass an eventual jurisdictional review.[88]

Denmark adopted an official list of 'safe countries', compiled in co-operation with the Danish Refugee Council.[89] However, there was no legislation establishing the principle, so its legal status was unclear. Germany introduced the principle when it amended its Constitution and the Foreign Ministry decided which countries were to be put on the list.[90] However, there was no parliamentary control of such a list. Finland amended its asylum law in 1993 to include the safe country principle. A list (drafted by the Foreign Ministry – with no independent scrutiny) was compiled in that year and remained unchanged. However, this list only included Western European Countries, the Baltic Republics and Central European States. No African or Asian country was included.

The United Kingdom amended its Asylum and Immigration Act in 1996 to include the principle. The Home Office decided the contents of the so-called 'white list', but the compilation was to be monitored by Parliament.[91] In theory, the fact that a country was on the white list would only have implications for the appeal procedure, but in practice it could be assumed that many applicants from 'safe countries' were rejected outright. Luxembourg included the principle in its asylum legislation, but specifically avoided drawing up any list. The Netherlands introduced the 'Safe countries of origin' Act in 1995. The States Secretary of Justice was given the power to decide which countries were to be included in the list, but the list itself was not included in the Act in order to ensure flexibility. Interestingly, a distinction in assessment criteria was introduced between Europe and Africa, the criteria of the latter being less stringent in so far as fundamental liberties were concerned. Austria introduced the principle in 1992, but never compiled an official list.

In all cases the lists (where they were made public) did not seem very long. Discrepancies in assessment criteria were evident, though, as for instance in the cases of countries like Senegal or Ghana. Only Germany promptly removed the two from the list, while the UK, the Netherlands and Denmark (Senegal only) kept them on their lists. On the whole, the application of the 1992 Conclusion appeared so fragmented as to cast serious doubts on the validity of the principle.

---

88. See for instance the case of Italy. Since the Italian Constitutional Court is also the ultimate interpreter of the GC, doubts had been raised during parliamentary discussions as to the compatibility of the 'safe country principle' with Art. 3 GC.

89. The Danish Refugee Council seems to have considerable influence over the assessment process: the Gambia was removed from the list in 1994 due to its pressure.

90. For the amendments to the German Constitution, see Chapter II.2 and also G. Noll, 'The non-admission and return of protection seekers in Germany' (1997) 9 IJRL, p. 415. Monitoring of foreign political situations appeared very attentive. In 1994, the day after a military coup, the Gambia was immediately removed from the safe list and Senegal was suspended in 1996 following reports from Amnesty of persistent Human Rights abuses.

91. The so-called 'white list', however, existed long before it was formalised in 1996 and attracted numerous criticisms throughout the years.

III.4. INFORMATION EXCHANGES: THE SETTING UP OF CIREA AND ITS ACTIVITIES

Art. 14 of the 1990 DC provided for extensive exchange of information between Member States of different kinds of asylum data.[92] Its purpose was to overcome the inherent differences in the asylum policies of the Member States without necessarily having to achieve a total harmonisation of procedures and contents. The 1991 Maastricht Report had underlined the importance of such exchanges of information for the purpose of implementing concepts such as 'host third country' or 'safe country of origin'. Since the ratification process of the DC appeared to be quite tortuous, the idea of establishing a specific centre in charge of such matters was strongly supported by the Twelve. The Ad Hoc Immigration Group presented a draft proposal on the establishment of the *Centre d'Information de Réflexion et d'Echange en matière d'Asile* (CIREA)[93] in May 1992, which was subsequently approved at the following June Lisbon European Council.[94]

The CIREA was set up as an informal forum without any executive powers, composed of representatives of the Member States dealing with questions of asylum in the Council, officers in charge of implementing policies on asylum and the Commission. It was assigned a wide-ranging brief which basically coincided with the areas listed in Art. 14 of the DC, but because it had no permanently assigned staff, its operational capability was quite limited at first.[95] Their first progress report was presented in May 1993[96] and it showed the magnitude of their mandate. The collection of information on Member States' asylum legislation and practice was well under way and a statistical system recording monthly arrivals of asylum seekers and their nationalities had been

---

92. In particular it listed: 1) national legislation and practices on asylum; 2) statistical data on monthly arrivals of asylum applicants and their breakdown by nationality, to be circulated through the Secretariat of the Council to the Member States, the Commission and UNHCR; 3) information on new trends in application; 4) information on the countries of origin or provenance of applicants.

93. SN 2781/92 (WGI 1107) of 21/5/92.

94. In parallel with CIREA, the Member States also set up CIREFI (Centre for Information, Discussion and Exchange on the Crossing of Frontiers and Immigration), whose task focused on gathering data concerning mainly illegal immigration and expulsion. CIREFI became operational in 1995, but very little is known of its activities, although it has been criticised, mainly in the context of the setting up of EUROPOL, because of inevitable sensitive data duplication.

95. At its first meeting in November 1992 a complaint was recorded by the Presidency of the difficulty faced by staff in charge in combining this additional task with their 'normal' obligations (The Clearing House – First Meeting – Future work – Note by the Presidency, SN 4682/92 WGI 1270, of 16/11/92, at p. 2).

96. Ad Hoc Immigration Group, First activity report from CIREA to the Ministers responsible for Immigration, SN 2834/93 (WGI 1505), of 14/5/93.

set up.[97] A compilation of national case law concerning asylum seekers was being studied, including related cases at the ECtHR. Out of five reports on refugees' countries of origin or provenance that had been requested, three were being completed, but no countries were named. Other issues remained listed for future examination, such as the indications available for early warning, routes taken by asylum seekers, the involvement of intermediaries and finally information on new trends in asylum law. It was also decided which categories of acts should have been made available to the public and the matter appeared quite controversial. Only general information on asylum law and practice could be publicly accessed, while access to the rest was subject to permission by Member States. Country reports, the most vital type of information, were to remain strictly confidential.[98]

A second activity report was presented in June 1994[99] and it contained some notable developments. Firstly, the confidentiality rule had been toned down so that most information was now available to interested parties, such as refugee organisations. Furthermore, Annex III.4 established that national asylum authorities could make use of the country reports, but also that 'depending on national procedures, these [country] reports may be made available to the parties involved in a dispute when there is an appeal against a decision by the authorities responsible for matters concerning asylum and aliens'. Specific guidelines for the drawing up of such reports were attached. They included criteria such as the general political situation; respect of Human Rights and civil liberties; specific information on persecution for reasons of race, religion, nationality, membership of a particular social group or political opinion and whether the persecution was State-originated or perpetrated by other forces; and finally, the possibility of fleeing within the State. Other elements listed were clearly more of 'practical control' use for Member States and related to the possibility of obtaining false documents; the general economic situation; the attitude of the state to the return of its nationals (whether it would persecute them); compliance with the 1951 GC and other international Human Rights Conventions. Two reports were prepared along these guidelines on Ethiopia/Eritrea and Romania, while other reports were in the pipeline on Bulgaria, China, Iraq, Vietnam and Zaire. It was remarkable that the countries which had been the subject of a report were finally being named.

The activity report lacked a precise indication of any future work other than

---

97. The Commission, in its 1994 'Communication on asylum and immigration policy' (COM (94)23 final), noted however that this information was not always directly comparable (at p. 12).

98. These reports could have been essential in the case of Court proceedings dealing with asylum seekers, perhaps involved in accelerated procedures. The decision not to make them available was highly questionable as it gave Member States' immigration authorities an unfair advantage.

99. Text adopted on 20/6/94, in OJ 1996 C274/55. Strangely, no further activity reports have been presented to this date.

a generic reference to the continuation of previous work. The CIREA continued its role as an information exchange on asylum and producing country reports. However no annual report on its activities was made available after 1997.[100] The criteria to be used in the assessment of a country were judged very positively, but unfortunately no feedback on the use of its country reports by Member States or other organisations was made available.

III.5. CONCLUDING REMARKS

From the Member States' point of view, the Maastricht Treaty was a positive step towards the development of more efficient asylum coordination. The Third Pillar codified and streamlined the old EPC co-operation structures. Co-operation remained of an intergovernmental nature, but some elements of the Community framework were also introduced. These consisted mainly in the participation of Community institutions, such as the Commission and the EP, and the built-in possibility of transferring some competence to the First Pillar. From the point of view of refugee protection, however, the new Treaty was less positive. The choice of an intergovernmental framework entailed an increase in the secrecy of negotiations, a lack of democratic accountability and of public scrutiny. The respective roles of the Commission and the EP were very limited compared to their traditional ones and the Twelve failed to introduce any form of jurisdictional control.

Following the TEU, Member States continued to develop their asylum initiatives along the path set by the Schengen and Dublin initiatives. It was slowly becoming evident that those Conventions would not be able to function properly without further support measures. The Maastricht work-programme illustrated well the growing dichotomy between what even Member States perceived as the 'correct' choice in terms of refugee protection and what was simply considered politically feasible. The work-programme formally acknowledged the need for substantive harmonisation, only to subsequently ignore such need and proceed with proposing measures mainly aimed at controlling and curbing refugee flows. However, there were a few positive suggestions. The programme highlighted the need for exchange of asylum information in order to build a common platform for the DC. This proposal resulted in the setting up of the CIREA and the developing of country reports that were eventually made accessible – although grudgingly – to the public.

The Edinburgh initiatives did not represent any substantive harmonisation of national asylum laws. In the form of 'resolutions' or 'conclusions' they were only soft law initiatives that led to scarce and far from uniform implementation. The design of the Twelve to build what was commonly defined as 'Fortress Europe' started to slowly take shape. The 'accelerated procedures' principle openly disregarded many of the guarantees contained in the GC, such as not penalising

---

100. See OJ 1997 C191/29 and 33.

applicants attempting an illegal entry, or making contradictory statements. Highly disputable principles, such as the 'internal flight option', were pushed through in the face of popular opposition because the Third Pillar framework allowed governments the necessary secrecy.

Initiatives such as the one on 'host third countries' were undoubtedly aimed at creating a refugee 'orbit' around the Community (in direct contradiction with the claims of the DC). Moreover, the perimeter of this orbit kept being pushed further and further away by an ever more intricate web of readmission agreements. The hypocrisy of such a strategy was highlighted by the fact that Member States even resorted to 'bribing' neighbouring States with aid packages in order to dump their own unwanted refugees on them.

The 'safe country' principle was another keystone in the fortification of Europe's perimeter. Again, since Member States were not capable of agreeing a common list of 'safe countries', refugees ended up paying a heavy price due to the discrepancy between national policies. The various implementation surveys carried out showed that implementation could at best be described as erratic. This was symptomatic of one of the biggest flaws in the Third pillar co-operation, namely the fact that soft law did not guarantee implementation. This highlighted the inherent paradox of the asylum system that the Twelve were in the process of building. The Schengen and Dublin initiatives had created a hard law asylum framework that still needed several adjustments in order to function in practice. However, by subsequently adopting soft law initiatives to support it, Member States failed to understand that the inability to monitor or ensure implementation would undermine the whole framework. In this respect, the asylum policy EU Members were slowly trying to build could not be characterised as a very successful one from their own point of view. It took the Twelve some years, though, to realise this failure. From the refugee protection point of view however, this failure, produced a rather fortunate collateral effect, in that prospective asylum seekers were still able to take advantage of the differences in national asylum legislation.

Bearing in mind what Member States were trying to build, it should not be difficult to imagine the potential odyssey of hypothetical refugees. Even if they had overcome the hurdle of visa restrictions and carrier sanctions, they would still have to make sure not to go in transit via any other country, otherwise readmission agreements or the host third country principle might entail a potentially endless chain of expulsions. In the event of those refugees making it directly into the Community and managing to lodge a claim, DC members would first have to allocate among themselves the responsibility for their asylum claims. Furthermore, potential applicants would have to ensure that all their papers were in order and that their entry was not illegal. Their story would also have to be perfectly coherent and supported by heaps of admissible evidence – the burden of proof being most likely placed on them anyway. Finally, their account should not have contained the slightest contradiction, in order for their applications to avoid accelerated procedures or being thrown out for being 'manifestly unfounded' – a term so vague even their lawyers would have difficulty explaining it to them. Surely this scenario could not possibly have been the one the drafters of the 1951 GC had in mind. All this evidence pointed inevitably to the fact that EU Members were slowly abandoning their previous commitments towards true refugee protection.

4 Asylum Co-operation between Maastricht and Amsterdam

The Maastricht Treaty codified co-operation activities on asylum within the
Third Pillar framework. This co-operation was essentially of an intergovernmental nature, notwithstanding some concessions to the Community 'method'. The
momentum that accompanied the signing of the new Treaty led to a new wave
of soft law asylum initiatives designed to support the eventual implementation
of the DC. Unfortunately, those measures entailed a potential weakening of
refugee protection across the EU. The underlying plan of a 'Fortress Europe'
built upon the foundations of a border-free Internal Market was slowly beginning
to emerge.

The TEU eventually entered into force on 1 November 1993. The main
institutional and political players in the asylum arena focused their efforts into
continuing to hone their strategies for future developments. Hence, the
following December at the European Council in Brussels, the JHA Ministers
presented their first activity-report, including a priority work-programme for
1994.[1] The Commission on its part tried to put forward its own views through
a new Communication,[2] intending to complement the future action of the Union
in the asylum and immigration field with an up-to-date analysis[3] of the principal
issues involved. This document proved of extreme interest because of its ability
to transcend the more immediate action plans of the Immigration Ministers in
favour of drawing a broader picture of long-term solutions, which would have
involve the co-ordination of several levels of the European Union. For the first
time, the Commission also approached the subject of asylum and immigration
in the same context in order to develop a more comprehensive action strategy.
However, it correctly stressed that the humanitarian base of the asylum issue
deeply distinguished it from the immigration one. Therefore, the scope of action
of the Union in the asylum field was to be subjected to the international
obligations of its Members.

The Communication consisted of two parts. The first was devoted to a 'factual'

---

1. Not published. This analysis relies on the contents of the report as laid down in the
   Commission Communication (see below). The main areas identified for priority action
   appeared to be the 'harmonised interpretation of Art. 1 Geneva Convention' and the
   development of 'minimum guarantees for asylum procedures'.
2. Communication on asylum and immigration policies (COM (94)23 final, Brussels,
   23/2/94).
3. The last Communication had been in 1991 (see Chapter II.5).

analysis of the principal issues involved in the development of an asylum and immigration policy. The second was mainly 'policy-oriented'. The 'factual' analysis began with an interesting observation of how the public and political perceptions of these issues had changed in recent years, due to the growth of extremist political formations in the Member States and the lack of accurate and reliable information. Since the only substantial information available was on the number of asylum applications, public debate seemed to concentrate exclusively on these figures, instead of focusing on more urgent immigration issues. The Communication also analysed the 'operational' changes introduced by the new TEU (see paragraph V.8) and the initiatives adopted following the 1991 Maastricht work-programme. It observed that despite the report being aimed expressly towards harmonisation of national asylum policies, progress had nonetheless been very slow. It (bravely) criticised the choice of non-binding initiatives, such as those of 1992, because of the predictable problems caused by inconsistent national implementation. It also recognised that a wider international forum for asylum initiatives would be preferable, but practically difficult to bring about.

As in its previous Communication the Commission reiterated the concept that 'short-term control measures [...] need to be matched by long-term co-operation with countries and regions of origin [...].[4] Therefore, 'taking action on migration pressure' was becoming a fundamental part of a comprehensive asylum and immigration policy. Such a policy should take into account: a) the need for accurate information (hence the activities of the CIREA); b) the necessity of dealing with the root causes of migration pressure, such as economic disparities, demographic or environmental pressures and fighting the brain-drain phenomenon; and c) the obligation to tackle the abuse of Human Rights in the countries of origin. In order to achieve such a comprehensive approach, a 'co-ordination in the field of foreign policy, trade policy, development co-operation and immigration and asylum policy'[5] should be developed by the Union.

The Commission, however, also recognised the need to control increasing migration flows as part of a comprehensive action plan. In so far as the development of an asylum policy was concerned, it identified the most pressing issues as: 1) achieving a harmonised interpretation of Art. 1 GC; 2) the development of common minimum standards for asylum procedures; 3) the elaboration of a

---

4. See *supra* n° 2, p. 11.

5. See *supra* n° 2, p. 14. In particular six elements were listed as guidelines for this approach: 1) the preservation of peace and the termination of armed conflict; 2) full respect of Human Rights; 3) the creation of democratic societies and adequate social conditions 4) a liberal trade policy which should improve conditions in the countries of origin; 5) development aid aimed at encouraging social and economic development to alleviate poverty; and 6) co-ordination between foreign policy and economic aid. These principles had been drawn from a 'Declaration on principles governing external aspects of migration policy' adopted at the 1992 Edinburgh European Council.

Convention on manifestly unfounded asylum applications[6] and the implementation of the host third country principle; 4) temporary protection for non-GC refugees and burden-sharing among Member States; and 5) the development of a monitoring system to assist with situations of mass influx and transit in Member States and third countries. The last three points were really of an innovative nature and expressed an in-depth understanding of refugee issues. This work-programme also showed that the Commission was capable of envisaging the development of an asylum policy that was not simply aimed at satisfying the Member States' need for heavier controls. Instead it proposed an integrated system that would offer refugees more guarantees and more efficient solutions to their plight. This Communication therefore constituted an effective tool for measuring both Member States' progress in the asylum field and for assessing their subsequent choices. The fact that priority was given exclusively to 'control' measures[7] was a clear indication of the harmonisation path ahead.

IV.2. VISA REGULATIONS AND THEIR IMPACT ON ASYLUM CO-OPERATION

In the light of the Schengen example and its own interpretation of Art. 7a EC, the Commission tried to put forward some new proposals concerning external border controls and a visa Regulation. Although not directly connected to asylum measures, visa requirements had a deep impact on the ability of asylum seekers to lodge an application. In December 1993 the Commission attempted a concerted approach by presenting both a revamped 'Draft Convention on the crossing of external borders' and a 'Proposal for a Regulation determining the third countries whose nationals must be in possession of visas when crossing the external borders of the Member States'.[8] The Convention's legal base had to be updated and was now to be founded on Art. K.3 TEU, whereas the visa Regulation stemmed from Art. 100c EC. The progress of the Convention was unfortunately hindered by the dispute between the UK and Spain over the status

---

6. It is interesting that this idea of a convention was never taken up by the Member States. It could have proven very useful in overcoming the emerging disparities between accelerated procedures and the principles of 'host third countries' and 'safe countries of origin'. In essence, it could have finally helped to correct the disputed assumption that all Member States asylum adjudication systems were equal, an assumption on which the whole construction of the DC effectively rested.

7. More specifically, only 'some' control measures managed to be agreed upon; issues that were only indirectly connected to control, such as burden-sharing or the monitoring of mass-influx situations were given a much lower priority because of their more controversial nature.

8. COM (93) 684 Final, Brussels 10/12/93; OJ 1994 C11/5 and 6. On the history of the 'Convention on the Crossing of External Borders', first presented in 1989, see Chapter II.2, n° 23. On the impact that visa Regulations had on asylum flows, see Chapter II.3.D.

of Gibraltar, whereas the visa Regulation was eventually approved two years later in September 1995.[9]

However, the final Regulation was very different from the original Commission proposal. The competence over visa policy had been peculiarly distributed between the First and the Third Pillars. Art. 100c EC only regulated the drawing up of a common visa list and a uniform visa format. Art. K.1.a TEU did not mention the wording 'visa policy', but entrusted the Council with the possibility of regulating conditions of entry and movement of third country nationals into the Union. The Commission Regulation proposal included the drawing up of two lists. The negative list included the countries whose nationals would need a visa to enter the Union, whereas the positive list contained the countries whose nationals were exempted from such requirements. By June 1996, both lists would have been finalised, with Member States thus losing the possibility of maintaining separate visa requirements for countries that were off the negative list. Coupled with the establishment of a uniform visa format, this framework would, in time, have led to the establishment of a common visa policy of sorts.[10]

The Council held that the Commission had exceeded the scope of Art. 100c EC in its proposal and proceeded to approve a Regulation that contained merely a negative list of countries whose nationals were to be subject to visa requirements.[11] Virtually all countries affected by civil unrest, internal and external wars were listed, including entities that were not recognised as States by any of the Member States.[12]

In amending the Commission's proposal the Council omitted to consult the

---

9. Member States were undoubtedly pressurised into agreeing a common list within two years because of the qualified majority clause contained in Art. 100c.3 EC. The article stated that, as of January 1996, all decisions concerning the common visa list had to be adopted by qualified majority.

10. The Commission's design was clear. A simple negative list would only have acted as the lowest common denominator, leaving individual Member States free to establish further visa requirements for countries outside the negative list. A positive list, on the other hand, would have restricted Member States' room to manoeuvre to a minimum. The Commission argued that in the context of Art. 7a EC a mere negative list would not have been sufficient to fulfil the purpose of an internal border-free market. It also pointed out that the establishment of a common visa format as provided by Art. 100c.3 EC would only make sense in a mutual recognition context where both a negative and a positive list applied. The German delegation also presented a draft Regulation proposal along the same lines. It actually only provided for a positive list, relying on the presumption that all countries were subject to visa requirements unless they were on the positive list. See K. Hailbronner, 'Visa Regulations and third country nationals in EC law' (1994) 31 CML Rev., p. 969, at p. 985.

11. 'Council Regulation 2317/95 of 25/9/95 determining the third countries whose nationals must be in possession of visas when crossing the external borders of the Member States', OJ 1995 L234/1.

12. The list included countries like Somalia and Ethiopia, Myanmar, Algeria, Sierra Leone, Rwanda etc. The impact on the ability of refugees to reach safety was self-evident. The lack of a visa would have made any attempt at gaining asylum in one of the Member

EP any further on the issue. The EP successfully brought an action for annulment against the Council and the Regulation was repealed in 1997.[13] The Council approved a new Regulation in early 1999 which replicated almost entirely the previous one.[14] Member States remained free to decide whether or not to impose visa requirements for countries outside the common list. The only concession to a possible tighter co-ordination in the future was envisaged in Art. 3. It provided for the drawing up a progress report by the Commission on the harmonisation of national visa policies with regard to countries not on the common list in the first half of 2001. On the basis of this report, the Commission could present new proposals for further harmonisation in the field.[15]

The Council's attitude in the whole visa Regulation process had some subtle repercussions on the asylum co-operation field. The Commission had attempted to use the powers granted to it by the Treaty in drawing up visa proposals that would have furthered closer co-operation and eventually harmonisation of the common visa list. The Member States' negative reaction sent a clear signal to the Commission that its own role in the area had to be kept to a minimum. Initiatives that did not tow the national policy lines were obviously not welcome. This message had powerful implications for the future involvement of the Commission in asylum co-operation, since it only enjoyed a limited right of initiative and was mostly considered to be an observer. The Council displayed the same attitude towards the EP, by again approving the contested visa Regulation once the first one had been successfully annulled. Thus, the independent input the Commission had tried to put forward in the immediate aftermath

---

States an 'illegal entry' in itself. Worried by the enormous sanctions carriers would have tried to halt any attempt to enter the EU without a proper visa. Even if the applicant made it into the Community, 'illegal entry' often involved detention and had further negative implications in the case of accelerated procedures.

13. Judgment of 10/6/97, case C-392/95 [1997] ECR I- 3213. The ECJ upheld the EP's argument that the Council Regulation was a substantially different text from the Commission proposal and therefore it should have been consulted again. In the eyes of the Court the 'substantial' difference rested in the fact that the Commission proposal 'envisaged, after 30 June 1996, only a list specifically designating the third countries whose nationals must be in possession of a visa, whereas the Regulation authorises Member States to maintain, for an indefinite period, their list of third countries not appearing on the common list whose nationals are subject to that obligation'. The Regulation's effects were to be maintained until the Council could adopt new legislation on the matter.

14. Regulation 574/99, OJ 1999 L72/2.

15. The Commission anticipated its task by presenting a new proposal on the matter in September 2000 ('Proposal for a Council Regulation listing the third countries whose nationals must be in possession of visas when crossing the external borders and those whose nationals are exempt from that requirement', to be found in the EUROPE database under Community Preparatory Acts, Doc. 500PC0027. Approval of the regulation was still pending at time of writing). This proposal put forward again the idea of two lists.

of the Maastricht Treaty was so severely hampered that it practically ground to a halt for the next few years.[16]

IV.3. IMPLEMENTATION MEASURES OF THE DUBLIN CONVENTION

While rebuffing the Commission's attempts to play a constructive role within the Third Pillar asylum co-operation, Member States continued to focus their efforts towards the asylum objectives contained in the Maastricht work-programme. They were particularly concerned that the cornerstone of their asylum strategy – the 1990 DC – was appearing more problematic than initially foreseen. For starters, the ratification process was proving to be extremely slow. Moreover, it soon became apparent that, despite the extreme precision of the DC provisions,[17] further specifications would be necessary if the system was to function properly. In this respect most EU Member States could draw on the parallel experience of dealing with the implementation problems of the 1990 SC, which contained almost identical provisions with regard to States' responsibility for asylum applications.

IV.3.A. Means of proof in the framework of the Dublin Convention[18]

The DC laid down a hierarchical set of criteria for establishing which State would be responsible for examining an asylum application. The accompanying provisions indicated the means of proof Member States were to use in formulating their decisions. However, such means of proof were not described in particular detail. Numerous controversies had already arisen in the Schengen context on the interpretation of the very same provisions.[19] As a consequence, the JHA Council prepared a 'text'[20] laying down in great detail the type of proof to be

---

16. After the signing of the Maastricht Treaty, the Commission had enthusiastically taken up its new tasks. Hence, the proposals on the external borders Convention, on the visa Regulation and the 1994 Communication. Certainly a great chance was missed to introduce a more independent perspective into this strictly intergovernmental process.

17. The extreme preciseness had been necessary since there was no jurisdictional adjudication body in the event of a dispute

18. Text adopted by the Council on 20/6/94, OJ 1996 C 274/35. For a follow-up on this and other DC-implementation issues, see Chapter VI.4.

19. On this point, see an interesting assessment of the German Schengen experience in K. Hailbronner and C. Thiery, 'Schengen II and Dublin: responsibility for asylum applications in Europe' (1997) 34 CML Rev., p. 956, at p. 984 et seq.

20. The legal nature of this 'text' was not quite clear. Art. 18 of the DC established a 'Committee' composed of representatives of Member States which was in charge of any necessary revisions or changes. In this case it appeared that the JHA Council acted in place of the Committee, perhaps following Art. K.3.2.c TEU. This article envisaged the possibility of the Council drafting conventions in the fields listed in Art. K.1 TEU. However, the DC predated the adoption of the TEU. Moreover, the text did not specifically establish its legal nature. It wasn't drafted as one of the 'soft law' instruments at the

used in applying the DC. The first part concerned the 'principles regarding the collection of evidence' and it gave an interesting insight into the practical dynamics of the allocation of State responsibility. The logic behind these 'principles' was a clear indication of the Member States' mistrust toward each other. Behind the grand 'humanitarian' facade of the DC,[21] they feared that 'squabbles' on responsibility would jeopardise the whole system,[22] or that Member States which were more efficient in keeping records of asylum applicants would eventually be penalised.[23] Furthermore, there was an explicit reference to the need for 'a spirit of genuine co-operation' to allow the system to function properly. This reference gave the distinct impression that the DC had come to be seen more as an internal 'passing the buck' process rather than a responsibility allocation mechanism.

The text stated that the 'responsibility for processing an asylum application should in principle be determined on the basis of as few requirements of proof as possible'. Proof was divided into two types: the first was defined as 'conclusive' and could only be rebutted by strong contrasting evidence; the second was of 'indicative value' and of a secondary nature in case no conclusive evidence could be found. 'Indicative evidence' was to be weighed in each individual case and was entirely rebuttable. Lists were attached detailing types of act that could have constituted proof, for instance in the case of visas, residence permits, illegal entry or expulsion.[24]

Council's disposal, according to Art. K.3 TEU, nor was it explicitly defined as a DC 'implementing measure'. Therefore its legal force remained doubtful.

21. After all, in the words of the Member States, the system was set up to avoid putting prospective refugees into the plight of being in a constant 'orbit', without any State assuming definitive responsibility for their application.

22. The third paragraph of the text, *supra* n° 18, stated that '[i]f the establishment of proof carried excessive requirements the procedure for determining responsibility would ultimately take longer than examination of the actual application for asylum. In that case the Convention would fail totally to have the desired effect'.

23. See third paragraph, *supra* n° 22. 'Under a too rigid system of proof the Member States would not accept responsibility and the Convention would be applied only in rare instances, while those Member States with more extensive national registers would be penalised since their responsibility could be proven more easily'.

24. It was interesting to observe how much detail Member States were obliged to enter into, probably because of the absence of any arbitration system. So, for instance, in case of 'illegal entry' (Arts 6 and 7 DC) probative evidence would have been an entry stamp in a false/forged passport or exit stamp from a country bordering a Member State. Indicative evidence in the same instance would have been far more extensive: a declaration by the applicant; reports by organisations such as UNHCR; travelling companions or family members; fingerprints; tickets and hotel bills; entry cards for public or private institutions in Member States; appointment cards for doctors etc.; and information that showed the use of a travel agency (please note that the text specified that the list of indicative evidence was not exhaustive). However, it seemed very difficult to go into any more detail than this list. The obvious underlying aim was to avoid recriminations by Member States as much as possible.

IV.3.B. Harmonisation of expulsion policies

Another 'grey area' of the DC implementation involved the issue of expulsions. The need for concerted expulsion policies was inherent in the very concept of the Internal Market and the creation of an area without internal borders. If persons were to be allowed to move freely inside the Community without any kind of controls, it followed that Member States had to be able to rely on each other expelling unwanted aliens from the Common Territory. The Member States' awareness of this need was expressed by two provisions in the DC. The DC itself did not impose an absolute obligation on Member States to expel rejected asylum seekers, but it made them responsible for the rejected applicants' subsequent actions.[25] This provision meant that an efficient common expulsion policy became quite prominent on the Twelve's priority list.

In December 1992 at the Edinburgh summit the Twelve approved their first official initiative on defining some common principles on expulsion practices.[26] Art. 1 of the Recommendation opened with some rather unfortunate wording. It stated that 'Member States will ensure that without prejudice to Community law, their policies and practice with regard to expulsion are fully consistent with their obligations under the 1951 Geneva Convention […]. Account should also be taken of other relevant international instruments, including the 1950 European Convention for the Protection of Human Rights […]'. In what way the respect for Human Right instruments or of the GC could ever have prejudiced Community law appeared to be totally obscure. This reference arguably conveyed the idea that Member States were in fact intending to derogate from some basic rights and to cynically exploit some cryptic Community law obligation to justify such derogation. The Recommendation set out an obligation to expel unwanted or illegal aliens – including rejected asylum seekers – who were to be granted only basic appeal procedures. It also allowed for personal liberty restrictions and, most worryingly, for the person to be expelled during such proceedings. The key provision was that expulsion should take place to third countries and not another Community Member.

The JHA Council continued to develop a common expulsion policy, although the new measures were not primarily directed at asylum seekers. Subsequent

---

25. Art. 10.e put a State under the obligation of readmitting an alien whose application it had rejected and who was illegally in another Member State. This obligation ceased if the Member State 'takes and enforces the necessary measures for the alien to return to his country of origin or to another country which he may lawfully enter' (Art. 10 para. 4). The Ministers also approved another 'Recommendation concerning transit for the purpose of expulsion', OJ 1996 C5/5, which aimed at establishing close co-operation procedures between Member States in the case of an expulsion necessitating the transit of an unwanted alien through the territory of another Member State. The underlying principle was that whenever possible the alien should be expelled directly to a third state.

26. 'Recommendation of the Ad Hoc Immigration Group regarding practices followed by Member States on expulsion', SN 4678/92 WGI 1266 of 16/11/92.

measures all contained a standard exception for the respect of the GC and other Human Rights international instruments, while the unfortunate previous formulation was removed from the preamble of the later initiatives. By 1996, Member States had also agreed on the standard practice of inserting readmission clauses into association and co-operation agreements between the Community and third countries.[27]

Other issues concerning the implementation of the DC remained outstanding. In particular, a harmonisation of national asylum procedures would have represented a vital step for a uniform application of the Convention. Unfortunately, Member States were only able to agree on 'minimum standards' of asylum procedures (see further), although the point was finally introduced in the 1996 work-programme. The lack of jurisdictional control never really constituted a priority, although considerable improvements were eventually brought about by the Amsterdam Treaty.

IV.4. THE COUNCIL RESOLUTION ON MINIMUM GUARANTEES FOR ASYLUM PROCEDURES

The DC also confronted Member States with other sets of issues not directly connected with its implementation. As previously emphasised, the DC legitimacy *vis à vis* other international obligations rested on the assumption of the equivalence of Member States' asylum adjudication systems. In this respect, Immigration Ministers had already highlighted in the Maastricht work-programme the need to achieve some level of approximation of national asylum procedures. Although they had admitted that only substantive harmonisation would completely legitimise the DC, they had subsequently discarded this option as too time-costly to achieve. Thus, some degree of procedural approximation came to be seen as a viable intermediate objective. Moreover, there were other more pressing reasons for national interest in favour of greater procedural approximation. In a border-free area where the circulation of individuals was potentially greatly enhanced, the need to swiftly deal with asylum applications naturally became of paramount common interest. In this context procedural approximation became a way to ensure that all Member States would introduce more efficient procedures. This approach unfortunately had two major drawbacks. Firstly, its pragmatic nature left no space for legitimacy concerns and the interests of asylum seekers. Secondly, the subsequent choice of soft law instruments directly jeopardised the increased efficiency objective because of their low implementation rates.

---

27. See 'Council Recommendation on concerted action and co-operation in carrying out expulsion measures', adopted on 22/12/95, in OJ 1996 C5/3 and Environment Council press release of 4/3/96. On the 'bargaining' that went on during readmission and co-operation agreements, see Chapter III.3.B and S. Peers, *EU Justice and Home Affairs law* (Longman, London, 2000), p. 96. See also Chapter VI.4 on how the 'readmission' concept was emphasised at the Tampere summit.

Following the 'Resolution on manifestly unfounded applications' of December 1992,[28] in June of 1995 the JHA Council approved a 'Resolution on minimum guarantees for asylum procedures'.[29] According to Art. 1 this initiative was conceived as a follow-up measure based on the obligation to examine asylum applications within the meaning of Art. 3 DC.[30] The Resolution pledged to respect the main international instruments of refugee protection, the ECHR, and to take into account the Conclusions of the UNHCR Executive Committee and Recommendation R(81) of the Council of Europe. It specifically recalled the obligation of non-refoulement of Art. 33 GC by guaranteeing that no expulsion would be carried out while an asylum adjudication was pending (Art. II.2).[31]

Access to procedures, basic features of the asylum procedure itself, and designation of the responsible authorities were left to individual Member States' implementation.[32] The Resolution only set the minimum characteristic of these authorities, namely that they had to: a) be fully qualified in the field of asylum; b) be independent; c) have full disposal of specialised personnel, of up-to-date information from various sources, both of a governmental and non-governmental nature, and, if necessary, of expert external advice. An independent review of any negative decision had always to be offered, if possible by a Court (Part III Arts 3–9). This list of requirements could have appeared quite exhaustive. However, these criteria did not represent any novel effort to raise the overall level of guarantees offered to asylum seekers. The Commission's 1994 Working Paper[33] contained a note on the existing international standards in this area. It summarised the relevant provisions contained in the texts later quoted as a

---

28. See Chapter III.3.A. Following this Resolution, the Commission presented a 'Working Paper on minimum standards for asylum procedures', SEC(94)780, on 2/5/94. The Paper revealed that the development of minimum standards for asylum procedures was added by November 1993 to the 1994 JHA work-programme and that the Greek Presidency had subsequently presented a proposal on the matter to the Council.

29. Resolution of 29/6/95, in OJ 1996 C274/13. In November 2000 the Commission put forward a 'Proposal for a Council Directive on minimum standard for procedures in Member States for granting and withdrawing refugee status' that represented the theoretical transposition of this Resolution into a legally-binding measure (although heavily modified). See Chapter VI.6.

30. Art. 3.1 DC contained a generic undertaking by Member States to examine any asylum application presented at their border or within their territory, subject to the criteria establishing States' responsibility laid out in Arts 4–9. However, because of the third safe country principle, this obligation did not in fact entail a substantive examination of such applications (see Chapter III.3.B).

31. This provision was in direct contrast with the 'Recommendation on expulsion policies' adopted at Edinburgh in 1992, see supra n° 26, which allowed for expulsion to take place during appeal procedures.

32. It was mainly in these areas that the critics of organisations such as UNHCR or Amnesty focused (see later).

33. See supra n° 28.

reference in the preamble of this Resolution. These provisions had been entirely reproduced in the above-mentioned Part III of the Resolution.

Specific minimum rights to be granted to asylum seekers during examination, appeal and review procedures (Part IV) included: being effectively able to lodge an application; having their personal data properly protected, particularly in respect of their country of origin; being given, at all stages of the procedure, the assistance of a publicly paid interpreter, of a legal adviser, of the UNHCR and, if possible, of other refugee organisations; the opportunity to have a personal interview with a qualified official; having a decision on their application communicated in writing, including the reasons for an eventual rejection; and being given adequate time to present an appeal. During such proceedings, including those of appeal, an applicant would be granted permission to remain in the territory of the Member State. If the national legislation did not provide for this right during the appeal proceedings, the applicant would be given at least the right to appeal to a Court or a review authority for leave to remain. The UNHCR would be kept informed of all the stages of the procedures.

As those in Part III, these provisions did not show any discrepancies or omissions with regard to other relevant international obligations. However, many Member States were in practice far from complying with these provisions. Even in those cases where they had adopted these criteria into their legislation their practical implementation was still limited or worse non-existent.[34] In Germany, for instance,[35] the new Asylum Law explicitly excluded the possibility of suspending an expulsion order pending an asylum appeal if the applicant had entered via a so-called 'safe country'. In Austria, applicants entering from any neighbouring country[36] were automatically rejected and sent back to the country of transit if they attempted to lodge an application. In Denmark, no appeal procedure could provide relief from expulsion, whereas in more extreme cases, such as Greece, an asylum case was immediately rejected if an applicant did not

---

34. See a study by Amnesty and ECRE on *Minimum standards for asylum procedures*, first presented in June 1994 and updated in 1996. See also S. Peers, *Mind the gap! Ineffective Member State implementation of European Union asylum measures* (ILPA, London, 1998). Worse still, the provisions of the Resolution appeared at times to be the 'lowest common denominator' of all the most restrictive national practices. Danish provisions inspired the shortening of review procedures for 'manifestly unfounded' applications; French ones influenced the rules on refusal of admission at the border by a ministry or similar authority; and German practice was the model for allowing the rejection of applicants at the border on 'safe third country' grounds without possibility of review. On these examples, see J. Van Der Klaauw, 'Towards a common asylum procedure' in E. Guild and C. Harlow, *Implementing Amsterdam. Immigration and asylum rights in EC law* (Hart Publishing, Oxford, 2001), p. 165, at p. 171.

35. See S. Peers, *supra* n° 34, p. 15.

36. All of Austria's neighbouring countries had been declared 'safe', see S. Peers, *supra* n° 34, p. 16. Thus, the only way to be able to apply for asylum in Austria was to arrive by air. This appeared to be a clear case of 'denial of access'.

come 'directly' from the country of persecution.[37] No personal interview of the applicant was provided for. In Sweden, in particularly sensitive cases, the Asylum Act provided for the Immigration board to simply issue 'advice', the final decision resting with the government. In most of these cases, the final decision was generally not motivated, rarely translated[38] and did not even indicate if the opinion of the Immigration Board had been followed.[39]

In so far as practice was concerned, Member States' compliance with this Resolution scored even lower. Ireland, in most instances, did not have sufficient funds for the legal representation of asylum seekers so that they were often not represented at all at trials and, moreover, UNHCR was seldom informed. In France, on average less than 40 per cent of applicants had a full personal interview, again because of lack of funds. At the appeal stage very few benefited from legal assistance because of draconian qualification parameters – legal entry and at least one year of residence. Furthermore, the French Government dramatically cut the budget of OFPRA (French Office for the Protection of Refugees and Stateless Persons), the QUANGO in charge of providing legally-binding information on third country situations and other relevant documentation, making it almost impossible for this body to continue its normal activity. In Austria, the ability of applicants to confer with their legal assistants was in practice impossible because of the draconian detention conditions in which applicants were kept (phone calls were strictly not allowed).[40]

Two exceptional derogation clauses to these minimum guarantees were foreseen in this Resolution. The first exception concerned 'manifestly unfounded' applications as defined by the Edinburgh 1992 Resolution. To this purpose, appeal rights were restricted and expulsion measures subjected to a limited possibility of appeal.[41] As indicated by the above evidence, some Member States were already applying similar, if not even stricter, provisions anyway.

---

37. See S. Peers, *supra* n° 34, p. 17.

38. See S. Peers, *supra* n° 34, p. 15. Of all Member States, only Denmark and The Netherlands appeared to provide rejected applicants with a written translation of their decision. France, Italy, the UK and Portugal did not provide for a translation at all – although the UK would deliver the decision in a context where a translator was present. Finland, Sweden, Greece, Luxembourg, Austria and Germany did not have national provisions for translating decisions. However, in practice some sort of oral summary translation appeared to be provided in most instances.

39. See S. Peers, *supra* n° 34, p. 19.

40. For all the above information,see S. Peers, *supra* n° 34, pp. 18–19.

41. See S. Peers, *supra* n° 34, pp. 10–14. The author identifies a whole spectrum of Member States' practices in this context. Belgium and Luxembourg, for instance, did not allow any exceptions to the right to stay during an appeal. Countries such as the UK, Spain, Portugal, Sweden and the Netherlands theoretically allowed for expulsion during appeal procedures in some instances, but in practice provisional rulings deferring expulsion could be reasonably obtained. At the opposite end of the spectrum, countries such as France, Germany, Denmark or Finland had substantial exceptions to the right to stay during an appeal, both in law and in practice.

Interestingly, Art. 20 stated the there were 'no de jure or *de facto* grounds for granting refugee status to an asylum applicant who is a national of another Member State [...] a particularly rapid or simplified procedure will be applied to the application lodged by a national of another Member State, in accordance with each Member State's rules and practice'. The specification was introduced at the request of the Spanish delegation, but both the British and the Danish Governments had insisted in adding the second clause on the possibility of examining such applications anyway.[42]

The second exception to the application of minimum standards for asylum procedures concerned the asylum applications lodged at the border of a Member State. In these cases, State authorities were to carry out a preliminary evaluation of whether the application could be considered 'manifestly unfounded' or if there was a 'host third country' the applicant could be sent back to. In the instance of manifestly unfounded applications, however, the final decision had to be taken by a qualified 'central authority' (comparable to a ministry). This discrepancy of guarantees between decisions concerning manifestly unfounded applications and those on host third countries did not appear justified, since the outcome for the applicant in the event of rejection would have been the same: refusal of admission into the Member State's territory. The difference in these guarantees was reflected in the practice of several countries (Austria and Greece for instance) where the decision on whether a host third country could have been identified was remitted entirely to the border police, which could hardly be described as a 'fully qualified authority in the matters of asylum'.[43]

The Resolution also contained very welcome additional safeguards for unaccompanied minors and women. In so far as children were concerned, they were to be represented by an adult which would protect the child's interests. Curiously, Art. 27 stated that in considering a child's application, his 'mental development and maturity' would be taken into account. It was hard to envisage why age should have entailed a difference in the possibility of being persecuted.[44] Female

---

42. See the draft Resolution amendments by the COREPER, 5585/95 ASIM 78 of 14/3/95. Spain had had a long-standing interest in the matter due to its internal problems with Basque terrorism. Two Basque terrorists applied for asylum in Belgium in 1994 and a Belgian judge agreed to consider their case. This caused a major diplomatic incident between the two countries and brought the work of the Immigration Ministers to a virtual halt for months (see Chapter V.3.B at n° 65). However, it remained unclear why it was the British and the Danish delegations that introduced the exception clause to this text instead of the Belgian one.

43. The Resolution also provided for the 'safe third country' where the applicant was to be returned to be notified that the substance of the applicant's claim had not been considered. This provision appeared to have been widely disregarded in practice. Only Sweden and the UK envisaged some sort of notification procedure. See S. Peers, *supra* n° 34, p. 16.

44. From ILPA, *Commentary on draft minimum guarantees for asylum seekers and refugees* (London, March 1995), it appears that the original draft of Art. 27 was even stricter as it laid down that 'refugee status will depend on the child's degree of mental development and maturity'. This wording was modified at the request of the United Kingdom.

asylum seekers should have been assisted in the procedures by female staff wherever possible, especially in cases where, owing to their personal experiences or cultural background, they would have found it difficult to present the grounds for their applications. To this purpose Member States should have endeavoured to employ as many female staff as possible. UNHCR frequently complained that this provision was consistently being disregarded,[45] with often tragic consequences.

Finally, Art. 29 laid down the obligation to grant asylum to an applicant who fulfilled the criteria set out in Art. 1 GC and to grant residence in their territory. This provision appeared entirely superfluous since it was already contained in the GC itself to which all Member States were parties. Far more dubious appeared the provisions of Art. 30, which allowed an exception to the guarantees of this Resolution in the cases covered by point 11 of the 1992 'Resolution on manifestly unfounded applications'. Point 11 allowed Member States to apply an accelerated procedure 'if it is established that the applicant has committed a serious offence in the territory of the Member State, if a case manifestly falls within the situation mentioned in Art. 1.F GC, or for serious reasons of public security, even if the cases are not manifestly unfounded in accordance with point 1'. This definition was deliberately vague on what constituted a 'serious crime' – left entirely to national assessment – and furthermore deprived applicants of any minimum procedural guarantees in the event of being accused of such a 'serious' crime'.[46] On the positive side, Art. 32 recognised the guarantees laid down in this Resolution as being of a minimal nature and allowed for more favourable procedural guarantees in national legislation to be retained.[47]

Overall, this Resolution could hardly be qualified as a example of positive Third Pillar asylum co-operation. The measure appeared at times as the 'lowest common denominator' collection of some of the most restrictive national practices and therefore seriously flawed both in its contents and eventual outcome. Moreover, it failed to achieve both the Member States' objectives and to uphold good levels of refugee protection. The choice of merely agreeing some 'minimum' procedural standards meant that no equivalence could be established between national asylum adjudication procedures, and once again refugees were left to bear the brunt of such disparities. While the agreed minimum standards represented a mere reiteration of international obligation, compliance rates by

---

45. UNHCR, 'Fair and expeditious asylum procedures' (Explanatory Note, November 1994), p. 5.

46. The article did not define what was intended by 'if it [was] established' that the applicant had committed a serious crime: was this to be established through a formal trial, police accusation, witness testimony, or otherwise?

47. However, in this way the whole purpose of this Resolution was effectively defied. If the Dublin system could only function on the premise that the outcome of an asylum application would have been the same in any Member State, national legislation allowing more favourable procedural guarantees would still entail a distortion in the outcome of any such asylum application.

Member States were in fact abysmal. Certainly, no increased efficiency in national asylum adjudication procedures was ever gained by this Resolution. Finally, the derogation clauses raised serious doubts over the ability of Member States to strike a balance between their pursuit of their economic objectives, such as the Internal Market, and their willingness to comply with their international humanitarian obligations.

IV.5. The Joint Position on the Harmonised Definition of the Term 'Refugee' in Art. 1 of the Geneva Convention[48]

While trying to achieve some degree of procedural approximation, the Twelve also made another attempt at addressing the 'legitimacy' issue of the DC. As analysed in Chapter I, under international law the application of the 1951 GC was left entirely to individual signatory States through their national legislation. The GC only gave a very broad definition of who should be considered a 'refugee' and very little indication of how to assess this status. This resulted in extremely different applications of the GC throughout the world. Even among European States, diverging interpretations of basic legal concepts, such as 'persecution', led to very different definitions of the term 'refugee'. Since 1994, the JHA Council put at the top of its working priorities the development of a common definition of the term 'refugee' as expressed in Art. 1 GC. This constituted an interesting choice, since 'substantive' harmonisation had never been indicated before as a viable objective, both because it was too time-consuming and because it wasn't strictly essential to the functioning of the Dublin system (from a Member State point of view). It was arguably the first indication that asylum matters had slowly started to acquire an importance of their own, not always directly connected to the necessities of the Internal Market objective.

In March 1996, the JHA Council was finally able to present its conclusions on the matter in the form of a Joint Position (based on Art. K.3.2.a TEU),[49] the first one ever to be adopted in the asylum field. The preamble of the text contained one very innovative reference to the UNHCR Handbook as 'a valuable aid to Member States in determining refugee status'. Given Member States' past reluctance to involve or accept advice/criticism from the UNHCR, this formal acknowledgement constituted a welcome development. However, some of the provisions in this text blatantly disregarded the instructions of the Handbook. The initiative was presented as a collection of 'guidelines' for the application of criteria for the recognition and admission of an individual as a 'refugee'. These

---

48. Joint Position of the Council of 4/3/96, OJ 1996 L63/2.

49. It was the first time that such an instrument was used in the asylum field and one of the few times it was used in the JHA framework at all. The legal force of such an instrument was unclear (see the comments in Chapter III.1), although it was possible that it was perceived as being more forceful than a conclusion or a resolution. In any case, the ECJ would have had no jurisdiction over such a measure, unless it was contrary to Community law (see Chapter III.1 n° 21). See also *infra* n° 54.

guidelines should have been notified to the national asylum adjudicating bodies and adopted as a 'basis',[50] even though they would not have been binding on national legislative or judicial authorities. It therefore followed that the real scope of application of these provisions remained very obscure.

The guidelines referred to the interpretation of several of the criteria relating to the attribution of the status of 'refugee' as set out in Art. 1 GC. They specifically did not concern the circumstances in which Member States decided to allow applicants to remain on their territory because returning them would have been in breach of the Art. 33 GC non-refoulement obligation. They provided for the exclusive individual examination of each application, even in the event of 'mass influx', although in such cases examinations might have been limited to ascertaining whether the individuals belonged to the persecuted group in question. In so far as proof presented by the applicants was concerned, it rested upon them to submit the necessary evidence, but once their credibility had been established, they could be given the benefit of the doubt and exempted from giving confirmation of all the facts surrounding their application.

In dealing with the term 'persecution' the Council noted that the term was not defined in the GC, nor was there a universally-accepted definition available. Therefore it did not attempt a definition itself, but tried to summarise a few commonly agreed points of interpretation: 1) the acts suffered or feared had to be sufficiently serious (by their nature or their repetition); 2) they had to constitute an infringement of basic human rights and had to make it impossible for the applicant to continue living in that country; and 3) they had to be based on the grounds listed in Art. 1 GC (see further). A combination of acts that, taken individually, would not have amounted to persecution could do so if considered in combination.

Persecution was differentiated according to its origin. 'State-persecution' (by central or local authorities) could consist of the use of brute force or of judicial and/or administrative measures. The Ministers recognised that States sometimes found it necessary to adopt measures restricting certain freedoms in the public interest. It may be remarked that this declaration, coming from signatory States of the ECHR, was really quite astonishing and displayed considerable cynicism. It also did not appear consistent with the policy of conditioning development aid to the respect of Human Rights that the Community pledged to enforce. Even if accompanied by the use of force, these restrictions would only amount to persecution if they were directed in a discriminatory manner towards certain elements of the population for one of the grounds listed in Art. 1 GC. Similarly, measures restricting certain freedoms and only directed against one or more specific categories of the population might have been legitimate, unless their aim

---

50. A special clause was included, for the benefit of common law countries, specifying that the national case law on asylum matters and its relevant constitutional position was to be in no way prejudiced by these guidelines. However, how the latter could have been effectively applied in such instances was not very clear.

had been condemned by the international community, they were manifestly disproportionate or they were aimed at disadvantaging a section of the population. Judicial prosecution was also taken into account as 'persecution' when, although appearing lawful, it was in fact discriminatory and based on grounds that would lead to the award of refugee status. In the same terms, punishment which was disproportionate and discriminatory could also have counted as persecution. The case of an intentional breach of a criminal law provision in the country of origin was regarded as amounting to 'persecution' if it was 'an objective consequence of characteristics of the asylum seeker liable to lead to the granting of refugee status'.[51]

The GC only referred to State persecution. However, these guidelines included persecution by third parties as a legitimate ground to grant refugee status if it was 'individual in nature and encouraged or permitted by the authorities'.[52] Situations of civil war and of other internal or generalised armed conflicts would not generally have amounted to persecution, unless it could have been proven to be of an individual nature and based on the grounds of Art. 1 GC. Whether it stemmed from the State or third parties was judged irrelevant.

The grounds listed for persecution in the Joint Position, following Art. 1 GC, were race, religion, nationality, political opinions and belonging to a social group. All of these criteria were to be understood in the widest context possible. In the case of political opinions the applicant would have had to show that his State was aware of his opinions and would not have tolerated them.[53] In the instance of social groups, the Ministers accepted the notion that such a group could have been defined either by an objective criteria or by virtue of the prosecutor attributing membership to it for the victim.

The possibility of relocation within the country of origin was regarded as a preliminary consideration in the assessment of refugee status. In the event of applicants fearing persecution after having left the country of origin ('refugees *sur place*') because the situation in their country had changed, they would have had to demonstrate individual grounds for persecutions due to characteristics

---

51. On this point ILPA, *Comments upon the Presidency proposals for guidelines for harmonising the application of the criteria for the determination of refugee status in Art. 1 A of the Geneva Convention* (London 1996) noted that it wasn't clear how this principle was going to work for persons being prosecuted for characteristics which are subjectively held such as, for instance, political opinions (p. 49).

52. ILPA, *supra* n° 51, noted that this approach was at odds with the UNHCR Handbook, para. 65, which included in the definition of third party persecution also the instance where the authorities proved unable to offer effective protection. Most importantly, it was also in contradiction with established ECtHR jurisprudence (see Chapter I.4.C n° 99). For a general overview see B. Vermeulen *et alia*, *Persecution by third parties* (Nijmegen Catholic University, 1998). See also further comments *infra* n° 55.

53. ILPA, *supra* n° 51, p. 5, dissented on this point on the grounds that it should have been sufficient for an applicant to have shown 'reasonable fear' that his political opinions might have been discovered to prove persecution.

of which the State of origin was already aware. If the fear from persecution stemmed from activities the applicant undertook while away from the country of origin, these activities should have represented a continuation of beliefs he already held in his country of origin. If instead these beliefs were expressed with the sole purpose of obtaining refugee status, they could have constituted at most grounds for non-refoulement, but not for granting of refugee status. In the case of conscientious objection, absence without leave and desertion, 'persecution' could have been proven only if the conditions for performing military duties had amounted to persecution themselves or if the military activities would have led to acts such as crimes against humanity, serious non-political crimes or crimes against the principles or purposes of the United Nations.

The provisions regarding loss of refugee status replicated entirely those provided in the GC at Art 1.C-D-F. The co-operation of CIREA was advised in establishing if the reasons for persecution in one country had ceased. In the instance of exclusion clauses from the status of refugee (the applicant having committed a crime against humanity, a serious non-political crime or an act contrary to the purposes and principles of the United Nations), ILPA remarked that the burden of establishing whether they actually applied ought to have been passed to the body responsible for examining the claim for asylum, instead of resting on the applicant.

An effective assessment of the impact of the Joint Position proved very hard. The document represented a summary of the current legal interpretations and practices concerning the definition of 'refugee', thus it was already widely implemented at the time of its drafting. An examination of national jurisprudence revealed that few national authorities ever mentioned this Joint Position in their judgments[54] and most were not aware of its existence at all. The major discrepancy of interpretation seemed to rest in the definition of 'third party persecution'. France and Germany appeared to be the odd ones out among their EU partners, since neither of them fully accepted the concept.[55] Other important differences

---

54. Only the German and Dutch Courts mentioned the Joint Position a few times. The French *Conseil d'Etat* only ruled that the 1992 Edinburgh initiatives were not legally-binding and the same view would have presumably applied to the Joint Position. See S. Peers, *supra* n° 34, p. 23.

55. Both in France and in Germany 'persecution' had to emanate directly from the State or be imputable to it because it tolerated it. In France if the 'Third party' was a direct opponent of the State, then it could not be inferred that the State had tolerated its actions. In Germany any show of willingness by the authorities, however feeble, to fight the Third party would have been enough to exclude persecution. See S. Peers, *supra* n° 34, p. 22 and N. Blake, 'The Dublin Convention and rights of asylum seekers in the European Union' in E. Guild and C. Harlow (eds), *supra* n° 34, p. 95, at p. 113. Sweden recorded a formal objection to the lack of a definition of 'non-State' persecution in the Joint Position. Later on, these differences become of crucial importance when judges refused to transfer applicants back to Germany or France because of their different interpretation of Third party persecution. This endangered the whole mechanism of the DC. See cases reported in Chapter VI.4 n° 73.

of interpretation arose from the definitions of 'internal flight option' and 'particular social group'.[56] Applicants fleeing civil war conflicts were generally held by all Member States not to fall within the remit of Art. 1 GC unless they could prove 'individual' persecution. Overall, the guidelines of the Joint Position appeared to have very little impact on national authorities, leaving the disparities in national interpretations virtually intact. Only after the ratification of the Amsterdam Treaty did the Commission eventually acknowledge the need to introduce a binding initiative on the matter (see Chapter VI.2).

In hindsight, the importance of this measure in the context of EU asylum co-operation rested more on its relative 'irrelevance' to the Internal Market project, than on any impact it might have had. In this respect, it marked the departure from the pragmatic vision of asylum co-operation as a simple series of 'flanking' measures. Although still theoretically justified by the need to buttress the fundamental premise of the DC – namely the equivalence of national asylum adjudication systems – it constituted a clear acknowledgement that this premise could not be simply taken for granted. Hence, it implicitly endorsed the idea that such an equivalence had become an objective of its own and in this way laid the foundations for the development of the EU asylum policy that was subsequently enshrined in the Amsterdam Treaty.

IV.6. BURDEN-SHARING AND TEMPORARY PROTECTION ISSUES

Other developments also contributed to the progressive 'independence' of Third Pillar asylum co-operation from the Internal Market objectives. The 1951 GC definition of the term 'refugee' was confined to the fulfilment of a certain number of parameters, which reflected the reality of a bipolar world with two distinct spheres of influence. Large movements between power-blocks were not a realistic possibility, hence the accent on the parameter of 'individual' persecution. By the end of the Cold War, the world geo-political asset was vastly fragmented: the containment effect on local conflicts imposed by the logic of super-power antagonism thus came to an abrupt end. Moreover, the geography of conflict began to shift. Whereas in the past – from the Western perspective – super-power confrontations had taken place in far away theatres, the new era brought local conflicts much closer to home for Western Europe.

The crisis in former Yugoslavia acted as a catalyst, for the first time forcing Western European governments to realise their inability to face situations of mass influx. Their initial reaction was to impose visa requirements on all the countries where most asylum seekers originated from. For instance, since mid-1992 all Member States progressively imposed visas on nationals from

---

56. The latter particularly concerned the protection of women refugees, see G.S. Goodwin-Gill, 'The individual refugee, the 1951 Convention and the Treaty of Amsterdam' in E. Guild and C. Harlow (eds), *supra* n° 34, p. 141, at p. 154.

Bosnia-Herzegovina.[57] These tactics, however, failed to stem the flows. Over half a million people sought asylum in Europe, both in 1991 and in 1992, and most of them did not qualify for the GC status of 'refugee'. In 1992 the recognition rate was below 10 per cent in most European States.[58] Former Yugoslavia headed the list of the countries of origin in most European States in 1991–1992. The asylum applicants were mostly fleeing situations of civil war and internal armed conflict and therefore did not satisfy, in the eyes of Member States, the requirement of 'individual' persecution.[59] However, once they had arrived in the territory of a Member State, it proved impossible to remove them due to the obligation of non-refoulement contained in Art. 33 GC.

All Member States had developed some form of 'exceptional leave to remain' for persons who feared persecution outside the definition of the GC, but practices varied greatly. The acknowledgement of these differences was one of the factors that pushed forward the idea that some sort of harmonisation in the field was needed. However, by far the strongest motivational factor was the uneven distribution of these mass influxes. Germany alone coped with 80 per cent of all EU applications. In 1992, Germany and Austria received 450,000 refugees from former Yugoslavia, the Nordic Countries 110,000 and Spain, Italy, France and Great Britain together only 55,000. The strain on national resources was enormous and through Third Pillar asylum co-operation the worst hit Member States started to apply considerable pressure to promote the concept of 'burden-sharing'.[60]

The first timid JHA initiatives focused on specific situations. In December 1992, a 'Conclusion on people displaced by the conflict' was approved by the Edinburgh European Council.[61] Member States expressed their readiness to

---

57. For the implications of the developments of the common visa list ex Art. 100c EC, see Chapter IV.2.

58. Except in France (28 per cent), The Netherlands (23 per cent), Sweden (28.3 per cent) and Belgium (19.4 per cent). On the other end of the spectrum, recognition was well below 5 per cent in Germany and the UK (see Annex, Table 3).

59. This point has been highly disputed, since it was maintained by some that the GC did in fact cover civil war refugees when it mentioned persecution because of race, faith, nationality and social group (Art. 1). All of these criteria could have applied in the case of persons fleeing former Yugoslavia, but the problem in reality lay with the large numbers of people involved and the inability of Member States to deal with them effectively. For a summary of these views, see P. Rudge, 'The asylum dilemma – Crisis in the modern world: a European perspective' (1992) 4 *Journal of Policy History*, p. 93.

60. For statistical data, see Annex, Table 1. In this context, none of the previous asylum initiatives applied because they all related to 'refugees' within the context of the 1951 GC. The DC system, however, was not geared to pick up differences in refugee status. Since the allocation of responsibility preceded the examination of an application, States closer to the external borders ended up bearing the brunt of the mass influx, even when the applicants made it further into the Community, precisely because they had travelled through the border State first.

61. See Council Press Release 10518/92 (press 230).

accept, on a 'temporary basis', those nationals of former Yugoslavia who were coming 'directly' from combat zones, if they were within a Member State and could not return home as a direct result of the conflict and the Human Right abuses. This undertaking by the Member States was expanded in 1993 (Copenhagen June Council) in a 'Resolution on certain common guidelines with regard to the admission of particularly vulnerable groups of distressed persons from the former Yugoslavia'.[62] 'Vulnerable groups' were identified as prisoners of war at risk of life or limb; critically ill people who could not obtain treatment *in situ* and, likewise, persons who had been subjected to severe sexual assault; and generally people that were under direct risk to life or limb and could not be otherwise protected.

The 1994 'Commission Communication on asylum and immigration policies' had pointed out that despite the specific initiative for former Yugoslavia, no attempt had yet been made to harmonise national legislation on temporary protection (TP) or to set up an effective system of burden sharing.[63] It had therefore recommended the harmonisation of national TP schemes and the setting up of a monitoring system to help Member States in situations of mass influx to share the refugee burden. The German Presidency in the second half of 1994 put the issue high on its priorities agenda by presenting a draft Resolution on burden-sharing, but failed to reach a compromise.[64] The proposal was strongly opposed by the Member States that were dealing with small numbers of refugees and which according to the plan would have had to substantially increase their refugee intake. It was a sad display of extreme lack of Community solidarity.

A 'Resolution on burden-sharing with regard to the admission and residence of displaced persons on a temporary basis'[65] was finally adopted a year later in September 1995, followed in 1996 by a 'Resolution on an alert and emergency procedure for burden-sharing with regard to the admission and residence of displaced persons on a temporary basis'.[66] These two Resolutions represented a

---

62. See Council Press Release 548/93 (press 132).

63. The Commission noted that temporary protection schemes throughout the Community varied greatly. However, they all seemed to concern only mass influx situations and most schemes excluded the possibility of submitting an application for asylum. The ultimate aim of the scheme was to allow for rapid repatriation after the situation in the country of origin had gone back to normal. Conditions of reception also varied widely, ranging from permission to work and rights of family reunification to mere benefit support (COM (94)23 final, p. 8).

64. Presidency document 7773/94 ASIM 124. Germany was particularly keen to introduce a system of refugee quotas allocated for each country on the basis of their respective population, territory and percentage of EU gross domestic product. The only exceptions to these criteria were to be the population already present on the territory and eventual military expenditure deriving from peace-keeping/making exercises in the context of a refugee crisis.

65. Resolution of 25/9/95, OJ 1995 C262/1.

66. Resolution of 4/3/96, OJ 1996 L63/10.

're-arrangement' and generalisation of the two previous initiatives on former Yugoslavia, but bore little resemblance to the original German proposal. However, they made no reference to any harmonisation of national TP schemes. The 1995 Resolution only briefly mentioned that 'the effect that the differences between Member States' arrangements for displaced persons have on the destinations of migratory flows should be kept to a minimum' (preamble). The definition of persons in need of protection in a situation of armed conflict or civil war literally corresponded to that of 'vulnerable groups' of the 1993 Resolution. A strong emphasis was laid on the possibility of securing an 'internal flight' option, even if international action would have been necessary to achieve it. Instead of a setting up a burden-sharing mechanism, the Resolution proposed a series of 'guidelines' for assessing how to share the burden of refugees in situations of mass influx. Criteria included the contribution of each Member State to the solution of the crisis (including military intervention),[67] humanitarian assistance and all economic or political factors that might have reduced the capacity of a State to admit large numbers of refugees. Tellingly, the Resolutions closed with a provision on the non-retroactivity of such guidelines: in other words, people admitted during previous conflicts constituted no 'bargaining chip' for further refugees.

The 1996 Resolution attempted to set up a rapid response mechanism for situations of mass influx whereby the principles of the burden-sharing Resolution would be applied to a specific emergency situation. An urgent meeting of the K.4 Committee would be convened at the request of the Presidency, any Member State or the Commission and a report would be prepared on the situation in the light of the opinion of the UNHCR. The agenda for the emergency meeting would consider the feasibility of local intervention and how many refugees Member States would be willing to admit according to the criteria laid down in the 1995 Resolution. The detailed arrangements for admitting the displaced persons would be set up by each country.

Both Resolutions were put to the test during the Kosovo crisis. Although the emergency mechanism provided for by the 1996 Resolution was correctly started, it proved impossible to achieve any consensus on refugee quotas. This led to undignified 'squabbles' among Member States, proving once more that a better TP framework was urgently needed. The delays in approving this framework were a very clear indicator of the lack of consensus on the matter.[68]

As in the case of the 1996 Joint Position on the interpretation of the term 'refugee', the importance of these initiatives did not lie in their ability to achieve efficient results, but in the fact that they constituted a further departure from

---

67. This was a particularly difficult clause for the German Government because of the inability of Germany to intervene in international conflicts due to its Second World War legacy.

68. See further in Chapter VI.3. A general Joint Action on Temporary Protection should have substituted these two burden-sharing Resolutions. A draft proposal remained on the agenda for almost four years, but no consensus could be reached. Eventually, in March 2000 the Commission presented a new, radically altered Directive on TP (see Chapter VI.5).

the 'flanking' measure aspects of asylum co-operation. They proved that (at least some) Member States had come to realise the full potential of the generic definition of Art. K.1.1 and were willing to exploit it to tackle 'any' common concern on asylum matters and not just security issues derived from the Internal Market objectives. The fact that these new initiatives were so strongly resisted and eventually disapplied indicated that this expansion of the asylum co-operation field was still in a delicate transitional phase and many Member States still needed time to adjust to these new developments.

IV.7. New Priorities for Asylum Co-operation: An Assessment of the Third Pillar Working Structures and the New 1996 JHA Work-programme

The transition to a wider-scope asylum co-operation that took place between the entry into force of the Maastricht Treaty and the signing of the Amsterdam one was further highlighted by the crisis of the Third Pillar structures and the setting of new asylum priorities. The 1991 Maastricht work-programme had determined the priorities that were followed by the Immigration Ministers in the subsequent four and a half years. By 1996, most of the points on the programme had been formally tackled, but implementation of such measures was totally inadequate. Moreover, no initiatives had been taken on two of the listed priority areas, namely harmonisation of national treatment conditions for asylum seekers and of national temporary protection measures. The ability of the Third Pillar structures to cope with an ever increasing level of co-operation had also been severely tested. The overall performance results in the asylum field were not judged to be satisfactory.

The Third Pillar structure had consolidated itself into five levels of operation. The COREPER operated directly below the JHA Council. It was in charge of organising the meetings' agendas, of deciding on voting procedures (Points A and B) and was mainly concerned with the 'political' aspects of decision-making. Underneath the COREPER – but also sometimes in parallel to it – was the Co-ordinating Committee (so-called K.4 Committee) in charge of supervising and co-ordinating the work of the Steering and Working Groups. There were three Steering Groups (Immigration and asylum; Security, Police and customs co-operation; Judicial co-operation) that acted as supervisors in specific areas and reported to the K.4 Committee. The Immigration and Asylum Group in turn was divided in six Working Groups on 1) migration; 2) asylum; 3) visas; 4) external frontiers; 5) forged documents; and 6) CIREA and CIREFI. Any given initiative would have been discussed, planned and approved stage by stage throughout these five layers of bureaucracy. The inevitable result was a rather slow rate of progress, duplication of efforts, miscommunication and power struggles between the different structures.[69]

---

69. Criticism on the operational abilities of the Third Pillar came from various quarters. Politicians were quick to acknowledge these faults and put the reform of the Third Pillar

In so far as asylum policy was concerned, Art. K.9 TEU – the so-called *passarelle* clause – would have allowed a radical change of structure by transferring the subject area into the EC Treaty with the unanimous vote of the Council. The 'Declaration on Asylum' attached to the Maastricht Treaty provided for a revision of the issue by the Council by the end of 1993 and to this purpose the Commission presented a report to the Council in November 1993.[70] The report highlighted the advantages of such a transfer in terms of greater transparency and democratic control, faster implementation, wider choice of legal instruments[71] and the possibility of judicial control, but had to conclude that such a decision would have been premature.[72] In approving this report,[73] the Council agreed to review the matter by the end of 1995, but the discussion was subsequently abandoned in favour of a comprehensive revision by the IGC.

The 1996 work-programme[74] was intended to cover a span of two years, while the IGC negotiations were being finalised. Matters that had been neglected in the implementation of the 1991 work-programme appeared as high priorities, namely the harmonisation of conditions for the reception of asylum applicants and the tackling of TP and burden-sharing issues.[75] The work-programme also

---

structures onto the IGC agenda (see Chapter V). For an academic comment, see M. Den Boer, 'Justice and Home Affairs cooperation in the European Union: current issues' [1996] *Eipascope*, p. 12. The House of Lords European Communities Committee also highlighted the shortcomings of these structures twice, both in *Enhancing parliamentary scrutiny of the Third Pillar*, 6th Report, session 1997–98, HL Paper 25 (31/7/97), at pp. 45–47; and in *Dealing with the Third Pillar: the Government's perspective*, 15th Report, session 1997–98, HL Paper 73 (17/2/98) at pp. 5–8. The latter report in particular drew attention to the frequency and the scale of activities in the Third Pillar. A typical Presidency (Luxembourg, for instance) would have included two JHA Council meetings, six meetings of the K.4 Committee, eight meetings of the Steering Groups and 70 Working Groups' meetings. However, the record showed that during the Irish and Dutch Presidencies the Steering Groups met only once and confined their discussions to the future work programme.

70. 'Commission's Report to the Council on the possibility of applying Art. K.9 of the Treaty on European Union to asylum policy', SEC 1687 final, 4/11/93.

71. On this point the Commission had already stressed that the constant choice of non-binding instruments in the asylum field could have had negative repercussions on the level and quality of national implementation. This warning was to be prove very true indeed (*supra* n° 70, p. 6)

72. D. O'Keeffe, 'Recasting the Third Pillar' (1995) 32 CML Rev., p. 893, at p. 898, noted that the application of Art. K.9 constituted in fact a 'double lock' procedure, is so far as it was subject to the double requirement of unanimous voting in the Council and national ratification.

73. 'Council Conclusions of 20/6/94 concerning the possible application of Art. K.9 of the Treaty on European Union to asylum policy', OJ 1996 C274/34.

74. 'Council Resolution of 14/10/96 laying down the priorities for co-operation in the field of Justice and Home Affairs for the period from 1 July 1996 to 30 June 1998', OJ 1996 C319/1.

75. This priority was peculiarly formulated. It did not provide for action to be undertaken on harmonising TP status, but simply to 'examine' the problem. Consensus on the issue was obviously still very low.

re-listed some older priorities, a clear indication that achievements were regarded as unsatisfactory. Among the latter were implementation measures of the DC – no further specification was given – and the examination of forms of alternative protection (de facto protection and humanitarian leaves to remain). The harmonisation of national asylum procedures for granting the right of asylum appeared for the first time in a work-programme.[76] Finally, the development of EURODAC[77] was also included as a priority.

On the whole, however, this work-programme appeared to be of a temporary nature, a priority list that focused more on the 'examination' of issues rather than on concrete proposals for action. This attitude was obviously due to the complex negotiations that were taking place within the IGC framework and the uncertainty surrounding the future shape of Third Pillar co-operation. The new 1998 work-programme was in this respect much more forceful and contained a more precise calendar of initiatives (see Chapter V). However, the relative importance of this programme lay in the fact that it reflected quite accurately the final transitional period of Third pillar asylum co-operation. This co-operation was in a process of expansion, reflected by the mixed priorities contained in the programme. Hence, old 'flanking' measures, such as outstanding DC implementation issues, were listed together with newer initiatives, such as 'alternative' forms of protection, TP and burden-sharing. The main obstacle to such expansion lay in the inefficiency of the old Third Pillar co-operation framework. The IGC took this issue seriously and the results of this transition were to be seen eventually in the new provisions of the Amsterdam Treaty.

IV.8. CONCLUDING REMARKS

The Third Pillar asylum co-operation was severely tested in the aftermath of the Maastricht Treaty. The inevitable conclusion was that Third Pillar procedures appeared too cumbersome. Efficient decision-making was hindered by

---

76. It should be recalled that in 1991 the Immigration Ministers considered this point and discarded it as unrealistic because it was too time-consuming (see Chapter III.2). Four years later the outlook had eventually changed.

77. EURODAC (European Automated Fingerprinting System of Asylum Applicants) had been put forward since 1992 as an essential tool in the framework of the implementation of the 1990 DC. The first Meeting of CIREA in November 1992 (see Chapter III.4) had highlighted the need to study the feasibility of this option. However, progress was hindered by the necessity, for all Member States, of adopting the relevant international instruments for the protection of personal data (Brussels 1980 Convention, see Chapter II.2). Since 1996, all Member States had adopted such legislation, but further obstacles bogged down its progress. By 1998, the main obstacles appeared to concern the role of the ECJ, whether the Commission should have run it, and above all if it should have also included 'illegal immigrants' (the definition of this concept posed particular problems). See Council Press Releases 6889/98 (Press 73) of 19/3/98 and 8856/98 (Press 170) of 28–29/5/98. The Council tabled a 'EURODAC Draft Convention' by the end of 1998, but then decided to 'freeze' the text in order to adopt it as an EC measure once the Amsterdam Treaty came into

too many levels of bureaucracy and a pervasive atmosphere of mutual distrust among Member States. The Commission initially tried to take advantage of its new – albeit limited – status to carve out a more independent role for itself. These attempts were severely thwarted by the Council and valuable inputs, such as the 1994 Communication, were uselessly wasted. The EP showed willingness to fight its corner whenever possible (as in the visa action), but ultimately its opinion was never taken into account. Thus, opportunities to take advantage of the co-operation of Community institutions were missed. This co-operation could, for instance, have proved very useful in monitoring and enforcing implementation of the new asylum initiatives, a task the Commission would have been well equipped to tackle.

Lack of implementation was indeed one of the biggest problems of this period. From a policy-building point of view, the Third Pillar unfortunately provided Member States with the wrong choice of instruments. Soft law initiatives were by their very nature subject to scarce implementation. The seven year long ratification process of the 1990 DC had shown that conventions, although binding, were not an efficient alternative. The preference Member States displayed for non-binding measures was probably a symptom of a still low level of consensus. Agreement levels appeared higher around measures directly or indirectly concerning the implementation of the DC. This was probably due to the fact that the constantly emerging Schengen difficulties constituted a very powerful learning example. The whole asylum co-operation appeared to be caught in a vicious circle. In order to achieve some level of agreement, only soft law initiatives could be adopted. However, these initiatives subsequently remained largely unimplemented, thus raising the legitimate suspicion that no real consensus had been reached on them anyway. The obvious result was that progress in the asylum field was extremely slow.

It would be difficult to characterise these asylum initiatives as a 'policy'. However, some guiding principles had definitely started to emerge. The underlying philosophy appeared very much inspired to buttress the 'Fortress Europe' concept. All measures were invariably geared towards control and prevention of access, fast processing of applications and expulsion – at least into some sort of 'outer orbit'. Most issues were prioritised simply because they were necessary for the efficient implementation of the DC, as for instance the minimum guarantees initiative. However, requirements of international law were blatantly sacrificed and no real humanitarian concern motivated such decisions. Old recurring issues, such as the role of the ECJ, remained too controversial and kept being indefinitely postponed.

At the same time, new asylum issues were surfacing that went beyond the traditional Internal Market logic. Sometimes, such as in the case of the drafting of a common refugee definition, the new issues were indirectly linked to the

---

force. It was eventually approved as Council Regulation (EC) n° 2725/2000 on 11 December 2000 (OJ 2000 L316/1).

Dublin system, but had then become objectives in their own right. Other times, as in the instance of TP and burden-sharing, certain Member States successfully pursued at EU level their own pressing asylum issues, thereby implicitly widening the scope of EU asylum co-operation. Although such extended co-operation appeared capable of producing new initiatives, the Member States later miserably failed to face these new issues because of a total lack of solidarity among themselves. Their attempts at hiding the absence of consensus behind showpiece political initiatives – the two Resolutions on burden-sharing of 1995–96 – backfired badly when the initiatives were put to the test. Once more the brunt of this failure had to be borne by the very refugees the measures were designed to help.

From the refugee protection perspective the low implementation levels produced mixed consequences. Sometimes they counteracted the inherent restrictiveness of some of the measures. For instance, in the case of manifestly unfounded applications, the fact that some countries – such as Italy – never applied them eventually ensured the maintenance of higher levels of protection. Such cases, however, were rare, and in most instances Member States disapplied precisely those provisions that would have been beneficial to refugees (see, for instance, the lack of translated refusal decisions). Other times an effective implementation of the measures would have actually had a positive impact on refugee protection. The 1996 Joint Position on the interpretation of the term 'refugee' would have been of great benefit to asylum seekers lodging an application in France or in Germany and claiming non-State agent persecution. Instead, the Joint Position had no impact whatsoever on the practice of these two countries. Eventually, only the national Courts could act as a buffer against the iniquities of the DC system.[78]

By the end of 1996, it was clear that the Third Pillar asylum co-operation needed to be improved. Hopes were pinned on the possibility that the ongoing IGC negotiations might devise a more effective framework. During the negotiations, Member States appeared to be very aware of their past mistakes. However, the search for an overall consensus was still very difficult.

---

78. See Chapter VI.4.

5 The IGC and the Amsterdam Treaty

V.1. THE BEGINNING OF THE IGC NEGOTIATIONS ON THE THIRD PILLAR

Given their nature, there was a natural expectation that the problems surrounding Third Pillar co-operation would be addressed during the IGC negotiations that were due to take place in 1996. At the time of the Maastricht negotiations, Member States had been highly aware that some of the new provisions would cause considerable difficulties. Therefore, they had set a fixed deadline for revision in the hope that time would have allowed them to build a wider political consensus around some of the thorniest issues. Back in 1992, they had originally planned for the revision to focus on: 1) the Common Foreign and Security Policy (Art. J.4.6 and Art. J.10 TEU); 2) the extension of the codecision procedure (Art. 189b.8 EC); 3) how to add the energy, tourism and civil protection fields to the Community domain (Declaration n° 1); 4) examining the issue of the hierarchy of acts (Declaration n° 16); and 5) how in general to revise policies and other forms of co-operation in order to ensure the effectiveness of EU action (Art. B TEU).[1]

In the five years that followed the original signature of the Maastricht Treaty, the Union was faced with new challenges, notably the accession of three new Member States and the daunting prospect of a future enlargement to the East. It thus seemed logical to include these issues in the broader framework of the IGC negotiations. It was largely under the impulse of the new Member States[2] that a proposal to bring the Union closer to its citizens eventually gained momentum. Thus, issues concerning fundamental rights, internal security, employment, the environment, subsidiarity and transparency were also placed on the IGC agenda. As a consequence, the IGC's scope was radically reshaped from a mere 'technical' revision of possible malfunctions to a broad ranging Treaty-reshaping occasion.

The actual negotiations lasted for a year and a half under the Italian, Irish and Dutch Presidencies. In anticipation of these negotiations, the Corfu

---

1. This provision in particular served as a stepping stone for the revision of the Third Pillar co-operation measures. The Third Pillar had not been originally explicitly listed for revision because of Art. K.9 TEU. This passarelle clause had been intended as an in-built mechanism to allow internal change without a major Treaty revision. As Art. K.9 was never used, the inherent weaknesses of Third Pillar co-operation slowly came to light in the intervening years (see Chapter IV.8).

2. See H. Kortenberg, 'La négociation du Traité – Une vue cavalière' (1997) 33 *Revue Trimestrelle de Droit Européen*, p. 711.

European Council of June 1994 had instituted a Reflection Group composed of representatives of the Member States' Foreign Ministers and presided by the Spanish Minister, Mr. Westendorp. The group was charged with the drawing up a report covering the issues to be revised and the ensuing options available to the IGC. Before the Reflection Group began its proceedings, the EU institutions were asked to submit reports on the operation of the TEU. These reports were submitted during the first half of 1995 and constituted the first official assessment of the functioning of the EU two years after the entry into force of the TEU.[3]

The Reflection Group submitted its report to the Madrid European Council in December 1995. Its analysis on the shortcomings of Third Pillar co-operation was surprisingly frank and offered an interesting insight into the state of the negotiations. On some vital points, consensus building proved impossible and the report limited itself to merely 'registering' the various national disagreements. There was a general acknowledgement that 'the magnitude of the challenges is not matched by the results achieved so far in response to them'.[4] Three issues were pointed out as the main reasons for the inadequacies of JHA co-operation. The first one entailed the '[l]ack of objectives and of a timetable for achieving them. Instead of placing emphasis on the consolidation of an area of freedom and security in which there are no internal frontiers and where persons can move freely – the goal at which all action should be targeted – Art. K merely lists areas of common interest'.[5]

The lack of a coherent definition of the common goals of the JHA co-operation stemmed directly from the resistance of some Member States to the idea of formalising the previous EPC into the Treaty framework. Such Member States had particularly disliked the possibility – however remote – that a 'common policy' in the Community sense might eventually ensue from such co-operation. The fields listed in Art. K TEU where simply areas were Member States shared some common interests. The subsequent achievements in this field were more the result of the 'superimposition' of identical national wills than of a concrete effort of policy building. In many instances, the degree of agreement on an issue did not go beyond the formulation of the problem,[6] in more extreme cases the

---

3. The EU Commission, the Council, the EP, the ECJ, the Court of First Instance, the Court of Auditors, the Economic and Social Committee and the Committee of the Regions all submitted reports. The ECJ report can be found in (1995) 31 *Revue Trimestrelle de Droit Public*, p. 678, whereas the EP report is in OJ 1995 C151/13.

4. IGC Reflection Group's Report, SN 520/95 (REFLEX 21), Brussels, 5/12/95, p. 16, point 46.

5. See *supra* n° 4, p. 16, point 48. This point highlighted the inherent tension in the expansion of EU asylum co-operation from a mere collection of 'flanking' measures to a co-operation with its own independent objectives. This gradual transition was possible precisely because of the fact that Art. K.1.1 only contained a generic reference to 'asylum matters'. See Chapter IV.5–6.

6. See, for instance, the impossibility of agreement on common controls over the EU's external borders (the dossier had been blocked since the Commission proposal in 1993), the legal

mere 'perception' of the problem varied widely. The Madrid European Council, spurred on by the Westendorp Report had tried to address the lack of common objectives by requesting that JHA Ministers draw up a list of priorities for co-operation for the following two years. It took the Ministers one year to agree on the priorities and the annex to the Decision[7] reveals how common initiatives were well under way in most of the prioritised fields. Therefore, the Decision represented more of an effort to put past initiatives into a coherent shape, rather than to formulate future objectives.[8]

The lack of effective instruments for pursuing common action in JHA was the second problem highlighted by the Reflection Group report. Most of the instruments listed in Art. K.3 were originally formulated for the Second Pillar on Common Foreign and Security Policy. However, as the report pointed out 'external policy is rarely normative and requires flexibility of action, whereas

status of third country nationals resident in the EU, the EUROPOL dossier, the fight against drugs etc., all highlighted in H. Labayle, 'La coopération européenne en matière de justice et d'affaires intérieures et la Conference Intergouvernamentale' (1997) 33 *Revue Trimestrelle de Droit Européen*, p. 6; and also J. Monar, 'European Union – Justice and Home Affairs: a balance sheet and an agenda for reform' in G. Edwards and A. Pijpers (eds), *The politics of European Treaty reform – The 1996 Intergovernmental Conference and beyond* (Pinter pub., London, 1997), p. 328.

7. 'Council Resolution of 14/10/96, on laying down the priorities for co-operation in the field of Justice and Home Affairs for the period from 1 July 1996 to 30 June 1998', OJ 1996 C319/1. See comments on this work-programme in Chapter IV.7. The programme was nonetheless important because it highlighted the transition that was taking place in asylum co-operation (see *supra* n° 5).

8. In truth, one of the main reason for the lack of clear objectives lay in the age-old dispute over the interpretation of Art. 7a EC. The Reflection Group report briefly touched upon the issue, but failed to adequately stress it. In its general considerations on JHA co-operation the Report mentioned the 'context of a single market, an open society and the abolition of the Union's internal frontiers in accordance with the Treaty [...]' (p. 16, point 48). The Edinburgh European Council of December 1992 had to officially acknowledge that the free movement of persons, as provided by Art. 7a, could not be completed by 1 January 1993. That same year the EP started an action against the Commission under Art. 175 EC for failure to put forward the proposals necessary to dismantle national internal frontiers. As a response, in 1995 the Commission did present three proposals to the EU Council concerning the free movement of persons across the 'border-free' Community (the so-called 'Monti package': 'Commission Proposal for a Council Directive on the right of third-country nationals to travel in the Community', COM(95)346 final; 'Proposal for a Council Directive concerning the abolition of controls on persons at internal frontiers', COM(95) 347 final; 'Proposal for an EP and Council Directive amending Directives 68/360/EEC and 73/148/EEC', COM(95) 348 final). However, the measures were stalled once again because of national disputes over their legal basis. In this context, the Schengen framework enabled the majority of EU Member States to bypass this stalemate, but it did not offer a more effective alternative to the intergovernmental co-operation formula of the JHA. Schengen itself was in fact suffering some of the same shortcomings that affected the functioning of the Third Pillar.

matters relating to the security of citizens require legal protection and, therefore a legislative framework'.[9] At the time of the report the Council had never adopted any 'joint position' (Art. K.4.a), but it had agreed on two 'joint actions' (Art. K.3.b) and drafted one Convention on Extradition. It had nonetheless adopted over 50 Recommendations, Resolutions and Conclusions, all of which were 'old' instruments available before the TEU.[10] The slow ratification process of international conventions[11] and the inability to reach any compromise on the eventual competence of the ECJ over them – as provided by Art. K.3.c – effectively deprived Member States of the only legally-binding instrument in the Third Pillar. As possible alternative measures, the report mentioned that some national proposals highlighted the suitability of the directive instrument for this delicate area. Others, instead, put forward the idea of conventions entering into force once a certain number of ratifications had occurred. Most Member States seemed to agree that the overall requirement of a unanimity vote had proved to be the most formidable obstacle to any consensus building.

Finally, the report also pointed out that all Member States agreed on the working structures being too complex, thus making the decision-making process extremely cumbersome. The JHA co-operation lacked 'a true institutional driving mechanism',[12] since all the typical Community mechanisms had been severely limited in order to keep the nature of the co-operation intergovernmental. The Commission had a shared initiative in a number of fields only (Art. K.1.1–6), the EP could merely be 'consulted' and the ECJ had no competence at all. As the Commission pointed out in its own report, a Member State not holding the Presidency had used its right of initiative only once, the Commission itself only twice. All proposals and initiatives still emanated from the Presidency as in the past. Furthermore, the decision formation process was encumbered by two additional negotiating levels introduced by the TEU, notably the K.4 Committee and the Group of Directors,[13] the latter situated between the working groups and the K.4 Committee. Co-operation between COREPER and the K.4 Committee was notoriously uneasy,[14] due to very different working methods.

Whereas the Westendorp Report registered an overall agreement on the fact that the JHA co-operation was plagued by serious structural problems, national solutions varied immensely. In broad terms, there appeared to be three possible options. The first one would have been to take advantage of the Art. K.9 *passarelle* clause and transfer most Art. K.1 fields to the EC Pillar. No Member

---

9. See *supra*, n° 4, p. 16, point 48.
10. For a comprehensive overview of these acts, see the 'Commission's Report for the Reflection Group' of May 1995, pp. 94–98.
11. See, for instance, the 1990 DC whose ratification process lasted seven years.
12. See *supra* n° 4, p. 16, point 48, and also the Commission report, *supra* n° 10, p. 53 *et seq.*
13. See Chapter IV.7.
14. See M. Lepoivre, 'Le domaine de la Justice et des Affaires Intérieures dans la perspective de la Conférence Intergouvernementale de 1996' [1995] *Cahiers de Droit Européen*, p. 323, at p. 339.

State at any stage of the negotiations seriously put forward such a proposal. The second option would have been to maintain the current Pillar division and to develop practical solutions to improve co-operation. The United Kingdom, Ireland and Denmark were the strongest advocates of this position, but other Member States such as Sweden also initially supported this view. The underlying reasons for such a position obviously varied among the Member States and ultimately determined the complex structure of the new Treaty. The British and Irish opposition to any structural change was mainly conditioned by their interpretation of Art. 7a EC. This led them to fear that any 'communitarisation' of the Third Pillar fields would have inevitably entailed their obligation to abolish border controls. The Danish position was determined by the Edinburgh Declaration of 1992 which limited their participation in JHA solely to the intergovernmental framework. This Declaration had played an essential role in ensuring Danish ratification of the TEU in its second referendum and no politician was willing to risk opening a new debate. Sweden in its turn was bound by the Nordic Union and was worried about the repercussions of the abolition of EU internal borders on its Nordic partners. The accession of the Nordic Union Members to the SC in December 1996 considerably eased the Swedish position.

Finally, a majority of Member States appeared to support the third possible option, a partial 'communitarisation' of the Third Pillar. Most agreed that the areas to be transferred should have included the crossing of external borders and asylum and immigration policy and that majority voting should have been introduced. The issue of how to incorporate Schengen into the EU framework was also on their agenda. 'Flexibility' rapidly became the keyword, both to circumvent the strenuous British and Danish opposition and to accommodate the individual national views within the majority group. The idea of a flexible participation in the new provisions, coupled with the proposal of 'closer co-operation' among certain Member States within the Treaty framework was already being strongly promoted by the Franco-German partnership by December 1995.[15]

V.2. THE DUBLIN PROPOSAL OF DECEMBER 1996[16]

As requested by the European Council in Florence in June 1996, the Irish Presidency set out to prepare a 'general outline for draft revision of the Treaties'.[17] Three initiatives were to prove of fundamental importance in the shaping of the new provisions on the JHA co-operation. The first one was a courageous

---

15. The IGC preceding Amsterdam was incidentally the last one where the traditional Franco-German partnership functioned as a 'driving motor' for integration. See further, Chapter VI.7.

16. 'The EU today and tomorrow – Adapting the EU for the benefit of its people and preparing it for the future – a general outline for a draft revision of the Treaties – Dublin II', CONF 2500/96 CAB, EN, 5/12/96.

17. Florence European Council, Presidency Press Release, 1345/96, p. 5.

proposal presented by the Commission in September 1996.[18] It defined the new overall objective of JHA co-operation as the establishment of an 'area of liberty, security and justice' within the European Union. The second initiative consisted of a common Franco-German contribution towards the definition of the notion of 'closer co-operation',[19] to be included both in the EC Pillar and in the JHA co-operation. The final impulse to the Irish proposal came in December 1996 from a joint letter by Chancellor Kohl and President Chirac,[20] which stated that the 'security' dossier was to be given 'absolute priority' at the Dublin summit. It underlined that the creation of a 'European common juridical space' should entail clear objectives, common asylum, immigration and border control policies, extensive majority voting in these areas and a fixed progressive calendar of implementation (possibly of five years) with specific 'support measures' – a particular French priority throughout the negotiations. Enhanced 'flexibility of participation' would have been the key to overcome individual national resistance to further integration.

The document presented by the Irish Presidency at the Dublin summit of December 1996 contained extremely innovative proposals in the JHA field, including the communitarisation of sensitive Third Pillar matters, such as asylum and immigration. Not all of the proposals were retained in the course of the following negotiations, but the final draft of the Treaty signed in Amsterdam the following June certainly owed a great deal to the courageous proposals tabled by the Irish Presidency. It appeared remarkable that innovative developments even occurred in areas which the Irish Presidency had indicated as too controversial to be reformed, notably the jurisdiction of the ECJ.

The starting point of the Irish proposal was the realisation that the European Union should be better equipped to meet the challenges of the next century. Such challenges were defined as the ability to face the rapid evolution of international events, the globalisation of the world economy, terrorism, drug trafficking and international crime, migratory pressure and ecological imbalances. Consequently, the proposal considered five major fields to be reformed: the first one concerned the establishment of 'an area of freedom, security and justice', the second the enhancement of citizens' rights, the third foreign policy measures, the fourth the Union's institutions and finally there was to be a chapter on 'enhanced co-operation and flexibility'. The first and the last of these intended reforms were to have a considerable impact on asylum co-operation.

The Irish Government went to great lengths to explain the need to create the new objective of an 'area of freedom, security and justice'. The concept in their

---

18. CONF 3912/96 of 18/9/96. It constituted the final reshaping of ideas already put forward earlier that year in another Commission document, COM(96)90 of 28/2/96. The Commission proposal was seen as a 'blueprint' for a new approach to Union citizenship based on a 'European Social Model' of an inclusive nature (see J. Shaw, 'The many pasts and futures of citizenship in the European Union', 1997 22 EL Rev., p. 554 at p. 555).

19. See *Europe* n° 6836 of 19/10/96, pp. 3–4.

20. See *Europe* n° 6871 of 11/12/1996, p. 2.

view derived directly from the establishment of the Internal Market and was aimed at allowing EU citizens to take full advantage of the freedoms granted by the Treaty. At the same time the population had to be protected from threats to their personal security. In this context asylum initiatives were once again presented as mere 'flanking' measures for the establishment of the Internal Market. Their international Human Rights dimension was almost completely ignored when it was stated that 'issues such as immigration, asylum, visas and external borders [...] must be handled collectively if free movement in the Union is to be achieved without jeopardising the security of citizens'.[21] Unfortunately, in what way asylum seekers might have constituted a threat to the safety of EU citizens was left unexplained.

As part of this objective, new attention was given to the issue of the Union's commitment to fundamental Human Rights – asylum issues were obviously excluded from these concerns. Several Member States would have favoured the accession of the EU or of the EC to the European Convention on Human Rights.[22] However, since an agreement on this point seemed unlikely, a different solution was put forward. The Community, by unilateral initiative, would have respected fundamental rights as guaranteed by the ECHR. By inserting this provision into the EC Treaty it would have automatically fallen under the ECJ's jurisdiction.[23] A new procedure for suspending Member States found in serious and persistent breach of the Union's fundamental principles was also formulated. One third of Member States, the Commission or the European Parliament could propose the suspension of a Member State for the above-mentioned breach. The

---

21. See *supra* n° 16, p. 13. This passage highlighted the theoretical model on which the new area of freedom, security and justice was being conceived. It was mainly an intergovernmental-inspired vision of 'a liberal "freedom-from" polity' where the Union citizenship was seen as 'a minimal framework of civil rights' in the context of the 'Union's market-building vocation'. In such a vision European citizens were identified by separating them from the 'foreigners', who needed 'to be excluded in order to make [the citizens] feel "secure"' (J. Shaw, *supra* n° 18, p. 571). This model contrasted with the Commission's supranational vision of an inclusive model of 'Social Europe' (see *supra* n° 18), where citizenship would be characterised by extensive political, social and economic rights for all without exclusions. In this respect the area of freedom, security and justice was merely one of the many aspects of Union citizenship, whereas in the Irish proposal it actually constituted the starting point for all subsequent rights (J. Shaw, *supra* n° 18, p. 565).

22. On this point see ECJ, opinion 2/94 on the accession of the EC to the European Convention on Human Rights [1996] ECR I-1786. The Court concluded that the EC lacked the necessary competence to accede to the Convention. A reform of the EC Treaty would therefore have been necessary.

23. A similar solution was later inserted into the Amsterdam Treaty, except that the obligation to respect the rights included in the ECHR was founded on the new Art. 6.2 of the TEU. By virtue of the new Art. 46.d TEU the ECJ was given jurisdiction over the compliance of Community institutions with the ECHR.

Council was to decide by a two-thirds majority of its weighted votes which rights of the State concerned should be suspended.[24]

The Irish draft proposal supported the introduction in a revised Art. B TEU of a new Union objective, namely the establishment of a Freedom, Security and Justice Area. This objective would be pursued by means of a double strategy. On the one hand, a new Title on the 'free movement of persons, asylum and immigration' was to be inserted into the EC Treaty. On the other hand, the provisions in the JHA Pillar were to be strengthened to guarantee the greater security and safety of persons. The Presidency also suggested the insertion of 'an overall target date', possibly January 2001.

The idea of transferring some of the JHA Pillar fields to the EC competence had already been put forward by a certain number of Member States. Several members of the Reflection Group had declared themselves to be in favour of the communitarisation of the asylum and immigration fields. The Italian Presidency had highlighted these areas as suitable for Community competence in its progress report on the IGC on 17 June 1996.[25] Thus, the solution put forward in the Irish proposal consisted in the creation of a new Title in the EC Treaty, regulated by special rules concerning the scope of the ECJ's jurisdiction and the decision-making process. The reaching of an agreement on this transfer of competence to the Community was in essence made possible by the new rules on flexible participation.

Five new fields were suggested for the new EC Title: 1) border controls; 2) asylum policy, immigration policy and third country nationals' residence policy; 3) administrative co-operation; 4) fight against drugs; and 5) customs co-operation.[26] There was a general exemption clause that excluded any interference of this Title with the Member States' responsibilities concerning the 'maintenance of law and order and the safeguarding of internal security'. The provisions on the crossing of internal borders explicitly relied on the interpretation of Art. 7a EC as implying the total abolition of internal border controls, both for EU and non-EU nationals.[27] Therefore, numerous and detailed provisions on external border controls followed. They included standards and procedures for border checks, rules on short-term visas – part of which were already Community

---

24. This provision was entirely maintained in the new draft TEU, see Art. 7.

25. On these proposals, see J. Monar, *supra* n° 6, p. 336.

26. The new Amsterdam Treaty did retain fields 1–3 and added others, such as judicial co-operation in civil matters (former Art. K.6 TEU) and police and judicial co-operation in criminal matters, which overlapped with an identical competence remaining in the Third Pillar.

27. The United Kingdom's constant refusal to accept this interpretation (see Chapter II.1) eventually led to a special Protocol on Art. 7a EC being added to the new Amsterdam Treaty. This Protocol would allow its current border controls to continue (see Chapter V.3).

competence (ex Art. 100c EC) – and conditions for the free movement of third country nationals across the EU.[28]

The Irish draft article on the EC competence in the field of asylum and immigration was entirely retained in the final version of the Treaty.[29] The Council was to undertake action in a listed number of refugee and immigration issues. These mainly concerned States' responsibility for examining asylum applications; common standards of reception for asylum seekers; common rules in the definition of the notion of 'refugee'; common national parameters for granting or withdrawing refugee status; *de facto* refugees and burden-sharing measures; common entry and long-term residency rules, including family reunification; combating illegal immigration and common expulsion measures; and common rules on third country nationals' rights. There was a temporal deadline of two or three years for the adoption of such measures.[30]

The provisions on fighting drug trafficking, administrative and customs co-operation were barely sketched out and referred for further consideration by the IGC. The same applied to decision-making measures and the competencies of the ECJ. In this respect, the Irish proposal appeared as a structured recapitulation of the measures that, at that particular point, were acceptable to a majority of Member States. However, no effort was made to formulate possible solutions for the outstanding 'thornier' issues. Therefore, most of the progress was in fact achieved in the first half of 1997, in parallel with the definition of a new type of 'variable' participation in the Community process.

The Irish Presidency did summarise, in its proposal, the progress achieved up until the Dublin summit on the issue of 'flexibility'. It was defined as the 'possibility for a number of Member States less than the full membership to cooperate more closely in specific areas using the institutional framework of the Union'.[31] No sufficient consensus had been reached by December 1996 to formulate some draft Treaty articles, but different national suggestions had been tabled. The discussion appeared to centre on the ways to regulate such co-operation and on the problems of guaranteeing the uniformity of Community rules. Some proposals favoured flexibility being encoded into specific areas of the Treaty. Others suggested that it could be regulated by a special Protocol outside the TEU. The rest supported the introduction of specific conditions for regulating all such kind of co-operation in a general (non-operational) clause of the TEU. In the end, the latter option prevailed in the Amsterdam Treaty. The role of the Communities' institutions was also discussed and several Member States indicated a preference for the Commission and the EP to be involved in the process in some ways.[32]

---

28. The wording of this article was almost entirely replicated in the Amsterdam Treaty, but a new competence concerning rules on a uniform visa was added.
29. For an in depth analysis, see further at Chapter V.4.B.
30. This deadline was expanded in the Amsterdam Treaty to five years.
31. Dublin Proposal, *supra* n° 16, p. 129.
32. The outcome of these discussion was the new Title VII on provisions for closer co-operation of the Amsterdam TEU, which is examined in Chapter V.4.A.

In the framework of the Dublin proposal, the Third Pillar constituted the other essential part of the new area of freedom, security and justice. Its overall aim became to ensure the security and safety of persons. Following the numerous IGC proposals to improve the efficiency of the decision-making in the JHA sector, new instruments of action were proposed and the fields of competence expanded. Greater prominence was given to police co-operation, following the entry into force of the EUROPOL Convention in June 1996.[33] New fields of co-operation included combating paedophilia, racism, xenophobia and corruption, while others, such as customs co-operation and fighting drug trafficking, also appeared also in the new EC Title. Two new types of initiatives were proposed. The first consisted of 'decisions' to be adopted by unanimity and which were binding on Member States. The second involved 'framework decisions', very similar to directives and entailing only an obligation of result. Both these instruments were retained in the new Title VI of the Amsterdam TEU, but with the added specification that they should not entail any direct effect.

Finally, the proposal mentioned some other related issues that would need further consideration in the IGC negotiations. Two of those eventually appeared in the final drafting of the Treaty. The first one concerned the possibility of incorporating the SC into the EU framework, which was achieved at Amsterdam through a separate Protocol. The second one related to asylum applications of EU citizens and whether Member States should agree to refuse to process them. This issue was solved with the adoption of another separate Protocol.

The Dublin Draft Treaty proposals proved of great importance as a discussion platform for the final part of the IGC negotiations. In so far as asylum matters were concerned, the main Dublin objective of creating a Community area of freedom, security and justice was retained and competence over this field transferred to the Community sphere. A substantial amount of negotiation was necessary to define the points that could not be agreed at the Dublin summit. The most ground-breaking discussions took place in February 1997.[34] These concerned, on the one hand, the definition of the areas of majority voting – to be introduced after a transitional period of five years – the involvement of the ECJ with the EUROPOL formula[35] and provisions on closer co-operation. On the other

---

33. The EUROPOL Convention, a German proposal, had a troubled history and was finally signed in July 1995. Its entry into force was delayed by the lack of agreement over the ECJ's jurisdictional powers. Finally, a sort of *á la carte* jurisdiction was introduced, with the voluntary acceptance of the ECJ's jurisdictional competence. It was the first example of a selective jurisdiction solution in EU matters and it obviously proved inspirational for the voluntary jurisdictional clause introduced into the Third Pillar by the Amsterdam Treaty (see Art. 35 TEU).

34. See the results of the Noordwijk summit of 6/2/97 in *Europe*, n° 6909 of 7/2/97.

35. On the compromise of EUROPOL, see Europe, n°6755 of 23/6/96 and *supra* n° 33. The EUROPOL compromise allowed Member States to accept and possibly limit the ECJ's jurisdiction by means of national Declarations attached to the Convention. This solution, however, posed great problems for the uniformity of the Convention's application.

hand, a compromise on the incorporation of Schengen by means of a separate Protocol was finally found and finalised the following May.[36] As the negotiations went along, the positions of the Member States that totally opposed any further integration became firmly crystallised.[37] It was only when the May British elections brought about a new Government that an agreement based on a series of opt-out clauses was finally possible on the whole JHA co-operation.

V.3. THE AMSTERDAM TREATY PROVISIONS

The new Treaty was eventually agreed by the Amsterdam Council of June 1997. It retained the same three-pillared structure as the Maastricht TEU. In keeping with the Irish proposal, a new Art. 2 TEU listing the Union's objectives was introduced. Among its objectives, it set down the maintaining and developing of 'the Union as an area of freedom, security and justice, in which the free movement of persons is assured in conjunction with appropriate measures with respect to external borders controls, asylum, immigration and the prevention and combating of crime'. This overall objective was to be pursued both in the First and Third Pillar through a co-ordinated approach. A new Title VI was added to the TEU – a new Third Pillar in practice – dealing with 'Police and Judicial Co-operation in criminal matters'. New provisions on closer co-operation were also inserted in Title VII TEU. A radical change took place in the asylum field whereby refugee-related issues were transferred from the JHA framework to the Community competence. However, the new asylum provisions in the EC Treaty were regulated by a special regime that constituted an exception to the standard Community rules, especially in so far as the powers of the ECJ were concerned. Further exceptions were introduced by several Protocols that regulated the participation of some countries to the new Title and the integration of the Schengen framework within the Union.

V.3.A. The new Part III, Title IV of the EC Treaty

The greatest innovation in the EU approach to asylum issues was the introduction into the Amsterdam Treaty of a new EC competence on asylum policy. The new Part III, Title IV TEC (here and after referred to as Title IV TEC) dealt with visas, asylum, immigration and other policies related to the free movement of persons (Arts 61–69) and it was added to the section of the EC Treaty concerning 'Community policies'. This Title set, as a new EC objective, the progressive 'establishment of an area of freedom, security and justice',[38] echoing

---

36. See *Europe* n° 6970 of 8/5/1997, p. 3.
37. See *Europe* n°6909 of 7/2/1997, p. 4.
38. The use of the word 'area' was arguably the result of a precise choice of words. 'Community' could have been employed, but this term had 'important historical associations' of a supranational nature. It would therefore have not been adequate for matters which spanned both the First and Third Pillars and were 'thus subject partly to the Community method, and partly to the intergovernmental' one (J. Shaw, *supra* n° 18, p. 569).

the almost identical objective contained in Art. 29 TEU on Police and Judicial Co-operation. Part of this new EC Title consisted of fields of competence listed under the old Art. K.1.1–6 in addition to entirely new areas of intervention. As reflected by the heading, its legal justification stemmed from the necessity of guaranteeing the free movement of persons.[39] It was therefore firmly grounded in the overall objective of the establishment of the Internal Market. Thus, it put an end to the 10-year dispute over the interpretation of Art. 7a EC. The Amsterdam Treaty finally codified once and for all that the free movement of persons did necessarily entail an internal border-free Europe.[40]

Art. 61 TEC established the general scope of the new Community competence. This competence involved five different areas. It mainly concerned the establishment of an internal border-free area and its related measures,[41] thereby involving the asylum, immigration and crime control fields; judicial co-operation in civil matters – former Art. K.1(6); administrative co-operation and finally police and judicial co-operation in criminal matters. The establishment of a border-free Internal Market was directly related to Art. 14 TEC (former 7a EC). In this context, some asylum measures once again assumed the role of mere 'flanking' measures (Art. 61.a).[42] However, Art. 61.b TEC referred also to competence on

---

39. However, the new provisions were not inserted next to the traditional ones concerning the free movement of persons, but rather in a separate following Title. The reasons for this choice lay in the special regime regulating this particular area, in so far as it allowed selective Member States' participation and limitations to ECJ jurisdiction. This led certain commentators to qualify the new Title IV TEC as a 'ghetto' (see S. Peers, *EU Justice and Home Affairs law* (Longman, London, 2000), p. 2).

40. The solution to the dispute was, however, only superficial. The United Kingdom and Ireland introduced a separate Protocol on the interpretation of Art. 7a that allowed them to retain their border controls (see further). Therefore it would be more correct to claim that the different Member States finally agreed to disagree on the issue.

41. Two aspects were particularly interesting in this article. The first one regarded the 'progressive' aspects of the new Community competence, which was ensured by introducing a five-year transition period and by avoiding an automatic passage to the next phase (majority voting or codecision – see later). The second one concerned the French obsession with the need to flank the abolition of border controls with 'accompanying measures' to ensure a high level of security. This concern – a constant preoccupation also in the application of the SC – was fully accepted, even though the eventual wording was blander than that proposed by the French delegation. On this point, see H. Labayle, *supra* n° 6, p. 118. The timing was carefully planned to make sure that the 'accompanying measures' would have been in place by the end of the transitional period.

42. Art. 61.a introduced for the first time an interesting distinction between which asylum measures could be defined as 'flanking' and which were not of this nature. It specifically determined as 'flanking' measures those contained in Art. 63.1.a and 63.2.a. These two provisions concerned the rules allocating State responsibility on asylum applications (i.e. the DC) and measures relating to the introduction of an EU TP regime. If the choice of the first one seemed justified, the second one appeared more puzzling, especially in the light of the other asylum measures not defined as 'flanking' (see further).

'other' measures in the asylum field, listed further in Art. 63 TEC. For the first time, it also specifically mentioned 'the rights of nationals of third countries' as an additional field to those necessary for the establishment of the Internal Market. There was also an interesting overlap between part of the new EC competence and the one contained in the new Title VI TEU in the field of police and judicial co-operation in criminal matters.[43]

The measures concerning the crossing of external and internal borders and common visa rules were laid down in Art. 62. A transitional period of five years from the entry into force of the Treaty was set as a deadline for the Council to adopt all measures necessary for the setting up of a common external borders area,[44] including rules on border checks and short-term visas.[45] In practice, two factors could be foreseen as likely to facilitate the speedy implementations of these measures. The first one would derive from the eventual incorporation of the Schengen Convention and its *acquis* into the Union framework. By 1997 Schengen was fully operational, hence all mechanisms relating to external border controls and visa rules were already in place and could easily be transferred to the Community domain. The second important factor consisted of the fact that the only two non-Schengen members – the UK and Ireland – had obtained the possibility of maintaining their own border controls through separate Protocols. They would have had no interest therefore in raising any of their past objections.

Art. 63.1-2 TEC regulated the new EC competence in the asylum field. The measures, to be 'in accordance with the 1951 Geneva Convention and the 1967 New York Protocol and other relevant treaties', were restricted to a number of fields that were specifically listed. The careful wording chosen to define this list

---

43. Art. 61.e TEC defined this co-operation in such broad terms – while pointing at the relevant TEU provisions – that the Council would be virtually left with a choice of legal basis between the EC and the Third Pillar. This choice could have important repercussions in the scope of the ECJ's jurisdiction.

44. In respect of checks at external frontiers, see the added Protocol on external relations of the Member States with regard to the crossing of external borders. This Protocol preserved the competence of Member States to conclude agreements with third countries concerning their common borders (in this respect see also the vast and scarcely public area of the so-called 'readmission agreements' discussed in Chapter III.3.B). The Protocol was of particular importance because it explicitly underlined that Member States had not surrendered their 'external' competence over these matters and that therefore all previous ECJ ERTA jurisprudence did not apply.

45. Some of the rules concerning short-term visas (i.e. the list of countries whose nationals required visas to enter the EU and the uniform visa format) were already in place due to the previous Art. 100c EC (see Chapter IV.2). EC competence over visas was greatly expanded to include most areas of visa policy – common list, rules on visa-issuing, uniform visa rules, conditions regulating third country nationals' travels across the EU and finally long-term visa and residence permits. Interestingly, the latter provisions were listed in a separate article (Art. 63.a TEC) among the immigration measures. Overall, with the Amsterdam Treaty the Community could be deemed to have acquired full competence in the visa field.

indicated that it was to be considered exhaustive and not merely of indicative value. The asylum measures to be adopted within a period of five years[46] from its entry into force concerned mainly:

1. matters relating to the 1990 DC determining Member States' responsibility on asylum claims;
2. minimum standards of reception for asylum seekers in Member States;
3. minimum standards in the Member States' definition of the concept of 'refugee';
4. minimum standards for national procedures on granting or withdrawing refugee status;
5. minimum national standards of temporary protection for *de facto* refugees and displaced persons;
6. burden-sharing of refugee flows between Member States.[47]

Also included by Art. 63.3-4 TEC were immigration policy measures concerning long term visas, third country nationals residency rules and expulsion and family reunification rules. However, no Council action in the latter fields should prevent Member States from establishing or safeguarding national provisions which are compatible with the Treaty and with international agreements.[48] Interestingly, there was no five-year action obligation on burden-sharing decisions and on long-term visas and residency rules. This was a clear indication that the consensus level in this area was still very low.

The formulation of the future asylum policy action fields contained in Art. 63 TEC had obviously heavily relied on the past efforts of the K.4 Co-ordinating Committee. Most of the areas listed had been the subject of past initiatives.[49]

---

46. Measures on burden-sharing (Art. 63.2.b) were however excluded from the five-year rule. Solidarity among Member States was obviously still running very low.

47. Interestingly, TP and burden-sharing measures were not covered by the provision of Art. 63.1 TEC on the requirement to respect international instruments of refugee protection. In the eyes of Member States, this was no doubt justified by the fact that temporary protection measures were intended to help refugees that fell outside the scope of the GC. However, the issue of which refugees fell under the protection of the GC was quite a disputed one (see Chapter IV.6). By specifically excluding *de facto* refugees – the 'vulnerable groups' defined by the 1995 Resolution on burden-sharing and temporary protection as people generally fleeing internal conflicts (see Chapter IV.6) – from the clause in Art. 63.1, Member States made their interpretative choice very clear. Extremely large numbers of refugees that could have technically benefited from the protection of the GC were now formally excluded from it.

48. This specification was added to preserve a wide range of special agreements between Member States and third countries with whom they retain special historical or cultural ties, or other particular border agreements, such as the Nordic Union, for instance.

49. Some of the instruments necessary for the implementation of the 1990 DC were already in place (see Chapter IV.3). The 'Joint Position 96/196/JHA concerning the harmonised application of the definition of the term 'refugee'' (adopted on the basis of Art. K.3 TEU – see Chapter IV.5) laid down the possible convergence points among very diverging

The other areas covered by Art. 63, where no prior action seemed to have been undertaken, were all, however, mentioned in the 'Council Resolution laying down the priorities of co-operation in the field of JHA for the period from 1 July 1996 to 30 June 1998'.[50] As recalled earlier, Art. 61.b introduced a distinction between 'flanking' asylum measures and 'other' asylum initiatives. Only measures relating to the DC (Art. 63.1.a) and to temporary protection (Art. 63.2.a) were defined as 'flanking'. This left open the characterisation of the rest of the asylum provisions. Up until the Amsterdam Treaty, all asylum initiatives had been justified as compensatory measures to be put in place before the abolition of internal border controls. However, in the years following the Maastricht Treaty, a number of asylum initiatives had been adopted,[51] whose logical connection to the necessities of the Single Market appeared to be rather remote. By leaving open the definition of measures concerning the very essence of refugee status and burden-sharing,[52] Member States appeared to finally imply that asylum issues were to become a policy in their own right.

However, some very important exceptions to the application of this new Community competence were contained in Art. 64 TEC. It specifically laid down that nothing in Title IV 'shall affect the exercise of the responsibilities incumbent upon Member States with regard to the maintenance of law and order and the safeguarding of internal security'. This clause reflected the old Art. K.2.2 – now in Art. 33 TEU – and its inclusion was not surprising, given the early stages of

---

national jurisdictional interpretations. The same applied to the 'Council Resolution on minimum guarantees for asylum procedures' (see Chapter IV.4). Guidelines for burden-sharing action had been laid down both by the 'Council Resolution on burden-sharing with regard to the admission and residence of displaced persons on a temporary basis' and the subsequent 'Council Resolution on an alert and emergency procedure for burden-sharing with regard to the admission and residence of displaced persons' (see Chapter IV.6). Also in the immigration field, a great number of the measures to be undertaken had already been tackled in the past JHA co-operation efforts. For a list of these initiatives, see the EP study, 'The Third Pillar: an Overview' of 19/9/96 (EP 00342/96).

50. Adopted 14/10/96, OJ 1996 C319/1. See comments on the 'mixed' contents of this work-programme in Chapter IV.7.

51. Among those initiatives were for instance those concerning the uniform interpretation of Art. 1 GC, minimum standards for asylum procedures and burden-sharing (see Chapter IV). It was argued that these initiatives were necessary to guarantee the correct functioning of the 1990 DC, which in itself was a major asylum 'flanking' measure. However, the link to the removal of internal border controls was becoming increasingly remote and certain Member States successfully introduced new priorities of their own, notably in the field of TP and burden-sharing. The progressive harmonisation of national asylum policies was slowly becoming a goal in itself.

52. Those measures concerned Art. 63.1.b-c-d and Art. 63.2.b, i.e. minimum standards of reception; minimum standards with respect to the qualification of third country nationals as refugees; minimum standards on national procedures for the granting or withdrawing of refugee status; and burden-sharing in the reception of both GC and *de facto* refugees.

this new Community competence.[53] Furthermore, in the event of emergency situations (i.e. sudden refugee flows) the Council could adopt, by qualified majority on the proposal of the Commission, transitional measures – not exceeding six months – in favour of the State concerned. No consultation of the EP was to be required. The scope of this exception represented an extension of the old Art. 100c.2 EC on the introduction of emergency visa requirements.[54] The great latitude of the latter exception could potentially have a major impact on the operational mode of the Council and its decision-making ability. The ECJ would, however, be competent to judge on the opportunity of both exceptions.

Art. 67 TEC regulated the decision-making procedures applicable to this Title, as well as possible future involvement of the EP in these procedures. Even though most Member States had declared themselves in favour of an extended majority voting for the areas of this Title,[55] at the very end of the negotiations Germany decided to oppose an automatic passage to majority rule after the five-year transitional period. The German Government feared both unwanted supplementary budgetary expenses and a strong opposition from its *Laender*, notoriously very keen to preserve their specific areas of competence. Therefore, in the first five years from the entry into force of the Amsterdam Treaty, the Council was to act unanimously and Member States were to retain their shared right of initiative with the Commission, while the EP was to be compulsorily consulted. After this period, the Commission would have the sole right of initiative, but it would also have to examine requests submitted by Member States. Since there was no explicit indication of whether the Council was then to act by qualified majority or unanimity, presumably unanimity rule would continue to apply. Moreover, the exclusivity of the Commission initiative was partly limited by the fact that the unanimity rule rendered the special protection afforded by Art. 250 TEC to the Commission's proposals utterly superfluous.

After the five-year period, the Council could decide 'unanimously', after consulting the EP, whether to subject all or parts of the areas covered in this Title to the codecision procedure and whether to reform the powers of the ECJ in this field. The innovative potential of this provision was, however, hampered by two factors. Firstly, the difficulty of having to overcome the stringent requirement of unanimity was self-evident. Secondly, one had to take into account that the

---

53. See H. Labayle, 'Un espace de liberté, de sécurité et de justice' (1997) 33 *Revue Trimestrelle de Droit Européen*, p. 813, at p. 846. These exemptions were apparently strongly supported by the German and French Governments as a sort of counterweight to the attribution of new competence to the Community. In the future, though, it could have served as a supplementary national protection clause, should the United Kingdom, the Republic of Ireland or Denmark have decided to fully participate in this Title.

54. See D. O'Keeffe, 'Can the leopard change its spots? Visas, Immigration and asylum – following Amsterdam', in D. O'Keeffe and P. Twomey (eds), *Legal issues of the Amsterdam Treaty*, (Hart Publishing, Oxford, 1999), p. 271, at p. 281.

55. See Chapter V.2 and the results of the Noordwijk summit, *supra* n° 34.

list of intervention areas in Art. 63.1-2 TEC was exhaustive and that the Council was supposed to legislate in these areas during the five-year interim period. Therefore, it was not clear what areas would be left to legislate on with the participation of the EP. Presumably, all the fundamental principles would have already been set unanimously by the Council, possibly with the exception of burden-sharing issues that were not subject to the five-year rule. Eventually, it could be foreseen that only further implementation provisions would have been decided by codecision.

There were two exceptions to the above-mentioned decision-making procedures and timetables. The first one concerned the common visa list and the uniform visa format, which would be subject to qualified majority since the entry into force of the Treaty, on proposal of the Commission and after consulting the EP. This exception was obviously necessary, since these areas were already subjected to such procedures by the previous EC Treaty. Finally, the second exception regarded national procedures and conditions for issuing visas and rules on a uniform visa, which after five years from entry into force should be subject to the codecision procedure. The ratio of this decision probably lay in the importance that visa issues assumed in the context of the safety of the EC 'internal space', hence the necessity to reach a wider consensus.

The scope of the ECJ's jurisdiction was regulated by Art. 68 TEC. The attribution of jurisdictional powers to the ECJ in this field represented a major reform, given the strenuous opposition the idea had faced in the past.[56] All the areas covered by Title IV were subject to ECJ jurisdiction. However, the scope of Art. 234 EC was restricted and allowed only national Courts of last instance or tribunals to request an ECJ preliminary ruling on the validity or interpretation of acts of the institutions based on this Title. This restriction of the ability of a party to question the validity of Community acts had far reaching implications for the protection of fundamental rights within the Community jurisdiction, as it went against the principle of effective remedies guaranteed by Art. 13 of the ECHR. Moreover, the effects of this restriction were further compounded by the probable inability of individuals to bring annulment actions in this field. Finally, the established *Foto-Frost* jurisprudence on the ability of national Courts to suspend the validity of national measures implementing community law was also seriously jeopardised by the inability of lower Courts to request a preliminary ruling.[57]

A multitude of reasons laid behind this restriction of the scope of Art. 234

---

56. See Chapters II.3.C and III.1. Every effort was made during the Dutch EU Presidency to reach an agreement on this subject, but some national resistance proved too great to be overcome (see Council Press release 1605/97). How this national resistance was finally overcome in the IGC negotiations – given that the issue was not even on the official agenda – remained unclear.

57. *Firma Foto-Frost* v. *HZA Lubeck Ost*, case 314/85 [1987] ECR 4199. For these comments, see P. Eeckhout, 'The European Court of Justice and the 'area of freedom, security and justice': challenges and problems' in D. O'Keeffe *et alia* (eds), *Liber Amicorum Slynn*,

TEC. Firstly, immigration and asylum appeals represented an enormous caseload for national tribunals. Member States probably feared that this caseload would filter through to the ECJ, further slowing down national procedures at a time when the streamlining of asylum adjudication procedures had become a key Community concern.[58] Secondly, given the particularly sensitive nature of the field, Member States would have been naturally reluctant to allow widespread jurisdictional questioning of their initiatives by all levels of national Courts. Unfortunately, this exception meant that individual rights would have been less effectively protected. Most of time, asylum applicants lacked sufficient resources to pursue their case as far as a Court of last instance.[59]

Whether the ECJ had acquired the competence to judge the compatibility between EC action in the asylum field and other international obligations remained unclear. Art. 63.1 TEC explicitly mentioned the 1951 GC and other related treaties as a parameter for Community action. It provided for EC measures on asylum to be 'in accordance with the 1951 Geneva Convention [...] and other relevant treaties' and therefore appeared to allow the ECJ to interpret the 1951 GC. Moreover, in laying down such a vague definition of the 'other

---

Judicial review in European Union Law (vol. I, Kluwer Law International, The Hague, 2000), p. 153, at pp. 157 *et seq.* As indicated by the Commission (see Chapter VI.2), most future asylum initiatives would take the form of directives and thus not be challengeable. Even in the event of the DC being turned into a regulation, it would be hard to imagine how the stringent criteria of Art. 230 EC could be met by an individual. The ECJ jurisdiction was also further limited by Art. 68.2 TEC. It specifically provided that no national measure or decision taken in connection with the abolition of internal border controls (Art. 62.1 TEC) could be subjected to the ECJ's jurisdiction if it was justified by the maintenance of law and order or the safeguarding of internal security. As H. Labayle, *supra* n° 53, p. 846, pointed out, this exception could make it impossible for the ECJ to apply all its well-developed jurisprudence on the national use of the 'public order clause'. This exception was related to the similar provisions contained in Art. 64 EC which provided, as a general rule, that nothing in Title IV should affect Member States responsibilities' concerning internal law, order and public security.

58. This concern had been reflected in every official working programme of the K.4 Committee and in both the 1991 and 1994 Commissions' Communication on asylum. All these documents invariably referred to the enormous pressure of ever-increasing asylum applications on national adjudication procedures. Consequently, one of the main common aims became ensuring the swift processing of such demands. See also the concern expressed on the point in the Irish Presidency proposal, *supra* n° 16, p. 32, where it was stated that '[t]he large number of cases which come before national Courts in the areas of asylum and immigration suggests that many applications for interpretation of provisions in this area by way of preliminary ruling would be submitted to the ECJ by national Courts at the request of parties involved in such cases. This would lead to a considerable increase in the workload of the Court and delay national proceedings'. Concerns were also raised about the potential inability of the ECJ to face such enormous increase in caseload (see p. Eeckhout, *supra* n° 57, p. 154).

59. See A. Arnull, 'Taming the beast? The Treaty of Amsterdam and the Court of Justice' in D. O'Keeffe and P. Twomey (eds), *supra* n° 54, p. 109, at p. 116.

relevant treaties' it could potentially allow the ECJ even wider freedom of interpretation. This definition could in future be stretched to include, for instance, the 1984 CAT or Art. 3 ECHR. These provisions were often invoked during national asylum adjudication cases to prevent instances of refoulement. The potential for challenging EU action, because it was incompatible with the 1951 GC, was enormous.[60]

According to Art. 68.3 TEC the Council, the Commission and any Member State could request the ECJ to give a ruling on an interpretation issue concerning either the content of this Title or acts of the EC institutions based on this Title. The European Parliament was unfortunately excluded from this list of institutions. It was possibly expected to rely on the services of the Commission to forward its requests for interpretation. However, the exclusion of the EP certainly indicated an uneasiness of the Council to allow increased democratic scrutiny in this field. This was probably due to the EP being seen as the Institution most likely to raise 'delicate' interpretative questions. In future, the EP's inability to demand an interpretative ruling in its own rights might be the subject of a legal challenge. This reluctance of Member States to allow a greater EP role cast a negative shadow on the prospective application of the codecision procedure after the five-year interim period as provided by Art. 67 TEC.[61]

Art. 68.3 echoed similar provisions found in other instruments, but the precise legal force of these interpretative rulings appeared uncertain.[62] One possible reason for its introduction could have been the fact that this area relied on a

---

60. See, for instance, the issue of whether the 1951 GC imposed on Member States an individual obligation to examine asylum applications. The Dutch Council of State took the position that the obligation was to be interpreted as falling upon each individual Member State. Hence, it questioned the very basis of the 1990 Dublin Convention. The question remained of what would happen if the ECJ chose to uphold this interpretation. See also the position of the ECtHR on this point in Chapter V.3.B. On the general issue of fundamental liberties, the ECJ had already affirmed in its case law the need to respect such liberties as embodied in international law texts and in the constitutional traditions of Member States, despite its negative opinion on the ability of the EU to join the ECHR (Opinion 2/94 on the accession of the EC to the European Convention on Human Rights [1996] ECR I-1786). For a review of the jurisprudence of the ECJ in the Human Rights field see Chapter III.1 n° 13. The EU participation in the ECHR had in fact been put on the IGC agenda. The outcome of the IGC negotiations reflected the compromise advocated by the Irish proposal of December 1996. The ECJ was given a special competence to judge over whether Union institutions were respecting the fundamental rights guaranteed by the ECHR (see Art. 6.2 and Art. 46.d Amsterdam TEU). However, the Union was given no specific competence to join the ECHR.

61. Art. 68.3 TEC was left unaltered by the Nice Treaty revision (see Chapter VI.7).

62. Such as the Protocols on the interpretation of the Brussels and Rome Conventions. On this point, see A. Arnull, *supra* n° 59, p. 117. The author also argued that Art. 68.3 was unlikely to be used often, because its frequent use would have defied the purpose of restricting the applicability of Art. 234 TEC. See also S. Peers, *supra*, n° 39, p. 44. On the relative force of such rulings see P. Eeckhout, *supra* n° 57, pp. 157 *et seq.*

number of related Conventions, such as the 1990 DC, the SC and other international instruments of refugee protection. These all lacked a centralised arbitration authority and therefore it would have been natural for the ECJ to fulfil this role. However, it would be difficult to predict how widely used this provision might be in the future, bearing in mind Member States' historic reluctance to submit the 1990 DC to the ECJ's jurisdiction.

V.3.B. The Protocol on asylum for nationals of EU Member States

In addition to the new Title IV TEC, the Amsterdam Treaty introduced another major asylum reform. It consisted of a Protocol that regulated the asylum applications lodged by EU nationals in any EU Member State. The 1967 New York Protocol had specifically removed the old geographical limitation clause on the origin of asylum seekers.[63] The Amsterdam Treaty in practice reintroduced the opposite rule, by radically limiting the ability of EU nationals to lodge an asylum application in another Member State.[64] These provisions were in keeping with previous measures on 'safe third countries' and in some way constituted the logical follow up to the 1992 initiatives.[65]

The issue of granting asylum to EU citizens had been a long-standing problem for Member States. It had caused some very heated diplomatic disputes in the past and as a consequence of one particular instance, the works of the K.4 Committee were brought to a halt for several months during 1995.[66] As a

---

63. The 1951 GC was originally intended to cover only 'refugees coming from Europe'. However, this clause was widely disregarded in the 50s and 60s and formally removed in 1967 (see Chapter I.2).

64. The Protocol also explicitly contradicted the undertaking of Art. 2 DC where it stated that '[t]he Member States reaffirm their obligations under the Geneva Convention, as amended by the New York Protocol, with no geographic restriction of the scope of these instruments [...]'. It might be left to the ECJ to possibly arbitrate on this contradiction under the new provisions of Art. 68.3 EC.

65. See Chapter III.3. These initiatives were based on the presumption that some countries could be assumed to be 'safe' and therefore less likely to generate prospective asylum seekers. Therefore, applicants originating from these countries were to be automatically placed in speedier adjudication channels reserved for 'manifestly unfounded' applications. Countries like Germany had actually embodied their 'safe countries' list in their Constitution: it included all EU countries. All of these elements – 'safe third countries' and 'manifestly unfounded' procedures – were found in the new Protocol. Moreover, the 1995 Resolution on minimum guarantees (Chapter IV.4) had already explicitly stated that there were no foreseeable reasons for EU Members to grant asylum to an EU national.

66. The case concerned two Basque separatists who had fled to Belgium and applied for asylum. Due to their particular constitutional requirements, Belgian Courts had to examine all asylum applications. Therefore, their demand was deemed admissible, even though they were wanted in Spain in connection with terrorist activities. Diplomatic links were severely strained for several months, while Spain blocked all asylum-connected activities in the EU Council for almost six months during 1995. The asylum application of the two Basques was eventually turned down and the men were extradited to Spain. However, a precedent

consequence, the Spanish Government had raised the issue right at the beginning of the IGC negotiations. When, in the latter part of 1996, the IGC focus shifted to the reform of the JHA co-operation, Spain promptly presented a discussion paper aimed at inserting a new asylum clause for EU nationals in the Treaty itself.[67] The heart of the controversy lay in Art. 33 of the 1951 GC, which prohibited the return of asylum seekers to a country where they might have faced persecution. States such as Belgium had a constitutional obligation to examine asylum applications in order to comply with Art. 33 and thereby had already ended up giving involuntary shelter to suspected terrorists.[68] The matter was further complicated by the refusal of certain Member States to accept a specific clause in the Treaty[69] and general political concern on future enlargements. In the end, the Dutch Presidency successfully convinced the Spanish delegation to accept a separate Protocol on the matter by annexing it directly to the EC Treaty.

The Protocol's main justification for restricting the right to asylum of EU nationals rested on the Treaty's new provisions on the respect for Human Rights. These included, first of all, the new ECJ jurisdiction over the conformity of all EU institutions' acts with the ECHR. This new competence followed the already established principle that membership and the respect for the ECHR was a fundamental pre-requisite for obtaining membership of the European Union (Arts 6 and 49 TEU). The new Amsterdam provisions added a suspension mechanism for Member States that were in 'serious and persistent breach' of the fundamental principles on which the EU is based on' (Art. 7 TEU). The new suspension procedure involved both the EP and the Commission in the assessment of this breach.

Drawing on these new Human Rights provisions, the EC Protocol laid down in its single article that Member States were to regard each other as 'safe countries of origin'. Therefore, all asylum applications of EU citizens should be

---

had been created and the issue remained unsolved on the negotiation table. The Basque case should not be viewed as an isolated exception, since, for instance, during the late 70s and early 80s numerous Italian Red Brigades terrorists were granted a sort of 'temporary protection' in France.

67. CONF/3925/96 and, for a further proposal in February 1997, see *Europe*, n° 6923 of 27/2/97. The essence of the Spanish proposal consisted in a modification of Art. 8 Amsterdam TEU to include the impossibility for an EU citizen to seek asylum in another Member State. This amendment was to be an integral part of the new provisions on the Union's respect for fundamental rights.

68. The fact that terrorists were excluded from the GC had never been disputed and a specific European Convention on the repression of terrorism was already in force among EU Member States.

69. Some of these States were traditionally in favour of a broad interpretation of the right to seek asylum, notably Denmark and Austria. Others, such as Ireland, had particularly sensitive terrorist problems, or were particularly concerned about their ability to repress terrorist activities (Greece). See H. Labayle, *supra* n° 53, p. 853.

declared inadmissible for processing. Only two exceptions to the general principle were envisaged. The first one concerned nationals of countries found in persistent breach of fundamental principles or against whom the procedure for persistent breach had been initiated. The second exception concerned the possibility of a Member State unilaterally accepting an application for consideration.[70] The Council had to be immediately informed of the unilateral decision. In these cases, the application should have been presumed to be 'manifestly unfounded'. However, it was specifically stated that this presumption would not have affected the decision-making power of the State concerned. Thus, the possible impact of this Protocol was considerably reduced. Moreover, a Belgian Declaration annexed to the Amsterdam Treaty underlined that Belgium considered it a 'Convention obligation' under the 1951 GC to examine all asylum applications, but that the Belgian Government would have nonetheless endeavoured to apply the Protocol.

The reaction to this Protocol by other concerned organisations was rather hostile. The UNHCR stated that the new Protocol went against the 1951 GC as it denied 'unqualified access to asylum'.[71] In their eyes, the European Union had set a dangerous new precedent that could be followed by countries with a less clean Human Rights record. The same view was shared by Amnesty, which pointed out that on the eve of enlargement the EU, should have been more careful about setting dangerous examples for the future.[72] It called for more Member States to follow the Belgian example and retain control over their discretion to examine an asylum application.

The relation between this Protocol and the 1967 New York Protocol relating to the status of refugees also remained unclear. The introduction of a 'geographical restriction clause' clearly appeared to run contrary to the spirit of the 1967 agreement. In this respect, an uneasiness about this contradiction was already apparent in the wording of the EC Protocol's preamble. Instead of inserting a standard reference to the 1951 GC,[73] Member States simply preferred to assert that the Protocol respected 'the finality and the objectives' of the GC. No mention was made of the 1967 New York Protocol. By virtue of its new competence in the asylum field, the ECJ could be called upon in the future to give an interpretative ruling on this apparent contradiction.

---

70. This exception had to be introduced because of the constitutional requirements of countries such as Belgium or the Netherlands. It was similar in some ways to the exception clause contained both in Schengen and in the 1990 DC. It concerned the possibility for a Member State to consider an asylum application despite not to being responsible for it under the terms of the Convention (see Chapter II.3).

71. See *Europe*, n° 7001 of 23–24/6/97, pp. 4–5. In this context the UNHCR also reiterated the same reservations and objections it had expressed a few years earlier vis à vis the 1992 initiatives (see III.2).

72. See *Europe*, n° 7006 of 1/7/97, p. 4.

73. By then, such a reference had become standard in the preambles of all EU asylum initiatives, as well as in the new Art. 63 TEC.

V.4. FLEXIBILITY AND CLOSER CO-OPERATION MEASURES:
     THEIR IMPACT ON THE ASYLUM FIELD

The need to accommodate Member States' different paces of integration had been a constant factor in the life of the European Community.[74] Sometimes accommodating the wish for further integration within the context of the Union proved impossible. Hence, the resorting to alternative frameworks, as in the Schengen case. With the Maastricht Treaty, the British 'opt-out' from the Social Protocol and the EMU became typical examples of *á la carte* participation. As several Member States opposed further integration, 'flexibility' quickly became a fundamental keyword in the new IGC negotiations. However, the new 'flexibility' concept did not have an easy birth. Members receiving cohesion funds were suspicious of closer co-operation and feared losing political clout in the decision-making process. Countries like the UK or Denmark were in favour of specific exceptions for themselves but not of a general 'closer co-operation clause'. They feared either being marginalised by their eventual refusals to participate or being pushed to participate anyway simply because some measures had proved to be extremely successful. Sweden shared these concerns.[75]

The idea of closer co-operation was first mentioned in the Franco-German initiative of December 1995 and it was further developed in the Dublin Report. The Commission also seized on it and presented a detailed paper at the beginning of 1997.[76] At the same time, an Italian proposal put forward the positions of smaller Member States.[77] The concerns of reticent countries were finally overcome by the even greater fear that experiences such as Schengen could eventually become the norm. In such instances, no controls could be applied to these types of 'closer co-operation'. Moreover, the prospect of the forthcoming enlargement of the Union also played a relevant part. The existing Member States viewed closer co-operation as the only viable option to break and eventual future deadlock due to the excessive heterogeneity of the Union. Out of necessity, the idea that some Member States should be allowed to move forward within the EU framework became the preferred option. Hence, by March 1997, the essential conditions for closer co-operation had been finally agreed upon. First of all, there were to be some general provisions regulating the possibility that a certain number of Member States could achieve closer co-operation within either the First or the Third Pillar framework. Secondly, some instances of 'predetermined flexibility' were inserted into the Treaty by means of different Protocols. These

---

74. Early examples of different integration speeds could be found in the temporary derogation clauses included in several accession treaties, or in Art. 100a.4 introduced by the Single European Act. For these examples see H. Kortenberg, 'Closer co-operation in the Treaty of Amsterdam' (1998) 35 CML Rev., p. 833, at pp. 833–34.

75. See H. Kortenberg, *supra* n° 74, at pp. 844–45.

76. CONF/3805/97.

77. *Europe*, n° 6894 of 17/1/97, pp. 2–3.

Protocols regulated the position of the UK, Denmark and Ireland, as well as the incorporation of the Schengen framework into the Union.

V.4.A. The general provisions on 'closer co-operation'

Title VII TEU laid down the general principles that governed closer co-operation. Further provisions specifically regulated closer co-operation either within the EC framework (Art. 11 TEC), or in the Third Pillar (Art. 40 TEU).[78] All these provisions concerned Member States that wished to establish closer co-operation between themselves by making use of the institutions, procedures and mechanisms laid down by the Treaties. Obviously, the conditions between the two Pillars varied – the EC provisions being much stricter – but the under-lying principles were broadly the same. Art. 43 TEU set out the general condi-tions for recourse to closer co-operation. In principle, it had to aim at furthering a Union objective. In this respect, it could not exceed the competence of the Union or of the Community.[79] A majority of Member States was required to begin such co-operation and it could only be employed as a last resort measure.[80] It was required to maintain respect for the Union framework, principles and *acquis communautaire*. It had to be open to subsequent accession by other Member States and it was required not to prejudice the interests of those that were not part of it. On the other hand, non-participating States had a duty not to impede the co-operation being undertaken.

Art. 44 TEU laid down the essential operational rules, to be supplemented by the more specific provisions of Art. 11 TEC and 40 TEU. Closer co-operation measures had to be adopted in conformity with the relevant Treaty provisions that formed their legal base. Non-participating Members could be present during deliberations to deliver their opinions.[81] The voting method would have to be adapted to the number of participating States.[82] Administrative costs had to be borne by the Community budget, whereas operating costs only had to be borne by the participating States. According to Art. 45 the EP had to be regularly informed on the progress of closer co-operation.

Art. 11 TEC laid down the specific conditions for closer co-operation within

---

78. There were no provisions for closer co-operation in the Second Pillar, except for Art. 23 TEU, the so-called 'constructive abstention'. See, G. Gaja, 'How flexible is flexibility under the Amsterdam Treaty?' (1998) 35 CML Rev., p. 855, at pp. 857–58.
79. In other words, it could not constitute a disguised way to amend the Treaty.
80. The preoccupation of smaller Member States being that this provision could have been used to support a very elitist group of countries. However, the requirement of a 'majority' of Member States was in fact lower than the 'qualified majority' required to authorise closer co-operation.
81. This would have presumably facilitated their participation at a later stage.
82. However, the voting rules for the EP were not amended. The idea was explored during the IGC, but dropped when the EP expressed its firm opposition to the idea. See G. Gaja, *supra* n° 78, p. 866.

the Community framework. It therefore also applied to the new provisions in Title IV TEC. Closer co-operation did not have to concern fields of exclusive competence of the Community. It did not have to affect Community policies, actions or programmes. It had to remain within the Community areas of competence and not constitute an obstacle or a discrimination to trade, or a distortion of competition. The field of European citizenship was excluded from any possible closer co-operation due to its delicate nature and such co-operation could not discriminate between nationals of Member States. The co-operation had to be authorised by the Council deciding by qualified majority[83] on a proposal of the Commission after consulting the EP. The Commission's exclusive right of initiative meant that it could in practice block any closer co-operation effort. A national veto 'Luxembourg style' was astonishingly reintroduced to counterbalance the qualified majority rule. It allowed a Member State to block the vote on an authorisation for 'important and stated reasons of national policy'. In such cases the Council could, by qualified majority, demand the intervention of the European Council.[84] The ECJ was given jurisdiction to review the conditions for resorting to closer co-operation both under Title VII TEU and Art. 11 TEC.[85] The extent to which the Court would be competent to judge on the national justifications for the imposition of a veto remained unclear.[86] If any Member State intended to join this co-operation agreement at a later stage, it had to notify the Commission. The latter had the exclusive power to decide on the authorisation[87] and any eventual conditions to be satisfied.[88]

Several issues would have had the potential to hamper the future use of the closer co-operation measures within the Community framework. To begin with, Member States willing to proceed with further integration could have perceived

---

83. Earlier proposals had suggested a unanimity clause, but it quickly became clear that it would have paralysed most co-operation efforts.

84. This new veto, however, differed from the old Luxembourg one because the 'reasons of national policy' had to be explained. Moreover, the European Council could be asked to arbitrate on the matter. Therefore, the Member State imposing the veto would have to be prepared to argue its reasons in public.

85. Thus, an action for annulment could have been brought under Art. 230 TEC against a decision by the Council to authorise a closer co-operation measure because the criteria of Art. 43 TEU or Art. 11 TEC had not been met.

86. On this point, see the remarks in favour of such competence by V. Constantinesco, 'Les clauses de "coopération renforcée"- Le protocole sur l'application des principes de subsidiarité et de proportionnalité' (1997) 33 *Revue Trimestrelle de Droit Européen*, p. 751, at p. 762. Against this interpretation see G. Gaja, *supra* n° 78, at pp. 864–65.

87. In this event, the Commission would only have to notify its opinion to the Council and would be subsequently free to decide on the authorisation. It appeared peculiar that this power of decision should have rested exclusively with the Commission given that the initial authorisation decision had to be taken by the Council.

88. The conditions for closer co-operation laid down in the Third Pillar varied slightly due to the different nature of the intergovernmental framework. According to Art. 40 TEU, two requirements had to be met for this co-operation to be endorsed: firstly, they had to

other Members as inadequate and therefore would not have liked the obligation to keep the co-operation open to all. Equally, the requirement to involve a majority of Member States might have acted as a disincentive. Most importantly, both the Commission and each Member State had some sort of veto power over the whole process. Finally, the knowledge that closer co-operation would have inevitably entailed a complex 'fragmentation' of the Community legal framework would also be a factor against its deployment.[89]

The potential application of closer co-operation measures in the asylum field presented particular complications. Art. 63 TEC did not give the Community a general competence on asylum matters, but only a specific one in the fields explicitly listed by the article. The countries with the greatest reservations in these fields had already obtained special opt-outs by way of separate Protocols.[90] The rest of the Member States were also under the obligation to undertake initiatives in these fields within a five-year time limit.[91] Therefore, it is difficult to foresee a great recourse to closer co-operation, other than possibly for the more controversial issue of burden-sharing. The prospective of a more hetero-geneous Community after the next wave of enlargement could potentially lead to closer co-operation becoming more relevant. However, by the time of the next enlargement most of the asylum fields listed in Art. 63 TEC will be at least partially harmonised. In Conclusion, further co-operation in the asylum field appears more likely to happen outside the remit of Art. 11 TEC. This would mainly be due to the wish to proceed with harmonising asylum matters outside the Community competence.

V.4.B. The Protocols on the position of the United Kingdom, Ireland and Denmark and the Schengen Protocol

Apart from the general clauses on closer co-operation, the Amsterdam Treaty contained several examples of specific *á la carte* participation. In relation to the general regime introduced by Title VII TEU and Art. 11 TEC, those examples could have been defined as instances of 'predetermined flexibility'. To overcome national resistance over some of the Union's new areas of competence, the

---

respect the powers of the EC and the objectives of Title VII TEU; secondly, they had to aim at a faster development of the Union into an area of freedom, security and justice. The Council had to authorise such co-operation by qualified majority after consulting the Commission and informing the EP. The same national veto possibility as in Art. 11 TEC was envisaged, but – most exceptionally for the intergovernmental framework – it was also subjected to the arbitration of the ECJ. As in the EC Treaty similar rules were laid down for Member States wanting to subsequently join such co-operation, the difference being that the decision power rested firmly in the hands of the Council.

89. For an in-depth analysis of these reasons, see G. Gaja, *supra* n° 78, at pp. 858–67.

90. These countries were the UK, Denmark and Ireland. For these Protocols – which consti-tuted a sort of 'predetermined flexibility'- see Chapter V.4.B.

91. The only exception was Art. 63.2.b TEC, which concerned burden-sharing measures.

participation of the United Kingdom, Ireland and Denmark to the Amsterdam Treaty was regulated by a series of special Protocols. These Protocols concerned mainly the interpretation of the old Art. 7a EC, the incorporation of the Schengen framework into the Union and the participation of these countries in the new Title IV TEC. In so far as border checks were concerned, the United Kingdom and Ireland were allowed to retain their border controls on the European Economic Area and third country nationals.[92] In derogation to the application of old Art. 7a EC, the other Member States of the European Union were allowed to carry out border controls on travellers coming from the United Kingdom or Ireland.

Special Protocols also regulated the participation of the United Kingdom, Ireland and Denmark with regard to Title IV TEC. The Protocol on the position of the United Kingdom and Ireland stipulated that neither country would in principle take part in the new Title IV EC measures.[93] However, both countries had the option at any time to participate in any of the measures adopted under this Title if the matters being decided were of interest to them. This position could therefore be summarised as a total 'opt-out' with selective 'opt-in' possibilities. The two countries had to notify their wish to take part in the adoption and application of a Title IV TEC measure within three months of a proposal for action having been presented to the Council. Their intention to participate, however, could not be used to block the adoption of a decision. If a decisional compromise could not be found after a 'reasonable period of time' (Art. 3.a UK-Ireland Protocol), the Council could adopt the decision without their participation. In this event they would not be bound by such decision. According to the Protocol, Ireland had the further opportunity of completely renouncing this Protocol and taking part fully in Title IV TEC.[94] In the event of the UK or

---

92. Protocol on the application of certain aspects of Art. 7a of the EC Treaty to the United Kingdom and to Ireland. The United Kingdom and Ireland presented the Protocol together because of their mutual special travel arrangements. However, the position of Ireland was slightly different. During the negotiations, Ireland had made it clear that it did not oppose the abolition of internal border controls and that it supported the majority interpretation of Art. 7a EC. Nonetheless, due to its historical Common Travel Area agreement with the UK it consented to maintaining its border controls. This difference in position between the UK and Ireland was obvious in the wording of Art. 2 of the Protocol. There it was stated that Ireland would only maintain such controls as long as the Common Travel Area agreement was in place. No such clause was applicable to the British position. It could be argued that by requesting a separate regime on border-crossing, the United Kingdom implicitly accepted – after 10 years of opposition – that the Commission's interpretation of Art. 7a was actually correct.

93. Therefore, in principle no measure adopted under this Title, no decision of the ECJ on these matters and no international agreement agreed on this basis would have been applicable to them. The voting methods of the Council were to be amended accordingly.

94. Once again the position of Ireland was different from the UK, but inevitably conditioned by the Common Travel Area Agreement. Therefore, Ireland always reserved for itself the possibility of abandoning the Protocol's provisions in the event of the travel agreement

Ireland wishing to join a measure already adopted under Title IV TEC, the procedure laid down in Art. 11 TEC would be applicable. The Commission would have to issue an opinion on their request to the Council and would subsequently be free to decide on whether to authorise the request and on any other specific requirement to be met by the applicant countries.[95] No specific exception in the total 'opt-out' allowed by the Protocol was made for the provisions of the old Art. 100c EC concerning the common visa list and the unified visa format. Hence, the UK and Ireland retained the choice of whether to participate in any future amendments of the provisions that were already adopted under the old Art. 100c.[96]

The position of Denmark according to its Protocol could be defined as a complete 'opt-out',[97] without any possibility of 'opt-in', except in the case of measures based on the Schengen *acquis*. Unlike the UK and Ireland, an express exception was made for the provisions relating to the common visa list and the uniform format for visas (old Art. 100c EC), which remained within the remit of the Community competence. However, the Danish position was further complicated by its membership of Schengen and its inability to accept its incorporation into the Union's framework. As in the Irish case, Denmark also had the opportunity to renounce its 'opt-out' agreement and take part fully in Title IV TEC.[98]

The integration of Schengen into the TEU was eventually achieved by a separate Protocol. The issue had been discussed since the beginning of the IGC negotiations and various solutions had been put forward. The SC had always presented itself as a useful 'laboratory' for further EU co-operation and therefore

---

with the UK coming to an end. Ireland made it clear during the negotiations that it wished to join all EU asylum initiatives and so far has done so.

95. Thus, an instance of 'predetermined' flexibility, such as this Protocol, effectively came to rely on the more general Treaty clauses on closer co-operation.

96. For these measures, see Chapter IV.2. This Protocol therefore reverted a Community competence back to the British and Irish national prerogatives. The 'clawing back' of such competence could be explained by the slightly different wording employed by Art. 62.1.b.i TEC, as it referred to both 'negative' and 'positive' visa lists, whereas Art. 100c EC made no such distinction. The Commission had argued that the wording of Art. 100c implicitly referred to the possibility of drawing up two lists, but the UK had never accepted such an interpretation. However, even if this explanation for the 'clawing back' of the visa list competence had been correct, the British and Irish governments still regained the competence on the uniform visa format (Art. 62.1.b.iii TEC), whose wording had remained unaltered from Art. 100c EC.

97. It should be recalled that, due to its particular constitutional arrangements, Denmark had particular difficulties in participating in the Maastricht provisions. After one unsuccessful national referendum to ratify the Treaty, Denmark obtained considerable concessions on its participation with regard to the Third Pillar (see Edinburgh summit Council Press Release 1867/92).

98. Denmark also had a further 'opt-out' clause from the common defence arrangements laid down by Art. 13.1 and Art. 17 Amsterdam TEU.

its incorporation into the TEU did not present any particular ideological problems. However, Schengen was also undeniably an alternative forum created to escape the institutional and democratic constraints of the Union, a way to achieve consensus without the traditional opposition of some EU Member States. By being outside the Union's fold, Schengen contradicted the very essence of the new rules on institutionalised flexibility. It thus needed to be brought into the framework of the Union under a special set of flexibility rules similar to the other national Protocols. Moreover, from a practical point of view, incorporating the successes of Schengen was seen as a way to compensate for the failures of the Third Pillar.

Three solutions had been discussed during the IGC negotiations. The first one consisted of the complete incorporation of Schengen into the EC framework, but a substantial number of Member States (the Nordic new partners, France, Germany and above all Denmark) opposed this option. Integration into the Third Pillar appeared to be the favourite option until the development of the negotiations made it clear that the Schengen domain was going to fall within both the remit of the EC and the intergovernmental framework of the new Treaty. Thus, the third solution was developed, consisting of the idea of a 'progressive' integration of Schengen. The whole Schengen framework was to be first placed within the domain of the Third Pillar. Subsequently, the Council would allocate the relevant legal basis to each of the Schengen provisions, deciding whether they belonged to the First or Third Pillars. The summit of Noordwijk finally laid down the principles for the incorporation of Schengen along these progressive lines in a separate Protocol.

The Protocol integrating the Schengen *acquis* into the framework of the European Union was explicitly based on the new provisions on closer co-operation. Therefore, formal permission was granted to Schengen Members to establish closer co-operation among themselves within the scope of the Schengen *acquis*.[99] The Council was charged, after the entry into force of the new Treaty, to replace the Executive Committee and to decide by unanimity vote the legal base of each of the Schengen provisions. Until no formal vote was taken, all Schengen provisions were deemed to be based on Title VI TEU.[100]

---

99. The *acquis* was defined as the 1985 Schengen Agreement, the 1990 SC, all the Accession Protocols and all the Decisions and Declarations adopted by the Executive Committee.

100. Presumably, the ECJ would exercise its jurisdiction in accordance with the chosen legal base of the provisions. According to Art. 35.6 Amsterdam TEU it could also have arbitrated over the choice of the legal base itself. In any case, it could not exert its jurisdiction on any measure concerning the safeguarding of public order and of internal security. This exclusion clause was much broader than the one of the new Art. 68.2 EC because it was not limited only to the measures concerning the crossing of national borders. Certain Member States, notably France, attached great importance to the 'safeguarding measures' provided by the Schengen framework (see, for instance, the French dispute with the Netherlands over the so-called 'drugs-tourism') and strenuously refused any jurisdictional control over such clauses.

Finally, the acceptance of the Schengen *acquis* would have constituted a necessary prerequisite for any future candidate for accession to the EU. This provision appeared particularly iniquitous given that three Member States had been granted important exceptions in this context.

Specific provisions covered the participation of non-Schengen Member States, such as the UK and Ireland, as well as Denmark. Although a member of Schengen, a specific exception had to be made for the latter. Due to its particular constitutional requirements – introduced to allow the Maastricht ratification process – Denmark could not allow any JHA co-operation outside the intergovernmental framework. Any Council decision to base a Schengen provision on Title IV TEC could not therefore apply to Denmark. Neither could it accept any provision in Title VI TEU introducing a new ECJ jurisdictional competence. Therefore, Art. 3 of the Schengen Protocol stated that Denmark was to maintain its Schengen obligations purely within an intergovernmental framework. Art. 5 of the Protocol on the position of Denmark allowed the country six months after the adoption of a measure building upon the Schengen *acquis* to decide whether to accept it and implement it.[101] A positive Danish decision in this case would have created an obligation 'under international law' between the States participating in the decision. In the event of Denmark deciding against the implementation of the measure, the other EU Members would have considered 'appropriate measures to be taken' (Art. 5.2).

According to the Schengen Protocol, the United Kingdom and Ireland could at any time request to participate partly or in full in the provisions of the Schengen *acquis*.[102] The Council was to decide on these requests by unanimity vote with the participation of the requesting Member.[103] This meant that the Protocol conferred no explicit 'right' to the two countries to opt-in the Schengen provisions. This was in strong contradiction to the spirit of the closer co-operation provisions. At the Amsterdam Council, the UK and Ireland disputed the fact that the unanimity rule had been previously agreed. However, it

---

101. The choice of legal base would therefore have enormous implications for Danish participation. Given the overlap between many of the provisions of the Schengen *acquis* with the new Title IV TEC (for instance, in visa policy, border controls, immigration etc.), basing a measure on the Schengen *acquis* would give Denmark the option to participate. Otherwise, basing it on Title IV TEC would totally preclude Danish participation. On the other hand, the choice to base a measure on the Schengen *acquis* could have had serious implications for the UK or Ireland, since their participation in it was subject to the unanimous assent of the Schengen Members and not just a Commission authorisation (see further).

102. This constituted an exception to the general closer co-operation procedures as they only envisaged full participation of the Member State wishing to access the co-operation agreement.

103. Again, another difference from the 'ordinary' regime, where the decision was to be taken by majority vote and with no participation of the acceding Member State. Furthermore, there was no provision for the opinion of the Commission or consultation of the EP.

appeared that the unanimity clause had been inserted at the express request of Spain, still locked in a dispute with the UK over Gibraltar.[104] After strongly voicing their concerns, a Declaration was added in which the Schengen Members asserted that they would do their best to allow British and Irish participation in the Schengen *acquis* and that the opinion of the Commission would be sought prior to a decision of the Council.[105]

The integration of Schengen into the TEU posed numerous problems, the biggest being the determination of what constituted the Schengen *acquis*. Given the secretive nature of most of the Executive Committee Decisions, by the time of the signature of the Amsterdam Treaty in October 1997, the extent of the *acquis* was still not clear.[106] This was clearly incompatible with the new commitment to transparency in the Amsterdam Treaty. By the end of May 1999, 20 days after the entry into force of the Amsterdam Treaty, the Council adopted a Decision assigning the legal basis of all the Schengen *acquis* provisions.[107] No provision was actually based on Art. 63 TEC,[108] so the impact on asylum co-operation was actually minimal. However, the provisions on visa policy and the Schengen Information System (SIS) were all capable of having potential transversal effects on refugee rights in the future.

Overall, the insertion into the Treaty of a complicated web of general closer co-operation clauses, predetermined flexibility in the shape of national opt-outs and opt-ins and the integration of the Schengen framework were likely to cause a high degree of legal uncertainty. Arbitration by the ECJ - where at all possible – would therefore imply the careful navigation of an intricate maze of different sets of *acquis* applicable to different Member States. The potential for the fragmentation of the Community's legal order could therefore be enormous. In this respect, many of the advantages acquired by the communitarisation of the asylum competence could be lost.

V.5. CONCLUDING REMARKS

The IGC negotiations began with a brutally frank analysis of the institutional and operational shortcomings of the past Third Pillar asylum co-operation.

---

104. See *Europe*, n° 7014, of 11/7/97, p. 2.
105. Declaration 45 on Article 4 of the Protocol integrating the Schengen acquis into the framework of the European Union.
106. Some national ratifications actually took place without the *acquis* having been determined. On the concerns over the secrecy of Schengen Decisions, see House of Lords, Select Committee on the European Communities, *Incorporating the Schengen acquis into the European Union*, 31st Report, session 1997–98, HL Paper 139, at pp. 30–31.
107. This actually involved the agreement by unanimity of the legal base for over 3,000 pages of *acquis*. The process was so strenuous that the new term 'ventilation' was actually coined; see J. Monar, 'Justice and Home Affairs in the Treaty of Amsterdam: reform at the price of fragmentation' (1998) 23 EL Rev., p. 320, at p. 333.
108. This was actually due to the fact that the 1990 DC had already substituted all the Schengen asylum provisions contained in Chapter VII of the Convention. (Bonn Protocol of 26/4/94, see Chapter II.4 n° 101; and also House of Lords, *supra* n° 106, at p. 32).

Lack of transparency, of democratic accountability and of judicial control, as well as a limited role for the Commission, constituted the main institutional problems. On the operational side, the lack of efficient instruments and an overly complex decision-making process severely hampered progress in the asylum field. The scope of national responses to these issue spanned from the full transfer of competence to the Community Pillar to a retaining of the intergovernmental framework with a few operational improvements. Countries like Denmark were bound to their irremovable positions by their past Maastricht commitments. Others, like Germany, were prevented from supporting full communitarisation by their internal federal arrangements. Finally, countries like the UK feared that any progress might hamper their ability to retain national border controls. Eventually, the looming prospect of a considerable future enlargement of the Union made the necessity for reform an unavoidable imperative.

The progress in the asylum co-operation field achieved at Amsterdam was by any standards exceptional. The transfer of the asylum competence to the Community Pillar was an event of historic proportions, which a mere five years earlier would have been unthinkable. In this respect, the heavily criticised Maastricht asylum provisions were vindicated as a necessary stepping stone for further evolution. Communitarisation meant that past institutional problems were considerably diminished. Democratic accountability, judicial control, the rule of Community law, a legitimate role for the Commission and principles on openness and transparency all applied now to the new asylum provisions. From an operational point of view, Community legislative instruments represented a healthy antidote to previous ineffective action.

However, the previous national resistance to a full transfer of the asylum competence led to some important – and potentially very disruptive – exceptions being introduced into Title IV TEC. This meant, for instance, that the Community was not given a general competence on asylum, but rather an 'exhaustive' list of intervention fields. A five-year transitional period had to be introduced in order to 'smooth' Member States into the new regime. During this period, the EP had only consultation rights, and the power of initiative of the Commission was hindered both by the Council's unanimity requirements and the Member States' concurrent right of initiative. Title IV TEC contained some in-built evolution mechanisms such as the possibility of extending the use of the codecision procedure after the transitional period, subject to a unanimity vote. However, whereas in the Commission's case its sole power of initiative was guaranteed after a five-year spell, the EP still had to depend on the uncertain outcome of a unanimity vote. Moreover, in the event of the Council being unable to reach a unanimous consensus on codecision, no provision was made for at least a shift to qualified majority voting. Thus, the right of initiative of the Commission could be voided of its significance indefinitely.

Special rules of judicial control were introduced for Title IV TEC. Only national Courts of last instance were given the right to demand a preliminary ruling, but such a demand was mandatory. On the positive side, the Court was given further powers of interpretation (Art. 68.3), but the EP was specifically excluded from this provision. The possibility of subjecting the compatibility of Title IV TEC provisions with the GC and 'other relevant treaties' (Art. 63.1) to judicial review opened up new avenues for the protection of refugee rights. However, general provisions on the necessity for Member States to safeguard 'the maintenance of law and order' (Art. 64.1) – reminiscent of the old Third Pillar terminology – continued to apply. The jurisdiction of the Court was further limited by the new provisions on closer co-operation and several national Protocols granting different opt-out and opt-in possibilities. This new enhanced flexibility had been the inevitable price for progress in the communitarisation of the asylum field, but the inherent risk of fragmentation of the Community legal order was very high indeed.

Overall, momentous progress was made in the asylum field at Amsterdam. Confirming the slow transition which had taken place in the years following the Maastricht Treaty, new areas of co-operation were introduced that did not specifically relate to the objectives of the Internal Market. Harmonisation of national asylum policies – or at least aspects of them – had finally became an objective in itself. The new Title IV TEC did not lay down any substantive harmonisation principles, but it 'equipped' the Community with the necessary instruments to fulfil its new asylum objective. The contents of such instruments, as well as the final target of such co-operation would have to be defined during the course of the transitional period.

From the refugee protection point of view the potential impact of the new provisions on asylum was of a mixed nature. Communitarisation undoubtedly displayed all the advantages that past intergovernmental co-operation had lacked. Democratic accountability, judicial control and a more independent role for the Commission were certainly key aspects of the development of a fairer refugee policy. The opportunity for the ECJ to rule over the compatibility of EC asylum initiatives with other international refugee obligations had tremendous future potential. The very existence of the special asylum exception agreed for EU nationals might in future be subjected to the review of the Court. Although not comprehensive, the list of asylum fields contained in Art. 63 TEC was in some ways a good start. It was still clearly inspired by a policy of 'access prevention', but it constituted a serious attempt at some much-needed substantive harmonisation. The real problem ahead would once again be the contents and effectiveness of such initiatives.

Among the measures conspicuously missing in Art. 63 TEC were those concerning the national integration of refugees. These could have greatly benefited a fairer European refugee protection. The Title IV TEC restriction of the scope of Art. 234 TEC could also have a negative impact on the majority of asylum seekers who might not be able to pursue their case all the way to a Court of last instance. Likewise, the inability of the EP to raise interpretative questions under Art. 68.3 TEC deprived asylum seekers in Europe of the help of one of their most outspoken supporters. Given the Commission's poor past record, one could only hope that an increased level of independence would lead it to raise 'unpopular' interpretative questions under Art. 68.3. Finally, real democratic accountability and the abandonment of the 'culture of secrecy' so cherished by Schengen Members could only take place if in the future the Council renounced its unanimous decision-making in favour of codecision. Therefore, the five-year interim period envisaged by the Amsterdam Treaty would prove to be of pivotal importance.

6 After Amsterdam: Towards an EU Asylum Policy?

VI.1. THE AUSTRIAN STRATEGY PAPER ON MIGRATION AND ASYLUM POLICY

The asylum provisions of the Amsterdam Treaty were hailed as a new dawn in the building of a proper EU asylum policy. The ratification of the new Treaty was completed in barely two years,[1] without the widespread opposition the Maastricht Treaty had faced a few years earlier. The new Art. 63 TEC laid down the specific fields on which Community action on asylum should focus and gave a precise timetable to realise such initiatives, namely a five year span.[2] The article did not, however, establish an order of priorities in the field and the development of a new work-programme quickly became imperative.[3]

Despite the draconian Treaty deadline, refugee issues were brought back into the EU limelight only in the second half of 1998 during the Austrian Presidency. The Austrian Government made it clear from the very beginning that asylum and immigration matters were to take a top priority in their Presidency agenda. Different reasons might have motivated their determination to pursue these matters and guarantee tangible progress. Austria and Germany had been the countries most affected by the Bosnian crisis of the early 90s. Their geographical proximity to the Former Republic of Yugoslavia inevitably made them the natural countries of first reception for refugees fleeing the Balkan civil wars. Together, both countries had hosted more than a half a million Bosnian refugees. They had also been deeply affected by the criticism and opposition that surrounded their refugee repatriation programmes to Bosnia once the conflict was over.[4] EU action on this issue had been slow and generally there had been no

---

1. The Amsterdam Treaty came into force in May 1999.
2. With the very notable exception of initiatives on 'burden-sharing' (Art. 63.2.b), which were specifically excluded from the five-year timetable. The lack of consensus on this matter continued to slow down further progress (see further Chapter VI.3)
3. The Cardiff European Council of June 1998 formally acknowledged this need and asked the Commission and the Council to draw up an Action Plan to be presented at the Vienna Summit the following December.
4. In December 1995, when the Dayton peace agreement was signed, there were circa 350,000 Bosnians in Germany. By the end of 1998, 200,000 had returned as part of an 'incentive' programme run by the German authorities. However, 10 to 20 per cent of them failed to be convinced by the programme and had to be forcibly deported (see 'Germany: CSU takes a hard line', *Migration News Sheet*, 5/8/98). On the repatriation of Bosnians from the Union, see M. Walsh *et alia*, 'Repatriation from the European Union to Bosnia-Herzegovina: the role of information' in B. Black and K. Koser, *The end of the refugee cycle? Refugee repatriation and reconstruction* (Berghan Books, New York, 1999), p. 110.

agreement on any workable solution.[5] Dramatic reports in early 1998[6] of the rapid deterioration of the internal situation in the Serb province of Kosovo would naturally have led the Austrians to fear a repetition of the Bosnian crisis.

The Austrian sense of urgency in these matters was further heightened by the establishment of a true internal border-free area within the framework of the SC, whose provisions were now to be incorporated into the new Amsterdam Treaty. In their view, the absence of border controls facilitated the movement of illegal immigrants/refugees across Europe without necessarily penalising the countries responsible for the initial illegal crossing into the Schengen area.[7] The Austrians were further encouraged to broaden their scope of action by the fact that their Presidency was to be followed by the German one, Germany being a country that notably shared their concerns.

The Austrians began to approach these matters by formulating a 'Strategy Paper on migration and asylum policy' that was secretly distributed to Member States during the first meeting of the K.4 Committee in the summer of 1998. By the following September, the document had been leaked by an Austrian newspaper, causing extreme alarm amongst Human Rights experts across Europe. The intense criticism that surrounded the paper – it was never intended for public consumption – caused several Member States to officially distance themselves

---

5. The two main initiatives relating to persons 'displaced' as a result of internal civil wars were adopted in 1995 and 1996, well after the Bosnian crisis was over. These measures on principles of 'burden-sharing' and emergency mechanisms to deal with 'burden-sharing' were mainly intended to co-ordinate EU action in future emergencies (see 'Council Resolution of 25/9/95 on burden-sharing with regard to the admission and residence of displaced persons on a temporary basis', OJ 1995 C262/1, and 'Council Resolution of 4/3/96 on an alert and emergency procedure for burden-sharing with regard to the admission and residence of displaced persons on a temporary basis', OJ 1996 L63/10). The Austrians and the Germans were well aware of the shortcomings of such instruments, as amply demonstrated by the Kosovo crisis. For an analysis of these measures see Chapter IV.6, for their failure to operate during the Kosovo crisis, see further in Chapter VI.3.

6. See, for instance, the ECRE Report of June 1998 on *The situation of refugees from Kosovo*. The report stressed that the 'large scale movements of war refugees now involved [...] all segments of the population [...] not only Kosovo Albanians [...] but also Kosovo Serbs, Montenegrins, Roma and Muslim Slavs. The vast majority of refugees have fled to Northern Albania and Montenegro, with an even larger number of internally displaced within Kosovo' (p. 1).

7. The hundreds of thousands of Kurdish refugees settled in Germany and Austria were a perfect case in point. Their main ports of entry into the Schengen area were generally Greece or Italy, who were effectively unable to efficiently patrol their extensive shorelines. However, the latter were mainly 'transit' countries crossed in order to reach the above-mentioned large Kurdish communities settled in Germany or Austria. The Austrian Presidency made very forceful use of this example in its Strategy Paper (see later) in order to argue for a sweeping reform of States' responsibility for allocation and of external border control practices.

from the Austrian perspective and the Presidency was eventually obliged to withdraw it and completely reformulate its position.[8]

The main aim of this Strategy Paper was to summarise the current status of past EU asylum initiatives and, in the light of the new Amsterdam provisions, to define a path for future developments. The choice of title indicated an intention to treat refugee issues within the broader framework of migratory problems, but only once, towards the end of this very lengthy proposal, did the authors acknowledge that there should be 'a clear analytical distinction between the accepted legal concepts of asylum and immigration'.[9] Throughout the proposal, the two terms were used interchangeably, with a marked predominance of the words 'immigration/ migration'.[10]

The Austrian Presidency adopted the 1994 Commission Communication on immigration and asylum policies (COM (94)23 fin) as the starting point of its main argument, namely that very few of the asylum (or 'migration') initiatives of the past decade had produced any lasting results. In this respect, the Strategy Paper represented the most scathing critique a Member State had ever dared to put forward of EU asylum and immigration co-operation.[11] It was this willingness to mercilessly expose the inadequacies of past EU asylum initiatives that made this document very important. It would have otherwise been impossible to gain an official insight into the degree of implementation of EU asylum initiatives. The main Commission proposals of 1994 were used as a benchmark

---

8. Of the original proposal, only short extracts and summaries provided by the press were available for analysis. The language was characterised as blunt, the contents as reiterating once again a paranoid vision of a 'Fortress Europe' under assault. The main Austrian idea appeared to be the need for a unilateral rewriting of the GC. In short, it appeared as a clumsy diplomatic disaster. The revised version certainly displayed a more 'politically correct' tone and references to unilateral revisions of the GC had been tactfully dropped. It remained, nonetheless, a very powerful proposal, very different in tone and content from previous EU asylum initiatives.

9. 'Strategy Paper on migration and asylum policy', Council of the European Union, 9809/98 REV 1, Brussels, 29 September 1998, point 51. The order of the wording in the title (migration first, asylum policy last) was clearly hinting at the fact that EU attention had decisively shifted towards migration issues (see later).

10. It could be argued that refugee movements were in fact 'migratory' movements, but only in so far as they both entailed a physical displacement of people from one country to another. Unfortunately, this was not the way the term 'migration' was used in the text. Instead, the three terms 'asylum', 'immigration' and 'migration' were considered in the Strategy Paper to be equivalent from every point of view. This phenomenon raised obvious concerns on the angle chosen by the Austrian Presidency to present these issues.

11. The Strategy Paper had such a poor reception among Member States partly because the latter were certainly not impressed by such a public display of their own shortcomings. In this context it should be remembered that the 'Council Decision on monitoring the implementation of instruments adopted concerning asylum', of 26/6/97, OJ 1997 L178/6, was itself never fully implemented, arguably because Member States already knew its eventual outcome.

to measure EU progress in the previous four years and the results were far from encouraging. CIREA and CIREFI were assessed as inefficient and incapable of delivering quick or precise answers to policy-related questions. Accurate information on refugee or immigration flows was still impossible to obtain. Numbers of 'manifestly unfounded' asylum applications were unaltered, even if there had been a drop in asylum applications.[12] The 1992 Edinburgh Resolutions had remained largely unimplemented. The DC was displaying serious problems of application, readmission agreements were not working properly, external border controls had not been standardised and therefore were still rather inefficient in certain Member States. Finally, repatriation programmes and expulsion measures were largely ineffective and temporary protection and burden-sharing issues were still waiting for a consensus solution.

Following this desolate appraisal of past EU asylum efforts, the Presidency very bluntly admitted that in the last few years the focus had shifted from asylum questions onto general issues of migration and 'problems of combating facilitator networks and expulsion issues' (point 14). The 1994 Commission advice to employ a common external policy to fight the root causes of migration had also gone unheeded, but in this new context it assumed an even greater importance. Eliminating 'push factors' appeared to be the main focus of the whole proposal. It envisaged a dual approach which, on the one hand, tried to ensure once and for all the correct functioning and implementation of all the above-listed initiatives. On the other hand, it developed an 'external strategy' consisting of a model of 'concentric circles of migration policy'. At the centre of this policy would be the Schengen States, characterised by 'intensive and extensive' control measures. A second circle of countries would include associated States and the Mediterranean area, which would be brought 'increasingly in line with the first circle' standards, particularly with regard to 'visa, border controls and readmission policies' (point 62). These criteria would be made a precondition for future EU membership. The third circle (for instance the CIS, some of the FRY countries, Turkey and North Africa) would concentrate mainly on 'transit checks and combating facilitator networks'. Any economic co-operation would have to be linked to the fulfilment of such obligations. Finally, the fourth circle (Middle East, China, sub-Saharan Africa) would have to deal with eradicating push

---

12. This was the first time the EU had ever acknowledged a drop in asylum applications. This admission was of particular importance because in the same paragraph the Presidency underlined that the total number of illegal immigrants was on the rise. Thus, one of the Member States' favourite arguments, namely that asylum channels were increasingly becoming an alternative to traditional immigration ones – and that therefore most asylum seekers were in fact 'economic' migrants – appeared to have been empirically disproved. However, the Presidency did not seem to be aware of this contradiction, as it reiterated the old argument of 'bogus refugees' several times throughout the proposal. Even more mystifying was the fact that on several occasions the Presidency also strongly complained about the lack of reliable data on all aspects of migration into the EU (see for instance point 74). On what basis did they then reach the above conclusions on 'bogus refugees'?

factors with the help of the EU and economic aid could be conditioned to achieving such aims.

It was this very idea of the 'concentric circles' policy and the crude way it had been formulated that caused the greatest public outcry at the time when the document was first leaked to the press. It survived virtually unchanged in the rewriting of the paper, indicating that this was in fact the Presidency's core vision of a future EU asylum policy. It was unclear how many Member States shared this 'vision' of the way forward. In any case, it would be hard to define it as a positive kind of 'vision'. Eurocentric, racist, obsessively protectionist and tainted with economic imperialism, were just a few of the adjectives that could have been used to define such a policy. Unfortunately, the issue of ensuring the respect for Human Rights in third or fourth circle countries was only explored in passing. This demonstrated once again the inability of the Presidency to fully comprehend the basic differences between asylum and immigration.[13]

On the internal policy side, the Presidency advocated a streamlining of EU institutions dealing with asylum matters and the concentration of all migration competencies into a single body. The 'soft law' approach that had characterised past Third Pillar co-operation had led to adopted positions not being effectively implemented. Therefore, the Presidency called for a translation of these past measures into new binding instruments, such as the ones available under Title IV TEC. These new initiatives would be envisaged as part of a comprehensive approach to develop a new 'overall entry control concept'. Outstanding obstacles to a real common visa list were seen as a high priority, as well as harmonisation of national carrier sanctions[14] and the development of effective readmission agreements. Remarkably, although the proposal was quite detailed about the necessities of a common approach to carrier sanctions across the EU, no mention was made of the obstacles such sanctions represent to effective 'access' to asylum procedures for would-be applicants. The report could have, for instance, suggested that in harmonising relevant national legislation, those with provisions exempting carriers from their responsibility in the case of asylum seekers should have been taken as leading examples.

In forcefully reasserting the need for a harmonised, fast and streamlined treatment of asylum applications across Europe, the Presidency also put forward the novel idea of first 'putting back the individual on the other side of the border' (point 93) in all cases of illegal entry, before even beginning to consider an asylum application. Once again, the formulation of the proposal appeared very

---

13. Refugees seek asylum in other countries precisely because their fundamental Human Rights are being denied to them. Simply aiming at improving the economic infrastructure of these countries might not necessarily improve their Human Rights record. Furthermore, it would be very hypocritical of the EU not to stress the universal importance of Human Rights since the introduction of the new Art. 6 TEU and the subsequent introduction of an EU Charter of Fundamental Rights. How these concerns fitted in with the Austrian proposal did not appear at all clear.

14. See Point 88.

ill conceived and crudely expressed. What seemed to emerge from the Presidency plan was a vision of Europe transformed into a giant transnational police State, where access to territory would effectively become impossible.

On the matter of TP, the Presidency took a very clear position on the inadequacy of the 1951 Geneva Convention. It was argued that new forms of protection were needed for the majority of the 90s refugees, who were generally fleeing situations of ethnic conflict.[15] These new forms of protection would simply 'supplement' the Geneva Convention and prove an effective way of relieving overburdened official asylum channels.[16] Given the similar parallel negotiations on TP that were going on at the time, this was one of the rare parts of this proposal where the Presidency seemed to be effectively in touch with the vision of the majority of Member States.

The importance of this Strategy Paper should not be undervalued as it represented the first global vision of a future EU asylum policy to be officially expressed after the signing of the Amsterdam Treaty. It was arguably a very controversial and often ill-conceived one, which probably did not necessarily represent the majority opinion on these matters. Although it was never adopted at the subsequent Vienna Council as a common policy statement, it undoubtedly influenced the parallel drawing up of the new Action Programme demanded by the Cardiff Council in June 1998.

VI.2. THE ACTION PLAN ON ESTABLISHING AN AREA OF FREEDOM, SECURITY AND JUSTICE

A new 'Action Plan on establishing an area of freedom, security and justice' was approved at the Vienna Summit in December 1998. In line with the deadlines set by the new Treaty, it laid down the priority areas on which the Council should focus its initiatives in the following five years. The general philosophy behind the plan was the acknowledgement that neither of the three ultimate goals, 'freedom, security and justice', could be attained without the other.[17] Therefore a balance had to be achieved between them.

---

15. No reason was given as to why the 1951 refugee definition would not cover individuals fleeing ethnic persecution and this presumption was heavily disputed. Nonetheless, this assumption remained at the heart of all subsequent EU attempts at defining a common regime of temporary protection. See further Chapter VI.3.

16. The way the Presidency structured its argument was quite unfortunate. It gave the impression that relieving 'quantitatively overburdened asylum procedures' was to be the main aim of these new forms of protection, rather than the necessity of guaranteeing a wider protection than that afforded by the 1951 GC.

17. Point 5 stated that '[f] reedom loses much of its meaning if it cannot be enjoyed in a secure environment and with the full backing of a system of justice in which all citizens and residents can have confidence. These three inseparable concepts have one common denominator – people – and one cannot be achieved in full without the other two. Maintaining the right balance between them must be the guiding thread for Union action'.

The Plan clearly stated that asylum policy and immigration were to be subjected to different considerations as a matter of principle, although it did not specify what such 'considerations' might be. It pointed out, quite correctly, that past asylum initiatives had been crippled by two main weaknesses: their lack of binding effects and the absence of adequate monitoring mechanisms. The transfer of the asylum competence to the EC field opened up the opportunity to correct such weaknesses with new legally-binding instruments. Therefore the transposing of such initiatives into new legal forms were to take a high priority. Finally, the Action Plan was seen to be of particular importance in the 'pre-accession strategy' as it would set out 'for the benefit of the applicant countries a clear and comprehensive statement of the Union's priorities in this area' (point 21).

A number of principles were chosen to act as selection criteria for the new priorities. Apart from the obvious guidance given by the Amsterdam Treaty and the principle of subsidiarity, solidarity and operational efficiency were both seen as extremely important. The latter, in particular, referred to the continuation of successful working methods, such as those tested within the Schengen framework. The principle of the respect for Human Rights, as contained in Art. 6 TEU was also to be taken into full account and consultation with the UNHCR encouraged. On the whole, the Action Plan seemed to fill all the regrettable voids left by the Austrian Presidency Strategy Paper.

Priorities were to be divided in measures to be taken within a two-year span and those that would require a five-year period of elaboration. Highest on the urgency agenda were measures concerning the development of EU TP provisions for displaced persons and mechanisms to guarantee effective solidarity among recipient countries.[18] The entry into force of EURODAC was also seen as imperative.[19] In so far as the 1990 Dublin Convention was concerned, the

---

18. The Austrian Presidency had obviously succeeded in making its most pressing concern the top of the EU agenda.

19. EURODAC was envisaged as a database, set up at the Commission, to which Member States would communicate fingerprints taken from asylum applicants and certain other illegal aliens, in order to control whether a person had already applied for asylum in another Member State. The creation of this database was put forward as an essential part of the implementation of the 1990 DC. However, in practice it proved very difficult to negotiate a text until the December 1998 Vienna summit when a draft Convention was finally agreed. The proposal was then 'frozen' in order to wait for the coming into force of the new Treaty, so that it could be adopted as a Community legal instrument. An amended proposal was presented by the Commission in March 2000 ('Amended proposal for a Council Regulation concerning the establishment of 'Eurodac' for the comparison of the fingerprints of applicants for asylum and certain other third-country nationals to facilitate the implementation of the Dublin Convention', OJ 2000 C29E/1) and then approved as Council Regulation (EC) n° 2725/2000 on 11 December 2000 (O.J. 2000 L316/1). Both Britain and Ireland notified their wish to take part in it. Denmark declared in October 1999 that it would take part in EURODAC on an intergovernmental basis. It remained unclear to which degree the creation of this database would help overcome the considerable problems of implementation the DC had encountered so far (for an analysis

improvement of its effectiveness was judged to be essential. Particular attention was drawn to the need to alter the provisions on responsibility for dealing with members of the same family and this suggestion constituted a great victory for the Human Rights advocates across Europe who had been campaigning on this point for years.[20] Two of the past Third Pillar initiatives were put forward for urgent transposition into Community instruments, namely the 1995 Resolution on minimum guarantees for asylum procedures, and the 1996 Joint Position on the harmonised definition of the term 'refugee'.[21] The former, in particular, was seen as lacking specific provisions on the duration of asylum procedures, and achieving faster adjudication processes was suggested as a sensible reform. Finally, a study was to be undertaken urgently on the possibility of establishing a single European asylum status.[22]

Among the measures that were deemed less urgent – arguably because more controversial – there were the definition of minimum standards on the reception of asylum seekers and the harmonisation of national carriers' liability laws.[23]

---

see further in Chapter VI.4). Part of the problems seemed to stem from the serious lack of solidarity and co-operation Member States displayed in their dealings with each other (see, for instance, French 'refugee dumping' on the EUROSTAR to Britain in N. Rufford, 'French pay refugees to seek asylum in Britain' *The Sunday Times*, 25/7/99). Thus, 'good faith' would play an essential role in a data system that would rely exclusively on Member States' 'voluntary' data contributions.

20. According to the DC, States were responsible for asylum applications presented by the family members of an individual who had already been recognised as a 'Convention' refugee by them (Art. 4). Human rights campaigners argued for years that the provision should be amended so as to allow for the asylum applications of members of the same family to be considered together, even if none of them has already been officially recognised as a refugee. (See *ECRE, Guarding standards – Shaping the agenda* (London, May 1999), p. 9).

21. See 'Council Resolution of 29/6/95 on minimum guarantees for asylum procedures', OJ 1996 C274/13, and 'Council Joint Position of 4/3/96 on the harmonised definition of the term 'refugee' in Art. 1 of the Geneva Convention', OJ 1996 L63/2.

22. This idea of the single European asylum status was to gather considerable momentum in the course of 1999 and was to be one of the central tenets of the Tampere European Council of October 1999 (see further Chapter VI.4).

23. These were measures to be adopted within a five-year span. As in the Austrian Presidency Strategy Paper, there was no mention of the fact that in harmonising carriers' liabilities, special attention should be paid to the situation of asylum seekers. The same omission surfaced later when, in September 2000, the French Presidency presented a 'Directive proposal on the harmonisation of carriers' liabilities'. Only in the preamble was there a mention of the fact that penalties against carriers should not be applied if the third-country nationals were asylum seekers. However, no specific provision to this purpose was inserted into the actual text (see 'Initiative of the French Republic with a view to the adoption of a Council Directive concerning the harmonisation of financial penalties imposed on carriers transporting into the territory of the Member States third-country nationals lacking the documents necessary for admission', OJ 2000 C269/8).

The European Parliament, commenting on the Action Plan,[24] indicated that supplementary measures on data protection should also have been included in the five-year time frame. It called upon the Commission to present proposals on the 'setting up of an authority to monitor the treatment of personal data in the work of the Institutions' (Art. 286 TEC) and on how to ensure that the levels of data protection afforded by national legislation would be comparable to those of the EU Institutions.

On the surface, the Action Plan appeared to be a fairly good starting point for the development of a stronger EU asylum policy. The reasons for defining the relative urgency of measures were not, however, sufficiently explained or clearly thought out. As with past work-programmes, the outcome seemed more the result of a 'reactive' approach than that a 'proactive' comprehensive strategy. Perhaps, on this occasion, more than in the past, the mixed reception of the Austrian Strategy Paper had highlighted the fact that no ultimate shared vision of a future EU asylum policy existed yet.[25]

In order to ensure a more speedy implementation of the priorities of the Action Plan and possibly to overcome the apparent lack of direction the Vienna Council agreed to create a European Task force on Immigration and Asylum that would report to the special October Council in Tampere. Among its tasks were the preparation of a series of reports on a number of countries that were great sources of migration to the EU ('migration' intended as an influx both of asylum seekers and immigrants). The initial five countries chosen were Albania, Afghanistan, Morocco, Somalia, Sri Lanka and Iraq. The Task Force was instructed to follow a 'horizontal' approach by integrating political, economic and development co-operation instruments in devising the best strategy to fight root causes of migration. The creation of this Task Force no doubt echoed some of the suggestions contained in the Austrian Strategy Paper, although a more targeted approach seemed to be the preference.[26]

---

24. See the 'EP Resolution on the draft Action Plan of the Council and Commission on how best to implement the provisions of the Treaty of Amsterdam on an area of freedom, security and justice', OJ 1999 C219/61, in particular p. 64.
25. Past working-programmes had seldom coherently reflected their accompanying reports (see for instance the comments made in Chapters II.5 and III.2 on the Maastricht Report of the Immigration Ministers and the Maastricht working-plan). This was possibly the reason why, between 1994 and 1998, no general Strategy Papers were issued together with the working-programmes. In this context, the adoption of a totally new framework, such as Title IV TEC, appeared in hindsight to be an attempt to overcome the political stalling and achieve a new vision in the asylum field.
26. Also the choice of countries did not seem to have been dictated by the 'circles' theory, otherwise only Afghanistan and Sri Lanka would have qualified for this approach. Again, though, the approach seemed to lack a comprehensive vision. It remained questionable whether a more general 'horizontal' policy would not have been preferable in terms of efficiency and fairness.

VI.3. THE NEW CHALLENGES: TEMPORARY PROTECTION AND BURDEN-SHARING IN THE LIGHT OF THE KOSOVO CRISIS

Both the Austrian Strategy Paper and the Commission Action Plan had set the issues of TP and burden-sharing at the top of the new asylum agenda. Although these issues had been on the table ever since the Bosnian crisis, it had proved impossible to achieve an overall consensus.[27] Once again, Member States seemed unable to agree on a comprehensive strategy, instead preferring small, topical solutions to individual crises. The initial focus had been almost exclusively on the thorny problem of burden-sharing. In this respect, the big disproportion in the reception of refugees across the EU during the Balkan conflicts had clearly dominated the agenda. Over the years a concept of 'financial solidarity' began to gather consensus, notably due to relentless German lobbying. In essence, the solution envisaged consisted of setting up contributions from the Community budget to help Member States with their expenses for the reception of refugees. Initially, however, there was no attempt to define the categories of refugees beyond a generic definition of 'displaced persons'. Their actual determination was still left to the legislation of Member States.

The first two of such measures were adopted in 1997.[28] According to Art. 1.1 of these Joint Actions, they were to be implemented on an 'experimental' basis during 1997, although they were renewed unaltered both in 1998 and in 1999.[29]

---

27. On how the EU had tackled temporary protection since 1992, see Chapter IV.6. Member States had slowly and reluctantly progressed from specific guidelines on the admission of Bosnian refugees to a very generic Resolution on burden-sharing in 1995 and the setting up of an ill-defined 'emergency' procedure the following year to trigger an EU burden-sharing mechanism (see *supra* n° 5). Both initiatives miserably failed the test of the Kosovo crisis (see further).

28. See the 'Joint action 97/477/JHA of 22/7/97 adopted by the Council on the basis of Art. K.3 of the Treaty on European Union, concerning the financing of specific projects in favour of displaced persons who have found temporary protection in the Member States and asylum seekers', OJ 1997 L205/3 and the 'Joint Action 97/478/JHA of 22/7/97 adopted by the Council on the basis of Art. K3 of the Treaty on European Union, concerning the financing of specific projects in favour of asylum seekers and refugees', OJ 1997 L205/5.

29. See the 'Joint action of 27/4/98 adopted by the Council on the basis of Art. K3 of the Treaty on European Union, concerning the financing of specific projects in favour of asylum seekers and refugees', OJ 1998 L138/8, and the 'Joint action of 27/4/98 adopted by the Council on the basis of Art. K.3 of the Treaty on European Union, concerning the financing of specific projects in favour of displaced persons who have found temporary protection in the Member States and asylum seekers', OJ 1998 L138/6. The 1999 Joint Action was slightly amended to include both measures in one text and to specifically include Kosovo refugees, see 'Joint Action of 26/4/99 adopted by the Council on the basis of Art. K.3 of the Treaty on the European Union, establishing projects and measures to provide practical support in relation to the reception and voluntary repatriation of refugees, displaced persons and asylum seekers, including emergency assistance to persons who have fled as a result of recent events in Kosovo', OJ 1999 L114/2.

These measures provided for the financing of two main types of projects: those dealing with 'improving admission facilities' for asylum seekers and refugees and those aiming at facilitating the 'voluntary repatriation of displaced persons who have found temporary protection in the Member States and asylum seekers'.[30] Both initiatives were mainly aimed at 'displaced persons' rather than traditional asylum seekers.[31] The term 'displaced persons' had hitherto been used to define persons who were not perceived to be covered by the GC, but who were nonetheless in need of protection. They constituted the great majority of the refugees that had fled to Europe during the Balkan conflicts of the early 90's.

It was clear from the situations covered by these initiatives that Member States intended their protection to be only of a 'temporary' nature, hence the stress on 'repatriation'.[32] Thus, 'reception' and 'repatriation' became the two fundamental tenets of the new TP equation. The development of this equation was further reinforced when, in 1999, the two Joint Actions were finally combined in a far more elaborate initiative, which for the first time included a clear reference to 'temporary protection'. The intervening Kosovo crisis undoubtedly played a large role in increasing the sense of urgency to implement the measure. A comparison between the initial Commission proposal in January 1999[33] and the final text approved the following April[34] shed an interesting light on the complexities of the negotiations going on at the time.

On the surface the new 1999 Joint Action appeared to be a streamlined integration of the two old ones. On a closer view, a great deal of new definitions had been added. Most importantly, a distinction had been drawn between 'displaced persons' and 'asylum applicants'. The first were defined as 'persons granted permission to stay in a Member State under temporary protection, or under subsidiary forms of protection in accordance with Member States' international obligations and national law, and persons seeking permission to remain

---

30. Both quotations are taken from Art. 1.1 of both the 1997 and the 1998 Joint Actions, see *supra* n° 28 and 29.

31. See Art. 1.2 of the 1997 and the 1998 Joint Actions, where explicit reference was made to the fact that the financed projects had to aim at implementing the 1995 Resolution on burden-sharing with regard to the admission and residence of displaced persons on a temporary basis, OJ 1995 C262/1.

32. As recalled in Chapter VI.1 Germany, Austria and also many of the Nordic countries had been particularly criticised following the controversies surrounding their repatriation programmes of Bosnian refugees. The main critique levelled at them was that most of the repatriations – especially in the German case – had basically been forced ones (see *supra* n° 4). These types of Joint Action, focusing mainly on financing repatriation were also serving the indirect purpose of giving official sanction to the idea that repatriation was an unavoidable part of affording protection.

33. See the 'Proposal for a Council Decision on a Joint Action establishing measures to provide practical support in relation to the reception and the voluntary repatriation of refugees, displaced persons and asylum applicants', submitted 13/1/99, COM (98)733 final in OJ 1999 C37/4.

34. See *supra* n° 29.

on such grounds, who are awaiting a decision on their status' (Art. 2.1.a). 'Asylum applicants' were instead those individuals who had lodged an asylum claim under the 1951 GC and whose application was still pending. This distinction was of particular importance to the development of the concept of TP as a 'parallel track' to the 1951 Convention refugee status.[35]

The new Joint Action specified in much greater detail the concept of 'reception' and 'repatriation' measures. Under the first term, projects to receive Community financing would have to aim at improving reception infrastructures, enhancing the 'fairness and efficiency of asylum procedures',[36] ensuring basic standards of living conditions, affording special assistance to vulnerable groups and enhancing public awareness (Art. 4). Under the term 'repatriation' the measures included were those aimed at the collection and dissemination of information on the economic/legal/political situation in the country of origin, at providing counselling, training and education, as well as those covering repatriation transport costs and post-repatriation monitoring (Art. 5). In the final version of the Joint Action another section was added to cover projects relating to emergency assistance in Member States (Art. 6) to persons displaced as a consequence of the Kosovo crisis. These contributions were, however, only limited to those countries who received a 'significant number of refugees' and for a maximum period of six months.[37] They covered basic emergency needs, from accommodation to health care and means of subsistence.

The main differences between the Commission proposal and the final approved text consisted firstly in the removal of most references to 'solidarity and burden-sharing' among EU Members.[38] Secondly, there was a considerable tightening of the Council's political control on the distribution of the financial contributions.

---

35. The issue of who would be covered by the 1951 GC has been analysed in Chapter I. Most EU Members contended that the majority of the refugees of the last decade were in fact not 'Convention refugees', because their grounds of persecution did not fall under those listed in the Convention, or because they could not prove 'individual' persecution. This assumption was widely criticised both by academics and Human Rights groups (see ECRE, *Guarding standards....*, *supra* n° 20). This issue will be discussed further on.

36. This would be achieved by 'the provision of: legal assistance and other counselling services; interpretation services; information on the procedure to be followed, and rights and obligations of the asylum applicant during the procedure; access to precise and up-to-date country information' (Art. 3.b). The level of meticulousness in the definition of such projects was astonishing, considering that in the previous two years no guidelines had been given at all. This change could have been justified by the increased budget – the 1999 Joint Action had no fixed budget cap. However, it was more likely that the strains on the relatively new concept of 'financial solidarity' were already beginning to show.

37. The wording was intentionally vague, 'significant numbers' being very hard to define. The period limit of six months was equally surprising, given that Member States could have no idea of how long the Kosovo crisis was going to last.

38. In this respect the Commission proposal was permeated by strong sense of 'solidarity'. Point (9) of the preamble, for instance, was watered down in such a way that it no longer expressed the idea that such types of Joint Action would necessarily foster the sharing of

Rules of 'comitology' had already applied to the 1997/98 Joint Actions, but they were not of a very restrictive kind.[39] In the final version of the 1999 initiative only very small financial contributions were subjected to a simple comitology procedure (less that EUR 50 000), all other financing having instead to be expressly approved by the committee of representatives of the Member States. Only in the case of emergency projects for displaced Kosovars was the Commission allowed some degree of freedom of choice (up to EUR 1 million). Finally, the Joint Action's application was limited to the end of 1999. The caution that surrounded every aspect of this initiative was probably the most visible symptom that consensus on burden-sharing, even if only in the simple form of financial solidarity, was still viewed as extremely contentious. This lack of consensus was further highlighted by the fact that this Joint Action was intended as an isolated initiative, not as part of a multi-annual funding programme, such as the Community ones on research or regional aid.[40]

Together with the 1999 Joint Action proposal, the Commission presented an initiative to establish an Action Programme to promote the integration of refugees.[41] This was done in the framework of the objectives laid down by the Social Action Programme 1998–2000 in the field of social integration and was to be legally based on Art. 235 TEC. Whereas the Joint Action was to target displaced persons and asylum seekers, this Community action programme was aimed at recognised 'Convention' refugees and other refugees legally settled in a Member State. Financing would take place on a complementary basis to existing national projects aimed at developing integration structures or encouraging transnational co-operation and exchanges of information. The EP expressed a favourable overall opinion on the measure.[42] It pointed out that it represented a novel way to give the concept of financial solidarity greater latitude, so that it would not always be linked simply to emergency situations, such as violent civil conflicts in one of Europe's peripheries. In this respect, this initiative was certainly an integral part of the Commission's attempts to finally create a

---

responsibility between Member States. In Art. 7 (financing criteria) the first criterion 'achieving an equitable balance of responsibility between Member States' was entirely removed, whereas cost-effectiveness and value for money were bumped up into second place.

39. See rules contained in the 'Council Decision laying down the procedures for the exercise of implementing powers conferred to the Commission', OJ 1987 L197/33.
40. It took the Commission another two years to introduce the idea that a Refugee Fund could be envisaged as a comprehensive multi-annual funding programme (see further Chapter VI.5).
41. 'Proposal for a Council Decision on establishing a Community Action Programme to promote the integration of refugees', submitted 13/1/99, COM (98)731 final, OJ 1999 C36/11.
42. See the 'Proposal for a Council Decision on establishing a Community Action Programme to promote the integration of refugees, EP Amendments', OJ 1999 C219/79.

comprehensive strategy for the reception of refugees in Europe, focusing initially on those not covered by specific international conventions.[43]

The Commission had already set about trying to achieve this comprehensive strategy by presenting, back in 1997, a proposal on the 'temporary protection of displaced persons'.[44] This was to take the shape of a Joint Action on the basis of Art. K.3 TEU. Recalling all the preceding initiatives on asylum adopted by the Council, the Commission highlighted the dangers that situations of mass influxes of displaced persons posed to the internal security of Member States[45] and the ensuing threat to human life, thus asserting the need for 'prompt and co-ordinated action' in a spirit of solidarity. This action would consist in the creation, at Union level, of a TP regime to be applied to specific emergency circumstances. This regime would also lay down the minimum contents of rights relating to its status and the decisions implementing the Joint Action would be taken by qualified majority voting. It also contained a generic provision on 'how best to support' Member States which were being affected by mass influxes of refugees (Art. 5).

The TP regime would apply to all persons in need of 'international protection'. These persons were defined as those who had fled their country of residence and could not return there because the current situation would have made their 'safe return, under humane conditions' impossible (Art. 1.b). This referred in particular to either people fleeing 'armed conflict and persistent danger', or to people at risk of 'systematic or widespread Human Rights abuses, including those belonging to groups compelled to leave their homes by campaigns of ethnic or religious persecution' (Art. 1.b).

The latter definition seemed, unfortunately, particularly inconsistent. TP was designed by its very nature to apply to people 'falling outside' the definition of the 1951 GC. Member States had long since maintained that the Convention's definition had become obsolete in the face of the rapidly changing geopolitical asset of the post Cold War world. The Austrian Strategy Paper had put this particular point across both bluntly and extensively.[46] In this context, this

---

43. The idea of an action programme was subsequently abandoned and substituted by a more comprehensive European Refugee Fund (see further Chapter VI.5).

44. See the 'Proposal for a Joint Action concerning temporary protection of displaced persons', COM (97)93 final, submitted 27/3/97, OJ 1997C106/7.

45. Interestingly, this notion was also acquiring some weight in the United Nations context. Several times during the 90s, the UN Security Council referred to large movements of refugees as an important element of the 'threat to the peace' as provided by Art. VII of the UN Charter. This happened in the case of the Iraqi Kurds (UN Security Council Resolution 688 – 1991 – Security Council Official records, Resolutions and Decisions, vol. 46, p. 31), of Bosnia-Herzegovina (UN Security Council Resolution 752 – 1992 – as above, vol. 47, p. 13), of Somalia (UN Security Council Resolution 897 – 1994 – as above, vol. 49, p. 55) and also in the case of the Kosovo crisis in spring 1999. NATO actually tried to justify its intervention on this point.

46. See Chapter VI.1 and *supra* n° 15.

initiative on TP appeared to be a laudable attempt to fill the last decade's refugee protection vacuum. However, it was trying to do so by effectively denying access to the Convention's protection to people who would have rightfully been entitled to it and by diverting them instead to the 'alternative' protection channel that the EU intended to create. Since the Convention's grounds of persecution were clearly listed as 'race, religion, nationality, membership of a particular social group or political opinion' (Art. 1.2), it was evidently absurd to try and deny that 'ethnic cleansing' or religious persecution would not fall under the above-mentioned grounds.[47] On the other hand, a widespread situation of lawlessness would not have fallen under the Convention's criteria. However, since it could have given rise to Human Rights abuses, it should have been rightfully included in the TP scheme. Unfortunately it wasn't, probably because this kind of situation did not appear to be the most recurring example of civil conflict. A bird's eye view of the internal conflicts of the last decade would reveal that the majority of them could be ascribed to 'ethnic cleansing' or religious persecution.[48]

Ethnic cleansing and religious persecution were probably included in the TP scheme because of the negative past experience of having to deal with enormous numbers of applications at the same time. Most Member States had tried to solve this logistical nightmare by bypassing traditional asylum channels and granting these refugees a leave to remain on compassionate or humanitarian grounds. In these instances, applications for asylum under the GC had been actively discouraged or barred. Unlike the specific reception conditions laid down by the 1951 GC for 'recognised' refugees, reception measures for 'other persons in need of protection' varied greatly across the EU. This disparity had, in the eyes of Member States, encouraged refugees to gravitate toward the most generous countries.[49] Hence the need to harmonise such reception conditions in an EU measure on TP.

---

47. A frequent argument in support of the theory that these instances would fall outside the GC was that it would be difficult to prove either individual persecution or 'State-led' persecution. For these arguments, see the analysis in Chapter I. In this context it is sufficient to recall that most EU Members accepted non-State persecution as a valid reason for granting protection under the GC. Also, in the case of ethnic cleansing or of religious persecution, the need to prove 'individual' persecution would become irrelevant, since the belonging of the individual to a particular ethnic group or religious faith would be enough to generate persecution.

48. See, for instance, the persecution of the Iraqi Kurds or of the Turkish Kurds, the massacres of Tutzis in Rwanda, the Balkan wars between Serbs and Croatians or Muslim and Serb Bosnians; the Kosovo crisis and the Algerian experience. Only in the case of Somalia and some of the African post-independence conflicts, such as Angola or Mozambique, could it perhaps be argued that clear motives of persecution were hard to define.

49. All EU Members' legal systems envisaged some kind of 'humane leave to remain' model (similar to the one in the UK), mainly to protect those who could not be 'refouled' under the terms of Art. 33 GC. However, the reception conditions varied greatly. The more liberal Scandinavian countries granted these refugees generous social security and permission to work. German legislation provided for generous reception conditions, but granted

The Commission proposal did indeed contain provisions to harmonise the treatment of persons falling under the EU TP. They were to be entitled to all the same benefits reserved for Convention refugees.[50] In this respect, the EU appeared to be undertaking a sincere effort to fill the alleged gap in the GC refugee protection regime. Unfortunately, the circumstances under which the TP scheme would be applied appeared far more problematic. In the event of a mass influx of people in need of international protection (or else of a 'strong probability that such a situation may soon arise', Art. 1.c) the Council, 'taking into consideration whether adequate protection can be found in the region of origin' would decide on the opportunity of establishing a TP regime (Art. 3.1) by qualified majority voting (Art. 12). 'Mass influx' was vaguely defined as a 'significant number of persons' (Art. 1.c). The TP regime could not exceed a total duration of five years and a review would be carried out at least once a year on the opportunity of phasing it out (Art. 4). Asylum applications under the GC could be suspended if this was allowed under national law, but not deferred for more than three years (up to five years if the TP regime was being phased out). A negative decision on an asylum application could not, however, overrule the TP status (Art. 10.1–3). Exclusion clauses similar to those of the GC also applied.[51] In the event of the TP status not being phased out after five years, the adoption of long-term measures was left entirely to the discretion of individual Member States (Art. 13).

If the purpose of this TP regime was purportedly to fill the gaps left by the obsoleteness of the GC, then it was insufficiently equipped for its task. Firstly, it conditioned the possibility of approving a TP regime in favour of a certain country because of an ill-defined concept of 'mass influx of refugees'.[52] In practice,

---

no work permits. Italy, Greece and Spain had no provisions for specific assistance, although they created 'refugee camps' in cases of mass influx (as during the Kosovo crisis). Although Member Sates recurrently hinted at 'benefits motivated' infra-European refugee movements, these allegations were never effectively substantiated. Proving such wide-spread allegations would have been difficult, given the Austrian Presidency Paper acknowledgement that the collection of refugees' statistical data across the EU was highly inefficient.

50. For an analysis of such benefits, see Chapter I. They included mainly family reunification, housing allowances, health care, education, social security, and working permits.

51. See Chapter I. These included individuals that had committed crimes against peace, war crimes or crimes against humanity; a serious non-political crime; or that had been guilty of 'acts contrary to the purposes and principles of the UN'. Likewise, an individual who posed a danger to the security of a Member State or to its community due to having been convicted of a particularly serious crime, could equally be excluded from the enjoyment of TP status (Art. 11).

52. What would in practice be a 'significant' number of refugees: hundreds, thousands or millions? The squabbles that ensued from the attempts to reach an equitable distribution of Kosovar refugees sadly illustrated the relativity of this concept. Britain was constantly publicising its incredible generosity towards hosting great numbers of Kosovars, but in the end the final figure amounted to a mere three thousand people. In the light of the German or Austrian experiences during the Bosnian crisis, a 'significant' number would have been more likely to entail hundreds of thousands of refugees.

this meant that only areas in the EU periphery could eventually qualify for it, since large masses of refugees could only travel relatively short international distances. Moreover, by virtue of the new provisions in Title IV TEC, this concept would be subject to the judicial scrutiny of the ECJ. Therefore, any Member State outvoted on the decision to grant TP status could have asked for a judicial review of the decision based on the absence of a 'significant influx' of refugees. This meant that the TP proposal was hardly the 'comprehensive' solution it had been hailed as.[53] Instead, the 'real' scope of the proposed EU TP scheme was simply to deal efficiently with individuals that could pose a sufficient 'logistical' problem to Member States, a very self-centred vision of the issue indeed. Secondly, the presumption that the offering of an alternative 'protected' status could effectively suspend a Member State's obligation to examine an asylum application under the GC was in itself open to questioning. Finally, the efficiency of qualified majority decision-making was severely hampered by the parallel proposal, concerning financial solidarity, that the Commission submitted the following year.[54]

This proposal was developed to be applied in conjunction with the TP regime. The final provisions of both initiatives linked their respective coming into force with each other. The solidarity proposal, a Joint Action based on Art. K. 3.2.b TEU, was mainly focused on the modalities of assisting Member States subjected to a 'mass influx' of refugees, in the event of a TP scheme having been approved. The preamble clearly pointed out that 'financial assistance' was to be the preferred primary option. Physical distribution of the beneficiaries of TP was merely envisaged as a 'subsidiarity point' and could only take place before the arrival of such refugees into the EU. Financial assistance would consist mainly of contributions from the Community budget towards the emergency costs of providing food, shelter and health care for the initial three months of TP. Alternatively, contributions could be used to supplement national initiatives aiming at guaranteeing the basic rights provided by the TP Joint Action. All decisions concerning financial solidarity were to be taken unanimously, despite

---

53. This was made clear by the inherent paradox of the Member States' arbitrary choice to exclude certain categories of refugees from the protection of the GC. For instance, in the case of the Rwandan massacres, Tutzi individuals that might have made it to Europe would have been left virtually unprotected. In the Member States' view, ethnic cleansing would apparently not have been acceptable as a ground for persecution under the GC. At the same time TP could not have been declared because of the small numbers of individuals concerned. Thus, individuals persecuted purely on the basis of their belonging to an ethnic group would have been left at the mercy of the various different types of national legislation to be able to remain on humanitarian grounds.

54. 'Proposal for a Joint Action concerning solidarity in the admission and residence of beneficiaries of temporary protection of displaced persons', submitted 26/6/98, OJ 1998 C268/14. The Commission put forward this proposal in the context of the 1998 amendments to the TP draft Joint Action, mainly because the burden-sharing provision of the original 1997 TP proposal had been severely criticised by certain Member States.

the fact that the main reason for adopting a joint action in the first place was generally to be able to take all subsequent decisions by majority voting (see Art. K.3.2.b).

The maintenance of unanimity voting had severe implications for the functioning of the proposed EU TP regime. Even though the Joint Action on TP itself envisaged majority voting, the fact that it had been operationally linked to that on solidarity made both initiatives rely in practice on achieving a unanimous consensus.[55] In a field were the major concepts had been voluntarily ill-defined and consensus on solidarity was notoriously scarce, the prospect of such a regime ever being able to function properly was very dim indeed. Also, the fact that physical redistribution of refugees had been defined as a 'subsidiary point' could have had extremely disruptive consequences. In the event of a really 'significant' influx of refugees, financial help would not necessarily be an all-solving panacea. There would always be objective limits to the logistical capacity of Member States and the solidarity Joint Action proposal definitely failed to properly address them.

Both initiatives obviously lacked basic levels of consensus, since they were reshuffled several times between the Commission, the Council and the EP. Eventually, the funding initiative was subsumed into the new European Refugee Fund and a radically revised TP proposal was put forward in the spring of 2000.[56]

Lessons from the Kosovo crisis were arguably a major factor in the revision of such measures. A pivotal role was played by Germany, who held the EU Presidency during the crisis. Germany was the country that accommodated the largest number of refugees during the Bosnian conflict. This no doubt accounted for the forcefulness of the EU initiative during the crisis. However, it should be acknowledged that the 1995 burden-sharing initiative and the 1996 emergency procedure on burden-sharing remained dead letters. Called to finally show the degree of solidarity they had reluctantly agreed upon just two years earlier, EU Members failed miserably. Not only did they fail to implement their 'soft law' approach, but they got into undignified public 'squabbles' about the distribution of refugees. The German Presidency presented a plan on refugee quotas, which also included the notion that countries unwilling to host refugees would have to pay for the ones that were ready to do so. Unfortunately, the plan faced such a wall of opposition that it was finally left to the UNHCR to slowly and painfully

---

55. Thus, vital refugee protection decisions could be held at ransom by one dissenting Member State. Even worse, the granting of financial assistance would not have been automatic. Art. 2 or the solidarity initiative actually stated that 'the Council [...] may adopt decisions implementing solidarity mechanisms'. The whole idea of an EU TP status was resting on the fact that, in exchange for granting extensive, harmonised rights to refugees (supposedly) outside the protection of the GC, the Community budget would have footed a substantial part of the bill. If the financial part of the equation were suddenly not available, why should Member States be keen to implement a TP status that considerably increased their financial obligations?

56. See further VI.5.

extract concessions from Member States.[57] The logistical inability to cope efficiently with large number of refugees was also highlighted by the crisis. Although huge resources were mobilised at the height of the Kosovar exodus, the horrendous realities of the refugee camps became a tragic daily recurrence in the European press. Huge financial contributions could not always make up for failing infrastructures. Therefore, it was clear that often there would be no substitute for the physical redistribution of refugees. Considering this factor as a mere 'subsidiary point' would stand in the way of future effective action.

On the positive side, the Kosovo crisis certainly proved that a good co-ordination of foreign policy and the will to devise a unanimous front in security matters was able to make an enormous difference in the solution of refugee crises. The introduction of the role of the High Representative for Foreign Policy in the Amsterdam Treaty in order to ensure a better co-ordination of the CFSP was certainly an encouraging element. In this respect, Kosovo also showed that the military had an important role to play in the everyday management of refugee crises and that this aspect would need careful future consideration.

VI.4. THE TAMPERE EUROPEAN COUNCIL: TOWARDS A 'COMMON EUROPEAN ASYLUM SYSTEM'

The poor reception of the Austrian Strategy Paper had highlighted the lack of a true shared vision on the future contents of an EU asylum policy. As a result, the Vienna summit of December 1998 had agreed on the need to call a special meeting of the European Council in October 1999 to focus discussions on the future of the EU area of freedom, security and justice. In the meantime, the German Presidency kept the asylum issue high on the agenda, notably because of the tremendous refugee implications of the Kosovo crisis.

The Finnish Presidency took up the challenge of the Vienna European Council and organised a summit in Tampere in October 1999. The focus of the meeting was to be the creation of an area of freedom, security and justice and to this purpose 'a number of policy orientations and priorities' were agreed.[58] These were rooted in the Union's reaffirmed 'commitment to freedom based on Human Rights, democratic institutions and the rule of law'. These principles included the right to 'move freely throughout the Union [...] in conditions of security

---

57. The German proposal was better known as the 'Bonn Plan' and it envisaged the possibility of hosting hundreds of thousands of refugees across Europe. The UK, for instance, was to take 80,000 refugees whereas in the end it only took between two and four thousand, arguing that it had already borne a large amount of the costs for the military campain. See I. Traynor (et alia), 'German fury at 'mean' Britain' *The Guardian*, 30/4/99, p. 3. In the end, Germany accepted circa 15,000 refugees (but was ready to take up to 20,000), Austria circa 5,000 and Norway 6,000. It was obvious that the relative size of a country was not a consideration in their generosity.

58. See the 'Presidency Conclusions of the Tampere European Council', 15 and 16 October 1999, n° 200/99.

and justice'. This freedom was to be granted to all, included those drawn to Europe because such basic rights were denied to them in their own country. The European Council, in a true milestone declaration, stated that '[i]t would be in contradiction with Europe's traditions to deny such freedom to those whose circumstances lead them justifiably to seek access to our territory. This in turn [would] require the Union to develop common policies on asylum and immigration'. It was clear from such a statement that the justifications for an EU asylum policy had finally changed. The transition from mere 'flanking measures' for the realisation of the Internal Market towards an independent objective rooted in the new Human Rights dimension of the Union was finally complete. It was no coincidence that the Tampere Council also instituted the body that was going to draft the EU Charter of Fundamental Rights, approved a year later at the Nice summit.

The overall aim of a future EU asylum policy would be 'an open and secure Europe, fully committed to the obligations of the Geneva Refugee Convention and other relevant Human Rights instruments, and [the ability] to respond to humanitarian needs on the basis of solidarity'. The main tenets of this policy were to be a 'partnership with the countries of origin' and the creation of a 'common European asylum system'. On the first point, the Council stated once again the importance of addressing the root causes of migration, namely political, economic and Human Rights issues, in the countries of origin. Partnership with those countries should always aim at combating poverty, improving living and working conditions, securing democratic institutions and the respect for fundamental rights, in particular those of minorities, women and children. For this purpose, Member States were called to increase their efforts to achieve a greater co-ordination of the internal and external policies of the Union.[59] The High Level Group on Asylum and Migration's mandate was continued in view of its positive contributions.[60]

On the second point the Council made a surprisingly strong commitment towards the establishment of a Common European Asylum System (CEAS) based on respect for the 1951 GC and the principle of non-refoulement.[61] In the

---

59. This suggestion probably referred to the ongoing discussions on how to achieve true participation of the EU at the international level, especially in the UN, where France and the United Kingdom are extremely reluctant to abandon their individual seats on the Security Council.

60. This Group, instituted by the Vienna Council, echoed the Ad Hoc Group of the pre-Maastricht era and the K.4 Committee. It appeared that in the asylum field certain instruments – predominantly designed as vehicles of Member States' control – had a distinct tendency to self-perpetuate.

61. This point wasn't a real novelty as it was already mentioned in the 1998 Action Plan. The Plan, however, included simply the drawing up of a feasibility study on a CEAS as a priority for the next two years. The impetus to adopt this goal so quickly was probably due to the growing expectations of bold progress that had been building up before the Tampere summit.

short term an integral part of this new system would have been a 'clear and workable' determination of States' responsibility for asylum applications, common standards for asylum procedures and for conditions of reception for refugees and the 'approximation of rules on the recognition and content of the refugee status'. The CEAS would also need to be complemented by 'measures on subsidiary forms of protection' for refugees falling outside the definition of the Geneva Convention.

In the long term, the CEAS would have entailed common asylum procedure rules and a uniform refugee status across the Community. The Commission was asked to prepare a communication on all these matters within a year. On the issue of TP, the Council called for a stepping-up of the efforts to reach an agreement. The Tampere summit was actually widely expected to deliver a consensus on TP, but in this respect the Council disappointingly confirmed that a compromise was still out of reach. The Council did, however, make a new proposal in this respect by hinting at the possibility of instituting 'some form of financial reserve available in situations of mass influx of refugees for temporary protection'. This idea might have been based on the European Parliament's proposal to reunite all the asylum budget lines for 1999 in a so-called 'Refugee Fund'.[62] Finally, the European Council also mentioned the new competence of the Community 'in the field of readmission' (based presumably on Art. 63.3.b TEC). It invited the Council to continue its policy of concluding readmission agreements or else of including standard readmission clauses in other association or co-operation agreements. This point was an obvious reminder that the 'security' concerns that had so typically characterised the first phase of EU asylum co-operation were far from being abandoned.

The Tampere summit constituted a real turning point in the development of an EU asylum policy. In the first place, it gave this policy a truly independent dimension by basing it on the new EU commitment to Human Rights. This could also potentially lead to a change of perspective in EU asylum initiatives, with a greater emphasis laid on the respect for international obligations, rather than the obsessive control of 'access to territory'. Secondly, the Tampere Council honestly assessed where old interventions had gone wrong and successfully articulated all the domains where future EU asylum policy interventions would be needed. It did not put forward radically new concepts, but it introduced an overall, comprehensive target with a great driving force: the CEAS. The acknowledgement that Europe needed a CEAS represented the closure of a circle opened in 1990 by the Dublin and Schengen Conventions. Both Conventions had been severely criticised.[63] The allocation of responsibility for an asylum application to a single Member State had been seen as a breach of the GC Signatories' obligation to individually examine asylum applications.[64] Furthermore, vast

---

62. The Fund was eventually approved in October 2000. See further in Chapter VI.5.
63. For an in-depth analysis of these criticisms see Chapter III.
64. See the opinion of the Dutch Council of State, reported in Chapter II.3.C.

differences between national asylum adjudication systems and legal inter-pretations of the GC meant that outcomes on asylum applications and national recognition rates varied enormously across the EU. Finally, the concept of 'safe' country[65] that was first put forward by the DC resulted in a severe 'territorial' limitation of the right to seek asylum.[66]

The ideas at the heart of the CEAS had already been put forward at the beginning of the 90s. Back then, Member States already had, at least in theoretical terms, a clear idea of the way to proceed in asylum matters.[67] This way wasn't very different from the one laid down at Tampere. The difference was that back in 1990, Member States chose to ignore concerns over the consequences of their choices and pushed ahead with issues that were seen as more pressing from their security point of view.[68] The DC was, in this respect, the cornerstone on which all subsequent initiatives of this kind were to be built.

However, just a few years later, the shakiness of the foundations Member States had laid was overwhelmingly apparent. Three years after the coming into force of the DC it was clear that the system was not operating effectively. Several problems plagued its application. Firstly, asylum seekers mainly travelled with-out any sort of documentation and this made it virtually impossible to conclu-sively prove their first port of entry.[69] Mutual distrust between Member States meant that almost none of them actually complied with the guidelines issued by the Dublin Executive Committee on acceptable standards of proof.[70] In this respect, it remained doubtful whether EURODAC would ever make a consider-able difference, since most asylum seekers did not necessarily apply for asylum until they reached the country of their choice. The only way to bypass this problem would have been to insert illegal immigrants into the database as well

---

65. Art. 3.5 of the DC stated that '[a] ny Member State shall retain the right, pursuant its national laws, to send an applicant for asylum to a third State'. This provision had been the cornerstone of all subsequent initiatives on 'safe third countries', see Chapters III.3.B-C and IV.4.

66. Refugees fleeing persecution rarely take a direct route to freedom. The neighbouring states of their country of origin might not necessarily be their best option because of lack of stability in the region. However, the 'safe' country concept would in practice prevent them from fleeing further afield because they would always be ultimately 'bounced back' to the territory to which they first fled.

67. See the Palma Document or the Maastricht Report of the Immigration Ministers, in Chapters II.1 and III.2.

68. The chief concern remained access and protection of the national territory. In this respect, all the measures of the early 90s related to this concern. In practice, 'protection' of the territory sadly outweighed the 'protection' of refugees.

69. States have been most unco-operative on this point, sending refugees back and forth over internal borders several times. Also on this point, see the 'dirty tricks' displayed by certain Member States, *supra* n° 19.

70. See A. Hurwitz, 'The 1990 Dublin Convention: a comprehensive assessment' 1999 (11) IJRL, p. 646, at pp. 670–672.

and this was eventually agreed in March 2000.[71] Other issues hampering the implementation of the DC concerned the random application of both the humanitarian and the opt-out clauses, especially in cases of family reunification where a breach of Art. 8 ECHR was often a prospect.[72]

Moreover, as judicial bodies across Europe were seized over the legitimacy of the DC criteria, their decisions represented further nails in the 'Dublin coffin'. These decisions were mainly based on the argument that other national asylum laws did not afford the same level of protection as those where the applicant was seeking refuge.[73] Doubts about the equivalence between Member States' asylum systems and their removal practices also came from government sources.[74] Finally, even the ECtHR rejected the Member States' contention that they could legitimately rely on the assumption that all EU asylum adjudication

---

71. See the 'Amended Proposal for a Council Regulation concerning the establishment of EURODAC for the comparison of the fingerprints of applicants for asylum and certain other third-country nationals to facilitate the implementation of the Dublin Convention', OJ 2001 C29E/1. This amendment caused a considerable amount of controversy due to jurisprudence of the ECtHR establishing certain criteria on fingerprinting (see *Freidl* v. *Austria* (1996) 21 EHRR 83 and S.Peers, *EU Justice and Home Affairs law* (Longman, London, 2000), pp. 116–117.

72. See A. Hurwitz, *supra* n° 70, pp. 659–663. The humanitarian clause referred to the possibility for a Member State not responsible for the application to ask the responsible Member State to transfer the application. The opt-out clause referred instead to the possibility for a Member State to examine an application lodged in its territory, even if it was not technically responsible for it.

73. See, for instance, the ruling of the UK House of Lords of 19/12/2000 in the case of *Regina* v. *Secretary of State for the Home Department, Ex Parte Adan* and *Regina* v. *Secretary of State for the Home Department, Ex Parte Aitsguer*, available at 'http://parliament.the-stationery-office.co.uk/pa/ld200001/ ldjudgmt/jd001219/adan-1.htm'. The decision involved two asylum-seekers (a Somali and an Algerian respectively) who had come to Britain via France and Germany. The Somali claimed to fear persecution from another tribe, whereas the Algerian applicant was on the target list of the main Islamic terrorist group in Algeria. In both cases their respective governments were powerless to protect them from such threats. The judges upheld the decision of the Court of Appeal and ruled that the applicants could not be sent back to France or Germany because those countries had a very limited concept of 'non-State' persecution that was not compatible with the wider UK interpretation of 'persecution agents'. For an in-depth analysis, see G. Noll, 'Formalism vs. Empiricism. Some reflections on the Dublin Convention on the occasion of recent European case law' forthcoming (2001) 70 *Nordic Journal of International Law*. See also N. Blake, 'The Dublin Convention and rights of asylum seekers in the European Union' in E. Guild and C. Harlow (eds), *Implementing Amsterdam. Immigration and asylum rights in EC law* (Hart Publishing, Oxford, 2001), p. 95 for a review of British DC-related jurisprudence. Another 218 court challenges have been pending since July 1997 in Britain, 194 relating to Germany and 24 to France, see C. Dyer, 'Straw asylum veto ruled illegal' *The Guardian*, 24/7/99, p. 12.

74. See the Swedish *Minority Bosnian Case*, analysed by G. Noll, *supra* n° 73. The Swedish government, against the advice of its own Aliens Appeal Board, decided not to return

systems did generate identical results.[75] It concluded that the Contracting States carried an individual responsibility under the GC to examine asylum applications and such responsibility could not be passed over to other States. In the future, this jurisprudence could have far-reaching implications in the event of the ECJ being asked either for a preliminary ruling or for an interpretative opinion of an EU measure based on the DC. Given the agreement between the overwhelming majority of commentators and the opinion of the ECtHR on the illegitimacy of the DC's fundamental presumption, it would appear highly unlikely that the ECJ would endorse a different interpretation.[76]

It was also becoming apparent that the DC criteria were inevitably fostering a very unbalanced distribution of responsibility among Member States. Since the DC cornerstone idea was that Members were individually responsible for controlling the 'external' borders of the Union, each country became inherently responsible for all, legal or illegal, crossings of its external border. Thus, the Member States placed along the external borders of the Union were inevitably left to shoulder most applications.[77]

---

some Bosnian asylum seekers to Germany, which was responsible for their asylum applications under DC rules. The Swedish authorities declared that use of the DC opt-out clause should be made 'to determine an asylum claim from a citizen of Bosnia-Herzegovina, who has been present in Germany before her arrival in Sweden, in cases where, according to practice, a residence permit is granted in Sweden, while it is denied in Germany' (Translation provided by G. Noll).

75. *T.I.v. UK*, Decision as to the admissibility of application n° 43844/98, unpublished, reported by G. Noll, *supra* n° 73. It involved the case of a Sri-Lankan national fearing persecution both from the Tamil Tigers and the Sri-Lankan government. T.I. had first applied for asylum in Germany and subsequently in the UK. The UK sought leave to return the applicant to Germany and the ECtHR declared his appeal against his deportation order inadmissible. However, the Court also stated that '[t] he Court finds that the indirect removal in this case to an intermediary country, which is also a contracting State, does not affect the responsibility of the United Kingdom to ensure that the applicant is not, as a result of its decision to expel, exposed to treatment contrary to Art. 3 of the Convention. Nor can the United Kingdom rely automatically in that context on the arrangements made in the Dublin Convention concerning the attribution of responsibility between European countries for deciding asylum claims. Whereas States establish international organisations, or mutatis mutandis international agreements, to pursue co-operation in certain fields of activities, there might be implications for the protection of fundamental rights. It would be incompatible with the purpose and object of the Convention if Contracting States were thereby absolved from their responsibility under the Convention in relation to the field of activity covered by such attribution' (quote taken from G.Noll).

76. In this sense, given the high probability that such a case will come under the ECJ's scrutiny in the near future, the building of a CEAS appears to be a real race against time for Member States.

77. For a more in-depth analysis of this problem, see C. De Jong, 'Is there a need for a European asylum policy?' in F. Nicholson and P. Twomey (eds), *Refugee rights and realities. Evolving international concepts and regimes* (CUP, Cambridge, 1999), p. 357, in particular at pp. 359–61.

The Dublin system would definitely need to be reformulated in order to overcome these problems. The Tampere Council expressed the belief that in rewriting the rules on the allocation of States' responsibility for asylum applications the big 'injustice' of this system would finally be overcome. By achieving a single European asylum status, it would no longer matter where an application was lodged, because outcomes would be identical everywhere. It remained unclear, however, whether Member States were really committed to full asylum harmonisation, or whether they would simply opt for a half-hearted agreement on 'minimum standards' for a CEAS. The Commission's own 'scoreboard' was not at all clear in this respect.[78]

Tampere also highlighted that the development of 'complementary forms of protection' remained another great challenge of a future EU asylum policy. The EP had already expressed its views on the subject a few months earlier.[79] It had emphasised the risk that the extremely difficult negotiations concerning TP and burden-sharing could lead to the marginalisation of a more comprehensive approach. The EP recalled how the proposed Union TP regime fell seriously short of providing protection to refugees supposedly outside the scope of the GC. The EP proposal contained a far more accurate and comprehensive definition of such refugees. Two general categories of people in need of protection were outlined:

1. 'Persons [...] threatened by widespread violence, foreign aggression, internal conflict, large-scale violation of Human Rights or other circumstances which have severely disrupted public order';
2. 'Persons who [...] have justified fears of being tortured, subjected to sexual violence or violence on account of their sexual orientation, inhuman or degrading treatment, capital punishment or other violations of their fundamental rights'.

No mention was made in the proposal of the victims of ethnic cleansing or religious persecution, thus endorsing the notion that these two categories justifiably fell under the protection of the GC. Furthermore, the EP stressed that in the context of a war or internal conflict the victims of 'systematic gender-specific persecution', in particular women, as members of a 'social group' should be recognised as refugees within the meaning of the GC. Finally, the notion of non-State persecution should also always be included in the correct interpretation of the GC. The EP maintained that completion of the CEAS could only be achieved by agreeing a complementary form of refugee protection which would also

---

78. 'Communication from the Commission to the Council and the European Parliament. Biannual update of the scoreboard to review progress on the creation of an area of 'Freedom, Security and Justice' in the European Union', COM (2000)782 final, Brussels 30/11/2000.
79. 'European Parliament Resolution on the harmonisation of forms of protection complementing refugee status in the European Union', OJ 1999 C150/203.

include clear standards of reception across the Union. In this respect, TP would become a solidarity instrument to be adopted only in extreme cases.

Overall, Tampere was the first real milestone in the creation of an EU asylum policy after the entry into force of the Amsterdam Treaty. It revealed a willingness to acknowledge past mistakes and to learn from them in order to build a truly comprehensive asylum policy for the future. The idea of a CEAS was the embodiment of such a vision. The formulation of the specific contents of this system was remitted to the Commission, but it was clear that all aspects of asylum policy had to be a part of this project. Therefore, the new asylum system would necessarily include a revision of the DC, a harmonisation of asylum procedures, asylum status, reception conditions and complementary forms of protection. It was truly an immense task, requiring the balancing of security interests with the respect for international asylum and Human Rights obligations that Member States had been shunning since the middle of the 80s. The good faith of the Tampere declarations would be severely tested in the following years.

VI.5. The European Refugee Fund and the Temporary Protection Directive

The Tampere summit was of fundamental importance to the development of an EU asylum policy. Building on the new reforms of the Amsterdam Treaty, it laid down clear objectives for the future and adopted the timetable suggested by the Commission in its earlier Action Plan. In the wake of the tremendous momentum generated by the summit, the first asylum initiative followed in just a few weeks. Aware of the delays surrounding the TP proposal, the Tampere Council had emphasised the need to create a financial instrument suited to emergency situation of 'mass influx' as part of the new CEAS. The EP had already repeatedly suggested the unification of all the different budget lines relating to refugees into a single budget heading entitled 'European Fund for Refugees'.[80] The Commission followed up these requests by presenting in December 1999, a proposal for a comprehensive five-year funding plan for all refugee-related initiatives.[81]

The proposal was to cover all the same areas that had been previously funded

---

80. The 1999 Joint Action funding refugees' reception and repatriation measures (see *supra* n° 33), had been followed by two separate funding proposals. The first concerned an Action Programme to promote the integration of refugees (see *supra* n° 41), the second was a proposal on financial solidarity (see *supra* n° 54) linked to the TP initiative. The EP suggested to link these two initiatives into a broader single fund. See the Europa site, at http://europa.eu.int/comm/justice_home/project/erf_en.htm.

81. This new proposal explicitly substituted the action programme for the integration of refugees proposal. It did not specifically mention the financial solidarity initiative, which at the time of the proposal was still not approved. Since the new initiative specifically linked up with the TP proposal in Art. 6, it should be presumed that the financial solidarity initiative had by then been abandoned.

through specific projects. It envisaged a system of financial redistribution to balance the refugee burden borne by Member States. It offered support in the following areas: a) improvement of reception conditions in terms of infrastructure and services (accommodation, material and social assistance, assistance with asylum formalities); b) integration of recognised refugees and others benefiting from stable protection forms; c) voluntary repatriation and reintegration into the country of origin (access to reliable information, advice, vocational training and assistance in resettlement); and d) emergency measures in the event of a mass influx of refugees (accommodation, food, healthcare, administrative and transport costs). The fund was designed to cover a very wide range of people, from recognised refugees and otherwise protected displaced individuals including those under TP status, to asylum seekers and those seeking TP status.

Member States would have to apply for funding on a yearly basis. The Commission would then decide on these applications,[82] while Member States would subsequently be in charge of managing and selecting the individual projects. The distribution of the fund's resources between Member States would be proportional to the number of asylum seekers they had received (65 per cent) and the number of recognised refugees and displaced persons they sheltered (35 per cent).[83] Projects could only be co-financed for up to 50 per cent of the costs, or 75 per cent in the case of Member States qualifying for cohesion funds.

As for the funding of emergency measures, a double decision-making process was envisaged. As long as the TP initiative had not been approved, the Council was to decide on the financing by acting unanimously on a proposal of the Commission. After the entry into force of the TP Directive, the Council was to act by qualified majority following the same decision-making procedure envisaged for declaring TP. Financing in these cases could not exceed 80 per cent of the project costs and could only last for six months. The resources had to be distributed according to the numbers of people having entered each Member State during the mass influx.

The Refugee Fund proposal indicated a change of perspective on the TP issue. By the end of 1999 it was clear that too many Member States were dissatisfied with the original 1997 TP proposal. In November 1998, the Austrian Presidency had presented a new TP draft Joint Action, which echoed the 1994 German one, but this too was considered unacceptable. Relying on a few fundamental points established by the German Presidency as a basis for negotiations, in the spring of 2000 the Commission presented a brand new initiative.[84] The TP regime being

---

82. The Commission was to be assisted by a committee under the 'advisory procedure' laid down in Art. 3 of the new 'comitology' decision (Council Decision 1999/468/EC in OJ 1999 L184/23). The powers of the committee in question were to be much reduced in comparison with those envisaged in previous funding instruments in this field.

83. In addition, a relatively small amount of resources would be allocated to each Member State every year. The amount was to decrease on a yearly basis.

84. 'Proposal for a Council Directive on minimum standards for giving temporary protection in the event of a mass influx of displaced persons and on measures promoting

suggested was considerably different. To begin with, its length had been shortened to a maximum of two years. The decision to declare a TP status would be taken on the proposal of the Commission only, but Member States could make requests to the latter on this matter. Decisions on adopting or withdrawing TP could be taken at any time by qualified majority. The original deeply controversial terms referring to 'ethnic and religious persecution' as grounds for protection were fortunately dropped. They were replaced by 'armed conflict', 'endemic violence' and 'systematic or generalised violations of Human Rights' (Art. 2.c). On a further positive note, consultations with the UNHCR were instituted at all stages of the procedure and the concept of family reunification extended. This was widened to include non-married partners (if recognised by the Member State's national legislation) and all dependants of any age. A TP decision had to be based on a set of specific criteria, but unfortunately they appeared intentionally generic and lacked any specific guidelines (Art. 5.2).[85] In this respect, it would have been far more preferable to link the adoption of a TP regime to a Commission decision, possibly to be taken in co-operation with the UNHCR. Access to asylum procedures could be temporarily suspended in the event of a mass influx, but had to be granted at the end of TP. The turning down of an asylum application could not overturn the effects of TP while it was in effect. Finally, TP status beneficiaries would be granted the same level of benefits as GC refugees.

The proposal contained some remarkable new provisions on solidarity among Member States in the reception of refugees. Solidarity rules of a financial nature were obviously linked to the Refugee Fund. Measures of a physical nature, entailing the distribution of refugees across the Community were envisaged both before and after the adoption of the TP regime. In the initial phase, Member States would be requested to indicate – 'in figures or in general terms' (Art. 25.1) – their respective reception capacities. Subsequent additional capacities would

---

a balance of efforts between Member States in receiving such persons and bearing the consequences thereof', to be found at 'http://europa.eu.int/eur-lex/en/com/dat/2000/en_500PC0303.html'. Approval of this Directive was still pending at time of writing. For the Austrian and German Presidency proposals, see G. Noll and J. Vedsted-Hansen, 'Temporary protection and burden-sharing: conditionalising access suspending refugee rights', in E. Guild and C. Harlow (eds.), *supra* n° 73, p. 195, at pp. 207 *et seq.* For the 1994 German proposal, see Chapter IV.6.

85. The same lack of a proper definition of what would constitute 'mass influx' appeared in the new proposal. Some general criteria were added in Art. 5.2. However, they merely referred to taking into account the 'scale' of the population movements, the 'advisability' of establishing a TP regime and information from Member States, the Commission and the UNHCR. Hence, declaring a TP regime still boiled down to a decision of pure political convenience. In this respect, the provision on qualified majority should also be viewed with some scepticism, as it would be difficult to envisage the possibility of a Member State being outvoted on such a 'sensitive' matter.

also have to be communicated to the Commission.[86] Following the entry into force of the TP regime, Member States could also request to transfer excess refugees between them. A specific format for the transfer pass was included in the annex to the proposal. These transfers would obviously have to rely on the 'solidarity' spirit of less affected Member States. This necessity appeared the greatest weakness of this provision, given that the Commission itself had stated in its proposal that the major resistance to approving the previous TP package had been caused by its solidarity provisions. In the new proposal, the only positive commitment consisted of the initial capacity declaration. However, it appeared obvious that it would not be in the interest of any Member States to declare generous capacities.

The European Refugee Fund was eventually approved in September 2000.[87] The decision was based on Art. 63.2.b TEC dealing with burden-sharing and it applied also to the UK and Ireland, but not to Denmark. Overall, the consolidation of all previous funding initiatives into a single instrument structured along the lines of most other Community funding programmes was indeed a tremendous advance in the building of a true EU asylum policy. As in the case of most other Community policies, comprehensive funding had always played a pivotal role in their consolidation. One of its most important consequences would certainly be the strengthening of the Commission's role and of its independence. It was also remarkable that Member States could eventually overcome their resistance to abandoning unanimity voting in favour of qualified majority.[88]

However, the European Refugee Fund would only be able to have a positive impact on building a fairer system of burden-sharing if its resources proved adequate to its task. Considering that only EUR 216 million were allocated to this fund over a five-year period, the sums involved appeared unlikely to have any relevant impact on the majority of Member States. The UK alone spent more than 1 billion EUR on asylum seekers in the year 2000.[89] Suggestions to improve the fairness of the financing distribution also went unheeded.[90] A distribution mechanism that took into account the ratio between numbers of refugees entering the territory of a Member State and the latter's population would have been fairer than the chosen one based only on absolute numbers of

---

86. This provision strongly recalled the 'Bonn Plan' presented by the German government during the Kosovo crisis, see *supra* n° 57, as well as the Austrian Presidency 1998 proposal, see *supra* n° 84.

87. OJ 2000 L252/12.

88. In the previous proposal of financial solidarity, Member States had insisted on maintaining unanimity voting, even though they had accepted qualified majority rule for declaring TP status. See Chapter VI.3.

89. According to Home Office figures the UK spent GBP 835 million on asylum seekers in 2000, roughly equivalent to EUR 1 billion and 285 million. See M. Prescott, 'Refugee bill soars to £835m' *The Sunday Times*, 11/02/01, p. 1.

90. Suggestion put forward by the UK immigration minister Barbara Roache, see A. Travis, 'EU scheme to fund repatriation of failed asylum seekers' *The Guardian*, 14/3/2000, p. 8.

refugees in the previous three years. Moreover, the distribution of resources was disproportionately tilted in favour of measures concerning asylum seekers instead of recognised refugees and other displaced persons. This could have been seen as a clear warning message to Member States not to increase their refugee recognition rates. Similarly, restricting emergency aid to a mere six month time-limit also appeared to be an indirect encouragement for Member States to dispose of sudden mass influx in a speedy manner which might not always be compatible with good levels of protection. Finally, the European Refugee Fund bore no mention of any 'physical' solidarity measure, implicitly referring this instance to the application of the TP Directive. However, the small amount of financial contributions envisaged would certainly not make up for failing national infrastructures in the future. Likewise, most often in the event of a real mass influx, there might be no substitute for a physical redistribution of refugees. In the context of the doubts raised by the eventual implementation of the TP directive rules on refugee 'redistribution', the concept of Community 'solidarity' appeared far from being effective.

VI.6. THE DRAFT DIRECTIVE ON MINIMUM STANDARDS FOR GRANTING AND WITHDRAWING REFUGEE STATUS

Following the principles of the 1998 Action Plan, Tampere had advocated the harmonisation of national asylum procedures as an integral part of the new CEAS. In March 1999, the Commission had already taken up this challenge by presenting the Working Paper 'Towards common standards on asylum procedures'.[91] It also stated its intention to prepare a proposal concerning a legally-binding instrument involving a certain degree of harmonisation of asylum procedures across the EU, following the priorities laid down by the Action Plan.

The Commission declared that the Paper was to be a sounding board for Member States, NGO's and the UNHCR to put forward their specific ideas and concerns. The wide consultations carried out by the Commission[92] indicated that the Commission was finally beginning to shed the culture of secrecy that had characterised the previous asylum initiatives. It was also symptomatic of its higher level of confidence and independence brought about by the communitarisation of the asylum field.

In the Paper Commissioner Gradin stressed that 'increased efficiency in handling asylum applications must not mean a lowering of our ambitions when it comes to safeguarding a fair and equal treatment for all'. The initiative pointed out that there would be a choice between two general approaches. The first one would consist of an instrument establishing minimum procedural safeguards and

---

91. SEC (1999) 271 final.
92. The Commission actually consulted the UNHCR, ECRE, Amnesty International, Save the Children, The Refugee Legal Centre, The Medical Foundation for the Care of the Victims of Torture and the Immigration Law Practitioners' Association.

guarantees compulsory for all Member States, while leaving them relative freedom in the adoption of procedural tools and their national administrative arrangements. The second one would entail a more 'prescriptive approach' whereby precise procedures to be followed would be laid down, thus achieving a greater level of harmonisation. The Commission indicated its preference for the first approach, because its implementation chances appeared considerably greater. Nonetheless, it conceded that the second approach would be more consistent with a future comprehensive CEAS. In this sense, the caution expressed by the Commission seemed to indicate that the possibility of achieving a uniform European asylum adjudication system was still considered quite remote.

The working document attempted to lay down a comprehensive list of the issues open for discussion. These included important outstanding problems that the EU had either failed to address in the past, or had done so in an unsatisfactory manner. The questions involved: a) how to relate eventual new legally-binding initiatives to the old 'soft law' instruments; b) ways to achieve an effective application of the DC; c) additional safeguards for the implementation of the concept of safe third country; d) how to restrict the concept of 'manifestly unfounded' applications; e) which time limits should be imposed on asylum procedures; f) how to simplify the appeal systems; and g) how to deal with repeated applications. The Paper also emphasised the need to address major national differences on the standard of proof and went as far as suggesting the abolition of the 'safe country of origin' concept. It also stressed that special attention should be given to particularly vulnerable groups, such as women, children and sexually persecuted individuals. The Commission's proposal generated a great deal of discussion and in some instances met with outright opposition by the Member States. This opposition focused on the suggestion of abolishing the 'safe country of origin' concept, on the harmonisation of the means of proof and on the attempts to restrict the application of the notion of 'manifestly unfounded' claims.

Having taken the Member States' comments on board, in the autumn of 2000 the Commission presented a proposal for a 'Council Directive on minimum standard for procedures in Member States for granting and withdrawing refugee status'.[93] Thus, the Commission obviously opted for the first option envisaged in its previous Working Paper and aimed at establishing minimum procedural safeguards and guarantees compulsory for all Member States, while leaving them relative freedom in the adoption of procedural tools and their national administrative arrangements. The 'prescriptive approach' option, laying down a defined set of compulsory procedures, was abandoned as impractical. However, the result of this option would inevitably be a lower level of harmonisation. To

---

93. The draft Directive can be found at 'http://europa.eu.int/eur-lex/en/com/dat/2000/en_500PC0578.html, document n° 500PC0578'. Approval of the Directive was still pending at time of writing.

counteract this criticism, the Commission made it clear that this was to be considered only as 'a first measure on asylum procedures'.

The purported aim of the Directive was to set out a 'simple and quick' system for dealing with asylum applications. The Commission repeatedly emphasised that the proposal would not aim at obliging Member States to apply uniform procedures, or forcing them to implement concepts or practices against their wishes. Unfortunately, the latitude of implementation Member States would be allowed under this proposal cast important doubts over the eventual adoption of 'real' common procedural standards. The choice of a directive as a legal instrument was also justified by the impracticality of a 'prescriptive approach'. The scope of the proposed Directive did not, unfortunately, appear to be in line with the requirement of a comprehensive CEAS affirmed at Tampere. These provisions were to apply only to asylum applicants within the meaning of the GC and it was left to the discretion of Member States whether to extend their application to persons in need of protection outside the remit of the GC.

The proposal suggested Art. 63.1.d TEC as a legal base for the Directive, which basically contained three different sets of provisions. The first set dealt with minimum procedural guarantees for asylum seekers. These were designed to 'approximate notions of procedural fairness among Member States'.[94] The provisions echoed in many respects the ones of the 1995 Resolution,[95] but a great amount of detail and specification was added. Asylum seekers were to be given an 'effective opportunity' to lodge an asylum application (Art. 4.2) and the possibility of remaining at the border or in the territory of the Member States as long as the application was being examined. Unfortunately, a lot of the terms used in the Directive were too vague. So, for instance, Art. 6 stated that decisions on applications had to be taken 'individually', 'objectively' and 'impartially', but the translation of these terms in the national asylum adjudication systems could give rise in practice to very different national implementations. Other provisions appeared contradictory.

Art. 7 laid down the right of asylum applicants to an interpreter when submitting their application, this service being paid by public funding.[96] All subsequent decisions would have to be communicated to the applicant in writing, but only positive decisions would have to be translated. Other minimum rights to be granted to asylum seekers included the opportunity of a personal interview,[97] free legal assistance and, in principle, the right not to be detained. However, the latter was subject to such severe limitations so as to be stripped of any significance.[98] Also the subsequent provision guaranteeing regular reviews of the

---

94. See *supra*, n° 93, p. 3.

95. Resolution on minimum guarantees for asylum procedures, see Chapter IV.4.

96. This was one of the most disregarded provisions of the 1995 Resolution on minimum guarantees, see Chapter IV.4.

97. Special provisions applied in the case of people not able to attend interviews because of particularly traumatic experiences (Art. 8.5).

98. According to Art. 11.1, detention was to be allowed if it was necessary to: i) ascertain or verify the identity or nationality of the applicant, especially in the event of the applicant

detention orders appeared to be inspired by the habeas corpus right contained in Art. 5.4 ECHR.[99] Special provisions covered the applications of unaccompanied minors and dependants of one family. Finally, a very vague provision covered the need to supply 'basic training' to all personnel coming into contact with asylum applicants, the obligation to keep all information concerning applicants confidential and the rights of the UNHCR. The latter was to be granted access to applicants and to their files and the possibility of making representations to the authorities.[100]

The second set of provisions contained in the draft Directive concerned the setting of minimum standards in the decision-making process. A distinction was introduced between a 'regular procedure' and an 'accelerated' one.[101] All procedures would be subject to a three-tier system of adjudication and appeals. The initial level would be constituted by an authority competent to take first instance decisions on asylum applications. A reviewing body would hear appeals against initial decisions. This authority could be of an administrative or judicial nature, but it would have to be competent to hear appeals on points both of fact and of law. An Appellate Court would constitute the final tier. Only if the second tier was already a judicial body could the Appellate Court be restricted to hear only appeals based on points of law. The 'regular' procedure was not subjected to any particular time limits.[102] The only requirement imposed by the proposal requested those limits to be 'reasonable'. Once again the vagueness of the terminology cast serious doubts on the effectiveness of such measures. The cancellation or withdrawal of refugee status was only to be undertaken under the 'regular' procedure.[103]

---

himself having disposed of his travel documents; ii) 'to determine the elements on which his asylum application is based which in other circumstances would be lost' (point c) – the meaning of this provision being very 'obscure'; and iii) to verify the applicant's right to enter the territory. It was obvious how the broad scope of these exceptions effectively nullified the right not to be detained.

99. In fact the very idea of detaining refugees could be in breach of Art. 31 GC (whereby refugees should not be penalised for illegally entering the country of refuge), Art. 5 ECHR and specific UNHCR guidelines. See, for instance, the 1999 High Court decision in the UK declaring that the jailing of asylum seekers constituted a breach of Art. 31 GC in C. Dyer, 'Home Office faces huge bill for ignoring rules by jailing refugees' *The Guardian*, 7/2/2000, p. 7.

100. These rights were already enshrined in the UNHCR's mandate anyway. See Chapter I.3.

101. In this case, the proposal also echoed earlier measures. It constituted a comprehensive restructuring of the principles contained in the three 1992 Edinburgh initiatives and the 1995 Resolution (see Chapters III.3 and IV.4).

102. With regard to 'regular' procedures, the only specific time limit to appear in the proposal concerned the filing of grounds for a first appeal, which should not be shorter than 20 working days (Art. 34.1) and 30 working days for a further appeal (Art. 38.5).

103. No grounds for withdrawal or cancellation of refugee status were given. Presumably these were remitted to the discretion of Member States and the general provisions of Art. 1.C-F GC.

'Accelerated' procedures, on the other hand, were subjected to very specific time requirements.[104] They were to be applied to inadmissible or manifestly unfounded applications. According to Art. 18 inadmissible applications were those: a) where another Member State was responsible for the application under the DC; b) where a third country could be considered as a country of first asylum for the applicant; and c) where the applicant could be sent back to a safe third country.[105] A first asylum country was a country where the applicant had already been admitted as a refugee. Art. 28 defined applications as manifestly unfounded if: a) the applicant had submitted false information about himself; b) the applicant had not produced identity or travel documents or he had in bad faith destroyed them; c) the application was lodged so as to delay deportation order; d) the applicant's claim for protection fell outside the scope of the GC or Art. 3 ECHR;[106] e) the applicant came from a safe country of origin; or f) the applicant submitted a new application which raised no relevant new facts. In considering whether the application was unfounded Member States could not take into account the fact that the applicant could have pursued an internal flight option or that there could be serious grounds to believe that Art. 1.F GC might concern the applicant.

Therefore, 'accelerated' procedures entailed a considerable restriction of applicants' rights compared to the 'regular' ones. Apart from the strict time-limits, under accelerated procedures applicants would not be guaranteed legal representation at their personal interview (Art. 9.3). Their application would almost certainly be subjected to an automatic review, the Appellate Court could decide not to grant them leave to appeal and examine their appeal under an abbreviated procedure (Art. 36).[107] Finally, the general principle that appeals should have suspensive effect did not necessarily apply.[108]

---

104. According to Art. 29, under the 'accelerated' procedure applicants had to be interviewed within 40 working days; a first instance decision had to follow within 25 days of this personal interview (65 days from the lodging of the application if no interview had taken place). A reviewing body was given 65 days to review first instance decisions (Art. 35). No time limits were set for Appellate Courts. If at any stage of the procedure the time limits prescribed were not respected, the case would automatically revert to the 'regular' procedure.

105. The definition of safe third country and of safe country of origin constituted the third set of measures that characterised the proposal (see further)

106. This provision appeared incredibly innovative as it was the first time that Art. 3 ECHR was expressly mentioned in the asylum context. For the importance this article has had in the expansion of the right to non-refoulement, see Chapter I.4.C.

107. Art. 36 contained a startling contradiction to the provisions determining whether an application could be considered unfounded. Art. 28.2.b specifically stated that Art. 1.F GC could not constitute grounds for declaring an application unfounded. However, Art. 36.3.c, in dealing with the possibility of allowing an automatic review in 'manifestly unfounded' cases, specifically mentioned Art. 1.F GC as grounds.

108. According to Art. 33, Member States could derogate from the general suspensive effect rule in safe third country cases, in the event of manifestly unfounded applications and on

The third set of measures contained in the draft Directive proposal concerned the definition of certain key principles such as 'safe third countries' and 'safe countries of origin'. Annex I listed the main criteria for the designation of safe third countries. These rested on two main requirements: safe third countries had to observe both international standards for the protection of refugees and basic standards of international Human Rights law. The first requirement on standards of international protection would necessarily have to entail: a) the ratification of the GC; b) asylum procedures prescribed by law and decisions taken objectively and impartially;[109] c) the right to remain on the territory as long as the asylum application was being processed; d) the right to a personal interview and the assistance of an interpreter; e) the opportunity to communicate with the UNHCR and the latter enjoying all the rights conferred by its mandate; and f) the possibility of appealing against a first instance decision either to an administrative body or a Court of law.[110] Membership of the GC would not be necessary if the third country was a member of the OAU Convention or it followed the 1984 Catagena Declaration and in both cases co-operated with the UNHCR. As for the basic standards of Human Rights law, the third country had to have ratified either the ECHR, or both the 1966 ICCPR and the 1984 CAT.[111] Countries could be designated as safe on the basis of all available sources of information, such as diplomatic and NGOs reports and information supplied by the UNHCR and other international organisations. According to Art. 22, any national laws or regulations concerning the designation of safe third countries had to be notified to the Commission.

Annex II listed the criteria designating a country of origin as safe. Those criteria entailed the respect of international Human Rights,[112] democratic institu-

---

grounds of national security or public order. The latter instance, however, could be incompatible with Art. 33 GC and Arts 3 and 13 ECHR. In *Chahal* v. *UK* (1997) 23 EHRR 413, the ECtHR maintained that the claim of 'national security grounds' had to be in itself subject to judicial scrutiny, otherwise a breach of Art. 13 ECHR (right to an effective remedy) might occur.

109. The further specification of the word 'individually' contained in Art. 6 was missing from this provision.

110. No three-tier adjudication system was required of safe third countries, not even for the reviewing authority to be a judicial body.

111. They also had to respect: the right to life; freedom from torture, cruel, inhuman or degrading treatmen; freedom from slavery and servitude; the prohibition of retroactive criminal laws; the right to recognition as a person before the law; freedom from being imprisoned merely on the grounds of inability to fulfil a contractual obligation; and freedom of thought, conscience and religion.

112. These rights were defined as the right to freedom of thought, conscience and religion; the right to freedom of expression; the right to freedom of peaceful assembly; and the right of freedom of associations with others, including the right to form and join trade unions and the right to take part in government directly or through freely chosen representatives (Annex II, I.A).

tions, the rule of law[113] and effective remedies against the violation of those rights. The country also had to be regarded as 'stable'. Sources similar to those employed in the designation of safe third countries were to be used. Echoing Art. 22, Art. 30 provided for any national rules on safe countries of origin to be communicated to the Commission. Overall, there appeared to be substantial discrepancies between the criteria determining 'safe third countries' and 'safe countries of origin'. The respect for certain fundamental rights appeared compulsory for the first category, but not for the second and vice versa, while other important rights such as family or property ones were excluded without any apparent logic.

The Commission suggested, as an implementation date for the draft Directive, 31 December 2002. The creation of a Contact Committee was also suggested. The Committee's tasks would be to facilitate the implementation of the Directive and to promote further approximation in the future, paving the way for a transition from 'minimum standards on procedure to a common procedure' (Art. 4.1 of the financial statement). The proposal suggested the Committee would need to meet for these purposes at least three times a year.

This draft Directive was intended as a cornerstone in the overall project of a CEAS. However, this proposal fell short of reaching its purported target on several counts. The DC had been shown to be ineffective and clearly illegitimate. National and international judicial interpretations had clearly indicated that the roots of such illegitimacy lay in the lack of harmonised asylum adjudication systems.[114] The Tampere idea of a CEAS also stemmed from the need to correct the illegitimacy of such premises in the context of the Union's new Human Rights dimension. Unfortunately, the tools chosen by the Commission appeared to be totally inadequate. Firstly, the draft Directive was not addressed to all persons in need of protection, but only to GC refugees. Secondly, controversial aspects, such as the harmonisation of the means of proof, had been conveniently side-stepped. Finally and most importantly, minimum standards fell sorely short of substantive harmonisation and certainly could not guarantee the required identity of result in national processing of asylum applications. The Commission appeared conscious of the shortcomings of its choice when it declared the proposal to be only 'a first measure on asylum procedures'. However, the sincerity of this statement was patently contradicted by its later affirmation that 'once minimum standards on asylum procedures are in place, the operation of, *inter alia, an effective system for determining which Member State is responsible for considering an asylum application is fully justified'.*[115] As on previous occasions, the Commission appeared to have correctly identified the ultimate goals of a

---

113. The rule of law entailed respect for the right to liberty and security of person, the right to recognition as a person before the law and equality before the law. (Annex II, I.C)

114. See Chapter VI.4 and the 1991 Opinion of the Dutch Council of State, Chapter II.3.C.

115. See *supra* n° 93, p. 5.

fair common asylum policy, but then seemed to have been pressurised into finding some 'quick-fix' solutions.

The overriding concern of the proposal appeared once again to be 'access control' and ultimately prevention of such access. This was evident in the excessive emphasis laid on 'accelerated' procedures throughout the draft Directive. Minimum rights and decision-making standards were established for asylum applicants only to be derogated from in the event of an 'accelerated procedure'. Given that most asylum seekers would have transited at some point through other countries, in practice 'accelerated procedures' would have applied to the majority of applicants, thus becoming the standard procedure. The very premises of 'accelerated' procedures were in contradiction with the spirit of the proposal purporting to guarantee uniform fundamental rights for all applicants. Even the guarantee that these procedures would apply mainly to 'safe third country' and 'safe country of origin' cases appeared problematic. Despite the lengthy and detailed annexes on the designation of such countries it was evident that the standards required from them were well beneath those expected from EU Members. Yet, it would be considered acceptable to return applicants to those countries, moreover under an accelerated procedure entailing as few rights as possible.

Some elements of the proposal nonetheless showed interesting potential. The catalogue of applicants' rights – notwithstanding its inherent contradictions – was in itself a considerable step forward. Although most of these rights had already been included in previous initiatives, their national implementation had been abysmal.[116] In this context, the formulation of a legally-binding instrument could hopefully bring about some long awaited implementation. The creation of a Contact Committee also appeared positive, provided it would be given enough standing and resources to play an effective promotion and liaising role.

VI.7. THE REFORMS OF THE NICE TREATY

During the negotiations of the Amsterdam Treaty, it proved impossible to build a consensus around some major issues of institutional reform. Rather than delay the signature of the new Treaty, Member States agreed to reconvene an IGC in the year 2000 to examine the outstanding problems. These pertained mainly to the future of EU decision-making in relation to the impending enlargement of the Union. The 1999 Cologne Council concluded that the future IGC's main tasks should deal with issues such as the size and composition of the Commission, the weighting of votes in the Council and the possible extension of qualified majority voting in the Council. The prospect of enlargement was particularly daunting for the field of asylum, given the formidable problems posed by the

---

116. See Chapter IV.4. For an example of how national asylum procedures might be impacted by the provisions of this draft Directive (specifically, in the UK case) see House of Lords, Select Committee on the European Union, *Minimum standards in asylum procedures*, 11th Report of session 2000–2001, 27/3/2001, HL Paper 59.

harmonisation of more than 20 different types of national asylum legislation.[117] The inherent danger was that the content of the Amsterdam reforms could be watered down. In the impossibility of producing legally-binding agreements, soft law instruments might have made an unwanted comeback and refugees would be left to bear the brunt of the Union's failure to manage its enlarged decision-making process.

The IGC negotiations were officially opened by the Portuguese Presidency in February 2000, but consensus on the scope of the reforms was not within easy reach. Germany became the main motor of a radically more 'integrationist' vision of Europe, even going as far as demanding a new IGC in 2004 to fundamentally revise the Treaties of Rome.[118] France struggled to keep up with the German pace and the traditional Franco-German axis showed for the first time in 40 years considerable signs of strain. Germany was determined to strengthen its voting power based on the considerable increase in its demographic base since the unification. France was determined to resist German requests in order to maintain the traditional balance between the two powers. France was also particularly determined that majority voting should be extended to virtually all Community decision-making. Eventually, in the final round of negotiations in December 2000, Germany performed a policy U-turn similar to the one that took place at Amsterdam. After having supported the introduction of qualified majority rule in Title IV TEC, it then suddenly changed its mind, rallying behind the British position. The result could be best termed as a hybrid reform.

In the first place, Art. 68.1 TEC remained unaltered. Therefore, the much criticised restriction in Title IV TEC of the right to request a preliminary ruling by limiting it to Courts of last instance remained intact. Instead, Art. 67 TEC on decision-making procedures for Title IV TEC was eventually amended, but in a much more limited manner than originally intended. The French would have preferred to simply modify Art. 67.1–2 (second indent) by replacing the unanimity requirement with that of a qualified majority. In this way, during the transitional period the Council would adopt its decisions by qualified majority, including eventually the decision to transfer areas of this Title to the codecision procedure. Instead, the Nice negotiations resulted in the creation of a new paragraph 5 in the old Art. 67. The second indent in this new paragraph had direct relevance to decision-making in the asylum field. Measures in Art. 63.1.a-d and 63.2.a TEC were to be adopted by codecision procedure, but only after the Council had unanimously adopted 'Community legislation defining the common

---

117. The current EU Members could possibly make use of the new provisions on 'closer co-operation' to bypass the resistance of newer Members (see Chapter V.4.A). However, serious doubts have been cast on the practical implementation of such instruments (see H. Kortenberg, 'Closer co-operation in the Treaty of Amsterdam' (1998) 35 CML Rev., p. 833 and G. Gaja, 'How flexible is flexibility under the Amsterdam Treaty?' (1998) 35 CML Rev., p. 855).

118. For a summary of the new German position, see J. Hooper and I. Black, 'Showdown over Europe', *The Guardian*, 23/6/2000, p. 1.

rules and basic principles governing this issue'. Measures on 'burden-sharing' according to Art. 63.2.b TEC were excluded from this rule, just as they had previously been excluded for the five-year transitional rule.

The Commission scoreboard[119] mentioned – forthcoming and already presented – proposals in most of these areas, but it appeared uncertain whether all of these proposals would qualify under the strict requirements of the new Art. 67.5. It was also doubtful whether just one initiative would be sufficient to set all 'the common rules and basic principles' of a particular field. In this respect, it would have been reasonable to indicate which pieces of future legislation were to be considered the 'common rules and basic principles' in the area. In the event of a lack of such specification, subsequent initiatives approved under unanimity rule would no doubt be open to judicial review. In the end, the impact of the new procedures was to be considerably reduced in comparison to the original proposals, since the basic tenets of the asylum field would still have to be approved by unanimous consent. Moreover, the potential implications of an eventual passage to codecision might produce the opposite effect to the one originally intended. Instead of simplifying the achievement of consent, the temptation to reduce subsequent unwanted EP intervention might lead Member States to introduce extremely detailed provisions, thereby making it even harder to reach an agreement.

The provisions on 'closer co-operation' were also the subject of extensive amendments. In June 2000 the Portuguese European Council had already highlighted the necessity of easing the implementation of closer co-operation procedures.[120] The result of the Nice negotiations was a streamlining of these instruments and a simplification of the procedures involved. The common provisions contained in Title VII TEU were modified so as to synthesise both lists of requirements contained previously in Art. 11 TEC and Art. 40 TEU. A new provision was added requiring that closer co-operation was not to undermine the Common Market or economic and social cohesion. Most importantly, the previous requirement that closer co-operation should always involve 'a majority of Member States' was dropped in favour of a reduced minimum number of just eight countries. To presumably counterbalance the lowering of the participation standards, a 'last resort' clause was added, whereby Members might resort to enhanced co-operation only if their objectives could not be attained within a reasonable period by applying the relevant Treaty provisions. The Council and the Commission were charged with ensuring the consistency of the activities undertaken on the basis of closer co-operation with the policies of the Union.

Subject to these amendments, the Community article dealing with closer co-operation concerned only procedural issues. In the event of the Commission refusing to submit a proposal on closer co-operation to the Council, a new

---

119. See *supra* n° 78.
120. See the 'Presidency's report to the European Council on the IGC for institutional reforms', CONFER 4750/00, of 14/06/2000, at point 8.1.

clause was added obliging the Commission to explain its reasons to the Member States. Assent of the EP would now be required for closer co-operation in areas covered by the codecision procedure. This new clause could prove a potential discouragement of future closer co-operation attempts in the asylum field. Procedures were considerably simplified by the dropping of the veto clause. The amended article only referred to the possibility for a Member State to refer the matter to the European Council. The latter should decide by qualified majority except in codecision cases.[121]

Overall, the new conditions and procedures for taking advantage of the possibility of 'closer co-operation' were considerably streamlined. This showed considerable foresight in view of the forthcoming enlargement of the Union. In this context, reducing the number of participating countries to a minimum of eight greatly enhanced the possibilities of its adoption. On the other hand, however, reducing the number of participating countries also heightened the risk of further fragmentation of the Union's *acquis*. In this respect, the Commission's gateway role in the process should hopefully ensure that all conditions would be fulfilled before its acceptance. Given the improbable adoption of asylum 'closer co-operation' in the near future, the EP would eventually also be involved through the codecision procedure in scrutinising the fulfilment of such conditions.

Other changes introduced by the Nice Treaty with potential repercussions on asylum co-operation consisted of granting the EP the full right to bring an annulment action and the amendment of Art. 7 TEU. Art. 230 TEC only gave the EP the ability to bring an action of annulment 'for the purpose of protecting [its] prerogatives'. The new Treaty, instead, would allow the EP the same wide scope of annulment actions previously granted only to the Council, the Commission and the Member States. Given the EP's past willingness to strongly support refugee protection, in the future this provisions could give it a powerful tool to challenge the conformity of EU initiatives with international refugee obligations. In this respect, it was unfortunate that the EP still remained excluded from the ability to request the ECJ to give an interpretation of Title IV TEC or of EU initiatives based on it (Art. 68.3 TEC), especially because such judgments were not subjected to the temporal limitations imposed by Art. 230 TEC.

Art. 7 TEU was amended to include the possibility of a 'preventive procedure' aimed at declaring 'a clear risk of a serious breach by a Member State of the principles mentioned in Art. 6.1' TEU. The Council was to act 'by a majority of four-fifths of its Members after obtaining the assent of the European Parliament'. This amendment had potential implications for the Protocol on asylum for nationals of EU Member States, which contained a specific exception to its application relating to Art. 7.1 Amsterdam TEU. According to Art. 1.b-c of the Protocol, Member States were allowed to examine an asylum application of EU

---

121. It remained ambiguous how the codecision procedure could be applied in the case of the European Council having to take a decision on the matter, given that the President of the Commission takes part in this body.

nationals if their country had been found to be in violation of the fundamental principles of the Union contained in Art. 6 TEU or if the procedure to ascertain such a breach had been initiated. However, the Protocol was not amended at Nice in order to include the new 'preventive procedure' among its exceptions. Hence, the hypothetical possibility remained that an EU national of a country that had been declared at serious risk of breaching the Union's fundamental rights could be denied asylum in the rest of the EU.

Overall, several amendments of the Nice Treaty might have a potential impact over EU asylum co-operation. Some amendments could have very positive implications, such as the streamlining of 'closer co-operation' rules and the strengthening of the EP's ability to bring an action for annulment. However, the impact of other provisions, such as the new Art. 7 TEU, remains ambiguous. This new article could potentially widen the scope for protection of EU citizens requesting asylum in another Member State, but only if the relative EC Protocol is amended to include the new exception. Finally, the chance for some important reforms was unfortunately missed. The right to request a preliminary ruling ex Art. 68.1 TEC remains restricted to Courts of last instance. The EP is still excluded from the scope of Art. 68.3 TEC and as a consequence an important opportunity to test the legitimacy of EU asylum initiatives has been effectively overlooked. Most importantly, the 'cosmetic' reform of Art. 67 TEC still falls sorely short of allowing real democratic control over the EU legislative process on asylum.

VI.8. THE EU CHARTER OF FUNDAMENTAL RIGHTS AND REFUGEE PROTECTION

The 1999 Cologne Council concluded that the forthcoming IGC should also deal with the issue of the EU's Human Rights dimension. Therefore, it approved a project to draft an EU Charter of Fundamental Rights. To this purpose, a Convention was nominated composed of representatives of Member States, national Parliaments, the EP and the Commission. The purpose of the Charter, according to the Cologne Council, was to make European citizens aware of the existence of a whole series of civil, political, social and economic rights that were dispersed in various international texts. By incorporating them into a single, easily accessible document the Union hoped to reaffirm its commitment to fundamental rights solemnly stated in Art. 6 TEU and to pave the way for the incorporation of the Charter into the Treaties.

The EU Charter of Fundamental Rights drafted by the Convention was eventually approved by the Nice Council.[122] This Charter marked a further stage in the process begun at Amsterdam of expanding the Union's competence toward new fields of a non-economic nature. As stated in its preamble, the Charter based its rights on the 'constitutional traditions and international obligations

---

122. OJ 2000 C364/1.

common to the Member States, the Treaty on European Union, the Community Treaties, the European Convention for the Protection of Human Rights and Fundamental Freedoms, the Social Charters [...] and the case law of the Court of Justice of the European Communities and the European Court of Human Rights'.

Two articles directly concerned the asylum field. Art. 18 stated that the right of asylum would be guaranteed with due respect of the GC, the NY Protocol and in accordance with the TEC.[123] Art. 19 contained a prohibition both of collective expulsions and of the possibility to remove somebody to a country where he or she might be at 'serious risk' of being subjected to the death penalty, torture or other inhuman or degrading treatment. The wording of this article, clearly inspired by the ECtHR jurisprudence, presented two sets of problems. Firstly, it did not define the term 'collective'.[124] Secondly, by referring specifically to the risk of being subjected to the 'death penalty', the article purposefully avoided the issue of non-State agent persecution. By definition, the death penalty could only be applied by a State. Art. 33 GC avoided the issue by prohibiting refoulment to a territory where 'life or freedom' would be threatened on account of the classic grounds of persecution. The ECtHR had always maintained in its jurisprudence that the prohibition of refoulement contained in the ECHR was greater than that of Art. 33 GC because it was not dependent upon a set of reasons for persecution,[125] but it never specified that it only applied to the death penalty. By insisting on the concept of the death penalty, the EU Charter would effectively shrink the wide scope of the protection against refoulement afforded by the jurisprudence of the ECtHR.

Despite high expectations, it was impossible at Nice to define the juridical status of the Charter. Only a third of Member States favoured the integration of the Charter within the TEU and as a result the adoption of the text amounted in practice to a political declaration.[126] Art. 51 clearly stated that only the Union's institutions and the Member States – when implementing Union law – were bound by the Charter. However, without incorporation within the TEU,

---

123. The article did not really contain any new element as the obligation for Community institutions to comply with the GC and the NY Protocol was already stated in Art. 63.1 TEC. Moreover, the obligations contained in Art. 63.1 were of a wider nature because the provision also mentioned the necessity of complying with 'other relevant treaties'.

124. 'Collective' could historically be referred to expulsions based on nationality criteria, such as the Armenian expulsion from the Ottoman Empire at the beginning of the 20th Century. However, in the context of modern mass-transport, could it also refer to the occupants of one particular vessel that enters a Member State illegally, such as, for instance, the boat-people fleeing the Vietnam war or, more recently, the boats carrying Kurdish refugees to Italian shores?

125. See Chapter I.4.C, n° 99.

126. On the development of negotiations on the Charter, see J. Dutheil De La Rochère, 'La Charte des droits fondamentaux de l'Union européenne: quelle valeur ajoutée, quel avenir?' (2000) 443 *Revue du Marché commun et de l' Union européenne*, p. 674.

there would be no opportunity to subject the actions of the EU institutions or of the Member States to judicial scrutiny.

Incorporation of the Charter into the Treaties also raised the issue of a conflict of competence between the Union and other international bodies, such as the ECtHR over provisions which the Charter had reproduced from other texts. This had particular relevance for the asylum provisions. To solve the potential conflict, Art. 53 of the Charter maintained that no provision should be interpreted so as to restrict or adversely affect Human Rights provisions contained in other international law provisions such as the ECHR. In respect of the latter, Art. 52.3 went even further by specifying that 'the meaning and scope' of any right of the Charter also found in the ECHR would be the same as its ECHR equivalent. However, attempts to include an explicit reference to the ECtHR jurisprudence in this article were strenuously opposed by certain Member States and in the end only a generic reference in the preamble was accepted.[127] As for the Charter provisions echoing those of the GC, possible conflict could in future arise with national Courts which had traditionally been entrusted to interpret the GC.[128]

In its present form the Charter's impact on the development of EU asylum policy would arguably be minimal. However, two Advocates General have already mentioned it in their opinions and the Court of First Instance has refused to pronounce itself on the Charter's potential implications on a mere technical ground.[129] Despite the judicial value the ECJ might attribute to it in the future, the Charter's real impact would still depend almost entirely on the modalities of its incorporation within the Treaties. It can only be hoped that future negotiations on this point would also include a workable solution to eventual conflicts of competence.

VI.9. TOWARDS A COMPREHENSIVE EU ASYLUM POLICY: SEARCHING FOR A LONG-TERM ACTION PLAN

On an ideal path towards an EU asylum policy, the Amsterdam Treaty provided the overall framework for action and the Tampere summit set the ultimate goals.

---

127. 'This Charter reaffirms[...] the rights as they result, in particular, from [...] the case law [...] of the European Court of Human Rights', para. 5. On the opposition to the insertion of this reference, see Editorial Comments, 'The EU Charter of Fundamental Rights still under discussion' (2001) 38 CML Rev., p. 1, at p. 5.

128. The Preamble of the Charter also referred to 'the constitutional traditions and international obligations common to Member States' in the same context of its para. 5, see *supra* n° 127. It is not clear, however, how this provision would solve eventual conflicts between the ECJ and national Courts.

129. Advocate General Tizzano in *BECTU* v. *Secretary of State for Trade and Industry*, case C-173/99 (pending) quoted the Charter as a 'substantive point of reference'. Advocate General Jacobs in *D'Agostino* v. *European Parliament*, case C-270/99 (pending) stated that 'whilst itself not legally-binding, [the Charter] proclaims a generally recognised principle'. The Court of First Instance, in a judgment of 20/2/2001 (case T-112/98), *Mannesmannröhren-Werke AG* v. *Commission*, available on the ECJ website), refused to be

However, the EU was still lacking a concrete and detailed blueprint to undertake such action. A year after Tampere the Commission put forward a Communication aimed at starting a debate on the direction of future EU asylum action.[130] The Commission explicitly emphasised that its intention was to 'set out an ambitious approach to all the questions [relating to the CEAS] and certain possible scenarios so that the Council, Parliament and the various organisations concerned by asylum policy can engage in a full discussion and come up with precise guidelines'.[131]

The Commission clearly set out the issues and challenges that the future asylum debate would have to tackle. First of all, the Commission remarked that since 1996 the number of asylum applicants in the EU being granted GC refugee status had been dropping dramatically, whereas the number of subsidiary protection cases had been steadily growing. Unfortunately, forms of subsidiary protection were very much dependent on national asylum systems and therefore varied greatly. In order to counteract this trend the Commission called for the adoption of definite protection principles firmly attached to the GC and the other relevant human rights instruments, the harmonisation of national admission and reception policies, and the approval of 'rapid high-quality decision-making'. This in turn would limit secondary movements of applicants influenced mainly by the disparities in national asylum legislation.

In the eyes of the Commission any future EU asylum system would need to balance together: a) the need to 'preserve the specificity of humanitarian admission and asylum in the European Union as distinct from other grounds for admission'; and b) the necessity to fight illegal immigration. Conscious of the ambitious nature of the Tampere objectives and in an attempt to propose some concrete guidelines the Commission suggested a two-stage strategy. During the first stage minimum standards would be set across the Community for the areas listed by the scoreboard.[132] These included asylum procedures, asylum status and subsidiary forms of protection, reception facilities and refugees status benefits.[133] This short-term stage would span at least until 2004 and possibly longer to give Member States the necessary time to implement the Community legislation. The success of this stage would be enhanced by achieving a considerable

---

drawn into 'the potential impact of the Charter', because the contested measure had been adopted prior to the proclamation of the Charter in December 2000 (point 76). Significantly, however, the Court refused to specify whether the Charter could have any impact at all.

130. See 'Communication from the Commission to the Council and the European Parliament: towards a common asylum procedure and a uniform status, valid throughout the Union, for persons granted asylum', COM (2000) 755 final, of 27/11/2000.

131. See *supra* n° 130, Preface to the Communication

132. See *supra* n° 78.

133. In this sense the proposed Directive on minimum standards for asylum procedures (see *supra* n° 93) should only be seen as part of the short-term measures.

improvement both of EU asylum analytical tools and of the administrative co-operation between Member States.[134]

In the second stage, the overriding aim would be to reach a final level of convergence leading to the CEAS called for at Tampere. The Commission acknowledged the ambitiousness of this project, but appeared confident that all the means for it had been provided by the Amsterdam Treaty. It envisaged the development of a single EU asylum status, possibly encompassing different types of protection.[135] To this purpose, the Commission also appeared to favour a 'one-stop-shop' procedure where the authorities would decide automatically which type of protection status best suited the merits of one particular application. Showing a remarkable sensitivity to the controversial nature of related concepts such as the 'safe country of origin' or the 'safe third country' the Commission suggested either the adoption of common lists or the abandonment of such concepts.[136] Finally, the proposal also hinted at the possibility of introducing an EU resettlement scheme to be operated in conjunction with the UNHCR. This scheme would not replace spontaneous arrivals, but would rely on the possibility of examining asylum claims outside the EU.[137]

This Commission Communication attempted to suggest its preferred path towards an EU asylum policy, even if many of its proposals were only intended as suggestions for further debate. The future EU asylum action strategy would still very much depend on the outcome of such debate. The crucial issue would as always remain the degree of harmonisation proposed as an ideal target. In this respect the Communication did not spell out in absolute terms its preferred final outcome. The overall tone appeared rather more tentative, arguably still

---

134. The Communication appeared very critical of how information had been collected by Member States in the past. It suggested that some Member States did not have sufficient know-how or resources to conduct clear and efficient data-collection. To this purpose, it suggested a radical overhaul of CIREA, redirecting its functions towards enhancing data-collection methods across the Community. It also called for increased co-operation strategies between national administrations. These were seen to be of particular importance for the gradual convergence of relevant national asylum case law.

135. The Commission recognised the need to develop subsidiary forms of protection for persecutory reasons other that those contained in the GC. For the sake of simplicity and transparency, it also appeared to favour the grouping of all protection statuses into one granting identical benefits.

136. The abandonment of such controversial concepts would constitute a real step forward towards achieving an EU asylum policy that was substantially in line with the other major international asylum obligations. This would, nonetheless, involve a major change in countries which have keenly adopted these concepts, and especially in Germany where it would even involve a constitutional reform (see Chapters II.2 and III.3.C).

137. According to the Communication, only four Member States operated resettlement schemes. The UK has been a very vocal advocate of such schemes. However, such schemes, which are common in the US, Canada, Australia and New Zealand, have often been criticised for being a 'cherry-picking' exercise, whereby only the refugees capable of making a positive economic contribution to the receiving State were being selected.

trying to assess the Member States' preferred integration pace. Moreover, some important aspects were left out of this analysis altogether. No mention was made, for instance, of the potential impact of the EU Charter of Fundamental Rights on the Community's future approach to asylum.[138] Equally, no consideration was put forward on the possible ways of integrating such an instrument into the Treaties.

Most importantly, the Commission gave no thought to the impact that the enlargement process might have on the ability of the Union to achieve these high-aiming goals. As the external borders of the EU will expand, so will the pressure to keep up the 'protection' of the territory. And if the prospect of harmonising fifteen different types of national asylum legislation wasn't daunting enough, the attempt to harmonise twenty or more might appear practically insane. In the impossibility of producing legally-binding agreements, soft law instruments might make an unwanted comeback, with serious implications for the EU level of refugee protection. In this scenario, time and a definite action strategy become of the essence. Keeping to the tight two-to-five year timetable of the Commission Action Plan would be a good starting point, but a clear long-tem strategy remains an absolute imperative. Only by setting a clear path towards achieving the CEAS and the harmonising of complementary forms of protection, before too many new Members gain full accession, can the budding EU asylum policy born at Tampere be given a fair chance of success. Unfortunately, two years after Tampere, the EU still appears to be searching for a clear and concrete plan of action in order to reach its asylum policy goals.

---

138. The Communication only contained a perfunctory mention of Art. 18 of the Charter in Part I, point 1.1.

7 Conclusions – Towards an EU Asylum Policy and the Future of Refugee Protection in Europe

In the last two decades an increasing level of asylum co-operation has taken place among EU Member States. The Amsterdam Treaty sanctioned the historical developments in this area by introducing a new Community competence on asylum. Following the setting of an overall goal for such a competence at the Tampere summit and the changes introduced by the Nice Treaty, a body of asylum legislative initiatives is slowly being put forward. However, these last two decades of EU asylum developments happened against a background of existing international refugee and Human Rights obligations, upon which they had a mostly negative impact. The Union seems to have only recently acknowledged the repercussions of its asylum co-operation on the levels of refugee protection in Europe and it remains to be seen whether it will act accordingly.

In analysing the historical evolution of the EU asylum competence, this work has focused both on the evolving nature of EU asylum co-operation and on the implications of the latter for refugee protection across the Union. In drawing some conclusions on these two pivotal aspects of such asylum co-operation, this research will also endeavour to put forward some recommendations for a balanced and comprehensive future EU asylum policy.

VII.1. EUROPEAN ASYLUM HARMONISATION: A TRUE EU POLICY?

Member States' interest in the co-ordination of their asylum policies was borne out of the logic of the Internal Market as put forward by the 1985 SEA. Due to the enormous geopolitical changes of the late 80s most Member States experienced an increasing pressure on their national asylum adjudication systems. The effects of this pressure were further worsened by the restrictive immigration practices Member States had put in place since the 70s economic crisis.

The prospective opening of the EC's internal borders envisaged by the creation of the Internal Market added a completely new dimension to the issue of refugee protection in Europe. Notwithstanding the differences of interpretation over the old Art. 7a EC, Member States increasingly viewed refugee protection in the context of the new controls to be imposed on the circulation of aliens within the Single Market, an essentially economic objective. Rather than emphasising the traditional Human Rights aspects of refugee protection, Member States increasingly focused on elements such as 'access to territory', 'access to procedures' and 'removal from the territory'. These elements were seen as the necessary 'flanking' or 'compensatory' measures for the abolition of internal border controls. Thus, the distinction between asylum and the traditional area of immigration became progressively blurred.

The dispute over the interpretation of the old Art. 7a EC meant that some Members were reluctant to allow any co-operation to take place within the established Community mechanisms. Moreover, the prevailing general perception was that immigration matters were still an essential national prerogative. The Community framework, with its inevitable publicity and loss of national decision power, was not the ideal playing field for reticent Member States. Traditional intergovernmental co-operation had the added advantage of allowing a very high degree of secrecy in the decision-making process, thus effectively bypassing the scrutiny of national legislators or public opinion. Hence, the choice of some Member States to establish the alternative Schengen co-operation framework.

However, co-operation on asylum measures also continued within the EPC framework, despite these national differences of interpretation and the setting up of the Schengen system. In this respect, great emphasis was laid on the definition of the 'compensatory' measures necessary for the establishment of the Single Market. They were viewed as a prerequisite for leading reticent Member States, such as the UK, to eventually accept the abolition of internal border controls. The result of these early efforts was the 1990 Dublin Convention, which represented the cornerstone of the future EU asylum co-operation.

While devising the future contents of their asylum co-operation Member States also focused their efforts on improving their ability to co-operate efficiently. They viewed the Maastricht Treaty as a positive step in this direction. The Third Pillar had the advantage of retaining most of the national prerogatives of the previous system, but at the same time it codified and streamlined the old EPC structures. Co-operation remained of an intergovernmental nature, but some elements of the Community framework were also introduced. These consisted mainly in the participation of Community institutions such as the Commission and the EP and in the built-in possibility of transferring some competence to the First Pillar. However, the respective roles of the Commission and the EP were very limited compared to their traditional ones. The choice of an intergovernmental framework still guaranteed the secrecy of negotiations and a lack of democratic scrutiny. The Twelve also failed to introduce any form of jurisdictional control, which was symptomatic of their reticence to allow any Community interference in the asylum field.

The Third Pillar asylum co-operation was severely tested in the aftermath of the Maastricht Treaty. The inevitable conclusion was that Third Pillar procedures appeared too cumbersome. Efficient decision-making was hindered by too many levels of bureaucracy and a pervasive atmosphere of mutual distrust among Member States. Opportunities to take advantage of the co-operation of Community institutions were repeatedly missed. Lack of implementation was one of the biggest problems afflicting EU asylum co-operation in the mid-90s. From a policy-building point of view, the Third Pillar unfortunately provided Member States with the wrong choice of instruments. Soft law initiatives were by their very nature subject to low implementation. The seven-year long ratification process of the 1990 DC showed that conventions, although binding, were not an efficient alternative. The preference Member States displayed for non-binding measures was probably a symptom of a continuing low level of consensus. Agreement levels appeared higher around measures concerning, directly or indirectly, the implementation of the DC. This was probably due to the fact that the constantly emerging Schengen difficulties constituted a very powerful learning example. The obvious result was that progress in the asylum field was extremely slow.

Overall, it would be difficult to characterise the EU asylum initiatives resulting from Third Pillar co-operation as part of a substantive policy. They still appeared more as a 'co-ordination' of national asylum policies. Nonetheless, due to the inevitable implications of a border-free Europe, some guiding 'policy-like' principles had definitely started to emerge. The underlying philosophy appeared very much inspired by the need to buttress the 'Fortress Europe' concept embodied by the 1990 DC. As a consequence, most measures were invariably geared towards control and prevention of access, fast processing of applications and expulsion – at least into some sort of 'outer' Community orbit. However, by the mid-90s the perception of the functions of asylum co-operation began to slowly evolve. Apart from being essential 'flanking' measures, asylum initiatives progressively came to be seen also as objectives in themselves, independent from the Single Market logic. Member States with particularly pressing asylum concerns started to successfully employ the wide scope of Art. K.1.1 TEU to pursue their own asylum objectives, such as burden-sharing and temporary protection.

Eventually, the failures of the Third Pillar asylum co-operation and the looming prospect of a considerable future enlargement of the Union made the necessity of reform an unavoidable imperative. The progress in the asylum co-operation field achieved at Amsterdam was by all means exceptional. The transfer of the asylum competence to the Community Pillar was an event of historic proportions, which a mere five years earlier would have been unthinkable. In this respect, the heavily criticised Maastricht asylum provisions were vindicated as a necessary stepping stone for further evolution. Communitarisation meant that past institutional problems were considerably diminished. Democratic accountability, judicial control, the rule of Community law, a legitimate role for the Commission and principles on openness and transparency all applied now to the new asylum provisions. From an operational point of view, Community legislative instruments represented a healthy antidote to previous ineffective action.

From a 'policy' point of view, Amsterdam created what could be termed a 'qualified-competence'. The Community was not given general competence on asylum, but rather an 'exhaustive' list of intervention fields. Special rules of judicial control applied to the asylum Title and the jurisdiction of the Court was further limited by the new provisions on closer co-operation and several of the national Protocols granting different opt-out and opt-in possibilities. A five-year transitional period had to be introduced in order to 'smooth' Member States into the new regime. Although not a general policy competence, such as in other traditional areas of Community action, in essence the new EC asylum competence was very similar to other competence fields present in the Treaty, notably environment or research and technological development. Normal rules relating to implied external competence would also apply. From a practical point of view, the number of intervention fields contained in Art. 63 TEC was so extensive that most essential aspects of a comprehensive EU asylum policy could be covered, except unfortunately measures directed at the national integration of refugees.

Although the new asylum competence was inserted into the EC Treaty, it had extensive connections to other parts of the TEU. Firstly, Title IV TEC was an integral part of the Union's objective of an 'area of freedom security and justice' which spanned across both the First and the Third Pillars. Secondly, the asylum regime to be applied to EU nationals was regulated by a separate Protocol (attached to the EC treaty) which in turn relied heavily on Arts 6 and 7 TEU. Finally, the recent EU Charter of Fundamental Rights contained two provisions on asylum that could have major implications for future asylum co-operation. For these reasons, the present and future asylum *acquis*[1] has been termed as an EU asylum policy to emphasise its comprehensive nature.

The subsequent Nice Treaty finally clarified the decision-making rules for Title IV EC and asserted the eventual progression towards codecision procedures. However, the fundamental principles ruling this field would still have to be adopted by unanimity and in the case of more controversial issues, such as burden-sharing, no specific time frame was set at all. Urged no doubt by the five-year deadline imposed by Art. 63 TEC, several initiatives were undertaken in the last three years. The probable contents of a future EU asylum policy were slowly emerging. The Tampere summit in 1999 gave the shaping of such a future policy a decisive impulse. The proposed CEAS would entail a pan-European refugee definition, unified asylum procedures and a single asylum status for different refugee categories (i.e. GC refugees, TP and complementary protection).

The Tampere and Nice Councils also changed the fundamental perspective of EU asylum co-operation. Amsterdam had in part emphasised the ties that bound such co-operation to the realisation of the Single Market (Art. 61.a TEC), but it had also acknowledged it as an independent objective (Art. 61.b TEC). At Tampere, the independence of the asylum objective was finally framed in its rightful context, the Union's new Human Rights dimension. The EU Charter approved at the Nice Council represented the final endorsement of this profoundly evolved perspective: asylum had now become one of the fundamental rights of the Union.

The eventual harmonisation level of the CEAS envisaged at Tampere might be such as to exclude the possibility of any subsequent national interventions. Therefore, the Community would in theory achieve a level of asylum integration

---

1. The past asylum *acquis*, having stemmed from Third Pillar co-operation, would remain EU *acquis* anyway.

almost comparable to the one reached in its traditional 'common policies', such as agriculture or fisheries. Unfortunately, early indications show that full harmonisation is still not considered a feasible objective, despite the Tampere declarations. The kind of initiatives proposed so far consist of the approximation of minimum standards either of asylum procedures or of a refugee definition. Although they might be enough to give shape to an EU asylum policy as qualified by the requirements of Art. 63 TEC, their impact on the overall level of refugee protection in the EU might not be altogether too positive.

VII.2. EUROPEAN REFUGEE INITIATIVES, INTERNATIONAL ASYLUM OBLIGATIONS AND HUMAN RIGHTS PROTECTION IN THE EU: THE BALANCE BETWEEN 'PROTECTION' AND 'CONTROL'

The development of asylum law from a purely national dimension – subject to an international discipline – into a Community concern had a profound impact on the level of refugee protection in Europe. The promotion of the Internal Market idea by the mid-80s meant that any possible future EU concept of refugee protection was inevitably to be envisaged as an aspect of the need to control the circulation of aliens within the Single Market. Member States mistakenly believed that asylum 'flanking' measures could be treated virtually as any other 'economic' integration provision, thereby ignoring the ensuing Human Rights and refugee protection implications. Asylum progressively lost its 'protection' component in favour of the logic of 'compensatory' measures.

Against the background of the secretive and strictly intergovernmental framework of the EU early asylum co-operation efforts, the choice of asylum provisions in the SC or DC appeared almost inevitable. However, it was hardly justifiable from the perspective of refugee protection and international obligations. In the name of their ultimate goal, a border-free Europe, Member States sacrificed refugees' rights on the 'altar' of compensatory measures. Since time was of the essence, only minimal co-ordination was possible, just enough to guarantee the smooth functioning of the 'Common Territory' structures. Hence, the urgent need to devise the criteria for the determination of States' responsibility on asylum applications as a cornerstone of the new asylum co-operation efforts.

Minimal co-ordination of national asylum policies unjustifiably sacrificed the rights of asylum seekers. National implementation of the 1951 GC without any jurisdictional control was hardly an ideal solution, but at least refugees could take advantage of disparities between national legislation. This option was subsequently precluded by the adoption of the SC/DC principles. These principles meant that similar cases were being treated dissimilarly because national asylum legislation still widely differed, both substantially and procedurally. Member States conveniently ignored their individual obligations under the GC. Minimal co-ordination necessarily required the mutual recognition of negative asylum decisions. However, differences in national implementations of the 1951 GC were still considered important enough to prevent mutual recognition of positive decisions. Asylum seekers were left to bear the brunt of this harmonisation gap.

The progressive shaping of a policy of 'access prevention' to the Common Territory led to other tragic consequences. It prompted a downwards spiral of national carriers' liability legislation, all competing to implement tougher sanctions. Governments obviously bore a large responsibility in the subsequent misconduct and abuses displayed by carriers in response to provisions that were in blatant breach of international obligations, such as the ICAO Convention. The use of visa policy as a tool to actively and purposefully prevent access to asylum procedures was probably the best example of the 'practical' approach Members States took to the preservation of their Common Territory.

Unfortunately, Member States did not appear in any hurry to proceed to more comprehensive harmonisation. Early 90s asylum initiatives appeared to follow the same Single Market logic as the DC provisions. Nor did the Maastricht Treaty achieve more than an 'institutionalisation' of the previous EPC structure. In the running up to the Maastricht negotiations, some national parliaments had keenly advocated a jurisdictional control mechanism that would at least partially redress the balance in favour of refugee rights. Unfortunately, this option was not to be considered until the following IGC.

Following the signing of the TEU, Member States continued to develop their asylum initiatives along the path set by the Schengen and Dublin initiatives. It was slowly becoming evident that those Conventions would not be able to function properly without further support measures. The Edinburgh initiatives did not represent any substantive harmonisation of national asylum laws. In the form of 'resolutions' or 'conclusions', they were only soft law initiatives that led to scarce and far from uniform implementation. These measures were, however, an important indication of the underlaying 'Fortress Europe' philosophy Member States had begun to develop as an integral part of the Single Market logic. The 'accelerated procedures' principle openly disregarded many of the guarantees contained in the GC, such as not penalising applicants attempting an illegal entry, or making contradictory statements. Highly disputable principles such as the 'internal flight option' were pushed through in the face of popular opposition because the Third Pillar framework allowed governments the necessary secrecy.

Notions such as 'host third countries' directly contradicted the purported aims of the DC, namely to end the refugee in orbit problem. The effect of these measures was instead to place refugees in an 'orbit' around the Community rather than within it. The perimeter of this orbit kept being shifted further and further away by an ever more intricate web of readmission agreements. The hypocrisy of such a strategy was highlighted by the fact that Member States even resorted to 'bribing' neighbouring States with aid packages in order to dump their own unwanted refugees on them. The 'Common Market of deflection'[2] inherent in the idea of a border-free Europe was slowly taking shape.

---

2. G. Noll, *Negotiating asylum. The EU acquis, extraterritorial protection and the Common Market of deflection* (Martinus Nijhoff, The Hague, 2000).

The 'safe country' principle was another keystone in the fortification of Europe's perimeter. Once again, since Member States proved incapable of agreeing a common list of 'safe countries', refugee protection inevitably suffered because of the discrepancy between national policies. All measures were invariably geared towards control and prevention of access, fast processing of applications and expulsion – at least into some sort of 'outer orbit'. Sometimes requirements of international law were blatantly sacrificed – as in the case of the minimum guarantees initiative. No real humanitarian concern motivated such decisions, because what were essentially Human Rights issues kept being observed through an economic 'lens'. Old outstanding problems, such as the role of the ECJ remained too controversial and kept being indefinitely postponed. As in the case of TP and burden-sharing, new asylum issues were surfacing that went beyond the traditional Internal Market logic. But Member States failed miserably to face these new challenges. The refusal by certain Members to correctly implement the DC procedures and to create an efficient burden-sharing system showed a concerning lack of mutual good faith, trust and solidarity. Their attempts at hiding the absence of consensus behind showpiece political initiatives – the two Resolutions on burden-sharing of 1995–96 – backfired badly when the initiatives where put to the test. Once more, the brunt of this failure had to be borne by the very refugees these measures were designed to help.

Different surveys clearly showed that implementation of most Third Pillar asylum initiatives could at best be described as erratic. From the refugee protection perspective the low implementation levels produced mixed consequences. Sometimes they counteracted the inherent restrictiveness of the some of the measures. For instance, in the case of manifestly unfounded applications, the fact that some countries – such as Italy – never applied them eventually ensured the maintenance of higher levels of protection. Such cases, however, were rare and in most instances Member States disapplied precisely those provisions that would have been beneficial to refugees (as, for instance, the translation of refusal decisions). At other times, an effective implementation of the measures could actually have had a positive impact on refugee protection, such as in the case of the 1996 joint position on the interpretation of the term 'refugee'. Instead, the measure had a negligible effect on national asylum authorities. To some extent, prospective asylum seekers were still able to take advantage of the differences in national asylum legislation. But the respite was to be only temporary. When the SC/DC mechanisms finally became fully operational, the level of EU refugee protection took a dramatic turn for the worse. The constant ignoring of refugee protection issues led to rising numbers of both international and national jurisdictional challenges. Eventually, only the national Courts and the ECtHR were left to act as buffers against the iniquities of the DC system.

One of the biggest flaws of the Third pillar asylum co-operation was the fact that soft law did not guarantee implementation. This highlighted the inherent paradox of the asylum system the Twelve were in the process of building. The Schengen and the Dublin initiatives had created a hard law asylum framework that still needed several adjustments in order to function in practice. However, by subsequently adopting soft law initiatives to support it, Member States failed to understand that the inability to monitor or ensure implementation would have undermined the whole framework. It subsequently took the Twelve some years to realise this failure.

Tremendous progress was made at Amsterdam in laying the foundation for a future EU asylum policy. From the refugee protection point of view, the potential of the new provisions on asylum was of a mixed nature. Communitarisation undoubtedly displayed all the advantages that the past intergovernmental co-operation had lacked. Democratic accountability, judicial control and a more independent role for the Commission were certainly key aspects for the development of a fairer refugee policy. The possibility for the ECJ to rule over the compatibility of EC asylum initiatives and other international refugee obligations had tremendous future potential. The very existence of the special asylum exception agreed for EU nationals might in future be subjected to the review of the Court. Although not comprehensive, the list of asylum fields contained in Art. 63 TEC was in some ways a good start. It was still clearly inspired by a policy of 'access prevention', but it constituted a serious attempt at some long-needed substantive harmonisation. The real problem ahead would once again be the contents and the effectiveness of these initiatives.

Among the measures conspicuously missing from Art. 63 were those concerning the national integration of refugees. These could have greatly benefited a fairer European refugee protection. The Title IV TEC restriction of the scope of Art. 234 TEC could also have a negative impact on the majority of asylum seekers who might not be able to pursue their case all the way to a Court of last instance. Likewise, the inability of the EP to raise interpretative questions under Art. 68.3 TEC deprived asylum seekers in Europe of the help of one of their most outspoken supporters. Given the Commission's poor past record, one could only hope that an increased level of independence would lead it to raise 'unpopular' interpretative questions under Art. 68.3. Finally, a move towards greater transparency would only take place once unanimous decision-making could be replaced by codecision procedures. Therefore, the five-year interim period envisaged by the Amsterdam Treaty would prove to be of pivotal importance.

Tampere and Nice were of fundamental importance for the shaping of the future EU asylum policy envisaged at Amsterdam. They each provided the goals and the (eventual) democratic decision-making process that this policy still lacked. The Tampere idea of a CEAS appeared to be the long-overdue answer to the imbalance created by the Dublin system and the 'economic' logic of the Single Market. The inclusion of asylum in the EU Charter finally put refugee protection within its proper Human Rights frame. In the context of a border-free Community and of the Union's commitment to fundamental liberties, EU asylum co-operation need not be necessarily detrimental to refugee protection, provided it entails substantial and, above all, comprehensive harmonisation. The degree of harmonisation would prove crucial: a half-hearted approximation of national standards would certainly not be enough.

VII.3. BUILDING AN EFFECTIVE EU ASYLUM POLICY WHILE ENSURING REFUGEE PROTECTION: HARMONISATION AND THE WAY FORWARD

Unfortunately, the short term strategy laid down by the 1998 Commission action plan does not appear to go beyond the setting of minimum standards. Recent initiatives tabled in the wake of the Tampere summit confirmed the lack of a real drive towards substantive harmonisation. These initiatives consist merely in attempts to define some minimum standards to be applied to national asylum policies. Likewise, solidarity initiatives were restricted to financial measures of a very limited impact. As indicated by the Tampere summit, substantive harmonisation appears to be the only answer, both to the need to comply with the Single Market project and to the restoration of adequate levels of refugee protection across the Community. To this purpose, harmonisation would necessarily have to be substantive in nature and comprehensive in scope. Partial harmonisation or legally-binding minimum standards might solve some of the past implementation problems, but would not be able to overcome mutual distrust and lack of solidarity. Ultimately, no mechanism in the world could oblige a Member State to take on the responsibility for one or several asylum applicants if it has refused to do so. Merely following a minimum common denominator would imply an unacceptable lowering of refugee protection levels, leading to further jurisdictional challenges in national and international Courts. Therefore, countries with lower protection levels, such as France or Germany, would necessarily have to rise up to the standards of the majority, instead of being afforded loophole clauses as in the past.

A comprehensive harmonisation would by definition entail one asylum procedure, one set of common definitions, one common asylum status covering different instances of persecution and eventually one 'asylum agency' to act as a first instance examiner of applications and as an effective jurisdictional control. However, it is obvious that the creation of the latter might encounter overwhelming problems, due to the extensive restructuring of national administrative and judicial systems that would be required.[3] Therefore, following a more practical approach, such an agency could at least focus on ensuring substantive uniformity among the various national examination procedures and asylum decisions. Such a comprehensive harmonisation programme would no doubt appear very ambitious, but it would be the only solution compatible with Member States' international refugee protection obligations. If the EU Single Market project really imposes on Member States the necessity of sharing such obligations, then the

---

3. See K. Hailbronner, *Immigration and asylum policy of the European Union* (Kluwer Law International, The Hague, 2000), p. 85.

only way this can be achieved is by a comprehensive substantive harmonisation subject to full jurisdictional scrutiny.

Burden-sharing will eventually be the ultimate good faith test for Member States. In a truly harmonised asylum system the lack of solidarity would no longer be acceptable. Since financial solidarity would not appear to be an entirely effective option, given the enormous economic implications, a new burden-sharing framework would necessarily entail 'people-sharing'. Eventually, this huge process of harmonisation would paradoxically make the very essence of the DC redundant. In an area with a CEAS and an effective solidarity framework, the Dublin criteria would cease to fulfill any purpose. Applicants' choices are naturally dictated by the presence of family support networks, language knowledge and the possibility of economic and social integration. In the context of an effective CEAS there would be no reason to discourage such choice incentives because the outcome of an application would be the same everywhere and effective solidarity mechanisms would ensure adequate compensation and fair distribution of asylum applicants. Surely, in the case of a successful application, the integration possibilities for the applicant would have to be considered of paramount importance.

A true CEAS should be the ultimate goal of a fair EU asylum policy. However, it should be clear that this scale of harmonisation would realistically require at least a decade, if not longer. In the interim period, some basic principles should apply. Firstly, the application of the DC should be suspended. Minimum standards cannot substitute substantive harmonisation and certainly would not guarantee identical results. Furthermore, the DC system was shown to unfairly penalise countries at the perimeter of the Community and could easily lead to a downward spiral of repressive measures by those countries. Its impact on the overall number of applications has been very limited so far (a mere 3 per cent of applications). The long delays applicants had to suffer as a consequence of the burdensome administrative process involved did not appear justified by the volume of exchanges. Serious complications could also arise with the next Community enlargement if the Dublin system was to be maintained. The EU perimeter would be shifted further outwards, but it remains doubtful whether the new Members could cope effectively with the increased pressure on their asylum systems.

Basic interim principles should also address the negative impact of visa provisions and carrier sanctions on EU refugee protection. Both types of measure should contain clear exceptions for asylum applicants – a mention in the preamble not being sufficient – and implementation should not be entrusted to carriers' personnel. Similarly, the safe third country principle should be rapidly subjected to a common and transparent regulation possibly by envisaging a stepping-up of the CIREA monitoring role. The UNHCR should be granted a greater role in the system. The eventual goal would be to permanently integrate the UNHCR within the EU asylum agency, thus ensuring a constant scrutiny of refugee protection standards across the Community by an independent and expert body.

Likewise, the limitations currently imposed on the opportunity to request an ECJ preliminary ruling within Title IV TEC should be lifted. Art. 68.3 TEC should be amended to include the EP. Great consideration should be given to ways of improving the ECJ's ability to cope with the resulting increase in the judicial case-load, especially in relation to urgent applications. Finally, scrupulous care should be taken in regulating the conflicts that could eventually arise between the ECJ and the ECtHR once the EU Charter of Fundamental Rights is incorporated into the TEU.

Naturally, an effective EU asylum policy should not only focus on protection from persecution, but also on the prevention of persecution. This objective has already to some extent been pursued through the incorporation of Human Rights clauses in the EU world-wide co-operation agreements. However, the inevitable links between Member States' foreign policies and refugee-generating situations remains largely ignored. Weapons used in civil conflicts around the globe originate predominantly from the West. Foreign policy decisions are primarily motivated by geopolitical strategic interests and commonly disregard Human Rights concerns, unless the latter offer a good pretext for intervention. The Gulf War represented a primary example of the duplicity of standards that still informs persecution prevention policies. Saddam Hussein's dictatorial regime could have been easily toppled during NATO's military intervention in Kuwait. However, strategic interests dictated that a crippled Saddam Hussein was preferable in the eyes of the West to the unknown scenario of his succession. An extensive embargo was supposed to permanently weaken the regime and favour internal change. A decade of embargos has had no impact on Saddam Hussein's authority, whereas the country has plunged into Middle Ages health and living conditions. Iraqis and Kurds (another of Saddam Hussein's targets the West was supposed to protect) have topped most of the EU's asylum applicant statistics for years: could this really be just a coincidence? Can Member States recriminate with a clear conscience every time a new contingent of these refugees reaches their borders?

A future EU asylum policy would therefore largely benefit from Member States exercising greater insight in formulating their foreign policy and adopting strategic decisions. Nor would some of the recent proposals put forward to appease public concerns over the rising numbers of applicants necessarily make up for poor foreign policy formulation. These proposals envisage the possibility of introducing permanent refugee quotas for different nationalities to be agreed in co-operation with the UNHCR. Although they could prove viable in mass influx cases, a generalised adoption of such schemes could lead once more to the blurring of the distinction between asylum and immigration. Prospective applicants might end up being included in the proposed quotas for reasons owing more to their particular qualifications or skills rather then their persecution problems. In the future, the Union will certainly have to address its need for increased immigration to make up for dwindling birth-rates. But it cannot hope to address this problem by transforming its burgeoning asylum policy into a surreptitious immigration one.

The Union portrays itself as a beacon of democratic principles and Human Rights values. It was precisely in the name of these principles and values that it undertook to provide protection from persecution. A border-free Community does not necessarily need to be a 'fortress': prevention of persecution and a better-formulated immigration policy would no doubt lift some of the current pressure on asylum adjudication channels. A better public information campaign on the roots of persecution and the relative insignificance of overall refugee numbers in the EU compared to world figures could also help contain the reactions of 'mass-hysteria' that most of the time characterise political discussions on asylum. The EU initiatives on the fight against racism and xenophobia are a welcome first step in this direction. Likewise, the EU Charter of Fundamental Rights represents a new era in the future nature of the Community, permanently adding a Human Rights dimension to the traditional economic one of the past. Therefore, the Community will in future be even better equipped to pursue the Human Rights implications of its border-free Single Market project. After all the formal declarations, it is time the EU showed that it really takes fundamental rights – and hence refugee protection – seriously.

Annex

STATISTICAL ASYLUM DATA

Notes on statistical information

The following tables contain statistical data relating to refugees across the EU over the last 10 to 15 years. Unfortunately, it is necessary to approach these statistics with caution as numbers tend to vary – sometimes greatly – according to different sources of information. The following tables have been compiled with data provided by the UNHCR, EUROSTAT and the UK Home Office. In this context, the term 'refugee' refers both to Convention Status and other humanitarian statuses as defined by national law.

TABLE 1

Asylum Applications in the European Union 1985–2000

	1985	1986	1987*	1988	1989	1990	1991	1992	1993	1994	1995	1996	1997	1998	1999	2000	TOTAL
AUSTRIA	6,724	8,639	11,406	15,790	21,882	22,800	27,300	16,200	4,700	5,100	5,900	7,000	6,700	13,800	20,100	18,284	212,325
BELGIUM*	5,387	7,644	5,976	4,510	8,188	13,000	15,200	17,600	26,900	14,400	11,400	12,400	11,800	22,000	35,800	42,691	254,896
DENMARK	8,698	9,300	2,726	4,668	4,590	5,300	4,600	13,900	14,300	6,700	5,100	5,900	5,100	5,700	6,500	10,077	113,159
FINLAND	18	23	49	64	179	2,700	2,100	3,600	2,000	840	850	710	970	1,300	3,100	3,170	21,637
FRANCE*	28,925	26,290	27,672	34,352	61,422	54,800	47,400	28,900	27,600	26,000	20,200	17,400	21,400	22,400	30,800	38,588	514,149
GERMANY*	73,832	99,650	57,379	103,07 $_b$	121,31 $_b$	193,10 $_u$	256,10 $_u$	438,20 $_u$	322,600	127,200	127,900	116,400	104,400	98,600	95,100	117,648	2,452,503
GREECE	1,400	4,300	6,300	9,300	6,500	6,200	2,700	1,900	810	1,300	1,300	1,600	4,400	3,000	1,500	3,083	55,593
IRELAND	#	#	50	49	36	62	30	40	90	360	420	1,200	3,900	4,600	7,700	14,796	33,333
ITALY*	5,400	6,500	11,000	1,300	2,240	4,800	26,500	6,000	1,600	1,800	1,700	680	1,900	7,100	33,400	14,000	125,920
LUXEMBOURG	32	92	98	44	87	114	238	120	225	165	155	266	427	#	#	#	2,063
NETHERLANDS	5,644	5,865	13,460	7,486	13,898	21,200	21,600	20,300	35,400	52,600	29,300	22,200	34,400	45,200	39,300	43,895	411,748
PORTUGAL*	70	118	178	252	116	80	260	690	2,100	770	450	270	250	340	270	202	6,416
SPAIN	2,300	2,300	2,500	4,516	4,077	8,600	8,100	11,700	12,600	12,000	5,700	4,700	5,000	6,700	8,400	7,926	107,119
SWEDEN	14,500	14,600	18,114	19,595	30,335	29,400	27,400	84,000	37,600	18,600	9,000	5,800	9,700	12,800	11,200	16,303	358,947
UNITED KINGDOM*	4,389	4,266	4,256	3,998	11,640	26,200	44,800	24,600	22,400	32,800	44,000	29,600	32,500	46,000	71,100	75,680	478,229
TOTAL	157,319	189,587	161,16 $_4$	209,00 $_u$	286,50 $_b$	388,35 $_b$	484,32 $_b$	667,75 $_u$	510,925	300,635	263,375	226,126	242,847	289,540	364,270	406,343	5,148,073

Source: EUROSTAT, UNHCR; * = excluding dependants (between 1985-1989); # = not available

214

TABLE 2

Indicative Number of Refugees, Asylum Seekers and Others Seeking Protection in EU Countries, end-2000

COUNTRY	NUMBER OF REFUGEES
AUSTRIA*	82,458
BELGIUM	63,834
DENMARK	76,216
FINLAND	13,276
FRANCE*	129,722
GERMANY	976,266
GREECE	9,032
IRELAND	15,566
ITALY	22,983
LUXEMBOURG*	700
NETHERLANDS	230,468
PORTUGAL*	410
SPAIN*	157,217
SWEDEN	85,122
UNITED KINGDOM	216,003
TOTAL	**2,079,273**

Source: UNHCR; * = estimates for end-1999

TABLE 3

Average Percentage Recognition Rate of Asylum Applications in EU Countries 1990–2000 (both for Convention Status and other forms of humanitarian leave to remain)

COUNTRY	1990	1991	1992	1993	1994	1995	1996	1997	1998	1999	2000	AVERAGE†
AUSTRIA	6.8	12.5	9.8	7.8	7.5	13.0	8.2	8.1	5.3	#	17.3	9.6
BELGIUM	30.3	22.1	19.4	21.8	24.0	24.6	22.5	19.7	24.6	31.2	21.3	23.8
DENMARK	#	#	#	#	#	86.7	81.7	58.3	54.5	51.8	42.6	62.6
FINLAND	32.1	73.3	35.1	59.6	45.6	46.8	58.6	52.1	44.1	18.2	25.0	44.6
FRANCE	15.4	19.7	28.0	27.9	23.7	15.6	19.6	17.0	17.5	#	#	20.5
GERMANY*	4.4	6.9	4.2	3.2	7.5	13.5	13.5	12.3	9.4	9.1	12.4	8.8
GREECE	19.4	4.5	5.7	5.3	11.9	16.1	15.7	12.9	17.4	26.5	19.4	14.1
IRELAND	#	#	#	#	25.0	34.8	56.8	52.3	12.0	9.2	4.8	27.8
ITALY	59.5	4.9	4.8	8.8	17.7	16.6	24.8	21.0	29.6	20.0	6.6	19.5
LUXEMBOURG	#	#	#	#	#	#	#	#	#	#	#	
NETHERLANDS	10.9	10.7	23.0	35.2	33.2	32.2	28.1	34.6	31.6	15.6	12.7	24.3
PORTUGAL	18.0	12.2	3.7	11.7	6.8	8.7	22.8	7.2	12.5	14.8	#	11.8
SPAIN	14.1	9.2	2.4	7.3	4.9	10.3	9.1	7.2	15.8	11.0	10.0	9.2
SWEDEN	41.7	45.4	28.3	41.5	69.0	37.6	43.1	58.2	49.8	31.6	40.4	44.2
UNITED KINGDOM	82.5	44.4	47.1	54.3	21.4	21.4	18.7	19.7	29.3	61.7	29.0	39.0
YEARLY AVERAGE	28.0	22.15	17.6	23.7	22.9	27.0	30.2	26.7	25.2	25.0	20.1	EU AVERAGE‡ 25.7

Source: UNHCR; # = not available; * = excluding administrative and judicial appeals decisions; † = for indicative purposes only; ‡ = based on EU countries average

216

TABLE 4

Asylum Seekers Per 1000 Inhabitants in the EU, based on the number of asylum seekers that applied in the EU in 1998

Country	per 1000 inhabitants
AUSTRIA	1.7
BELGIUM	2.2
DENMARK	1.1
FINLAND	0.2
FRANCE	0.4
GERMANY	1.2
GREECE	0.2
IRELAND	1.3
ITALY	0.1
LUXEMBOURG	1.0
NETHERLANDS	2.9
PORTUGAL	0.0
SPAIN	0.2
SWEDEN	1.5
UNITED KINGDOM	0.8
AVERAGE	**0.5**

Source:EUROSTAT

TABLE 5

Refugees Per 1,000 Inhabitants: Top 40 Countries, 2000 (EU Countries are highlighted in bold)

Country of residence	Refugees per 1,000 inhabitants	Country of residence	Refugees per 1,000 inhabitants
Armenia	84.2	FYR Macedonia	10.5
Guinea	67.5	Norway	10.3
Fed. Republic of Yugoslavia	47.1	Uganda	10.0
Djibouti	36.5	**Austria**	**9.8**
Liberia	32.7	Côte d'Ivoire	9.4
Azerbaijan	28.7	**TheNetherlands**	**8.2**
Iran	27.1	Pakistan	7.7
Zambia	22.5	Kenya	7.4
Tanzania	18.6	Croatia	6.3
Sweden	**17.5**	Guinea-Bissau	5.9
Bosnia and Herzegovina	16.5	Costa Rica	5.7
Central African Republic	13.6	Iraq	5.6
Congo	13.6	Democratic Republic of the Congo	5.5
Sudan	13.3	Nepal	5.3
Gambia	13.2	Algeria	5.2
Denmark	**13.0**	Rwanda	4.4
Gabon	12.3	Canada	4.4
Belize	12.0	Namibia	4.3
Germany	**11.9**	Turkmenistan	4.1
Switzerland	11.1	Ethiopia	4.1

Source: UNHCR

TABLE 6

Top 15 Countries/Territories of Origin of Asylum Seekers in Western Europe*, 1990–1999

COUNTRY	1990	1991	1992	1993	1994	1995	1996	1997	1998	1999	TOTAL
Former Yugoslavia	33,200	115,500	235,300	177,900	81,000	71,200	47,200	59,500	104,600	118,400	1,043,800
Romania	62,100	61,700	116,000	86,100	21,100	13,600	8,600	9,500	7,500	6,000	392,200
Turkey	48,800	45,500	37,100	25,500	26,100	41,400	38,300	32,900	20,900	19,400	335,900
Former USSR	4,800	10,300	16,400	28,300	16,300	18,100	20,800	23,100	21,400	37,100	196,600
Iraq	7,400	9,000	10,700	9,800	10,000	15,100	22,600	35,800	33,300	31,100	184,800
Sri Lanka	19,300	23,700	16,800	12,600	12,900	12,700	12,400	13,000	11,100	11,400	145,900
Somalia	12,200	11,100	14,600	13,300	12,400	11,800	7,500	8,500	11,900	14,000	117,300
Afghanistan	8,900	8,500	7,500	7,800	9,200	11,300	11,500	14,700	15,400	18,500	113,300
Iran	18,300	15,300	7,800	7,100	12,000	10,000	10,000	8,300	8,100	11,900	108,800
Bulgaria	13,00	16,900	33,800	25,100	5,200	3,500	2,900	3,200	1,400	1,300	106,300
Dem. Rep of the Congo	11,800	17,600	17,800	11,700	8,800	7,700	7,700	7,700	6,600	6,800	104,200
Pakistan	10,400	13,700	9,600	6,600	6,000	9,800	7,600	7,800	6,000	7,100	84,600
India	11,900	11,700	9,600	9,300	6,000	9,000	7,100	5,600	4,100	5,200	79,500
Vietnam	13,400	11,600	13,700	12,400	4,100	3,700	2,800	3,500	3,500	2,900	71,600
Nigeria	8,100	12,400	12,700	4,300	6,300	8,900	6,300	4,500	3,600	2,500	69,600

Source: UNHCR; * = Countries include EU Member States (excluding Ireland, Luxembourg and Portugal), Norway and Switzerland

Bibliography

Abell N., 'Compatibility of readmission agreements with the 1951 Convention' (1999) 11 IJRL, p. 60.

Achermann A. and Gattiker M., 'Safe third countries: European developments' (1995) 7 IJRL, p. 19.

Alston P., *The EU and Human Rights* (OUP, Oxford, 1999).

Anderson M. and Den Boer M., *Policing across national boundaries* (Pinter pub., London, 1994).

Arboleda E., 'Refugee definition in Africa and Latin America: the lessons of pragmatism' (1991) 3 IJRL, p. 185.

Arboleda E. and Hoy I., 'The Convention refugee definition in the West: disharmony of interpretation and application' (1993) 5 IJRL, p. 66.

Arboleda E., 'The Cartagena Declaration of 1984 and its similarities with the 1969 OAU Convention – A comparative perspective' (1995) 7 IJRL, p. 87.

Arnold H., 'The century of the refugee: a European century?' (1991) 3 *Aussenpolitik*, p. 271.

Bank R., 'Reception conditions for asylum seekers in Europe: an analysis of provisions in Austria, Belgium, France, Germany and the United Kingdom' (2000) 69 *Nordic Journal of International Law*, p. 257.

Baron Crespo E. *et alia* (eds), *Europa: l'impossibile status quo / un rapporto a cura del Club di Firenze* (Il Mulino, Bologna, 1996).

Bhabha J. and Coll G., *Asylum law and practice in Europe and North America* (Federal Publications Inc., Washington D.C., 1992).

Biber R., 'Die Abkommen von Schengen über den Abbau der Grenzenkontrollen' (1994) 47 *Neue Juristische Wochenschrift*, p. 294.

Black B. and Koser K., *The end of the refugee cycle? Refugee repatriation and reconstruction* (Berghan Books, New York, 1999).

Boeles P. *et alia*, *A new immigration law for Europe?: the 1992 London and 1993 Copenhagen rules on immigration* (Dutch Centre for Immigrants, 1993).

Boeles P., 'Effective legal remedies for asylum seekers according to the Convention of Geneva 1951' (1996) 43 *Netherlands International Law Review*, p. 291.

Bolten J. J., 'The right to seek asylum in Europe' (1989) 4 NQHR, p. 381.

Brok E., 'Intergovernmental Conference 1996: not a "Maastricht 2"'(1997) 34 CML Rev., p. 1.

Brownlie I., *International law and the use of force* (Clarendon Press, Oxford, 1963).

Bunyan T., *Statewatching the new Europe: a handbook on the European State* (Statewatch, London, 1993).

Care G., *A guide to asylum law and practice in the European Union* (ILPA, London, 1996).

Carlier J. Y. *et alia* (eds), *Who is a refugee?: a comparative case law study* (Kluwer Law International, The Hague, 1997).

Carlier J. Y. and Vanheule D., *Europe and refugees: a challenge?* (Kluwer Law International, The Hague, 1997).

Collinson S., *Migration, visa and asylum policies in Europe* (HMSO, London, 1996).

Clark T. and Crépeau F., 'Mainstream refugee rights. The 1951 Refugee Convention and international Human Rights' (1999) 17 NQHR, p. 389.

Constantinesco V., 'Les clauses de "coopération renforcée"- Le protocole sur l'application des principes de subsidiarité et de proportionnalité' (1997) 33 *Revue Trimestrelle de Droit Européen*, p. 751.

Council of Europe, *Problems raised by certain aspects of the present situation of refugees from the standpoint of the European Convention on Human Rights* (Strasbourg, 1997, Human rights files n° 9).

Crepeau F., *Droit d'asile: de l'hospitalité aux contrôles migratoires* (Ed. Bruylant de l' Université de Bruxelles, Brussels, 1995).

Cruz A., *Schengen, Ad Hoc Immigration Group and other European intergovernmental bodies* (CCME Briefing Papers n° 12, Brussels, 1993).

Cruz A., *Carriers' liability in the Member States of the European Union* (CCME Briefing Paper n° 17, Brussels, 1994).

Curtin D. and Meijers H., 'The principle of open government in Schengen and the European Union: democratic retrogression?' (1995) 32 CML Rev, p. 391.

Dacyl J., 'Europe needs a new protection system for 'non-Convention' refugees' (1995) 7 IJRL, p. 579.

Daya Amarasinha S. and Isenbecker M., 'Terrorism and the right to asylum under the 1951 Convention and the 1967 Protocol relating to the status of refugees – A contradiction in terms or do opposites attract?' (1996) 65 *Nordic Journal of International Law*, p. 223.

Dedecker R., *L' asile et la libre circulation des personnes dans l'Accord de Schengen* (CRISP, Brussels, 1993).

Dehousse F. and Van Den Hende L., 'Plaidoyer pour la réforme du troisième pilier' (1996) 403 *Revue du Marché Commun et de l'Union Européenne*, p. 714.

Dehousse F., *Les résultats de la Conférence intergouvernamentale* (CRISP, Brussels, 1997).

Dehousse F., 'Le Traité d'Amsterdam: reflet de la novelle Europe' [1997] *Cahiers de Droit Européen*, p. 265.

De Jong C.D., 'Elements for a more effective European Union response to situations of mass influx' (1996) 8 IJRL, p. 156.

Den Boer M., 'Justice and Home Affairs co-operation in the European Union: current issues' [1996] Eipascope, p. 12.

Den Boer M., 'Step by step progress: an update on the free movement of persons and internal security' [1997] Eipascope, p. 8.

Den Boer M. (ed.), *The implementation of Schengen: first the widening then the deepening* (European Institute for Public Administration, Maastricht, 1997).

Duff A., Pinder J. and Pryce R. (eds), *Maastricht and beyond* (Routledge, London, 1994).

Dutheil De La Rochère J., 'La Charte des droits fondamentaux de l'Union européenne: quelle valeur ajoutée, quel avenir?' (2000) 443 *Revue du Marché commun et de l' Union européenne*, p. 674.

Edwards G. and Pijpers A. (eds), *The politics of European treaty reform – The 1996 Intergovernmental Conference and beyond* (Pinter pub., London, 1997).

Ehlermann C.D., 'Différenciation, flexibilité, coopération renforcée: les nouvelles dispositions du Traité d' Amsterdam' [1997] *Revue du Marché Unique Européen*, p. 53.

Fosheim B. and Berg E., 'Broadening the definition of refugees in the light of recent developments in Europe?' (1995) 64 *Nordic Journal of International Law*, p. 413.

Gaja G., 'How flexible is flexibility under the Amsterdam Treaty?' (1998) 35 CML Rev., p. 855.

Goodwin-Gill G.S., *The refugee in international law* (2nd edn, Clarendon Press, Oxford, 1996).

Gorlick B., 'Human Rights and refugees: enhancing protection through international Human Rights law' (2000) 69 *Nordic Journal of International Law*, p. 117.

Gowlland-Debbas V., *The problem of refugees in the light of contemporary international law issues* (Martinus Nijhoff Publishers, The Hague, 1996).

Groenendijk C.A., 'The competence of the European Court of Justice with respect to intergovernmental treaties on immigration and asylum' (1992) 4 IJRL, p. 531.

Grahl-Madsen A., *The status of refugees in International Law* (Sijthoff, Leiden, 1966, vol. I & II).

Guggenbühl A., 'A contemplative view on the First Pillar of the new European Union' [1997] Eipascope, p. 2.

Guild E., *The developing immigration and asylum policies of the European Union: adopted conventions, resolutions, recommendations, decisions and conclusions* (Kluwer Law International, The Hague, 1996).

Guild E. and Harlow C. (eds), *Implementing Amsterdam. Immigration and asylum rights in EC law* (Hart Publishing, Oxford, 2001).

Harvey C, 'Restructuring asylum: recent trends in United Kingdom asylum law and policy' (1997) 9 IJRL, p. 60.

Harvey C., 'The European regulation of asylum: constructing a model of regional solidarity?' (1998) 4 *European Public Law*, p. 561.

Hailbronner K., 'Perspectives of a harmonisation of the law of asylum after the Maastricht summit' (1992) 29 CML Rev, p. 917.

Hailbronner K., 'The concept of 'safe country' and expeditious asylum procedures: a Western European perspective' (1993) 5 IJRL, p. 31.

Hailbronner K., 'Visa Regulations and third country nationals in EC law' (1994) 31 CML Rev., p. 969.

Hailbronner K. and Thiery C., 'Schengen II and Dublin: responsibility for asylum applications in Europe' (1997) 34 CML Rev., p. 957.

Hailbronner K., 'European immigration and asylum under the Amsterdam Treaty' (1998) 35 CML Rev., p. 1047.

Hailbronner K., *Immigration and asylum policy of the European Union* (Kluwer Law International, The Hague, 2000).

Hathaway J., 'Harmonising for whom? The devaluation of refugee protection in the era of European economic integration' (1993) 26 *Cornell International Law Journal*, p. 719.

Hathaway J. and Dent J., *Refugee rights: report on a comparative survey* (York Lanes Press, Toronto, 1995).

Hreblay V., *La libre circulation des personnes: les accords de Schengen* (PUF, Paris, 1994).

Hurwitz A., 'The 1990 Dublin Convention: a comprehensive assessment' (1999) 11 IJRL, p. 646.

Jacqué J.-P., 'La simplification et la consolidation des Traités' (1997) 33 *Revue Trimestrelle de Droit Européen*, p. 903.

Joly D., 'The porous dam: European harmonisation on asylum in the Nineties' (1994) 6 IJRL, p. 159.

Kanstroom D., 'The shining city and the fortress: reflections on the 'Euro-solution' to the German immigration dilemma' (1993) 16 *Boston College International and Comparative Law Review*, p. 201.

Kjaergaard E., 'The concept of 'safe third country' in contemporary European refugee law,' (1994) 6 IJRL, p. 649.

Kjaerum K., 'Temporary protection in Europe in the 1990's' (1994) 6 IJRL, p. 444.

Kjaerum M., 'Human Rights implications of the development of the concept of temporary asylum in the Nordic Countries' (1995) 64 *Nordic Journal of International Law*, p. 397.

Korella G. and Twomey P. (eds), *Towards a European immigration policy* (European Interuniversity Press, Brussels, 1994).

Kortenberg H., 'La négociation du Traité – Une vue cavalière' (1997) 33 *Revue Trimestrelle de Droit Européen*, p. 711.

Kortenberg H., 'Closer co-operation in the Treaty of Amsterdam' (1998) 35 CML Rev.p. 833.

Kuijper P.J., 'Some legal problems associated with the communitarization of policy on visas, asylum and immigration under the Amsterdam Treaty and incorporation of the Schengen acquis' (2000) 37 CML Rev., p. 345.

Labayle H., 'La coopération européenne en matière de justice et d'affaires intérieures et la Conference Intergouvernamentale' (1997) 33 *Revue Trimestrelle de Droit Européen*, p. 6.

Labayle H., 'La libre circulation des personnes dans l'Union Européenne, de Schengen à Amsterdam' (1997) 12 *Actualité Juridique – Droit Administratif*, p. 923.

Labayle H., 'Un espace de liberté, de sécurité et de justice' (1997) 33 *Revue Trimestrelle de Droit Européen*, p. 813.

Lambert H., *Seeking asylum: comparative law and practice in selected European countries* (Martinus Nijhoff, Dordrecht, 1995).

Laursen F. and Vanhoonacker S. (eds), *The ratification of the Maastricht Treaty* (European Institute of Public Administration, Maastricht, 1994).

Lavenex S., *Safe third countries: extending the EU asylum and immigration policies to Central and Eastern Europe* (Central European University Press, New York, 1999).

Lepoivre M., 'Le domaine de la Justice et des Affaires Intérieures dans la perspective de la Conférence Intergouvernementale de 1996' [1995] *Cahiers de Droit Européen*, p. 323.

Macdonald I. and Blake N., *Macdonald's immigration law and practice* (4th edn, Butterworths, London,1997).

Mahmood S., 'The Schengen Information System: an inequitable data protection regime' (1995) 7 IJRL, p. 179.

Marshall B., *British and German refugee policies in the European context* (Royal Institute of International Affairs, London, 1996).

Marx R., 'Non-refoulement, access to procedures, and responsibility for determining refugee claims' (1995) 7 IJRL, p. 383.

Marx R.and Lumpp K., 'The German Constitutional Court's decision of 14 May 1996 on the concept of 'safe third countries' – A basis for burden-sharing in Europe?' (1996) 8 IJRL, p. 419.

Meijers H. *et alia* (eds), *Schengen, Internationalisation of central chapters of the law on aliens, refugees, security and the police* (Kluwer Law International, The Hague, 1991).

Miles R. and Thraenhard T D., *Migration and European integration – the dynamics of inclusion and exclusion* (Pinter Pub., London, 1995).

Monar J. and Morgan R. (eds.), *The Third Pillar of the European Union* (European Interuniversity Press, Brussels, 1994).

Monar J., 'Justice and Home Affairs in the Treaty of Amsterdam: reform at the price of fragmentation' (1998) 23 EL Rev., p. 320.

Müller-Graff P., 'The legal basis of the Third Pillar and its position in the framework of the European Union Treaty' (1994) 31 CML Rev., p. 493.

Müller-Graff P., Justiz und Inneres nach Amsterdam: die Neuerungen in erster und dritter Säule' [1997] *Integration*, p. 271.

Nanz K.-P., 'Schengener Übereinkommen und Personenfreizügigkeit' (1994) 14 *Zeitschrift für Ausländerrecht und Ausländerpolitik*, p. 99.

Nascimbene B., *Da Schengen a Maastricht. Apertura delle frontiere, cooperazione giudiziaria e di polizia* (Giuffrè, Milan, 1995).

Nascimbene B., 'Gli accordi di Schengen e i problemi di applicazione in Italia' (1999) 46 *Jus – Rivista di Scienze Giuridiche*, p. 421.

Neuman G., 'Buffer zones against refugees: Dublin, Schengen and the German asylum amendment' (1993) 33 *Virginia Journal of International Law*, p. 503.

Nicholson F. and Twomey P. (eds), *Current issues of UK asylum law and policy* (Aldershot press, Ashgate, 1998).

Nicholson F. and Twomey P. (eds), *Refugee rights and realities. Evolving international concepts and regimes* (CUP, Cambridge, 1999).

Noll G., 'Prisoner's dilemma in Fortress Europe: on the prospects for equitable burden-sharing in the European Union' (1997) 40 *German Yearbook of International Law*, p. 405.

Noll G., 'The non-admission and return of protection seekers in Germany' (1997) 9 IJRL, p. 415.

Noll G., 'The democratic legitimacy of refugee law' (1997) 66 *Nordic Journal of International Law*, p. 429.

Noll G., *Negotiating asylum. The EU acquis, extraterritorial protection and the Common Market of deflection* (Martinus Nijhoff, The Hague, 2000).

Noll G., 'Formalism vs. Empiricism. Some reflections on the Dublin Convention on the occasion of recent European case law', forthcoming, (2001) 70 *Nordic Journal of International Law*.

O'Keeffe D. and Twomey P. (eds.), Legal issues of the Maastricht Treaty (Chancery Law, London, 1994).

O'Keeffe D., 'Recasting the Third Pillar' (1995) 32 CML Rev., p. 893.

O'Keeffe D. and Twomey P.(eds), *Legal issues of the Amsterdam Treaty* (Hart Publishing, Oxford, 1999).

O'Keeffe D. et alia (eds), *Liber Amicorum Slynn, Judicial review in European Union Law* (vol.I, Kluwer Law International, The Hague, 2000).

Pauly A. (ed.), *Les accords de Schengen* (European Institute of Public Administration, Maastricht, 1993).

Pauly A. (ed.), *Schengen en panne* (European Institute of Public Administration, Maastricht, 1994).

Pauly A., *De Schengen à Maastricht: voie royale et course d'obstacles* (European Institute of Public Administration, Maastricht, 1996).

Peers S., 'The visa Regulation: free movement blocked indefinitely' (1996) 21 EL Rev., p. 151.

Peers S., *Mind the gap! Ineffective Member State implementation of European Union asylum measures* (ILPA, London, 1998).

Peers S., *EU Justice and Home Affairs law* (Longman, London, 2000).

Phuong C., 'Internally displaced persons and refugees: conceptual differences and similarities' (2000) 18 NQHR, p. 215.

Pirjola J., 'Temporary protection as a future model for asylum' (1995) 64 *Nordic Journal of International Law*, p. 423.

Rotte R. et alia (eds), *Asylum, migration and policy coordination in Europe* (Ludwig-Maximilians-University, Munich, Discussion Paper 96–11, July 1996).

Rossetto J., 'La Convention de Schengen: controverses et incertitudes françaises sur le droit d'asile' (1994) 378 *Revue du Marché commun et de l'Union Européenne*, p. 315.

Rupperecht R., 'Justiz und Inneres nach dem Amsterdamer Vertrag' [1997] *Integration*, p. 264.

Sarooshi D., *The United Nations and the development of collective security* (Clarendon Press, Oxford, 1999).

Schermers H. *et alia* (eds), *Free movement of persons in Europe*, (Martinus Nijhoff, Dordrecht, 1993).

Silvestro M. and Fernandez-Fernandez J., 'Les orientations du Parlément Européen sur la Conférence intergouvernamentale et l'état actuel des negociations' (1996) 403 *Revue du Marché Commun et de l'Union Européenne*, p. 709.

Silvestro M. and Fernandez-Fernandez J., 'Le Traité d' Amsterdam: une évaluation critique' (1997) 413 *Revue du Marché Commun et de l'Union Européenne*, p. 662.

Shah P., 'Refugees and safe third countries: United Kingdom, European and international aspects' (1995) 1 *European Public Law*, p. 259.

Shaw J., 'The many pasts and futures of citizenship in the European Union' 1997 22 EL Rev., p. 554.

Spijkerboer T. *et alia*, *Persecution by third parties* (University of Nijmegen, Centre for Migration Law, May1998).

Steuer T.C., 'Protecting Human Rights in the European Union: an argument for treaty reform' [1997] *Fordham International Law Journal*, p. 916.

Toussaint M., 'EURODAC: un système informatisé européen de comparaison des empreintes digitales des demandeurs d'asile' (1999) 429 *Revue de Marché commun et de l'Union européenne*, p. 421.

Van Selm-Thoburn J., *Refugee protection in Europe: lessons of the Yugoslav crisis* (Martinus Nijhoff, The Hague, 1998).

Wachsmann P., 'Les droits de l'homme – le Traité d'Amsterdam' (1997) 33 *Revue Trimestrelle de Droit Européen*, p. 883.

Weiler J. and Lockhart N., '"Taking rights seriously" seriously: the European Court and its fundamental rights jurisprudence', Part I & II, (1995) 32 CML Rev., p. 51 and p. 579 respectively.

Wisskirchen C., 'Germany: assault on the constitutional right to asylum – Part I' (1994) 8 INLP, p. 87.

UNHCR

UNHCR, *Handbook on procedures and criteria for determining refugee status.*

UNHCR, *Overview of readmission agreements in Central Europe* of 30/09/1993.

UNHCR Executive Committee Conclusions.

UNHCR, Briefing on the Dublin and Schengen Conventions (Brussels,16/8/1991).

UNHCR, Briefing on the three Resolutions adopted at the Edinburgh Council on 3 December 1992 (Brussels, December 1992).

UNHCR, 'Readmission agreements, "protection elsewhere" and asylum policy' (Explanatory Note, Brussels, August 1994).

UNHCR, 'Fair and expeditious asylum procedures' (Explanatory Note, Brussels, November 1994).

UNHCR, 'Position on standard bilateral readmission agreements between a Member State and a third country' (Explanatory Note, Brussels, 1/12/94).

UNHCR, 'Concerned at a document adopted by the EU JHA Council on 30 November

1994 which could enable the transfer of asylum seekers to third countries' (Press Release, Brussels, 1/12/94).

UNHCR, *The state of the world's refugees*, 2000.

EU SOURCES (quoted in this work)

EC COMMISSION – INITIATIVES BY MEMBER STATES (in chronological order)

White Paper on the measures necessary to achieve the Common Internal Market, June 1985, COM(85)310.

Decision 85/381/EEC of 18/7/85 instituting a notification procedure of national measures concerning the entry, residence and employment of non-EC nationals, OJ 1985 L217/2.

Draft Directive aiming at co-ordinating rules concerning the right of asylum and the status of refugees, of 7/12/1988, COM(88)640 final.

Communication to the Council and the European Parliament on the right of asylum, of 11/10/91, SEC(91)1857 final.

Communication to the Council and the European Parliament on immigration, of 23/10/91, SEC(91) 1855 final.

Communication of the Commission on the abolition of border controls, of 8/5/92, SEC(92)877 final.

Commission's Report to the Council on the possibility of applying Art. K.9 of the Treaty on European Union to asylum policy, of 4/11/93, SEC 1687 final.

Draft Convention on the crossing of external borders and Proposal for a Regulation determining the third countries whose nationals must be in possession of visas when crossing the external borders of the Member States, of 10/12/93, COM (93)684 final, OJ 1994 C11/5 and 6.

Communication on asylum and immigration policy, of 23/02/1994, COM (94)23 final.

Working Paper on minimum standards for asylum procedures, of 2/5/94, SEC(94) 780.

Second Report to the Council and the European Parliament on the possibility of applying Art. K.9 of the TEU Treaty to asylum policy, COM(95)0566 final.

Commission Proposal for a Council Directive on the right of third-country nationals to travel in the Community, COM(95)346 final.

Proposal for a Council Directive concerning the abolition of controls on persons at internal frontiers, COM(95)347 final.

Proposal for an EP and Council Directive amending Directives 68/360/EEC and 73/148/EEC, COM(95)348 final.

Intergovernmental Conference 1996: Commission Report for the Reflection Group, EUR-OP, 1995 (cc-89-95-357-EN-C).

Proposal on 'closer co-operation', COM(96)90 of 28/2/96.

Discussion Paper on 'closer co-operation', CONF/3805/97, January 1997.

Proposal for a Joint Action concerning temporary protection of displaced persons, submitted 27/3/97, COM (97)93 final.

Amended proposal for a Joint Action concerning temporary protection of displaced persons, submitted on 24/6/98, COM (98)372 final.

Proposal for a Joint Action concerning solidarity in the admission and residence of beneficiaries of temporary protection of displaced persons, submitted 26/6/98, OJ 1998 C268/14.

Communication: towards an area of freedom, security and justice, of 14/7/98, COM (98)459 final.

Proposal for a Council Decision on establishing a Community action programme to promote the integration of refugees, submitted 13/1/99, COM (98) 731 final, OJ 1999 C36/11.

Proposal for a Council decision on a joint action establishing measures to provide practical support in relation to the reception and the voluntary repatriation of refugees, displaced persons and asylum applicants, submitted 13/1/99, COM (98) 733 final in OJ 1999 C37/4.

Working paper 'Towards common standards on asylum procedures', of 3/3/99 SEC (1999) 271 final.

Amended proposal of 15/3/2000 for a Council Regulation concerning the establishment of 'Eurodac' for the comparison of the fingerprints of applicants for asylum and certain other third-country nationals to facilitate the implementation of the Dublin Convention, OJ 2000 C29E/1.

Proposal for a Council Regulation listing the third countries whose nationals must be in possession of visas when crossing the external borders and those whose nationals are exempt from that requirement, (EUROPE database under Community Preparatory Acts, Doc. 500PC0027), 1999.

Working Paper, Revisiting the Dublin Convention: developing Community legislation for determining which Member State is responsible for considering an application for asylum submitted in one of the Member States, of 21/03/2000, SEC (2000)522.

Proposal for a Council Directive on minimum standards for giving temporary protection in the event of a mass influx of displaced persons and on measures promoting a balance of efforts between Member States in receiving such persons and bearing the consequences thereof, submitted 24/5/2000, to be found at 'http://europa.eu.int/eur-lex/en/com/dat/2000/en_500PC0303.html'.

Initiative of the French Republic with a view to the adoption of a Council Directive on mutual recognition of decisions on the expulsion of third country nationals, September 2000, OJ 2000 C269/1.

Initiative of the French Republic with a view to the adoption of a Council Directive concerning the harmonisation of financial penalties imposed on carriers transporting into the territory of the Member States third-country nationals lacking the documents necessary for admission, September 2000, OJ 2000 C269/8.

Draft Council Directive on minimum standard on procedures in Member States for granting and withdrawing refugee status, submitted October 2000, to be found at 'http://europa.eu.int/eur-lex/en/com/dat/2000/en_500PC0578.html, document n° 500PC0578'.

Communication from the Commission to the Council and the European Parliament 'Towards a common asylum procedure and a uniform status, valid throughout the Union, for persons granted asylum', of 27/11/2000, COM (2000)755 final.

Communication from the Commission to the Council and the European Parliament. Biannual update of the scoreboard to review progress on the creation of an area of 'Freedom, Security and Justice' in the European Union, COM (2000)782 final, Brussels 30/11/2000.

AD HOC IMMIGRATION GROUP – K.4 COMMITTEE – OTHER EU INTERGOV. BODIES (in chronological order)

Report of the Ad Hoc Group on Immigration to the Maastricht Summit, Brussels, 3/12/91, SN 4038/91 (WGI 930).

Draft proposal on the establishment of the *Centre d'Information de Réflexion et d'Echange en matière d'Asile* (CIREA), of 21/5/92, SN 2781/92 (WGI 1107).

Draft report on countries where there is generally no serious risk of persecution, of 26/10/92, SN 4282/92 WGI 1230.

Draft Resolution on manifestly unfounded applications for asylum. Progress report on discussions in the Asylum sub-group. Note by the Presidency, of 1/11/92, SN 3926/92 WGI 1195.

Recommendation of the Ad Hoc Immigration Group regarding practices followed by Member States on expulsion, of 16/11/92, SN 4678/92 WGI 1266.

The Clearing House – First Meeting – Future work – Note by the Presidency, of 16/11/92, SN 4682/92 WGI 1270.

Draft Conclusion on countries in which there is generally no serious risk of persecution, SN 3926/92 (WGI 1195).

First activity report from CIREA to the Ministers responsible for Immigration, of 14/5/93, SN 2834/93 (WGI 1505).

Second CIREA activity report, of 20/6/94, in OJ 1996 C274/55.

Draft Resolution on minimum guarantees for asylum procedures, amendments, of 14/3/95, 5585/95 ASIM 78.

IGC Reflection Group's Report, SN 520/95 (REFLEX 21), Brussels, 5/12/95.

Activity report on CIREA for 1996, OJ 1997 C191/29 and 33.

EU COUNCIL – EU PRESIDENCY (in chronological order)

Council Decision laying down the procedures for the exercise of implementing powers conferred to the Commission, OJ 1987 L197/33.

Resolution on a harmonised approach to questions concerning host third countries, of 19/11/92, SN 4823/92 WGI 1283.

Conclusion on countries in which there is generally no serious risk of persecution, of 1/12/92, SN 4821/92 WGI 1281.

Resolution on manifestly unfounded applications for asylum, of 2/12/92, SN 4822/1/92 WGI 1282.

Conclusion on people displaced by the conflict in Former Yugoslavia, December 1992, Council Press Release 10518/92 (press 230).

Council Resolution on certain common guidelines as regards the admission of particularly vulnerable groups of distressed persons from former Yugoslavia, June 1993, Council Press Release 548/93 (press 132).

Council Conclusions of 20/6/94 concerning the possible application of Art. K.9 of the Treaty on European Union to asylum policy, OJ 1996 C274/34.

Means of proof in the framework of the Dublin Convention, adopted on 20/6/94, OJ 1996 C 274/35.

Circulation and confidentiality of joint reports on the situation of certain third countries, adopted on 20/6/94, OJ 1996 C274/43.

Form of laissez-passer for the transfer of an asylum applicant from one Member State to another, adopted on 20/6/94, OJ 1996 C274/42.

Council Recommendation of 30/11/94 concerning the adoption of a standard travel document for the expulsion of third country nationals, OJ 1996 C274/18.

Draft Resolution on burden-sharing, German Presidency document 7773/94 ASIM 124, November 1994.

Resolution of 29/6/95 on minimum guarantees for asylum procedures, OJ 1996 C274/13.

Council Recommendation of 24/7/95 on the guiding principles to be followed in drawing up protocols on the implementation of readmission agreements, OJ 1996 C274/25.

Resolution of 25/9/95 on burden-sharing with regard to the admission and residence of displaced persons on a temporary basis, OJ 1995 C262/1.

Council Regulation 2317/95 of 25/9/95 determining the third countries whose nationals must be in possession of visas when crossing the external borders of the Member States, OJ 1995 L234/1.

Council Recommendation on concerted action and co-operation in carrying out expulsion measures, adopted on 22/12/ 95, in OJ 1996 C5/3.

Council Recommendation of 22/12/95 concerning transit for the purpose of expulsion, OJ 1996 C5/5.

Joint Position 96/196/JHA of 4/3/96 on the harmonised definition of the term 'refugee' in Art. 1 of the Geneva Convention, OJ 1996 L63/2.

Resolution of 4/3/96 on an alert and emergency procedure for burden-sharing with regard to the admission and residence of displaced persons on a temporary basis, OJ 1996 L63/10.

Guidelines for joint reports on third countries, adopted on 20/6/96, OJ 1996 C274/52.

Franco-German contribution towards the definition of the notion of 'closer co-operation', CONF 3912/96 of 18/9/96.

Council Resolution of 14/10/96 laying down the priorities for co-operation in the field of Justice and Home affairs for the period from 1 July 1996 to 30 June 1998, OJ 1996 C319/1.

The EU today and tomorrow- Adapting the EU for the benefit of its people and preparing it for the future- a general outline for a draft revision of the Treaties- Irish Presidency – Dublin II, CONF 2500/96 CAB, EN, 5/12/96.

Discussion Paper on asylum for EU nationals, CONF/3925/96.

Council Decision of 26/6/97 on monitoring the implementation of instruments adopted concerning asylum, OJ 1997 L178/6.

Joint action 97/477/JHA of 22/7/97 adopted by the Council on the basis of Art. K.3 of the Treaty on European Union, concerning the financing of specific projects in favour of displaced persons who have found temporary protection in the Member States and asylum-seekers, OJ 1997 L205/3.

Joint action 97/478/JHA of 22/7/97 adopted by the Council on the basis of Art. K3 of the Treaty on European Union, concerning the financing of specific projects in favour of asylum seekers and refugees, OJ 1997 L205/5.

Decision 1/97 of 9/9/97 of the Committee set up by Art. 18 of the Dublin Convention of 15/6/90, concerning provisions for the implementation of the Convention, OJ 1997 L281/1.

Decision 2/97 of 9/9/97 of the Committee set up by Art. 18 of the Dublin Convention of 15/6/90, establishing the Committee's rules of procedure, OJ 1997 L281/26.

Council Resolution of 18/12/97 laying down the priorities for co-operation in the field of justice and home affairs for the period from 1 January 1998 to the date of entry into force of the Treaty of Amsterdam, OJ 1998 C11/1.

Joint action of 27/4/98 adopted by the Council on the basis of Art. K3 of the Treaty on European Union, concerning the financing of specific projects in favour of asylum seekers and refugees, OJ 1998 L138/8.

Joint action of 27/4/98 adopted by the Council on the basis of Art. K.3 of the Treaty on

European Union, concerning the financing of specific projects in favour of displaced persons who have found temporary protection in the Member States and asylum-seekers, OJ 1998 L138/6.

Strategy paper on migration and asylum policy, Council of the European Union- Austrian Presidency, of 29/9/98, 9809/98 REV 1.

Joint Action of 26/4/99 adopted by the Council on the basis of Art. K.3 of the Treaty on the European Union, establishing projects and measures to provide practical support in relation to the reception and voluntary repatriation of refugees, displaced persons and asylum seekers, including emergency assistance to persons who have fled as a result of recent events in Kosovo, OJ 1999 L114/2.

Council decision of 20/5/99 determining in conformity with the relevant provisions of the Treaty establishing the European Community and the Treaty on European Union, the legal basis for each of the provisions or decisions which constitute the Schengen acquis, OJ 1999 L176/17.

Council Decision 1999/468/EC of 28/6/1999 laying down the procedures for the exercise of implementing powers conferred to the Commission, OJ 1999 L184/23.

Regulation 574/99 determining the third countries whose nationals must be in possession of visas when crossing the external borders of the Member States, OJ 1999 L72/2.

Portuguese Presidency's report to the European Council on the IGC for institutional reforms, of 14/06/2000, CONFER 4750/00.

Decision of 28/9/2000 establishing a European Refugee Fund, OJ 2000 L252/12.

Council Regulation (EC) n° 2725/2000 of 11/12/2000 concerning the establishment of 'Eurodac' for the comparison of the fingerprints of applicants for asylum and certain other third-country nationals to facilitate the implementation of the Dublin Convention, OJ 2000 L316/1.

EU Charter of Fundamental Rights, OJ 2000 C364/1.

EUROPEAN PARLIAMENT (in chronological order)

Working Paper, Immigration policy and the right of asylum in the Member States of the European Community, EN/DV/211/211924, 1992.

The Third Pillar: an Overview, of 19/9/96 (EP 00342/96).

Asylum in the European Union: the 'safe country of origin principle', 1997 (EP 166.466).

Proposal for a Joint Action concerning temporary protection of displaced persons, EP Amendments, OJ 1997 C339/146.

Amended proposal for a Joint Action concerning temporary protection of displaced persons, second consultation, EP Amendments, OJ 1998 C379/375.

Proposal for a Joint Action concerning solidarity in the admission and residence of beneficiaries of temporary protection of displaced persons, EP Amendments, OJ 1998 C379/380.

Proposal for a Council decision on establishing a Community action programme to promote the integration of refugees, EP Amendments, OJ 1999 C 219/79.

Proposal for a Council decision on a Joint Action adopted by the Council on the basis of Art. K.3 of the Treaty on the European Union, establishing projects and measures to provide practical support in relation to the reception and voluntary repatriation of refugees, displaced persons and asylum seekers, EP Amendments, OJ 1999 C219/83.

European Parliament Resolution on the harmonisation of forms of protection complementing refugee status in the European Union, OJ 1999 C150/203.

Resolution on the draft Action Plan of the Council and Commission on how best to implement the provisions of the Treaty of Amsterdam on an area of freedom, security and justice, OJ 1999 C 219/61.

Resolution on the strategy paper on the European Union's migration and asylum policy, OJ 1999 C219/73.

Working Paper, Asylum in the EU Member States, PE 168.631, January 2000.

EUROSTAT

Patterns and trends in international migration in Western Europe, April 2000.

European social statistics – Migration, 2000 edition.

OTHERS

Amnesty, *Europe: the need for minimum standards in asylum procedures* (EU Section, Brussels, 1994).

Amnesty, *Playing human pinball – Home Office practice in "safe third country" asylum cases* (British Section, London, 1995).

Amnesty, *Prisoners without a voice: asylum seekers detained in the United Kingdom* (British Section, London, 1995, 2nd edition).

Amnesty, *Slamming the door: the demolition of the right of asylum in the U.K.* (British Section, London,1996).

Commission Nationale Consultative des Droits De l'Homme, *Harmonisation des politiques d'asile. De nombreux acteurs* (Paris, June 1994).

Danish Refugee Council, *The effect of carrier sanctions on the asylum system* (Copenhagen, 1991).

Danish Refugee Council, *Safe Third Country: policies in European Countries* (Copenhagen, 1997).

ECRE, *Working Paper on the need for a supplementary refugee definition* (London, April 1993).

ECRE *A European Refugee Policy in the light of established principles* (London, April 1994).

ECRE, *Asylum in Europe: Review of refugee and asylum laws and procedures in selected European countries* (Vol. I & II, London, 1994).

ECRE, *The situation of refugees from Kosovo* (June 1998).

ECRE, *Position on the enlargement of the European Union in relation to asylum* (London, September 1998).

ECRE, *Guarding standards – Shaping the agenda* (London, May 1999).

ECRE, *Guidelines on fair and efficient procedures for determining refugee status* (London, September 1999).

ILPA, *Update on readmission agreements* (London, December 1994).

ILPA, *Commentary on draft minimum guarantees for asylum seekers and refugees* (London, March 1995).

ILPA, *Comments upon the presidency proposals for guidelines for harmonising the application of the criteria for the determination of refugee status in Art. 1 A of the Geneva Convention* (London, 1996).

House of Lords European Communities Committee, *Enhancing parliamentary scrutiny of the Third Pillar*, 6th Report, session 1997–98, HL Paper 25.

House of Lords, Select Committee on the European Communities, *Evidence by the Ministers of State, Foreign and Commonwealth Office, on the Amsterdam Treaty*, 9th report, session 1997–98, HL Paper 40.

House of Lords, Select Committee on the European Communities, *Incorporating the Schengen acquis into the European Union*, 31st Report, session 1997–98, HL Paper 139.

House of Lords, Select Committee on the European Union, *Minimum standards in asylum procedures*, 11th Report of session 2000–2001, HL Paper 59.

Table of Cases

Index

EUROPEAN MONOGRAPHS

1. Lammy Betten (ed.), *The Future of European Social Policy* (second and revised edition, 1991).

2. J.M.E. Loman, K.J.M. Mortelmans, H.H.G. Post, J.S. Watson, *Culture and Community Law: Before and after Maastricht* (1992).

3. Prof. Dr. J.A.E. Vervaele, *Fraud Against the Community: The Need for European Fraud Legislation* (1992).

4. P. Rawortli, *The Legislative Process in the European Community* (1993).

5. J. Stuyck, *Financial and Monetary Integration in the European Economic Community* (1993).

6. J.H.V. Stuyck, A.J. Vossestein (eds.), *State Entrepreneurship, National Monopolies and European Community Law* (1993).

7. J. Stuyck, A. Looijestijn-Clearie (eds.), *The European Economic Area EC-EFTA* (1994).

8. R.B. Bouterse, *Competition and Integration – What Goals Count?* (1994).

9. R. Barents, *The Agricultural Law of the EC* (1994).

10. Nicholas Emiliou, *The Principle of Proportionality in European Law: A Comparative Study* (1996).

11. Eivind Smith, *National Parliaments as Cornerstones of European Integration* (1996).

12. Jan H. Jans, *European Environmental Law* (1996).

13. Siofra O'Leary, *The Evolving Concept of Community Citizenship: From the Free Movement of Persons to Union Citizenship* (1996).

14. Laurence Gormley (ed.), *Current and Future Perspectives on EC Competition Law* (1997).

15. Simone White, *Protection of the Financial Interests of the European Communities: The Fight against Fraud and Corruption* (1998).

16. Morten P. Broberg, *The European Commission's Jurisdiction to Scrutinise Mergers* (1998).

17. Doris Hildebrand, *The Role of Economic Analysis in the EC Competition Rules* (1998).

18. Christof R.A. Swaak, *European Community Law and the Automobile Industry* (1999).

19. Dorthe Dahlgaard Dingel, *Public Procurement. A Harmonization of the National Judicial Review of the Application of European Community Law* (1999).

20. J.A.E. Vervaele (ed.) *Compliance and Enforcement of European Community Law* (1999).

21. Martin Trybus, *European Defence Procurement Law: International and National Procurement Systems as Models for a Liberalised Defence Procurement Market in Europe* (1999).

22. Helen Staples, *The Legal Status of Third Country Nationals Resident in the European Union* (1999).

23. Damien Geradin (ed.) *The Liberalization of State Monopolies in the European Union and Beyond* (2000).

24. Katja Heede, *European Ombudsman: Redress and Control at Union Level* (2000).

25. Ulf Bernitz, Joakim Nergelius (eds.) *General Principles of European Community Law* (2000).

26. Michaela Drahos, *Convergence of Competition Laws and Policies in the European Community* (2001).

27. Damien Geradin (ed.) *The Liberalization of Electricity and Natural Gas in the European Union* (2001).

28. Gisella Gori, *Towards an EU Right to Education* (2001).

29. Brendan Smith, *Constitution Building in the European Union* (2001).

30. Freidl Weiss and Frank Wooldridge, *Free Movement of Persons within the European Community* (2002).

31. Ingrid Boccardi, *Europe and Refugees: Towards an EU Asylum Policy* (2002).